Palestinian Refugee Repatriation

The repatriation of Palestinians is a highly topical issue, and a critical component of any future peace process for Israel and Palestine. Until now, the mechanics of repatriation has not been dealt with before in this detail. This book explores the notion that the Palestinian refugee case is exceptional. It does this through the comparative study of refugee repatriation, and by asking the following questions:

- To what extent can the Palestinian case be said to be unique?
- Where are the divergences, overlaps and points of similarity with other refugee situations?
- What lessons can be drawn from these comparisons?
- How can these lessons inform refugee organisations, the donor community and policy-makers?

In attempting to answer these questions, the expert contributors cover three main fields. Firstly, the contextual and methodological field, reviewing on one hand the main trends in forced migration and refugee studies and issues concerning policy transfer and comparative research; and on the other hand, the historical and political background of UNHCR and the negotiations around the Palestinian refugee issue. Secondly, the book offers a truly comparative approach with other case studies from around the world. It covers in-depth case studies of specific refugee situations – covering Cambodia, Guatemala, the Horn of Africa, Iraq, Afghanistan, Bosnia and Herzegovina – to reveal the key issues in the formulation of repatriation programmes. Finally, the book draws together the lessons learnt, and considers to what extent these lessons are relevant to the Palestinian–Israeli situation.

Michael Dumper is Reader in Middle East Politics at the University of Exeter. His previous publications include *The Politics of Jerusalem since 1967* and *The Politics of Sacred Space: the Old City of Jerusalem and the Middle East Conflict*. His research interests are the Permanent Status Issues of the Middle East peace process, religious institutions and the urban politics of the Middle East.

Routledge Studies in Middle Eastern Politics

Algeria in Transition
Reforms and development prospects
Ahmed Aghrout with Redha M. Bougherira

Palestinian Refugee Repatriation
Global perspectives
Edited by Michael Dumper

International Politics in the Gulf
A cultural genealogy
Arshin Adib-Moghaddam

Palestinian Refugee Repatriation
Global perspectives

Edited by Michael Dumper

Routledge
Taylor & Francis Group

LONDON AND NEW YORK

First published 2006
by Routledge
2 Park Square, Milton Park, Abingdon, Oxfordshire OX14 4RN

Simultaneously published in the USA and Canada
by Routledge
711 Third Avenue, New York, NY 10017

First issued in paperback 2014

Routledge is an imprint of the Taylor & Francis Group, an informa business

Transferred to Digital Printing 2007

Typeset in Baskerville by Prepress Projects Ltd, Perth, UK

British Library Cataloguing in Publication Data
A catalogue record for this book is available from the British Library

Library of Congress Cataloging in Publication Data
A catalog record for this book has been requested

ISBN 978-0-415-38497-1 (hbk)
ISBN 978-0-415-86017-8 (pbk)

Contents

Illustrations

Figures

Tables

Contributors

Professor Richard Black
Co-Director, Sussex Centre for Migration Research

Professor Rex Brynen
Chair, Middle East Studies Programme, McGill University

Dr Michael Dumper
Reader in Middle East Politics, University of Exeter

Dr Patricia Weiss Fagen
Senior Associate, Institute for the Study of International Migration, Georgetown University

Dr Laura Hammond
Assistant Professor, Department of International Development, Community & Environment, Clark University

Dr Sari Hanafi
Sociologist

Dr Nicholas Van Hear
Centre on Migration, Policy and Society, University of Oxford

Mr Michael Kagan
Lawyer; Instructor, Refugee & Asylum-Seeker Rights Clinic, Tel Aviv University Law School

Dr Menachem Klein
Senior Lecturer, Political Science Department, Bar Ilan University

Mr Peter Marsden
Former Coordinator, British Agencies Afghanistan Group Project, Refugee Council

Dr Christopher McDowell
Director, The Information Centre about Asylum and Refugees (ICAR), School of Social Sciences, City University, London

Paul Prettitore
  Legal Advisor, The World Bank, West Bank, Jerusalem

Ana Garcia Rodicio
  Researcher, Globalitaria Peace-Building Initiatives, Madrid

Dr Finn Stepputat
  Senior Researcher, Danish Institute for International Studies

Abbreviations

AHLC	Ad Hoc Liaison Committee
AI	Amnesty International
AUC	Autodefensas Unidas de Colombia
B&H	Bosnia and Herzegovina
CAP	Consolidated Inter-Agency Appeal Process
CCPP	Comisión Permanente de Refugiados (Permanent Commission of Refugees)
CEAR	Comisión Especial para la Atención a Repatriados, Refugiados y Desplacados (Special Commission for Assistance to Repatriates, Refugees and Internally Displaced Persons)
CIREFCA	Conferencia Internacional para Refugiados en Centro America (Central American Conference on Refugees)
CIVPOL	Civilian Police Force
CNR	Comisión de Reconstrucción Nacional (National Commission for Reconstruction)
CODAIC	Coordinador para el Desarollo Autónomo e Integral Comunitario (Coordinator for Integrated Communitarian Development)
COMAR	Comisión Mexicana de Ayuda a Refugiados (Mexican Commission for Refugees)
COMPAS	Centre on Migration Policy and Society
CONDEG	Consejo Nacional de Desplazados de Guatemala (Council for Displaced Persons in Guatemala)
CPA	Comprehensive Plan of Action
CRPC	Commission for Real Property Claims
CRT	Claims Resolution Tribunal
CTEAR	Comisión Técnica para la Ejecución del Acuerdo sobre el Reasentamiento de las Poblaciones Desarraigadas por el Enfrentamiento Armado (Technical Commission for the Resettlement of Populations Displaced by the Armed Conflict)
DfID	Department for International Development

DPA	Dayton Peace Agreement
DRC	Democratic Republic of Congo
ECHR	European Convention on Human Rights
EGP	Ejército Guerrillero de los Pobres (Guerilla Army of the Poor)
EU	European Union
FAO	Food and Agriculture Organization
FARC	Revolutionary Armed Forces of Colombia
FEA	food economy analysis
GNP	gross national product
GoE	government of Ethiopia
GoG	government of Guatemala
GoM	government of Mexico
GRICAR	Grupo Internacional de Consulta y Apoyo al Retorno (International Group for Consultancy and Support to the Return)
HEA	household economy analysis
HEP	Humanitarian Evacuation Programme
ICVA	International Committee of Voluntary Agencies
IDPs	internally displaced persons
IDRC	International Development Research Centre
IFIs	international financing institutions
ILO	International Labour Organization
IOM	International Organization for Migration
IRO	International Refugee Organization
JPKF	Joint Peacekeeping Force
LTTE	Liberation Tigers of Tamil Eelam
MDM	Ministry for Displacement and Migration
MINUGUA	United Nations Verification Mission in Guatemala
MOPIC	Ministry of Planning and International Cooperation
NATO	North Atlantic Treaty Organization
NGO	non-governmental organization
OHR	Office of the High Representative
ONUSAL	United Nations Observer Mission in El Salvador
OPTs	Occupied Palestinian Territories
OSCE	Organization for Security and Co-operation in Europe
PA	Palestinian Authority (sometimes PNA: Palestinian National Authority)
PDPA	People's Democratic Party of Afghanistan
PIC	Peace Implementation Council
PLIP	Property Law Implementation Plan
PLO	Palestine Liberation Organization
PPR	permanent place of residence
PRODERE	Development Program for Refugees, Displaced and Repatriated Persons
PRRN	Palestinian Refugee Research Net

QIPs	quick impact projects
ROI	Repatriación Organizada Individual (Organized Individual Repatriation)
RRTF	Returns and Reconstruction Task Force
RS	Republika Srpska
SCF	Save the Children Fund
SFOR	Stabilization Force in Bosnia and Herzegovina
SNM	Somali National Movement
TNI	Indonesian Army
UN	United Nations
UNBRO	United Nations Border Relief Operation
UNDP	United Nations Development Programme
UNGAR	United Nations General Assembly Resolution
UNHCR	United Nations High Commissioner for Refugees
UNICEF	United Nations Children's Fund
UNMIK	United Nations Mission in Kosovo
UNOCHA	United Nations Office for the Coordination of Humanitarian Affairs
UNOPS	United Nations Office for Project Services
UNRWA	United Nations Relief and Works Agency for Palestine Refugees in the Near East
UNSC	United Nations Security Council
UNSCO	Office of the United Nations Special Coordinator
UNTAC	United Nations Transitional Authority for Cambodia
UNTAET	United Nations Transitional Administration in East Timor
URNG	Unidad Revolucionario Nacional Guatemalteca (United National Revolutionary Party of Guatemala)
USAID	United States Agency for International Development
WBG	West Bank and Gaza
WFP	World Food Programme
WHO	World Health Organization

1   Introduction

The comparative study
of refugee repatriation
programmes and the Palestinian
case

Michael Dumper

Between 1992–3 and 1997–9, United Nations High Commission for Refugees (UNHCR) and other collaborating organisations repatriated some 400,000 people back to Cambodia. Following the completion of the programme in 2000, UNHCR commissioned a report into the lessons learnt from the programme. The purpose of the 'lesson drawing' was

> not so much to evaluate what should have been done, but rather to look at each case in these terms: *if staff knew then what they know now, what could they have done differently or similarly.* Ultimately, no two refugee situations are alike, though some may resemble others more closely. The degree to which lessons learned from one situation can be applied to other contexts depends on the expertise, experience, and collective wisdom of staff.
> (Ballard 2002: 10, emphasis added)

Given the enormous challenges UNHCR continues to face, the focus on learning from hindsight and feeding that knowledge into its policy and planning systems should be applauded. There is no doubt that over the years there has been an accumulation of expertise and a corpus of both policy and academic literature that has incorporated 'lessons learnt' from a wide range of UNHCR operations and programmes with refugees (Jamal 2000). The publication of two UNHCR handbooks on repatriation and resettlement and the 'Convention Plus' discussions in 2003–4 attest to this institutional learning process (UNHCR 1996; UNHCR 2003; Fagen and Rodicio in this publication).

The purpose of this book and the international workshop from which it emanated is to draw out the extent to which this international expertise and knowledge can be transferred to the Palestinian context. This chapter comprises four sections. First, it sets out the main contours of the Palestinian refugee situation in order to provide some essential background for those readers unfamiliar with the genesis and evolution of the Palestinian refugee issue. One focus of this section will be also to identify the key unique features of the Palestinian case. Second, it describes the purpose and main components of the overall comparative research project from which this study is derived. Third, it outlines the continuing relevance of the study in the light of recent political developments in the Middle East conflict. The chapter will conclude by introducing the contributions to this book and by indicating how they inter-relate in order to bring a broad perspective to the issue of Palestinian refugees.

What is the Palestinian refugee issue?

The Palestinian refugee issue is the most difficult of the outstanding problems in the conflict between Israel and the Palestinians. With a growth rate of approximately 3.1 per cent, the *registered* refugee population of over 4 million is increasing at approximately 124,000 per annum (UNRWA 2004). It is therefore an issue that will not fade away over time and delay only increases the magnitude of the problems to be solved. The personal suffering and political instability in the Middle East caused by the non-resolution of this issue is plain to see.

The Palestinian refugee issue began in 1948 as a result of fighting between Zionist Jewish settlers and the indigenous Palestinian Arab population and the surrounding Arab states. The causes of this conflict and the subsequent developments have been dealt with in great depth by a large number of writers and will not be covered in this introduction (Avineri 1981; Flapan 1987; McDowall 1994; Sayigh 1997; Rogan and Shlaim 2002; Kimmerling and Migdal 2003; Massalha 2003; Morris 2004). However, a few major events should be noted to provide some context for the following discussion.

Great Britain, authorised by the League of Nations in 1922 to be the Mandatory authority in Palestine, was unable to reconcile the conflicting aspirations of the two ethnic groups to self-determination. It handed the issue over to the newly formed United Nations who in 1947 passed Resolution 181 which declared that Palestine should be partitioned into an Arab and a Jewish state. The Palestinian side regarded the resolution as unjust and refused to accept it. In the ensuing hostilities they were defeated and over 85 per cent of the population forced to leave their homes (BADIL 2003: 23). The new Israeli state based on the borders in Resolution 181 also acquired land beyond the borders approved by the UN and quickly consolidated its position by transferring refugee land and property to state institutions. It embarked upon a rapid programme of immigration absorption in which Jews from Western Europe and the Arab world were encouraged to start new lives in the new state of Israel defined as a Jewish state. At the same time, the right of return of Palestinian refugees to their homes was accepted and supported by the United Nations in Resolution 194. However, the strategic goal of Arab states and the Palestinians to reverse the establishment of Israel and the refusal of Israel to accept significant numbers of refugees led to an impasse in which the region both refused to accommodate the creation of the new state of Israel but could not defeat it.

A further war in 1967 resulted in Israel occupying the remaining parts of historic Palestine, known as the West Bank and Gaza Strip. This situation lasted until the mid-1970s when the Palestinians under the leadership of the Palestinian Liberation Organization made tentative moves to recognise Israel. In turn, Israel realised it could not eliminate the PLO and finally, in what became known as the 1993 Oslo Accords, agreed to an interim stage of Palestinian self-government in the West Bank and Gaza Strip. This set the scene for detailed discussions on final status issues including the refugee issue. However, the collapse of the transitional Oslo arrangements amid a welter of mutual recriminations regarding the failure of Palestinians to control their militants and the Israeli refusal to halt colonisation activities in the West Bank and Gaza Strip has suspended for the foreseeable future official negotiations on these issues.

As a result of these hostilities the Palestinian refugee population continued to live mostly in exile. One-third of the registered Palestine refugees, about 1.3 million, live in 59 recognised refugee camps in Jordan, Lebanon, the Syrian Arab Republic, the West Bank and Gaza Strip (UNRWA 2004). They are administered by an *ad hoc* UN agency, the UN Relief and Works Agency for Palestinian Refugees in the Near East (UNRWA) which was also made responsible for service delivery (UNGAR 303 (IV), 8 December 1949). Socio-economic conditions in the camps are generally poor with a high population density, cramped living conditions and inadequate basic infrastructure such as roads and sewers. The other two-thirds of the registered refugees live in and around the cities and towns of the host countries, and in the West Bank and the Gaza Strip, often in the environs of official camps. Although most of UNRWA's installations such as schools and health centres are located in refugee camps, a number are outside camps and all of the Agency's services are available to both camp and non-camp residents (UNRWA 2004).

A number of indices, such as those of employment, poverty, mortality rates, health and education, will give an idea of conditions in the camps and among refugees. With regard to employment, a recent survey in 2003 has shown that

Table 1.1　Registered refugees in UNRWA area of operations

Field of operations	Official camps	Registered refugees	Registered refugees in camps
Jordan	10	1,740,170	307,785
Lebanon	12	394,532	223,956
Syria	10	413,827	120,865
West Bank	19	665,246	179,541
Gaza Strip	8	922,674	484,563
Agency total	59	4,136,449	1,316,710

Figures as of 31 December 2003.

the Palestinian refugee population is poorly integrated in the labour market. They are employed more within the private sector, have less job security, work for lower pay, and have access to fewer work related benefits than others (Jacobsen 2003: 58). Many camp dwellers are poor, with the proportion of people earning less than $2 per day per person ranging from some 25 per cent in Syria to 35 per cent in Lebanon. The very poorest families are those that do not qualify for UNRWA assistance and have no employed members. The refugees in Lebanon are worst off because they are excluded from the formal labour market and they have poorer health. They make up the highest proportion of families with no employed member and the remittances they receive do not compensate for this (ibid.: 9).

Infant mortality is generally in the range of 20–30 deaths per 1,000 live births, which is comparable to US rates in the late 1960s. Camps in Syria show particularly low rates, while the Lebanese rates are the highest. Maternal mortality rates are also highest in Lebanon (240 maternal deaths per 100,000 live births) and lowest in Syria (75). In general, due to the special hardship programmes of UNRWA, there is little acute malnutrition among children. There is, however, more reported psychological distress as well as somatic illness among adults in camps than elsewhere, and most of this occurs in Lebanon (ibid.: 10).

A remarkable feature of the Palestinian refugee experience is the high level of education attained. Adult literacy is much higher among refugees than in the region as a whole, especially for women, and attests to the relative high quality of the UNRWA education system. Indeed, anecdotal evidence points to high-ranking non-Palestinian officials often attempting to obtain entry into UNRWA schools for their children. Female literacy is most marked in Syria where 90 per cent of refugee women over 14 years are literate, compared with 60 per cent in the national population. Enrolment of camp refugee children in school is about the same across all fields. Nearly all (97 per cent) attend school at secondary level. Nearly all children living in refugee camps go to UNRWA schools for elementary and preparatory education. The exception is the chronically ill and disabled children, who receive very little education. Refugees in Lebanon fare particularly badly in this (ibid.: 12).

As one would expect for a refugee case which has lasted over 56 years, most Palestinian refugees, even those in camps, live in permanent housing, and less than 5 per cent live in temporary dwellings. In general, infrastructure in the camps is the responsibility of the host governments, but UNRWA has played a large role in financing and introducing basic infrastructure. Nearly all camps have electricity, water and sewerage, but the stability of supply of electricity and drinking water in the camps is considerably worse than in surrounding areas. In Lebanon this is particularly so. Despite this, the indoor environment is poor, in terms of ventilation, humidity and temperature control. Crowding is higher in the camps than elsewhere, and around 30 per cent of the households have three or more persons per room. The camps in

Jordan and Gaza Strip fare the worst, with 40 per cent of the households having three persons or more per room (ibid.: 13).

Readers not familiar with the Palestinian–Israeli conflict should be reminded that although most refugees live in host countries, that is Jordan, Syria and Lebanon, over one-third are residing in the rump of historic Palestine, the West Bank and Gaza Strip, also known as the occupied Palestinian territories (OPTs). Here they comprise nearly 15 per cent of the worldwide Palestinian population. They are refugees from the areas that became Israel in 1948 and following a peace agreement would aspire either to return to their homes in Israel or to be compensated. Although fully integrated in the OPTs, in the sense that they have been treated by the Israeli occupying authorities in exactly the same way as other Palestinians under occupation, there are some differences, in addition to their residence in camps, which in itself casts them as a separate category. For example, unemployment in the refugee camps is 4 per cent higher than the rest of the OPTs, 21.5 per cent compared with 17.5 per cent. An official census reveals that in the camps for every 100 economically active persons there are 590 dependants compared with 530 for the rest of the population. In addition, 32.8 per cent of Palestinians living in refugee camps are classified as poor, that is earning 1,460 New Israeli Shekels (less than $2) or below per day. In 1998, despite being only 15 per cent of the population, they constituted one-quarter of the poor in the Palestinian Territory. Nevertheless, as one would anticipate after three generations of exile, there is some accumulation of wealth and consumer goods. Most refugee families own a refrigerator, gas cooker, television set and washing machine, although only 12 per cent of families own a private car (Palestinian Central Bureau of Statistics 2002).

To some extent these indices of low employment, poverty, fragile health systems, high infant mortality, high literacy rates can be replicated in other refugee situations such as the Afghani refugee camps in Pakistan and Cambodian refugee camps in Thailand. However, a closer study of the Palestinian refugee issue suggests at least five aspects in which the Palestinian case can be regarded as particular or unique: its longevity, number, legal complexity, nature of the conflict and lack of territoriality.

Perhaps the most striking uniqueness of the Palestinian refugee situation is its sheer longevity. As we have seen Palestinian refugees were created as a result of the establishment of the state of Israel in 1948 – 57 years ago – and is the longest running refugee case in the world. The Palestinian case is thus a multigenerational one with a fourth generation of descendants of the original displaced Palestinians currently being born. The only equivalent cases can be drawn from other postwar partitions such as those of Germany and India where a political settlement has since been reached although individual refugees still nurse a sense of loss and grievance. In the case of Germany and German refugees from Eastern Europe, legal attempts are taking place. This longevity produces specific dynamics of exile. On one hand there are greater opportunities of integration and economic and social ties being established with the host community. On the other hand, there can be a greater forging of nationalist consciousness as communal solidarities are maintained in a foreign environment. It is clear that in the Palestinian case, while a degree of political and economic integration has been permitted in Syria and Jordan (but not in Lebanon), there has been a strong growth in nationalist feeling and Palestinian self-identity.

The second aspect is to do with demography. The exact number of people displaced by the 1948 war is disputed. Estimates range from 600,000 to 957,000 but the long duration has meant that the numbers have multiplied. At the end of 2002, it is estimated that there were more than 7 million Palestinian refugees and displaced persons. This includes Palestinian refugees displaced in 1948 and registered for assistance with UNRWA (3.97 million); Palestinian refugees displaced in 1948 but not registered for assistance (1.54 million); Palestinian refugees displaced for the first time in 1967 (753,000); internally displaced Palestinians in Israel (pre-1967 borders) (274,000); and internally displaced Palestinians in the areas occupied by Israel in 1967 and since the end of the war (150,000). (These figures are compiled by the BADIL Resource Centre for Residency Rights and Refugee Research, and there is a full breakdown of their calculations in Appendix 2.) This makes the Palestinian refugee and displaced persons population the largest refugee and displaced persons population in the world. It is more than the combined total for all refugees in Asia under responsibility of UNHCR (UNHCR 1997: 287). What is important to remember is that the proportion of refugees to the total Palestinian population is significantly higher than in most other refugee situations. In total, the Palestinian refugee and displaced population comprises nearly three-quarters of the entire Palestinian population worldwide of approximately 9.3 million.

A third aspect is the legal framework of refugee status and protection. Most Palestinian refugees are registered with UNRWA and not UNHCR. This occurred partly for historical reasons in that the creation of UNRWA preceded UNHCR by a few months and the mandate of UNHCR specifically excluded the Palestinian population under the mandate of UNRWA. It was also partly geographical in that UNRWA was given responsibility for Palestinian refugees in four locations: Lebanon, Syria, Jordan and the West Bank and Gaza Strip. Finally, it was partly political in that the legal protection mandate was given to another specialised agency for Palestinians, the UN Conciliation Commission for Palestine (UNCCP) (whose activities fell into abeyance), leaving UNRWA as primarily a humanitarian agency. This has meant that the provision of services and institutional development has been outside the UNHCR framework for over 50 years. In addition, it is important to stress that there is a mismatch, mentioned above, between the total displaced population and their descendants (more than 7 million) and the approximately 4.1 million currently officially registered with UNRWA. As a result, the definition of who is a Palestinian refugee is open to many interpretations. Is it only those registered with UNRWA, or also those who were forced to leave their homes and are now in exile but are not registered with UNRWA? What about those who were displaced from their homes yet remained in Israel, but are not allowed to return to their original homes? One needs to recognise that, whatever the legal definition, in terms of political action, it is the self-perception of being displaced or being a refugee that is important to the people concerned and which should be taken into account.

The fourth and fifth aspects are interconnected and are those which received the most emphasis in my discussions following the workshop with Palestinian refugee groups in the Middle East. The fourth area is the nature of the Palestinian displacement. Israel was established as a state of the Jewish people and the return of the indigenous Palestinian population would undermine its *raison d'être*. Ethnic cleansing is an emotive term and can be used loosely, but in the case of the creation of the state of Israel by Zionist settlers, there is no doubt that there was a practice of expulsion of Palestinians even if a deliberate policy cannot be documented (Flapan 1987; Massalha 2003; Morris 2004). While the ethno-centric elements of Zionism remain dominant in the Israeli state, a return of refugees to their lands and property in the borders established in 1948 is impossible. To put it simply, if Israel is to remain a Zionist and a Jewish state it cannot accept a large number of refugees. Thus the transition from refugee to citizen in the Palestinian case is more complex and politically charged than in many other refugee cases, involving as it does the dismantling of the Jewish nature of the state. The Palestinian case turns the principle of *non-refoulement* on its head. The issue is not whether the conditions are safe for repatriation as in many other refugee cases but whether they will ever be allowed to return. There are other refugee cases where the return of refugees is denied – Guatemala and Namibia spring to mind – but the denial is usually pending a political settlement. In the Palestinian–Israeli case, the denial is based upon religion and ethnicity, i.e. Palestinians are Arabs and non-Jews.

The fifth aspect concerns the lack of Palestinian sovereignty over its historic territory. Whereas there may be many other refugee cases in which displacement has occurred owing to secessionist conflict or occupation (e.g. East Timor, Cambodia, Eritrea), in these cases, repatriation has taken place at the same time as nation-building is being implemented. The Palestinian case is ostensibly similar. However, the lack of sovereignty over historic Palestine in the Palestinian case has an additional complexity. Because of the establishment of Israel on 72 per cent of the land of mandatory Palestine, the existing Palestinian leadership in the West Bank and Gaza Strip has responsibility over only part of the lands to which the refugees seek to return. This places it in an ambiguous position. Its main constituency is the refugee population, virtually all of whom have claims to return to an area that is within the 1949 borders of Israel and which is not under the actual or projected jurisdiction of the Palestinian leadership. Thus a repatriation programme permitted by Israel will be to a new state of Palestine which is not where the refugees have come from. In this sense, the term 'repatriation' is a misnomer. Much of the political discussion and policy planning is about repatriation not to place of origin but to a different part of Palestine. However, the term is retained since, as we shall see, UNHCR has introduced a more flexible definition of the term to incorporate a return to the homeland or country of origin.

Having identified the main areas in which the Palestinian case can be termed unique, we are confronted with the fact that most refugee situations are, indeed, unique to some extent. There is nothing so unique about the Palestinian uniqueness, so to speak. However, the argument being put forward in this study is that there is a collective international experience in repatriation which can be usefully applied to programme planning in the Palestinian case and which can take into account the unique Palestinian features. There is probably no dispute over the contention that we should not re-invent the wheel. The discussion is more on what are the most suitable wheels for the road conditions of the Palestinian case.

Purpose of the study

The main purpose of this study is to examine the extent to which international best practice in refugee repatriation can be transferred to the Palestinian context. In doing so it explores the argument that the Palestinian–Israeli conflict is unique and contends that this exceptionalist discourse has been an impediment to the formulation of policy options that can draw on international experience. Thus there has been the failure to utilise the experience of UNHCR, the World Bank, the International Organization for Migration (IOM) and other international NGOs. This in turn has led to a restricted range of policy options and operational planning. It is significant to note that much of the official planning of repatriation in Palestinian circles has been at the prompting of the World Bank and only belatedly has there been recognition of the World Bank's experience in other forced migration situations (World Bank 2003; Brynen 2003; Brynen in this volume). The project sought, therefore, to examine the view that there is a wealth of expertise, experience and collective wisdom available in the international community that is not being drawn upon by academics, practitioners, policy-makers and activists in the Palestinian context and fed into the planning of a putative Palestinian refugee repatriation programme. The evidence suggests that there is only a limited amount of exchange of ideas and experience and much valuable expertise is not being passed on.

With this purpose in mind, in June 2004, an international workshop entitled *Transferring Best Practice: the comparative study of refugee return programmes with reference to the Palestinian context* was organised at Exeter University, UK. Funding was obtained from the British government's Department for International Development (DfID) and the International Development Research Center (IDRC), based in Ottawa. Advice on participants was obtained from IDRC, the UNHCR Evaluation and Policy Analysis Unit, senior UNRWA staff, Palestinian refugee organisations and Israeli academics and researchers.

The overall purpose of the workshop was to take the notion of Palestinian *exceptionalism* and hold it under scrutiny through the comparative study of refugee repatriation programmes and return. It did so by asking the following questions:

- To what extent can the Palestinian case be said to be unique?
- Where are the divergences, overlaps and points of similarity with other refugee situations?
- What lessons can be drawn from these comparisons?
- How can these lessons inform refugee organisations, the donor community and policy-makers?

In attempting to answer these questions, the workshop covered three main fields of study. The first was the contextual and methodological field, reviewing on one hand the main trends in forced migration and refugee studies and issues concerning policy transfer and comparative research, and on the other hand the historical and political background of UNHCR and the negotiations around the Palestinian refugee issue. The second comprised in-depth case studies in which specific refugee situations were closely examined with a view to drawing out key issues in the formulation of repatriation programmes. Cases covered included Cambodia, Guatemala, Kosovo Albanians in Italy, the Horn of Africa, Sri Lanka, Somaliland, Iraq, Afghanistan, and Bosnia and Herzegovina. Finally, it also embraced a number of studies more closely linking the Palestinian case to the comparative framework. These included studies on compensation and Palestinian positions and options on return.

The gathering was specifically designed as a workshop in which sessions comprised the presentations of two related papers and contributions by at least two discussants and followed by ample time for focused discussion. The programme and invitations were designed to maximise the exchange of ideas, operational models and information between specialists in a range of different refugee situations and experts on and practitioners in the Palestinian refugee issue. In addition to the session discussions there were also two concluding panel sessions in which six participants were invited to sum up their conclusions from the workshop. A list of participants can be found in Appendix 1.

The main purpose of this book is not only to present the primary outcomes of the discussions but also to provide some of the tenor of the debate and the dilemmas being confronted. In essence it attempts to reconcile two opposing perceptions. It recognises the unique elements of the Palestinian case which has led to an *exceptionalist* discourse regarding Palestinian refugees. It contends that this uniqueness is crucial in the planning and preparation of any repatriation programmes. Without the unique elements being factored in there is little chance of a programme being implemented. Nevertheless, by the end of the two and a half days, a consensus emerged that there were areas of convergence with other refugee situations which are much more widespread than hitherto acknowledged.

There was not complete agreement amongst all the participants over the extent of that convergence. Some felt that the convergence was differentiated according to various fields. For example, there may be convergence of specific operational and logistical aspects, but there was less convergence in legal and political fields. Others thought that any emphasis on similarities with other cases would neglect the nature of the Palestinian displacement as a result of an exclusionist and Zionist vision of the state of Israel which to them was the key and over-riding difference. Others yet again held that by highlighting similarities the weight of international practice, which is broadly supportive of the rights of refugees, could be brought to bear on Israel to change its resistance to refugee repatriation. At the very least, there was broad agreement that mistakes have been made in the past, that the international community has learnt from them and that these lessons should be passed on or absorbed by those involved in the Palestinian context.

In addition to the papers and the workshop discussion, the project also included a dissemination and dialogue element. A summary of the workshop was compiled and a series of presentations were given to senior UNRWA staff, refugee organisations, government officials, academics and policy researchers in Jordan, Syria, Lebanon, Israel and the OPTs. These public meetings and small group discussions provided a good opportunity to bring into the public domain concrete issues associated with repatriation and to generate internal discussion.

Much feedback was received from these presentations and this has informed the compilation of this publication. Reactions ranged from outright hostility to the notion of comparison, in the light of continuing Israeli incursions, assassinations and evictions, through to a grudging acceptance that repatriation was implicit in many of the current policies of Lebanon and Jordan, and on to a cautious welcome, by a minority, of the mapping out of international frameworks for repatriation. From some quarters there was also concern that the study focused on the choice of cases which highlighted repatriation rather than other solutions to the question of refugeedom, while from others there were more pressing immediate concerns associated with conditions in the refugee camps and the ongoing occupation of Palestinian territory.

The impact of current events on the project

Before we go any further, we should examine the impact of the current developments on the project, such as the breakdown of negotiations between

Israel and the Palestinians, the Israeli re-occupation of the West Bank and Gaza Strip in 2002–4 and the death of the PLO leader and Palestinian Authority President, Yasser Arafat. First a bit of background: Discussions concerning the value of comparative work in the search for policy options for a Palestinian repatriation programme surfaced in the aftermath of the Camp David summit in 2000 and the Taba peace talks in 2001. In the absence of details to flesh out an Israeli–Palestinian agreement on the refugee issue, studies were commissioned by the World Bank, the European Commission and the Palestinian Authority's Ministry of Planning and International Cooperation (MOPIC) (Exeter Refugee Study Group 2001; Dumper 2003; Brynen in this publication). Following the change of government in Israel and the accession of Ariel Sharon to the premiership and arrival of a coalition of rightwing Israeli parties with maximalist positions to power, the already faltering peace process ground to a halt. The international community in the form of the Quartet, comprising the United States, Russia, the European Union and the United Nations, made attempts to re-launch it in the form of a reconstituted staged process known as the 'Road Map'. However, these have also failed in the face of disputes about the role of the Palestinian leader, Yasser Arafat, in supporting operations against Israeli civilians.

Israeli incursions against Palestinian residential areas, continued assassinations of party leaders and the construction of a wall down the middle of the West Bank have combined with the broader factors outlined above to create a new status quo where detailed discussion of refugee repatriation seems both irrelevant and a distraction. Policy-makers, the donor community, researchers and the refugees themselves can argue that there are more immediate tasks to hand. Intellectual efforts are best aimed, it could be said, at interim targets such as devising mutually beneficial security arrangements and confidence boosting measures or at fundamentals such as building up international support for the Palestinian refugee right of return. This view was certainly expressed to me during the tour of the region speaking to refugee representatives and UN officials mentioned above.

Clearly this is a legitimate position, and the re-ordering of research priorities in the light of changing circumstances (such as September 11 and the invasion of Iraq) is a constant feature of research in Middle East politics. Discussion of repatriation programmes that are to be implemented in a post-agreement phase when a negotiating process, let alone an agreement, is possibly some years hence, may at first appear premature, insensitive and unproductive. The details of a repatriation programme, it could be argued, are entirely contingent upon a political agreement, which in the Israeli–Palestinian case is fast receding. Indeed, the areas of overlap in the positions of the official Israeli and Palestinian negotiators that had been increasing during and after the Taba talks, and which may have provided the platform for some contingency planning, may no longer be the starting positions for any resumption of talks.

Nevertheless, there are two reasons why discussions around repatriation continue to be important. First, in the event of a political agreement, the repatriation of an unspecified number of Palestinian refugees will take place. This is a fairly safe assumption to make. I can foresee no circumstances in which a Palestinian leadership will sign up to an agreement where there is no repatriation involved. Whether there will be repatriation to pre-1967 Israel, or solely to the OPTs, and in what relative numbers, will be subject to the balance of power at the time of negotiations, but a peace agreement will undoubtedly contain some form of refugee repatriation.

In fact, as we will read in subsequent chapters, since the end of the Cold War, of the range of options traditionally available to refugees – integration into host countries, resettlement to third countries or repatriation to country of origin – repatriation has been the preferred option of the international community. UNCHR nominated the 1990s as the 'decade of repatriation'. This emphasis on repatriation drew criticism in the late 1990s. The criticism pointed to the lack of real choice available and the coercive nature of some of the programmes, the failure to take into account that many refugees had entered into new labour markets in exile and that many of the programmes were state-centred and top-down, which reduced the scope for refugee participation and initiative. Yet, despite such criticism, repatriation still holds a pre-eminent role in the constellation of options available to refugees. Indeed, since 11 September 2001, it is clear that repatriation will continue to be the preferred option of the international community. Fear of infiltration by terrorists has dramatically reduced the opportunities for the two other options contemplated: resettlement into third countries and integration into the host country. Although it may be the case that here is another situation in which the Palestinian–Israeli case is exceptional and bucks the trend, there is no doubt that repatriation remains on the medium-term agenda. International practice will continue to frame the debate over policy options for refugees and continue to put pressure on Israel to accept at least a limited number into Israel itself, and to accept that repatriation to the OPTs will be an essential part of any peace agreement.

In the light of this, those with access to data, to a network of researchers and to the necessary resources have an opportunity to carry out such medium-term policy research. The academic environment provides the opportunity to explore future dilemmas and challenges relatively free from political pressures and the daily pressures experienced by those under occupation or the threat of physical violence. The Palestinian refugee issue is an ongoing crisis. New refugees are being created currently by the continuing conflict and violence between the Israeli army and militant groups. Those immersed in these daily struggles and anxieties do not have the resources, the time or the mental energy to devote to medium-term planning. This is particularly the case in the Palestinian context as the small numbers of Palestinian academics and others equipped for such research are both under-resourced and over-stretched by more pressing issues. It is therefore both appropriate and responsible for those, concerned with the refugee issue, who are not subjected to the same pressures, to explore these themes and offer their insights. Any use of the opportunities for strategic research should not undervalue or denigrate the importance of other activities focusing on humanitarian, security and political rights. Rather it can be viewed as complementary and positive in that it provides guidance in terms of direction and hope in terms of a way out of the political impasse.

A second reason for the relevance of this study is derived from the role that the refugee issue played in creating a stalemate in the peace negotiations. Prior to the Camp David summit in 2000, most preparations had been focused on security and border issues, Israeli colonies, Jerusalem, water allocations, the nature of the interim administration, confidence building measures etc., and considerable progress had been made on them. As those who followed the progress of the Refugee Working Group set up by the Madrid Peace Conference in 1991 can attest, this was not the case on the refugee issue, which was dogged by lack of movement from the beginning (Peters 1996; Tamari 1996). As a result, most observers will agree the refugee issue was the 'deal-breaker' at both Camp David and Taba. Two major reasons for this were, first, the lack of preparedness by the negotiators and, second, the incapacity of the negotiators and their political masters to shift their respective constituencies. Closely held national myths, shibboleths, posturing and rhetoric imprisoned both sides when it came to addressing the issue at the heart of the conflict – the future of the Palestinian refugees. The right of return to their homes is enshrined in Palestinian notions of identity and justice whereas the fear of a demographic reversal, rendering the Jewishness of Israel meaningless, preoccupies the Israeli side. The demonisation of the Other on this issue has been a major contributing factor to the breakdown in trust and of the peace process.

The comparative study of refugee repatriation programmes helps to contextualise a Palestinian repatriation programme and the likely elements it will contain. Indeed, irrespective of the recognition of refugee rights, which are fundamental to a political agreement, comparative studies can be used to inject a dose of political realism into the debate about numbers of returnees. For example, the study shows that repatriation rarely entails a mass flow of refugees back to their homes, but is often a carefully managed process involving local institutional capacity building, training and human resource development, prior investment and a series of consultation mechanisms before the first refugee leaves their exile. Similarly, UNHCR statistics indicate that no more than 25 per cent of refugees have returned to their countries of origin. Global patterns of actual repatriation suggest that refugees, while desirous of achieving their political rights, are often circumspect in returning immediately to their place of origin after many years in exile.

In the Palestinian–Israeli context, the insights provided by comparative studies of figures such as these and the reality of repatriation programmes may be double-edged and offer assurances and alarm in equal measure to both sides. It may be disconcerting to many Israeli citizens to learn that repatriation programmes have taken place which do not have cataclysmic effects upon the society that is expected to absorb the returnees, and indeed may offer many advantages to it. Similarly, many Palestinians will be concerned to learn of the degree to which, despite the full backing of international law and the presence of external military forces, many repatriation programmes do not succeed in meeting the aspirations of the refugees and indeed fall considerably short of them. In this way, comparative studies can be used to penetrate some of the myths and fears associated with repatriation and point to a more evidence-based set of negotiations. Despite the deteriorating political situation, comparative work will not only remain a useful reference point for future planning and negotiation, but also assist in the humanisation of the Other which is a pre-requisite for a peaceful settlement.

Structure of the book

Regretfully not all the papers presented at the workshop have been included in this book. For reasons of space it was not possible to publish all the contributions. Papers were selected both to reflect the sense of the discussion and to ensure a degree of continuity and internal coherence. In the same way it was not possible to include a summary of the discussion at each session or for that matter between the sessions and at the end of each day. These were possibly as fruitful as the formal sessions themselves. Nevertheless, as editor I have striven to incorporate both the tenor and the substance of all these contributions in this introduction and the concluding chapter.

This book is divided into three sections reflecting the main themes of the workshop: an overview of general patterns and trends, case studies of a number of refugee repatriation situations and the lessons that could be learnt. In Part I, Professor Richard Black, co-Editor of the *Journal for Refugee Studies* and co-Director of the Sussex Centre for Migration Research, provides an overview of both the main trends in the study of refugee repatriation and repatriation itself. He highlights the disadvantages of a policy-driven research agenda which has neglected developments on the ground. The overall thrust of the chapter is to contextualise the study of Palestinian refugees to the wider literature and the debates that have taken place. Patricia Fagen, formerly a UNHCR official and now Senior Associate at the Institute for the Study of International Migration in Georgetown University, outlines the development of UNHCR policy and practice on repatriation since its inception. She discusses the challenges it has faced in exercising its mandate. These have ranged from conflicting political pressures and insufficient funding and institutional capacity to unrealistic expectations of what it can achieve. Nevertheless, her chapter points to a number of examples of good practice which have become international norms and have set benchmarks in the implementation of repatriation programmes.

Part I also includes two chapters which connect this overview to the Palestinian case. Professor Rex Brynen, chair of the Middle East Studies programme at McGill University and formerly a consultant to the World Bank and the Ministry of Planning in the Palestinian Authority, discusses the internal debates on the Palestinian refugee repatriation in both the Israeli and Palestinian policy communities and in the donor community. He attempts to delineate possible components of a repatriation strategy. Brynen also outlines the implications for repatriation contained in the Taba negotiations and the unofficial Geneva Accord of 2003. This is a theme developed in more detail by Dr Menachem Klein, Senior Lecturer in Political Science at Bar Ilan University, Israel, and former advisor to the Israeli Camp David negotiating team in 2000. In his chapter on negotiations between Israelis and Palestinians on the refugee issue he delineates approaches in which Palestinian refugees could be permitted to return to live in their former locales and ways in which such return would be forbidden. The chapter therefore links the overall context of repatriation to the detailed niceties of negotiations themselves and the political conditions that would allow a repatriation programme for Palestinian refugees. A common theme running through this section is that, despite the very serious political difficulties in reaching an agreement, repatriation both in the broader global context and in the Palestinian case is very much an option, particularly since September 11 and the rising concerns over immigration in the developed world.

Part II comprises a series of case studies ranging from Cambodia, Guatemala, the Horn of Africa and Afghanistan to Bosnia, but which at the same time highlight specific themes which throw light on the construction of a repatriation programme. The first case study by Dr Finn Stepputat, Senior Researcher at the Danish Institute for International Studies, examines refugee repatriation in Guatemala by examining the agreements and the institutional frameworks that bolstered them. Of particular relevance to the Palestinian case is his focus on the state-building implications of the whole process and the importance of recognising the role of refugees as economic actors in a broader labour market. Dr Laura Hammond, Assistant Professor in the Department of International Development, Community and Environment at Clark University, USA, continues the economic theme by focusing on the importance of an accurate assessment of the needs of refugees in returning to their countries of origin. Her chapter argues that, for a repatriation programme to be durable and achieve a measure of reintegration of the refugees, assistance packages have to be carefully tailored to the economic conditions. She proposes that household food economy analysis is a transferable technique for ascertaining the appropriate kind of refugee assistance.

The jointly authored chapter by Dr Christopher McDowell, Director of the Information Centre about Asylum and Refugees (ICAR) at the School of Social Sciences, City University, London, and Nick van Hear, Head of Research Programmes at the Centre for Migration, Policy and Society (COMPAS), University of Oxford, takes a broader perspective both thematically and through the comparison of five cases – East Timor, Sri Lanka, Georgia, Colombia and Burundi. In doing so it examines two important issues: first, the extent to which repatriation should be considered as a continuation of the management of 'forced migration emergencies' in the conflict to post-conflict phase, and second, the extent to which current trends in repatriation reflect the broader neo-liberal policies espoused by the international donor community.

The focus of the next three chapters is on the post-conflict phase. Paul Prettitore, formerly Legal Advisor in the Human Rights Department of the OSCE Mission to Bosnia and Herzegovina and currently Legal Advisor to the World Bank office in the West Bank, addresses another issue very relevant to the Palestinian case – that of property restitution in Bosnia and Herzegovina. He lays out the political frameworks and legal mechanisms that were put into place to ensure that most refugees were able to return to their homes and examines the extent to which this occurred. He demonstrates clearly that without international intervention down to the municipal level much of what had been agreed in the Dayton peace treaty regarding repatriation would not have taken place. The chapter of Ana García Rodicio, formerly researcher with the Jesuit Refugee Service in Cambodia and currently researcher on the Globalitaria Project 'Conflicts: Prevention, Resolution and Reconciliation' in Madrid, focuses on the importance of voluntary repatriation. In her study of repatriation in Cambodia she argues that unless voluntary repatriation is seen as part of post-conflict reconciliation process its durability will be brought into question. In addition, she contends that existing repatriation programmes focus on the juridical and legal (top-down) at the expense of the grassroots and psychosocial (bottom-up) elements of the return process. The third chapter of this group of post-conflict focus is by Peter Marsden, Coordinator of the British Agencies Afghanistan Group project at the Refugee Council in the UK, who examines the role of UNHCR in Afghanistan. He argues that UNHCR was forced to compromise on its refugee protection mandate as a result of host government and financial pressures. His analysis also reveals problems of conducting repatriation in conditions of a weak central government and poor coordination of the aid agencies, conditions which may prevail in the Palestinian case.

The final chapter in the case studies section is by Michael Kagan, currently an instructor at the Tel Aviv University Law School's Refugee and Asylum-Seeker Rights Clinic and formerly a lawyer in refugee legal aid programmes in Cairo and Beirut. His chapter focuses on the repatriation of Iraqis from Iran, Saudi Arabia and Lebanon in 2003 and brings the book neatly back to the Palestinian case by his probing of possible parallels. His focus is on the gap between UN-established standards of voluntariness in repatriation and the political pressures to set certain parameters of choice for refugees. In this way he is able to make an assessment of existing UN standards.

The final section offers two perspectives on lesson drawing. The first, by Dr Sari Hanafi, draws attention to international frameworks and patterns of trade and exchange in the analysis of refugee repatriation. He argues that a more accurate understanding of the dynamics of repatriation on both the social and economic level is to view it as a 'return migration'. This term brings out the dislocations occurring and new orientations required in the process of repatriation. The second perspective is by myself and attempts to bring together the main themes of the papers and the workshop discussions and incorporates feedback from the regional tour presenting the findings of the workshop. In it, I delineate five main elements which would provide the core principles for the construction of a repatriation programme for Palestinian refugees. As such there is an attempt to offer a checklist for policy-makers, activists and aid workers.

Before continuing into the substance of this subject, it is important to clarify the use of some terms. This project, which straddles the fields of forced migration studies and refugee studies *and* the study of the Arab–Israel conflict, has encountered a variety of identical terms which mean different things in the different fields. For example, *displaced persons*, which is used generically in refugee studies, has however a specific and more limited meaning enshrined in the agreements of the 1993 Oslo peace process in the Arab–Israeli conflict. Therefore a number of commonly used terms need to be defined.

In this book, the term *return* is used generically to encompass all elements of a refugee return including individual returns, 'spontaneous' returns and planned programmes of return. It also includes the integration of returnees in the country of origin. In contrast, the term *repatriation* is used as one element of return – the logistical and operational aspects of a large-scale repatriation programme. Thus this book refers to a *return process* of which a *repatriation programme* is a sub-set. The term *displaced persons* is used in three senses: a) generically as those who have been forced to leave their homes but not necessarily their countries or crossed any borders; b) as those Palestinians displaced by the 1967 Arab–Israeli war and referred to as such in the Jordan–Israel Peace Agreement of 1994; and c) Palestinians who have left their homes but still reside in Israel and are referred to as *internally displaced*. Displaced persons who have crossed an international border or ceasefire line are referred to as *refugees*. The term *resettlement*, or *tawtiin* in Arabic, refers in this book to the integration of refugees into their host countries. The term *returnee*, that is a refugee who has returned, is avoided as much as possible, not because it is wrong but because it may cause confusion. Instead the term returned *refugee* is used which has the added advantage of conveying the continuity in the status of refugees.

Finally, I would like to express my sincere thanks and profoundest gratitude to Shahira Samy, research PhD student at Exeter University, who acted as my assistant throughout this project. Her attention to detail and conscientiousness gave a much needed structure to my amorphous ideas. Assembling a high quality team of people required considerable research and discussion and in this task I would also like to acknowledge the help of the Workshop Steering Group, namely Roula al-Rifai from IDRC, Professor Black, Terry Rempel from BADIL Resource Centre for Residency Rights and Refugee Research and Dr Sari Hanafi. Others who provided essential ideas and contacts were Jeff Crisp, at the time Director of the UNHCR Evaluation and Policy Analysis, Karen Abu Zayyed, at the time Deputy Commissioner, now Commissioner-General of UNRWA, Hildegard Dumper, independent refugee consultant, and Michal Reifen from the Economic Cooperation Foundation (ECF), Tel Aviv. I am very grateful to all the participants of the workshop for the time and effort they put into coming to Exeter and for their contribution in making the project so worthwhile. In addition, the contributors to this volume have been outstanding in sticking to the tight deadlines I tyrannically imposed and worked hard to make sure this publication could be put into print so quickly. For help in arranging my tour in the Middle East to present the findings of the workshop I am very grateful to Karen Abu Zayyed, Salman Abu Sitta, William Lee, Raja Deeb, Lex Takkenberg, Simone Ricca, Jabber Suleiman, Salim Tamari, Mays Warrad and the staff of the Institute for Palestine Studies in Beirut, BADIL, Shaml and ECF. In Exeter I would also like to thank all my PhD students who assisted in the logistics and the hospitality involved in holding the workshop, particularly Awad Mansour, Maha Samaan and Ghada Ageel, Tim Harris for his conference-organising skills and Jan Evans, the Finance Officer of the School for Historical, Political and Sociological Studies. Finally I would like to thank my companion, partner and wife, Ann, and my family for their support and encouragement during a period when I was more distracted than ever.

This work was carried out with the aid of a grant from the Middle East Expert and Advisory Services Fund which is managed by the International Development Research Centre (IDRC), Ottawa, and financially supported by the Canadian International Development Agency and IDRC, in cooperation with the Department of Foreign Affairs and International Trade, Canada. An equal amount of funding was provided by the Department of International Development, United Kingdom. I am very grateful for their support.

References

Avineri, S. (1981) *The making of modern Zionism: The intellectual origins of the Jewish state* (London: Weidenfeld and Nicolson).

BADIL Resource Center (2003) Refugee return and real property restitution in Bosnia-Herzegovina – Lessons learned for the Palestinian case, press release of 28 January, available online at www.badil.org

Ballard, B. (2002) *Reintegration programmes for refugees in South-East Asia: Lessons learnt from UNHCR's experience* (Geneva: UNHCR: Evaluation and Policy Analysis Unit and Regional Bureau for Asia and the Pacific).

Dumper, M. (2003) "The Return of Palestinian refugees and displaced persons: The evolution of an EU policy on the Middle East peace process." Presented to the 2nd International Stocktaking Conference on Palestinian Refugee Research, International Development Research Center, Ottawa, July 2003.

Exeter Refugee Study Group (2001) "Study of policy and financial instruments for the return and integration of Palestinian displaced persons in the West Bank and Gaza Strip." Unpublished study prepared for the EU Refugee Task Force.

Flapan, S. (1987) *The birth of Israel: Myths and realities* (London: Croom Helm).

Jacobsen, L. B. (2003) *Finding means: UNRWA's financial situation and the living conditions of Palestinian refugees*, Summary Report, FAFO Report 415.

Jamal, A. (2000) *Refugee repatriation and reintegration in Guatemala: Lessons learned from UNHCR's experience* (Geneva: UNHCR: Evaluation and Policy Analysis Unit and Regional Bureau for the Americas and the Caribbean).

Kimmerling, B., and Migdal, J. (2003) *The Palestinian people: A history* (Cambridge: Harvard University Press).

McDowall, D. (1994) *The Palestinians: The road to nationhood* (London: Minority Rights Publications).

Massalha, N. (2003) *The politics of denial: Israel and the Palestinian refugee problem* (London: Pluto Press).

Morris, B. (2004) *The birth of the Palestinian refugee problem revisited.* 2nd edition (Cambridge: Cambridge University Press).

Palestinian Central Bureau of Statistics (2002) *Population characteristics of the Palestinian refugee camps* (Ramallah: Palestinian Central Bureau of Statistics).

Peters, J. (1996) *Pathways to peace: The multilateral Arab–Israeli peace talks* (London, Pinter).

Rogan, E., and Shlaim, A. (eds.) (2002) *The war for Palestine: Re-writing the history of 1948.* (Cambridge: Cambridge University Press).

Sayigh, Y. (1997) *Armed struggle and the search for state: The Palestinian national movement, 1949–1993* (Oxford: Oxford University Press).

Tamari, S. (1996) "Return, resettlement, repatriation: The future of Palestinian refugees in the peace negotiations", *Final Status Strategic Studies*, Washington, DC: Institute for Palestine Studies, http://www.arts.mcgill.ca/PRRN/papers/tamari2.html

UNHCR (1996) *Voluntary repatriation: International protection* (Geneva: UNHCR).

UNHCR (1997) *The state of the world's refugees: A humanitarian agenda* (Oxford: Oxford University Press).

UNHCR (May 2003) *Framework for durable solutions for refugees and persons of concern* (Geneva: UNHCR, Core Group on Durable Solutions).

United Nations Relief Works Agency (2004) http://www.un.org/unrwa (accessed in December 2004).

Part I

Trends and patterns in refugee repatriation

Overview and the Palestinian case

2 Return of refugees

Retrospect and prospect

Richard Black

'Refugee studies': key themes

The field of refugee studies has expanded considerably over recent decades, both in the form of new institutions and in terms of the volume of academic research and publications. Institutionally, the establishment of new research programmes and centres focusing on 'refugee studies' or 'forced migration studies' took off in the early 1980s and has expanded to the point at which strong institutions now exist not only in Europe and the Americas but also in poorer regions that are most affected by refugees (Black 2001a). The fact that many – perhaps most – of these centres have been established with funding from policy agencies and/or have developed an academic mission explicitly oriented towards analysis of policy questions and the provision of policy solutions, helps to explain the extent to which the emerging field of refugee studies as a whole has tended to be dominated by policy demands. This is reinforced by the structure of funding opportunities for refugee research, which has tended to be dominated by operational agencies and government policy departments seeking answers to policy questions. In particular, the United Nations High Commissioner for Refugees (UNHCR) has acted as both a focus and a funding agency for a considerable body of refugee studies research.

Policy research on refugees has taken a number of forms. This has included studies – often highly critical – of asylum policy in European and other 'northern' states, and the amassing of a considerable body of evidence of use in informing policies towards the integration and/or incorporation of refugees and asylum-seekers in host countries. It has also included a now substantial literature either focused on or of relevance to humanitarian assistance to refugees, which has sought to evaluate, inform and critique the work of governments and international agencies working in the field. There are theoretical contributions too, although these have often focused on typologies of forced migrants which themselves have taken their cue from political and legal definitions rather than building from first principles.

If a focus on policy is one key characteristic of refugee studies, another is arguably its tendency to exceptionalism. For example, much research in 'refugee studies' tends to take the category 'refugee' or 'asylum-seeker' as a given and proceeds from there to show (usually) how they are victimised or excluded, or treated in a particular way by public policy. Such research tends to deal with refugees in a relatively uncontextualised way, emphasising how the circumstances of particular refugee groups require specific solutions. From this perspective, refugee studies might be expected to have contributed little to comparative analysis or to the understanding of broader social questions. Where analysis has concentrated on setting out some key underlying theoretical questions for the field of refugee studies, a more robust basis for drawing wider conclusions from the 'refugee studies' literature does exist. Nonetheless, it is still a core element of the field that the focus is on the experience or situations of refugees as a group, however defined, often in isolation, or at best in contrast to other migrants or populations.

For example, an important paper by Stein and Tomasi at the start of the 1980s, partly in response to the Indo-Chinese refugee situation, called for 'a comprehensive, historical, interdisciplinary and comparative perspective which focuses on the consistencies and patterns in the refugee experience' – in other words, a research agenda was set out concerned with exploring the essence of *being* a refugee (Stein and Tomasi 1981). Similarly, a prospective of the field in the first issue of the *Journal of Refugee Studies* refers to the category of 'refugee' as an ascribed label that also has consequences which can be explored in comparative perspective (Zetter 1988). Although such a view has been critiqued by some (Malkki 1995a), the core of the field of refugee studies has arguably remained dominated by a policy-led and somewhat exceptionalist view of the refugee experience.

Both of these characteristics might help to explain why return has remained on the sidelines of refugee studies, lying, as it does, largely outside the core mandate of the key policy organisation involved with refugees – UNHCR – and after the period in which the distinctiveness of the 'refugee experience' might be expected to be most visible. Indeed, beyond a small number of edited books on refugee return (Allen and Morsink 1994; Black and Koser 1999; North and Simmons 2000), and one or two monographs (Hammond 2004), the topic of return has received surprisingly little attention from academics. For example, in the *Journal of Refugee Studies* since 2000, just seven out of a total of 90 published papers dealt with return; there were just seven articles on return out of 63 in the same period in the *International Journal of Refugee Law*, with five of these focused specifically on 'non-refoulement' as a legal concept. Meanwhile, just 10 out of over 100 UNHCR 'New Issues' papers are on return or repatriation, with relatively scant attention to the topic in the main migration journals, *International Migration Review* and *International Migration,* either. This is in spite of the existence of a growing body of 'policy-orientated, operational and basic studies' that have remained outside the core of peer-reviewed literature (Preston 1999).

Return of refugees in the 'decade of repatriation'

If the return of refugees has been a topic relatively neglected in the academic literature, the same cannot be said of the reality of refugee return on the ground. For example, over the course of the 1990s, it is estimated that over 12 million refugees had been repatriated to their countries of origin, in what the UN High Commissioner, Mrs Ogota, predicted in 1992 – accurately as it turns out – would be a 'decade of repatriation' (Ogota 1992). If it were not for new refugee movements – a big if, since almost as many people were newly displaced from their home countries over the decade – repatriation on such a scale would have all but eliminated the 'refugee problem' as it existed in the early 1990s, a true 'peace dividend' at the end of the Cold War. Moreover, this large-scale return movement also presents some interesting opportunities to learn lessons for the Middle East, since much of it took place in the context of high-profile mass returns to a small group of countries with highly visible peace processes often guided or supervised by the United Nations or other international actors (Table 2.1). Thus, whether we are talking about return of refugees to participate in UN-administered elections in Cambodia or Mozambique at the beginning of the 1990s, or return under the wing of UN-sanctioned multilateral military forces in Kosovo or Afghanistan at the end of the decade, there has been no shortage of assessment and analysis of these return movements, even if this has not yet had a significant effect on the field of 'refugee studies' (Emmott 1996; Marsden 1999; Petrin 2002; Turton and Marsden 2002).

One place in which this practical experience of return has been reviewed has been UNHCR's own overview of refugee issues, *The State of the World's Refugees*, which was published biannually through much of the 1990s. Here, we can identify changing approaches to return, and a mixed assessment of its potential to represent a genuine and relatively unproblematic 'durable solution' to refugee flight. For example, in its first issue in 1993, there was a major section on 'Going Home: Voluntary Repatriation', which highlighted returns to Cambodia, Mozambique and Afghanistan, and profiled 'Quick

Table 2.1 Mass repatriations, 1992–2002

Years	Country of return	Estimated number of returns (millions)
1992–3	Afghanistan	1.5
1992–3	Cambodia	0.4
1993–4	Mozambique	1.4
1996–7	Rwanda	1.6
1996–8	Bosnia and Herzegovina	0.3
1999–2000	Kosovo	0.9
2002 onwards	Afghanistan	1.9

Source: UNHCR Statistical Yearbook.

Impact Projects' (QIPs) as a key form of intervention in support of the return process (UNHCR 1993). This was arguably a time of great optimism for UNHCR as to what could be achieved by international intervention to support return processes, even if the return to Mozambique, for example, was largely effected by refugees themselves impatient to get back to their places of origin whether or not international assistance was there to help them (Winter 1994).

By the middle of the decade, a more cautious note was being sounded. For example, the 1995 edition of *The State of the World's Refugees* does not focus on return, although it does explore the concept of 'temporary protection', a notion which is premised on the expectation of return at the end of a hopefully short period of exile. The 1995 edition also highlights the need for 'rebuilding shattered societies' – a recognition that countries of origin are not unproblematically moving to peace, such that international intervention needs to make the peace, and not simply to facilitate repatriation (UNHCR 1995). As in the previous issue, a profile of return to Mozambique is included, along with what the organisation saw as its successful implementation of QIPs in this and other situations. However, discussion is also included of more problematic returns to Myanmar and Vietnam, undertaken in circumstances that were not necessarily voluntary.

The two most recent editions of *The State of the World's Refugees* in 1997 and 2000 come back to the issue of return, with a much more upbeat approach to the possibilities presented by return. Immediately prior to the 1997 edition, the largest return by far was of 1.2 million people to Rwanda, but this highly contentious return was not profiled by the report – even though it was referred to quite extensively in the text (UNHCR 1997). Instead, special sections highlighted the 'little noticed' but essentially successful return of Tuareg to Mali, and the then still nascent return to Bosnia, a return process that was to develop considerable political and ideological significance both for UNHCR and for other international actors in Bosnia. Moreover, whilst recognising that the 'circumstances confronting . . . returnees are fraught with difficulty', and that these include continuing social divisions, political instability, physical devastation and psychological trauma, overall the report stressed how return is symbiotically related to peace-building in conflict-torn countries.

In 2000, *The State of the World's Refugees* was based around a retrospective of the work of UNHCR over 50 years of humanitarian action, and again includes a major section on return. Here too, the focus is on the perceived 'success stories', in Namibia, Central America, Cambodia and Mozambique, with the argument put forward that UNHCR has moved from 'short-term and small scale' interventions to ensure safe return, towards 'UN peacebuilding operations, and humanitarian activities [which] were integrated into a wider strategic and political framework aimed at ensuring reconciliation, reintegration and reconstruction' (UNHCR 2000). This reflects the consolidation of repatriation as the preferred political solution to refugee flight not only for UNHCR but also for much of the international humanitarian community.

The trend since the 1990s towards return as the preferred option, rather than integration and resettlement, is relevant to the Palestinian case, and might be viewed as supporting pressure on the Israelis to consider this issue more seriously – especially in the context of closer dialogue and exchange between UNHCR and UNRWA than previously. However, whilst much of UNHCR's analysis of returns in the 1990s focuses on specific returns either as successes to be emulated or as events where successful and sustainable return represents a key element of a broader settlement, some rather different conclusions could also be drawn from this experience. For example, there is a striking comparison between the 2.4 million refugees who returned world-wide in 1992 (UNHCR 1993), and the 'nearly 2.5 million' returnees in 2002 highlighted in a 2004 special issue of UNHCR's *Refugees* magazine (UNHCR 2004). The fact that these returns were dominated in both 1992 and 2002 by returns to Afghanistan points to the limitations of linking return with post-conflict reconstruction. That broadly speaking the same people who were registering for return in 1992 were again registering in 2002 speaks both to the continuation of violence in Afghanistan, and to the at best transitory nature of the return. At worst, it speaks to return as a myth, as there is evidence that many of the 'returnees' in 1992, and also 2002, were actually people who registered for returnee assistance but then remained illegally in urban areas of Pakistan rather than moving to Afghanistan.

At the same time, the other countries that feature in the lists of key places of return for the two dates (Table 2.2) also reflect a wider pattern of messy, complicated returns, to countries still in conflict, with issues that led to displacement remaining largely unresolved. Few international organisations are likely to point to Angola, Sierra Leone, Somalia, or Burundi as 'successful' examples of return during the 1990s, but the reality is that all four countries saw complex patterns of return, renewed flight and internal displacement through the course of the decade.

Table 2.2 Significant return movements in 1992 and 2002[a]

1992	2002
Angola	Angola
Burundi	Bosnia and Herzegovina
Cambodia	Burundi
Iraq	East Timor
Mozambique	Eritrea
Sierra Leone	Liberia
Somalia	Rwanda
	Sierra Leone
	Somalia

Source: UNHCR (1993), UNHCR (2004).

Note
a Returns over 20,000 in number.

Return in public policy

The positions adopted in various editions of *The State of the World's Refugees* are best seen as a reflection rather than a statement of UNHCR policy on return, and also reflect some broader views on return within the international community over this period. Even amongst critics of the focus of international policy actors on return, there is acceptance of its importance of return as a solution, not least for many refugees themselves. For example, Allen and Morsink note that 'it is generally assumed that most refugees will eventually want to go home' (Allen and Morsink 1994), whilst Warner accepts that 'voluntary repatriation is the ideal durable solution', prior to launching a critique on the way in which repatriation is conceptualised (Warner 1994). Repatriation is one of UNHCR's three durable solutions, and as the other two (integration, resettlement) have become more politically difficult, it is not surprising that repatriation has become prominent in the 1990s, especially once the ideological imperative of not considering return to communist countries was removed by the end of the Cold War. But survey after survey also show that return remains overwhelmingly the aspiration of many refugees.

In this respect, UNHCR and other international humanitarian and development actors have increasingly tended to focus on the advantages of return and repatriation as part of a process of addressing the 'root causes' of refugee flight. As part of its 'Framework for Durable Solutions' initiative, UNHCR has developed a focus on what it calls the '4Rs' – repatriation, reintegration, rehabilitation and reconstruction. The idea is to address refugee issues in a comprehensive way that avoids an 'exilic bias' and sows the seed for a genuine long-term resolution of their plight, an aspiration that has been around for more than a decade (Coles 1989). In its latest incarnation, the emphasis on repatriation as a solution supports UNHCR's 'Convention Plus' initiative, although Convention Plus also includes measures to promote 'Development through Local Integration'.

Two specific concerns are often implied in the emphasis on reconciliation and reconstruction as part of refugee return. First, as the conflicts that produce refugees are increasingly perceived to involve the deliberate expulsion of populations not belonging to the same ethnic group as the perpetrators of violence, return has come to be seen as a way of righting the wrong of such 'ethnic cleansing'. Nowhere has this been more so than in Bosnia, where in spite of the acceptance of the administrative division of the country into two ethnically defined 'entities', the international community has also invested huge resources in so-called 'minority return' in order to promote the re-mixing of ethnic groups. In addition, there has also been some specific awareness of the fact that refugee populations often include quite a high number of professional and skilled individuals, especially where the country of asylum is relatively wealthy or education has been a priority in humanitarian assistance. What could be better than to use the skills of refugee doctors, teachers, administrators and businessmen in the reconstruction of conflict-ridden countries by promoting their return?

The desire to meet refugees' felt needs, reverse ethnic division and tap into a pool of skilled professionals are powerful enough policy reasons for an interest in promoting refugee return and repatriation. However, arguably more important than any of these this is the domestic context for returns in receiving countries. For example, in Europe, domestic considerations in Germany formed the primary context for the return of over a quarter of a million refugees to Bosnia after 1996, in conditions that were widely regarded as testing the boundaries of 'voluntariness', and which led to probably the majority of these returnees becoming internally displaced within their home country. Where Germany (and Switzerland) led, others have followed. In the UK, a Labour government has set a succession of removals targets designed to show that Britain is not a 'soft touch' on asylum, and that fraudulent claims will be met with robust action – in this sense return has become a part of the 'integrity' of the asylum system (Home Office 2001). This has been coupled with new and as yet still tentative interest in voluntary assisted return schemes implemented by the International Organization for Migration (IOM) both for refugees and asylum-seekers generally, and for refugees from Kosovo (briefly), Somalia and Afghanistan in particular, building on evidence that these are more cost effective (as well as more politically acceptable) than forced removals. In Kosovo, this 'voluntary return' formed part of an implicit package of measures adopted essentially as conditions for acceptance of refugees under the 'Humanitarian Evacuation Programme' (HEP), and saw over half of HEP arrivals return permanently to Kosovo within a year of the end of NATO military action. Similar measures have been adopted elsewhere, and clearly relate also to return assistance for migrants more generally adopted after the 'immigration stop' in Europe in the mid-1970s.

The significance of host countries' intention and action to return refugees to their countries of origin after the end of periods of conflict is particularly evident in Europe, but not limited to the continent, or indeed to richer countries of the north. For example, the return of refugees from Tanzania to Rwanda in 1996 reflected the impatience of the Tanzanian government with hosting such large numbers, and fears over the security implications of their presence, even though the return was encouraged and ultimately financed by international actors, including UNHCR itself (Whitaker 2002). Meanwhile, across Africa, Asia and the Middle East, there has been a hardening of government attitudes towards refugees and growing enthusiasm to ensure the temporary nature of refugee status – something that has always been the legal, if not physical, reality through much of the developing world.

Return of refugees: themes and discourses in the literature

The previous section has highlighted how refugee returns have been substantial over the last decade, and very much supported by policy-makers in UNHCR and other parts of the international community. To an extent, the refugee studies literature has followed these trends, seeking to document and analyse return movements and draw conclusions both about the consequences of return for refugees and home populations, and for wider policy development. It has explored the meaning of 'return' and 'home' for refugee populations themselves, which is often expressed in determination to return to their homelands, or at least maintain the right to return, at some stage in the future. However, in contrast to the perspective of policy-makers, which appears increasingly concerned with making return a practical reality, academic researchers have tended to adopt a much more negative perspective on return movements, in a literature that has tended to emphasise the failed, problematic or indeed impossible nature of refugee return (Harrell-Bond 1989; Chimni 1991).

The 'right' to return: a right denied

A first key theme of both academic and policy literature on the return of refugees is its growing focus on return as a 'right', even if this right might not be exercised in the short term. In the case of the Palestinian diaspora, this 'right to return' is a longstanding and prominent theme, articulated by a number of authors (Klein 1998; Abunimah and Ibish 2001; Aruri 2001; Hovdenak 2003). Yet talk of a right to return has also emerged in other contexts, most notably in the Balkans, following the war in Bosnia and Herzegovina from 1991 to 1996, and the NATO bombing of Kosovo in 1999. In Bosnia, the right to return emerged as a key discourse amongst groups of displaced persons in the aftermath of a war that has been characterised by observers as being primarily about promoting displacement in order to achieve ethnically 'pure' zones under the control of nationalist leaders (Black 2002). Thus, in contrast to considerable reticence amongst Bosnian refugees living abroad to return to Bosnia, displaced people within Bosnia have organised in considerable numbers to lobby for their right to return to their original places of origin, whilst international agencies have sought to counter a range of obstacles to the 'right to return' (International Crisis Group 1997). In particular, the 'Coalition for Return' has brought together a range of associations of displaced people lobbying for their right to return to pre-war homes, and often already actively engaged in the local politics of their 'home' locality as a result of an electoral law that allows people to vote in either their current or their pre-war place of residence if they have been displaced by the conflict. Meanwhile, in Kosovo, the 'right to return' has become a particular issue for minority Serb communities displaced as a result of NATO military action. (Rudge and Kapferer 1999; Frelick 2000).

In these and other examples, it is important to highlight what is often the intensely political nature of the 'right to return' as a concept, even if this right is expressed in different ways in different contexts. For example, in Bosnia, whilst the Coalition for Return constitutes something of a grassroots movement for return amongst displaced communities, and has focused on the exercising of an individual right to regain property, it cannot be considered outside the context of the work of the Returns and Reconstruction Task Force (RRTF) of the Office of the High Representative (OHR), the effective administration of a UN-controlled territory, or certain political groupings within Bosnia. Thus, RRTF's support – financial and political – to the Coalition for Return formed part of its broader objective of reversing ethnic cleansing and promoting the re-mixing of populations of different ethnicities, but also was effectively quite political in its nature. Meanwhile, for some return groups, the 'right to return' represented the concretisation of a political strategy to 'recapture' for one ethnic group a town that had been lost to another during the fighting. Nowhere was this clearer than in the town of Drvar, where the product of intense pressure to allow Serb 'minority' return to a town captured by Croat forces has subsequently led to the return *en masse* of many of the town's former Serb inhabitants, and the departure *en masse* of many of the Croats who had taken the town during the war, and who have now moved 'back' to Croatia.[1]

One interesting question here is the extent to which discussion of the 'right to return' can move from a symbolic or political aspiration to a more practical strategy, enshrined within a broader 'rights-based approach' to forced migration. Such a shift has been attempted by the United Nations Mission in Kosovo (UNMIK) and UNHCR in their return strategy for the province, which enshrines the right to a sustainable return in a 'Manual for Sustainable Return' (UNMIK and UNHCR 2003). Here, a 'rights-based' approach is seen as *de-politicising* the returns issue, and so reducing the propensity either for forced returns or for conditions to be placed on the right to return. The idea is that the process is both 'principled and practical', responding to demand for return from individuals to their pre-conflict homes.

Similarly, in Bosnia, considerable public expenditure has been devoted to promoting the re-mixing of residential patterns of different ethnic groups in Bosnia and Kosovo through highly bureaucratic and legalistic interventions, even at the risk of stalling the fragile peace process established by the Dayton Accords (Black 2001b). Gradually, people have been able to return to their original homes in Bosnia, through a combination of local negotiations backed up by robust policing by the international community. One recent study of return in and around Gorazde revealed complex arrangements, whereby some returnees have accepted return to houses still occupied by displaced people from a different ethnic group, with the returnee family living on one floor of the house and the displaced family on another (D'Onofrio 2004). Although hardly ideal, such arrangements are testimony to the extent to which practical solutions for return can be worked out by ordinary returnees. Yet this substantial international and local investment in return – both materially and symbolically – has not always resulted in significant advances, as practical obstacles and the determination of some nationalist politicians have continued to block returns in many areas. For example, returns have often involved primarily the movement back to rural areas of the elderly, and those who have maintained a foothold in their region of displacement to which they can return if necessary after a summer of reconstruction, or once they have sold their house. Worse, return has often been accompanied by violence and intimidation on the part of those opposed to the return process, and has had to be met with political responses from OHR.

Return as failure

Discussion of the 'right to return' in Bosnia leads on to a second key theme in the literature on return – that of return as the embodiment of failure. For example, not only are conditions for returnees often difficult, but at a very basic level, return can be seen as implicitly reflecting the failure of integration in countries or regions of destination. In this sense, for many observers in the destination countries for migrants and refugees, return is something that shouldn't happen – or at least something that should not be discussed lest it encourage governments and hostile host populations to restrict their commitment to policies of integration. Indeed, looking to the broader migration studies literature, one of four return 'types' identified in Cerase's oft-quoted typology of return migration is the 'return of failure', a risk or 'hazard' faced by classic economic migrants which can be seen as decreasing over time as migrants become more settled (Constant and Massey 2002). Even amongst refugee groups, there is a sense in which those who go back to their original homes are the ones who failed to 'make it' in their country of asylum.

However, it is also worth stressing that the return as failure is only *one* of four types of return migration for Cerase, whilst Constant and Massey stress a distinction between return as a hazard amongst 'income maximiser' migrants envisaged by neoclassical economics, and return as an objective amongst what they call 'target earner' migrants, as envisaged by theorists within the 'New Economics of Labour Migration' school. Amongst the former group – people who move to seek a better life elsewhere – those who do return are indeed negatively selected, as those without employment or on low wages, or with low occupational achievement. By contrast, within the latter group of people who go elsewhere ultimately to have a better life at home, return is positively associated with work effort. In other words, those who work harder will achieve their goals more quickly, and so be able to return home more quickly. The key point here is that, for refugees too, it is important to differentiate different groups who might have widely varied views on whether return constitutes a successful or an unsuccessful outcome – for those seeking temporary refuge and looking to return as soon as is safely possible, return is clearly a resolution of their problems, as envisaged by UNHCR's stress on repatriation as a 'durable solution'. Yet for others who are seeking safety above all else, once this is found, return may represent a perceived 'hazard' even if an objective assessment of conditions in their place of origin might encourage optimism about the prospects for return.

Meanwhile, for a number of other refugee researchers, return is problematic not just because it signals a failure of asylum and a welcome to strangers, but also because return confirms a nationalist, securitised view of the world as divided into a set of natural 'homes' that are rooted in particular places. For example, nearly a decade ago, Malkki called into question what she saw as the dominant discourse in favour of the return of refugees, which, she argued, effectively classified as 'dysfunctional' the position of refugees, and supported the notion that return involves a return to the natural or national order (Malkki 1995b). For Malkki, such return discourse was seen as supporting an outdated and potentially dangerous notion of states as separated into 'culture gardens' where people are naturally supposed to be and from which they are 'uprooted' in situations of refugee flight. Return then becomes a moral and spiritual, as well as a political and security matter, with a focus on the importance of a clearly delineated home encouraging the classification of refugees as 'pathological'.

Similarly, Warner noted the primacy of voluntary repatriation as a solution to refugees' problems, arguing that it assumes 'a world of order and symmetry that belies the problematic nature of the relationship between the individual and group, the group and the state, and the state and the territory, and fosters the idealization of a nostaliga for home' (Warner 1994). His response was to 'show problems in the concept of return to home', noting the 'temporal reality of our lives' and the 'changes [that] take place over time'. This is a theme that has been picked up in much of the literature on return within refugee studies since. For example, Stepputat has focused on the politics of return in Guatemala, arguing that transnational forms of existence have emerged as returnees have turned to longer-term labour migration, reflecting the difficulty of economic survival in return areas (Stepputat 1999). From a slightly different tack, Hammond has questioned whether return should be seen as connected to a 're-' anything; thus rather than 'reintegration', returnees must effectively 'integrate' anew in societies that have usually changed in their absence, sometimes beyond all recognition (Hammond 1999). From this perspective, return to an original 'home' is not simply an idealised myth, but may more importantly be a practical impossibility.

Of course, in addition to this literature that focuses on the idea of return as a conceptual failure, there is also a growing body of literature that charts how individual return programmes and processes have failed in practice, such that any process of learning lessons is one that needs to focus on 'worst practice' as much as 'best practice'. For example, in Bosnia, it is not just the identification of what constitutes 'home' for returnees that is problematic, but also the practical issue that a significant proportion of those returned to Bosnia from Germany, for example, have not ended up in their original towns or villages, but in other parts of the country where they are forced to remain as internally displaced people. As Prettitore (this volume) points out, this reflects the huge obstacles that have been placed in the path of so-called 'minority returns' – returns of individuals from one ethnic group to areas where they would now constitute an ethnic minority. Meanwhile, other return programmes have 'failed' in a much more basic sense, as they have simply led to only small numbers of returns. For example, the third phase of IOM's 'Return of Qualified African Nationals' succeeded in returning just 631 people over five years (IOM 2000).

The practice of return

A third strand of literature on return concerns itself less with evaluating whether return should happen, or whether it is 'successful' when it does, and seeks more to explain why some people return and others do not. Here, there seems to be an emphasis on the role of non-economic factors in return, compared with economic factors. For example, a recent review by King summarises return motivations for migrants in general as encompassing economic, social, family and life cycle, and political reasons, but stresses the importance of the social and political side, as well as the greater importance of 'pull' factors in the country of origin compared with 'push' factors from the country of destination (King 2000). In their study of migrants in Germany mentioned above, Constant and Massey also conclude that the strongest influences on return were attachments to country of origin – location of family, friends, frequency of contact etc. – rather than age, education, occupation or sex, although those not working were also more likely to return (Constant and Massey 2002). In her study of Ghanaian migrants in Canada, Manuh emphasises the importance of social ties as factors influencing return decisions (Manuh 2003). However, some authors disagree – for example, Dustmann and Kirchkamp (2002) suggest that return occurs sooner when host country wages and access to education for migrants are higher, although this conclusion partly reflects the economic basis of their study, whilst it is also arguably specific to economic migrants who are seeking to complete a 'migration project' (and can therefore complete it sooner, the better access to income and education they have).

If there is some agreement on the importance of social and political factors in return migration, and the particular importance of conditions in the country of origin, this is even more so in relation to studies focused specifically on the return of refugees. For example, a recent study by Refugee Action found that family reunion was the single largest reason for return given by those seeking return assistance in 1998 (29 per cent of responses), followed by nearly a quarter (23 per cent) mentioning changed conditions in their country of origin (Morrison 2000). In contrast, only one in five said they were not happy with their conditions in the UK. Meanwhile, a study of 200 Somali refugees in the UK looked instead at what prevented mass return at the present time, finding that political problems and uncertainty about the future of Somalia ranked highest (Bloch and Atfield 2002). Again, these reasons were followed by the (better) standard of living in the UK as the next largest obstacle to return.

Two recent studies at Sussex on the return – or non-return – of refugees reinforce these conclusions. Thus, an in-depth study of Bosnian and Eritrean refugees in the UK, Netherlands and Germany in 1999/2000 stressed how both economic and social problems in the home country play a major role in dissuading large numbers of refugees from returning, in spite of the end of armed conflict, although a desire to complete their children's education first also featured highly (Al-Ali *et al.* 2001). Meanwhile, a more exploratory study in 2002/03 with seven different refugee groups found respondents who wanted to talk about safety and security back home as the key influence on their willingness to return (Black *et al.* 2004). However, the latter study also focused on how different factors may be ranked in importance, or come to the fore at different points in the decision-making process. For example, peace and stability may be important as a first order issue preventing people re-turning, but if this factor is removed, economic and life cycle factors and the advantages of living in wealthier countries can take over as issues that still dissuade people from returning. Indeed, a global review by Kibreab suggests a clear correlation between whether a refugee flees to the north or the south, and whether they are eager to return or not (Kibreab 2003). Kibreab puts this difference down in part to the fact that most northern countries offer secure citizenship to those who are granted refugee status, whereas most southern countries do not. However, another interesting hypothesis would be to question whether *amongst those who flee to the north* secure status (i.e. acquir-ing citizenship) may actually encourage refugees to consider return, since it provides a guarantee to the individual that they would be able to re-emigrate should the return process not go according to plan.

Another issue in relation to the practice of return is the extent to which returns, when they do occur, are sustainable. Asking this question represents something more than considering the success or level of reintegration for in-dividual returnees, an issue referred to above, and on which there is a signifi-cant body of literature (Bovenkerk 1974; Gmelch 1980; Lepore 1986; King 2000; Ammassari and Black 2001). Rather, a distinction needs to be drawn between individual sustainability and the sustainability of a return process at a broader economic or societal level (Black *et al.* 2004). In its narrowest sense, the former might imply considering whether individuals are forced to flee again once they return home, although a definition of the sustainability of return adopted by UNMIK includes consideration of an individual's right to access services, shelter and freedom of movement. However, rather more interesting is the question of aggregate sustainability – what the impact is on countries of origin when significant numbers of people *do* return.

Conclusion

To ask about the success or sustainability of return, and what motivates individual returnees, is important whether we are considering state-sponsored attempts to encourage refugees to leave or the fulfilment of a decades-long aspiration to realise a right to return, as would be the case for any Palestinian return. To the extent to which existing literature has sought to answer these questions, the picture is not encouraging. Although heavily influenced by political factors, economics and family ties can also act as significant obstacles to return. Even where individuals and families wish to return, powerful forces often stand in opposition. When return occurs, this does not often – or indeed usually – lead to a process of unproblematic reintegration, such that return has often come to be characterised as a failure. This relates both to the changed circumstances of returnees and to the fact that 'home' itself is likely to have changed in their absence. For example, the jobs of refugees may well be filled by others during their absence, their homes occupied, whilst exiles themselves grow older, get married and have children, send their children to school and may gain or lose skills that will affect their life chances on return. In this sense, return can never be to the same place, whether emotionally, economically or politically. Hardly surprising, perhaps, that refugee scholars have often shied away from analysis of the return process, preferring to focus instead on integration and settlement in countries of asylum.

So what lessons are to be learned from the literature on refugee return, such as it is, that might be applied to the return of Palestinians? First, refugee scholars have critiqued the assumed simplicity of the return, and especially the link between return and reconstruction of war-torn societies. Even where return is a cherished goal of the refugees themselves, and where return of- fers the potential to reverse past injustice and bring motivated people back to their homelands to contribute to building society and the economy, the path ahead is unlikely to be smooth. In addition to the potential for change noted above, this is also because return – and the situation of those who were displaced – cannot be divorced from the domestic political, economic and social contexts of sending and receiving societies. Forced migration may contribute to tensions in home and host societies that return might resolve, but return may exacerbate, as well as relieve such tension.

Second, the potential for return to contribute to tensions relates to the fact that return is often a highly political act. To talk of a 'right to return' – whether in Bosnia, Kosovo or Palestine – may be to talk about a particular pattern of residence or settlement rooted in a particular point in time or political configuration. In realising this right, there are likely to be losers as well as winners – some for whom the return of exiles will mean a significant deterioration in their circumstances. In turn, those who stand to lose from a return process may well be motivated to resist this return, whether overtly through violence or public protest, or covertly through forms of everyday non-cooperation. Either could be highly problematic.

Yet, at the same time, the *right* to return often appears to be the key issue for refugees – not necessarily a reality of return, but the right to do so at some stage should the individual or family wish to do so. In this sense, although highly political in character, the right to return may not always bring with it the practical difficulties that appear to be associated with the realisation of that right. Refugees may be looking more for symbolic than practical return; indeed, they may also be looking for a return process that is enabling, and fundamentally temporary, rather than proscribed and permanent.

This leads us to a third area in which academic research may prove helpful in learning lessons for the Palestinian case: the emerging field that highlights the construction of 'transnational' lifestyles, rather than lives that are rooted in a single physical space. For some, 'transnationalism' and return might seem to be different and mutually exclusive courses that a refugee situation could take; in addition, the literature on transnationalism has paid relatively little attention to the situation of refugees, reflecting the relative difficulty faced by forced migrants in travelling and interacting across borders, particularly the borders of their host countries. Yet transnational strategies have been developed by refugees (Al-Ali *et al.* 2001), especially as the violence that forced people to flee is resolved or dies down. Moreover, the stimulus to develop transnational practices may be rooted precisely in the possibility of return, rather than in the process of initial migration, since it is only at the point of initial return that a would-be transnational migrant realises the full potential of two-way movement between home and host country.

Finally, it is important to recognise that neither the creation of a transnational lifestyle nor the transformation of a refugee's original home is inconsistent with the notion of a return there in the long run. Indeed, just as migration helps to create and shape places of destination, so too can return help to re-shape places of origin. As scholars, public policy-makers or others interested in human societies, we need to face the challenge not only of mobility in the contemporary world but also of return to a home that is likely to have changed, however long people have been away. That is the challenge of this volume, to explore best practice in relation to return programmes and also in relation to return outcomes. Given the diversity of refugee situations, and the complexity of the issues, it is not easy to identify patterns. Yet the goal – in this case, for a Palestine at peace with itself – is surely worthwhile.

Note

1 Moving 'back' or 'returning' is not perhaps the best way of characterising this movement, since many of the Croats of Drvar who have moved to Croatia had lived in towns and cities of Central Bosnia prior to the war, and had been driven out by Muslim–Croat fighting.

References

Abunimah, A., and Ibish, H. (2001) *The Palestinian right of return. ADC Issue Paper* 30 (Washington, DC, Arab-American Anti-Discrimination Committee).

Al-Ali, N., Black, R., *and Koser, K.* (2001) "Refugees and transnationalism: The experience of Bosnians and Eritreans in Europe", *Journal of Ethnic and Migration Studies* 27 (4), 615–34.

Allen, T., and Morsink, H. (eds.) (1994) *When refugees go home: African experiences* (Oxford: James Currey).

Ammassari, S., and Black, R. (2001) *Harnessing the potential of migration and return to promote development. Migration Research Series* (Geneva: IOM).

Aruri, N. (ed.) (2001) *Palestinian refugees: The right of return* (London: Pluto Press).

Black, R. (2001a) "Fifty years of refugee studies: From theory to policy", *International Migration Review* 35 (1), 55–76.

Black, R. (2001b) "Return and reconstruction: Missing link or mistaken priority in post-Dayton Bosnia and Herzegovina?", *SAIS Review* 21 (2), 177–99.

Black, R. (2002) "Conceptions of 'home' and the political geography of refugee repatriation: Between assumption and contested reality in Bosnia-Herzegovina", *Applied Geography* 22, 123–38.

Black, R., and Koser, K. (eds.) (1999) *The end of the refugee cycle? Refugee repatriation and reconstruction* (Oxford: Berghahn).

Black, R., Koser, K., Munk., K., Atfield, G., D'Onofrio, L., and Tiemoko, R. (2004) *Understanding Voluntary Return. Home Office Online Reports* (London: Home Office).

Bloch, A., and Atfield, G. (2002) *The professional capacity of national from the Somali regions in Britain* (London: Refugee Action and IOM).

Bovenkerk, F. (1974) *The sociology of return migration: A bibliographic essay. Publications of the Research Group on European Migration Problems 20* (The Hague: Nijhoff).

Chimni, B. S. (1991) "Perspectives on voluntary repatriation: A critical note", *International Journal of Refugee Law* 3 (3), 541–7.

Coles, G. J. L. (1989) "Approaching the refugee problem today", in Loescher, G., and Monahan, L. (eds.), *Refugees and international relations* (Oxford: Oxford University Press), pp. 373–410.

Constant, A., and Massey, D. S. (2002) "Return migration by German guestworkers: Neoclassical versus new economic theories", *International Migration* 40 (4), 5–38.

D'Onofrio, L. (2004) *Welcome home? Minority return in south-eastern Republika Srpska. Sussex Migration Working Papers* 19 (Brighton: Sussex Centre for Migration Research, University of Sussex).

Dustmann, C., and Kirchkamp, O. (2002) "The optimal migration duration and activity choice after re- migration", *Journal of Development Economics*, 67 (2), 351–72

Emmott, F. (1996) " 'Dislocation', shelter and crisis: Afghanistan's refugees and notions of home", *Gender and Development* 4 (1), 31–8.

Frelick, B. (2000) *Serbia: Reversal of fortune: Yugoslavia's refugee crisis since the ethnic Albanian return to Kosovo* (Washington, DC: United States Committee for Refugees): 24 pp.

Gmelch, G. (1980) "Return migration", *Annual Review of Anthropology* 9, 135–59.

Hammond, L. (1999) "Examining the discourse of repatriation: Towards a more proactive theory of return migration", in Black, R., and Koser, K. (eds.), *The end of the refugee cycle? Refugee repatriation and reconstruction* (Oxford: Berghahn), pp. 227–44.

Hammond, L. (2004) *This place will become home: Refugee repatriation to Ethiopia* (Ithaca, NY: Cornell University Press).

Harrell-Bond, B. (1989) "Repatriation: Under what conditions is it the most desirable solution?", *African Studies Review* 32 (1), 41–69.

Home Office (2001) *Secure borders, safe havens: Integration with diversity in modern Britain* (London: HMSO).

Hovdenak, A. (2003) "Palestinian refugees: The right to return", *Journal of Peace Research* 40 (6), 748–9.

International Crisis Group (1997) *House burnings: Obstruction of the right to return to Drvar. ICG Bosnia Report* 24.

IOM (2000) *Evaluation of phase III of the programme for the return of qualified African nationals* (Geneva: Office of Programme Evaluation, International Organization for Migration).

Kibreab, G. (2003) "Citizenship rights and repatriation of refugees", *International Migration Review* 37 (1), 24–73.

King, R. (2000) "Generalizations from the history of return migration", in Ghosh, B. (ed.) *Return migration. Journey of hope or despair?* (Geneva: IOM/UNHCR).

Klein, M. (1998) "Between right and realization: The PLO dialectics of the 'right of return'", *Journal of Refugee Studies* 11 (1), 1–19.

Lepore, S. (1986) "Problems confronting migrants and members of their families when they return to their countries of origin", *International Migration* 23 (1), 95–112.

Malkki, L. (1995a) *Purity and exile: Violence, memory and national cosmology among Hutu refugees in Tanzania* (Chicago: University of Chicago Press).

Malkki, L. (1995b) "Refugees and exile: From 'refugee studies' to the national order of things", *Annual Review of Anthropology* 24, 495–523.

Manuh, T. (2003) "'Efie' or the meanings of 'home' among female and male 'Ghanaian' migrants in Toronto, Canada and returned migrants to Ghana", in Koser, K. (ed.), *New African diasporas* (London: Routledge), pp. 182–210.

Marsden, P. (1999) "Repatriation and reconstruction: The case of Afghanistan", in Black, R., and Koser, K. (eds.), *The end of the refugee cycle? Refugee repatriation and reconstruction* (Oxford: Berghahn), pp. 56–68.

Morrison, J. (2000) *External evaluation of the voluntary return project for refugees in the United Kingdom 1998–99* (London: Refugee Action).

North, L., and Simmons, A. (eds.) (2000) *Journeys of fear: Refugee return and national transformation in Guatemala* (Kingston, ON: McGill-Queen's University Press).

Ogota, S. (1992) Speech at International Management Symposium, St Gallen.

Petrin, S. (2002) *Refugee return and state reconstruction: A comparative analysis. UNHCR Working Paper* (August 2002).

Preston, R. (1999) "Researching repatriation and reconstruction: Who is researching what and why", in Black, R., and Koser, K. (eds.), *The end of the refugee cycle? Refugee repatriation and reconstruction* (Oxford: Berghahn), pp. 18–37.

Rudge, P., and Kapferer, S. (1999) *Kosovo: Protection and peace building: Protection of refugees, returnees, internally-displaced persons and minorities* (New York: Lawyers' Committee for Human Rights): 15 pp.

Stein, B., and Tomasi, L. (1981) "Foreword", *International Migration Review* 15 (1–2), 5–7.

Stepputat, F. (1999) "Repatriation and everyday forms of state formation in Guatemala", in Black, R., and Koser, K. (eds.), *The end of the refugee cycle? Refugee repatriation and reconstruction* (Oxford: Berghahn), pp. 210–226.

Turton, D., and Marsden, P. (2002) *Taking refugees for a ride? The politics of refugee return to Afghanistan.* (Kabul: Afghanistan Research and Evaluation Unit).

UNHCR (1993) *The state of the world's refugees: The challenge of protection* (Harmondsworth: Penguin).

UNHCR (1995) *The state of the world's refugees: In search of solutions* (Oxford: Oxford University Press).

UNHCR (1997) *The state of the world's refugees: A humanitarian agenda* (Oxford: Oxford University Press).

UNHCR (2000) *The state of the world's refugees: Fifty years of humanitarian action* (Oxford: Oxford University Press).

UNHCR (2004) "Dreams, fears and euphoria: The long road home", *Refugees* 1.

UNMIK and UNHCR (2003) *Manual for sustainable return* (Pristina: United Nations Mission in Kosovo/United Nations High Commissioner for Refugees).

Warner, D. (1994) "Voluntary repatriation and the meaning of return to home: A critique of liberal mathematics", *Journal of Refugee Studies* 7 (2/3), 160–74.

Whitaker, B. E. (2002) "Changing priorities in refugee protection: The Rwandan repatriation from Tanzania", *New Issues in Refugee Research* (Geneva: UNHCR), available online at http://www.UNHCR.ch/cgi-bin/texis/vtx/research/opendoc. pdf?tbl=RESEARCH&id=3c7528ea4

Winter, R. P. (1994) "Ending exile: Promoting successful reintegration of African refugees and displaced people", in Adelman, H., and Sorensen, J. (eds.), *African refugees: Development aid and repatriation* (Boulder, CO: Westview).

Zetter, R. (1988) "Refugees and refugee studies: A label and an agenda", *Journal of Refugee Studies* 1 (1), 1–6.

3   UNHCR and repatriation

Patricia Weiss Fagen

The UN General Assembly approved the Statute of the Office of the United Nations High Commissioner for Refugees, UNHCR, at the close of 1950 (Res. 428 V). The UNHCR came into being primarily to resolve the still incomplete resettlement of World War II refugees. In 1951 the UN adopted the United Nations Convention Relating to the Status of Refugees which, with the Statute, provided a structure and standards for addressing refugee needs and protection (UNHCR 2000: 2). While the text of the Convention referred to refugees from Europe, its language affirmed the responsibility of states to protect and assist refugees in general. The geographical bias was corrected by the 1967 Protocol, which broadened the definition of refugees within the mandate of UNHCR to include persons anywhere in the world meeting the Convention definition. The UNHCR Statute limited its institutional tenure to three-year periods. The General Assembly clearly intended to create a small, temporary, decentralized agency with limited functions and minimal operating budget.

Over the years UNHCR has expanded its authority beyond the narrow confines of the Convention definition and has brought assistance and protection to groups deemed to be "of concern" to the agency who do not strictly meet the Convention definition. However, Article 1D of the 1951 UNHCR Convention omits from coverage those refugees who receive protection or assistance from other UN agencies. The UN General Assembly had established the United Nations Relief and Works Agency (UNRWA) in December 1950 (Res. 302 V) to continue the efforts previously initiated to extend aid and relief to Palestinian refugees in the Near East, in coordination with local governments and other UN bodies and NGOs (UNRWA 2004). Therefore, refugee protection under the Convention has not been made available to Palestinian refugees within the mandate of the UNRWA (discussed in Farah 2003: 163–5). Only Palestinians outside the jurisdiction of UNRWA may be protected by UNHCR, depending on their geographical and political situation.

The UNRWA mandate attends to the needs of those Palestinians and their descendents who "lost homes and means of livelihood as a result of the

1948 conflict with Israel." It serves Palestinians who have registered with the agency and live in occupied Palestinian territory, Lebanon, Jordan, and Syria (UNRWA 2004:). UNRWA has been operating since 1950 and primarily attends to health, education, relief and general social services. Although it has negotiated with Israel and other host governments regarding a wide range of problems facing Palestinian refugees, it is not charged to seek durable solutions for them. Unlike UNHCR, UNRWA does not have a protection mandate. The resolution of the Palestinian refugee problem, i.e. the durable solutions, is seen to depend on a political solution. Pending this political solution, and despite its longevity, UNRWA is categorized as a temporary agency within the UN system. It renews its mandate and funding yearly.

While there is no formally defined role for UNRWA in any eventual Palestinian repatriation or resettlement, it is logical that UNRWA experience and personnel would be fundamentally important in such operations. Nor is it clear what role, if any, UNHCR would play. Nevertheless precedents do exist for UNHCR to be given major responsibilities in the repatriation of groups of refugees not previously under its mandate. The most important in this regard is the repatriation of some 370,000 Cambodian refugees from Thailand 1992–3. The vast majority of these refugees had been living along the Thai–Cambodian border in camps under the control of military factions fighting in Cambodia. UNHCR did not have access to the refugees in these camps, but they were assisted by the UN Border Relief Operation, UNBRO. UNBRO, like UNWRA, was created to assist a specific population considered to be of international concern and, again like UNWRA, did not have a protection mandate. The 1991 Cambodian Peace plan gave UNHCR authority to oversee the repatriation. UNBRO was disbanded, but many in the UNBRO staff were incorporated into UNHCR to assist in the process. A similar role for UNHCR could be envisioned in the Palestinian case.

Repatriation policies and mechanisms

Becoming a priority

UNHCR's responsibility for finding durable solutions falls within its protection mandate. Article 1 of the UNHCR Statute affirms that part of its responsibility for finding durable solutions for the problem of refugees is to facilitate voluntary repatriation to countries of origin. Note, the term is "facilitate" not "promote". Repatriation was not a priority area for the agency prior to the 1990s. UNHCR spent the major part of its repatriation resources negotiating and organizing the repatriation movements and budgeted little for reintegration in countries of origin. Not until 1980 did the UNHCR Executive Committee confirm the need for post-repatriation assistance and integration projects (Conclusion No. 18) (Ruiz 1993: 27); still later, in 1985, the Executive Committee formally resolved that the agency should have full access to returnees in order to monitor security and ensure fulfillment of the legal conditions and guarantees previously agreed (Conclusion No. 40) (Ruiz 1993: 27). By 1985 UNHCR was already doing so.

During most of the Cold War, large numbers of refugees were fleeing from the then Soviet controlled states and from countries where leftist pro-Soviet forces held or were fighting to hold power. The western governments that supported UNHCR considered "voluntary" repatriation almost unthinkable for refugees from these countries, and made ample provision for the latter to be either settled in the countries where they first arrived or resettled elsewhere (UNHCR 1995: 83). UNHCR helped to negotiate individual voluntary repatriations, but did not organize return movements to Eastern bloc nations.

UNHCR did organize and assist fairly large African repatriations during the Cold War years, primarily involving the return of those who had become refugees because of the ongoing pro-independence struggles in a number of countries. The new governments in the countries that achieved independence during the 1960s and 1970s welcomed the return of refugees, and the latter faced few protection problems. Although UNHCR brought large numbers of refugees home, the majority preferred to return on their own. UNHCR negotiated with authorities to assure that returnees would recover legal status and basic rights, and gave short-term assistance to enable repatriating families to restart their lives. It was assumed all around that voluntary repatriation was the last act at the end of the refugee experience. UNHCR did not remain for long periods of time in the countries of origin, did little to monitor post-repatriation protection, and assumed that integration would take place as the newly independent states moved forward in the development process.

UNHCR faced a far more difficult situation with regard to African refugees who had fled because of civil strife and were returning before the situations in their home countries had stabilized. For example, there were serious internal conflicts during the 1980s in what was then Ethiopia and in the Sudan, and each country hosted refugees from the other. These refugees, in large part, were pawns in the shifting political relations in the region, which remained highly unstable. When groups from the Eritrean independence forces sought to return to Tigray from Sudan (1985–7), UNHCR and most of the international community opposed the actions on grounds that refugees should not return to regions still in conflict. Consequently, UNHCR provided minimal support or subsequent assistance (Hendrie 1995). Instead, support for the returnees was mobilized from bilateral and private sources. Not too long thereafter, during the late 1980s in El Salvador, UNHCR reversed its opposition to supporting repatriations in conditions of conflict. Under strong pressure from the refugees and NGO advocates, UNHCR brought the refugees back to contested areas then held by the guerrilla opposition. Even in this case, however, until the conflict was brought to a close, UNHCR assistance was limited largely to the legal area, while private and bilateral sources funded integration projects.

During its early years, UNHCR's mission to protect and assist refugees meant, primarily, protecting them from *refoulement* and assuring their legal status in new countries of settlement or resettlement. The ability to negotiate with governments in refugee receiving countries and, when repatriation was an option, with governments in countries of origin, has always been essential to these goals. Of course, UNHCR, directly and through its Executive Committee, must also respond to concerns of the donor country governments that fund refugee programs. Otherwise, for most of its history, the agency could and did operate with considerable independence from the rest of the international community. In this regard, UNHCR organizational culture changed significantly in the last decade of the twentieth century as it became more deeply involved in integration activities in countries of origin.

Repatriation mechanisms

As noted in the previous section, UNHCR both assists individuals who decide to repatriate to their countries of origin and organizes large-scale return movements. When individuals decide to repatriate but still have lingering fears, do not possess adequate documentation, or require financial assistance for the move, UNHCR will obtain government assurances of safety and restoration of status and rights, and will usually extend needed financial help. The large-scale refugee movements normally occur following either a cessation of conflict or a change of government.[1] Such returns require prior negotiations, which are sometimes quite protracted depending on relations between and among the governments involved and on the refugees' demands and needs upon arrival. The terms are established in a memorandum of understanding between refugee host country and country of origin governments. Before refugees return *en masse*, UNHCR officials inform the refugees of the conditions they are likely to face in their home countries and what assistance will be made available to them. It is common to bring refugee representatives on missions to observe the situation in their home countries and communities, so that they can accurately report the situation.

The actual repatriation may take place by land, using buses, trucks, and other forms of transportation for the refugees and their possessions; when refugee camps are located close to the border, able bodied refugees may walk home. On the other extreme, illustrated by Namibia in 1989, some 40,000 refugee repatriates were transported at high cost by air, because of both unsafe conditions en route and the need for speed. In most cases of large-scale returns, more refugees return spontaneously than are brought back formally by UNHCR, although refugee-returnees in both categories are usually able to take advantage of whatever post-return assistance is made available. Wherever there are returning refugees, however, there are almost always larger numbers of persons who have been internally displaced or otherwise have suffered as a result of conflict. Because there is an obviously unfair bias if assistance is available only to people repatriating from another country, returnee assistance practices have been evolving. Now, there are usually provisions for assistance to repatriates as well as other war-affected populations. These arrangements normally involve other agencies in addition to UNHCR.

Protection

It is a fundamental principle that UNHCR will facilitate a return process only when participants have affirmed that their return is undertaken voluntarily. There has always been concern as to how to assess voluntary decisions in mass movements. The degree to which each refugee decision is voluntary is of particular concern when refugee returns are strongly politicized, as in the so-called collective returns in Central America in the late 1980s and early 1990s; or when the return is mandated by a broader international peace agenda as in Cambodia, 1992–3; and, especially, in the increasing instances when host country governments and the donor community (and the refugee themselves) tire of protracted refugee situations and therefore promote repatriation despite extremely problematic conditions. These issues will be elaborated below.

Repatriations at the end of the Cold War

When the Berlin Wall fell, the two world powers withdrew support from ideological allies who had been waging proxy wars in a number of countries, and reduced barriers to cooperation on important global issues. The changing world views about Southeast Asian refugees illustrate this process.

The bitter and destructive Southeast Asian wars ended in 1978 but left a legacy of hundreds of thousands of refugees. They were pawns of Cold War politics but paradoxically also its beneficiaries. The countries of the region that received fleeing Vietnamese, Lao, and Cambodians were not signatories to the Refugee Convention and conditioned the provision of a safe haven upon rapid removal of the refugee population. Between 1979 and 1989, people able to flee Vietnam and Laos lived temporarily in camps in the region pending resettlement in Europe and (mainly) in the United States.[2] As they had in Eastern Europe, the countries of the west welcomed the Southeast Asian refugee flight as proof of the ills of communism, and the governments organized a burden sharing arrangement to meet the refugees' needs for resettlement. Until 1989, resettlement was commonly understood to be the only acceptable durable solution. In practice, the virtual promise of resettlement encouraged a continuing outflow.

When the Cold War ended, the situation dramatically changed, first for Vietnamese and Lao and later for Cambodians. In June 1989 the resettlement countries signed the Comprehensive Plan of Action, CPA. Among its provisions, the agreement foresaw that Southeast Asians would be treated the same as other refugees seeking resettlement. To be eligible for resettlement, they would undergo a screening process to determine if they met the refugee definition of a well founded fear of persecution elaborated in the Convention. The new rules ended the presumption of refugee status. Those in Southeast Asian camps who were not "screened in" faced repatriation because they could not stay where they were.

Perhaps even more surprising than the consensus among international leaders to allow repatriation was the fact that the Communist governments of Vietnam and Laos agreed to receive large numbers of returning anti-Communist refugees, and promised formally to respect their human rights. The new understanding on the refugee issue helped to open the way for improved international relations. The CPA agreement shocked some refugee advocates who had not anticipated that western governments would send people back to the oppressive regimes they had fled, and who distrusted the latter's promises to receive the refugees. Some maintained that the screening process being conducted by UNHCR officials was too stringent and disregarded human rights. To address the criticism, UNHCR mounted its first serious effort to monitor the human rights of returnees. Repatriations continued apace and the outflow of people subsided dramatically.

With the geopolitical changes of the 1990s, refugee repatriation came to be seen as both compatible with and necessary for other international efforts to promote post-conflict peace, reconciliation, and development. Moreover, for large groups of refugees who had passed a decade or more in camps and had little hope ever of gaining rights of citizenship anywhere else, repatriation to the country of origin became the only viable solution. High Commissioner Sadako Ogata (1991–2000) reiterated the message on several occasions, for example at the University of Notre Dame on 14 September 1991:

> For UNHCR voluntary repatriation of refugees is not only the most feasible solution, but also the most desirable. In a world where most refugees are confined to over-crowded, makeshift camps in conditions as dismal – if not more dismal – than the situation they have fled, the right to return to one's homeland is as important as the right to seek asylum abroad.
>
> (Ogata 1991)

The "right to return to one's homeland" in Ogata's formulation and in practice has been interpreted as the right to return to the country of origin, but not as a firm right to return to the actual place of origin. This potentially has an important bearing on the Palestinian case where, at the time of writing, the homeland has yet to be defined.

Advocates of repatriation in the 1990s counted on persuading governments in countries of origin to accept refugee return "in safety and dignity". Once the refugees were established in their homeland, it was expected that international peace-building and peacekeeping would serve to protect politically vulnerable populations, including repatriates, while an array of projects at local and national levels would build communities and reduce tensions among adversaries. At the same time, donor support for both reintegration and general development assistance would help to establish conditions for a better life for those who were returning.

The experiences of the early 1990s, although fraught with difficulties, seemed to support the hope that protracted conflicts could be ended and that persons displaced by these conflicts could return to productive lives. During the 1990s, internationally negotiated peace agreements opened the way for several large-scale repatriations, and were sustained by relatively success-ful UN-organized post-conflict missions. UNHCR played a fundamental role in obtaining government acquiescence for return, negotiating the rights of returnees and providing initial assistance for their reintegration. In Namibia (1989), Cambodia (1991), El Salvador (1991), and Mozambique (1992) the United Nations negotiated peace agreements that ended decades of Cold War conflict and permitted hundreds of thousands of refugees to return to their respective homelands. In each of these countries, refugee return was a cornerstone of the peace arrangements and the *sine qua non* for reconstruc-tion, reconciliation, and democratic government to proceed. In each of these cases, despite persistent difficulties and disappointments, peace arrange-ments basically held fast.

The easier cases gave way later in the decade to ever more problematic situations. UNHCR and its donors supported return movements to places in Asia, Africa, and Latin America where prevailing violence, corruption, and economic ruin made repatriation appear to be more an expedience than a so-lution. The expediency might have been more justified had the international community been expanding rather than cutting back on humanitarian relief programs, integration, and reconstruction aid to these same places (e.g. West Africa, Somalia, Tajikistan, Guatemala).

As repatriation and integration related activity has grown in the easy as well as the more complicated situations, UNHCR has faced unprecedented challenges to its longstanding practices and its traditional *modus operandi*.

Integration programs in countries of origin

Having successfully negotiated post Cold War peace agreements, the UN and its agencies began overseeing ambitious peace-building and reconstruction programs. Most wars of the 1980s and 1990s had been civil conflicts, and the victims largely civilian. Massive flight had left vast areas of the affected countries unproductive and almost without a civilian population. When the refugees repatriated to these war-torn countries, they could not count on meaningful economic support from their governments. Therefore, their reintegration required the support of UN agencies, NGOs, and donors. UNHCR and virtually all the major actors accepted the reality that reintegrating uprooted populations was a core component of post-conflict peace building, and essential both for consolidating peace arrangements and for reconstructing a country's economy and social fabric. Again, the September 1991 words of High Commissioner Ogata:

> Returning refugees can only be properly reintegrated if there are com-prehensive programmes for political, economic and social construction

or reconstruction. As such, ensuring the success of voluntary repatriation goes beyond the mandate or resources of UNHCR alone.

(ibid.)

During most of the 1980s, UNHCR devoted only 2 percent of its budget to repatriation activities. Between 1990 and 1996, however, UNHCR was channeling approximately 14 percent of its budget to activities related to returns. Expenditures for reintegration activities nearly doubled between 1994 and 1996 (Crisp 2001: 8).

The mass returns to Cambodia, El Salvador, and Mozambique during the early 1990s transformed UNHCR's traditional approach to integration activities, which hitherto had consisted of providing assistance packages to individual returnee families and interventions to secure legal guarantees. Despite a mandate limited to refugees, UNHCR increasingly participated in these countries in programs intended to benefit war-affected populations overall, especially IDPs. In addition to core legal concerns, UNHCR created projects for restoring infrastructure, improving local governance, and generating income. Although there were no massive repatriations in Bosnia and Herzegovina and Croatia, the Secretary General nonetheless asked UNHCR to serve as lead agency for humanitarian assistance in the post-conflict period. The assistance was made available to returnees, IDPs, and people affected by the war generally. This rapid expansion of UNHCR's role and the increasing complexity of the refugee returns have raised controversial issues of principle and priority that are still being debated.

Linking repatriations to broader peace-building programs

Prior to the 1990s UNHCR was able to operate solely on behalf of refugees and almost independently of other national or international programs. As UNHCR has become involved in negotiating and planning peace processes, however, the repatriation agenda is more often determined in collaboration with a number of other international bodies. The peace accords negotiated in Namibia, Cambodia, Mozambique, and Bosnia, for example, established time frames for the deployment of peacekeeping missions and dates for nationwide elections which, in turn, predetermined the timing of refugee return. The problem was to square the imposed time frames with the fundamental principles governing UN-organized repatriations, i.e. that they be voluntary and determined by individuals. By incorporating collective repatriations into peace agreements in these and other instances, the peacemakers inevitably have diminished the weight of individual decision-making among those who are slated to return. Although such post-conflict collective repatriations, for the most part, can reasonably be characterized as voluntary, both individual choices and realistic assessments of the home country's absorptive capacities tend to be subordinated.

The fact that UNHCR often has given less than full respect to individual decisions about where and when refugees return does not detract from the enormous achievements the large-scale repatriations represent. Refugees have left squalid camps to return to nations newly at peace and to participate in rebuilding their countries. When the international community also is committed to supporting rebuilding and assisting in the reintegration process, the net gain is substantial. International support, however, has been at best uneven and through the last decade has been declining.[3]

It is not possible at this juncture to forecast the fate of Palestinian refugees in the hoped-for peace agreement in the Middle East except that there is likely to be a mixture of repatriation, compensation, third country resettlement, and local integration. It is also more than likely that refugee choice among Palestinians, as among other refugee groups, will be subject to constraints imposed by negotiated compromises and economic viability.

Namibia was the first major example in which the United Nations negotiated a peace arrangement that encompassed refugee return as a key element. When the UN finally achieved recognition of Namibian independence and the right of refugees to return, the parties agreed to elections for November 1989. This agreement obliged UNHCR to accelerate the repatriation – at considerable expense – in order to meet the deadline for the first post-independence election. In other ways, however, the Namibia operation was run along traditional lines: The refugee organization remained fully in charge of the repatriation, but left before it could become involved in the subsequent integration process.

The Paris Peace Agreement of 23 October 1991, which brought peace to Cambodia and the decision to establish the United Nations Transitional Authority, UNTAC, was negotiated with full approval and involvement of the UN Security Council and had ample support from major donors. The regional actors participated in the process and the four rival armed Cambodian factions all agreed (albeit tentatively) to the terms. A repatriation unit was incorporated into the UNTAC structure under the direction of UNHCR, and its director reported both to the UN Secretary General and to the High Commissioner for Refugees.

Because the return of Cambodian refugees was fundamental to the success of the Paris Agreement and to the legitimacy of the Cambodian nation, the timing of repatriation was dictated by the negotiated date for elections, in this case May 1993. In vain, refugee experts recommended a longer preparation time, citing land mines, health risks, and the poor absorptive capacity of the country. Once the decision was taken, the repatriation of some 360,000 refugees from the Thai border (a population to which UNHCR had not previously had access as it was not recognized by the Thai government) became the major driving force behind initial efforts to rebuild the country. The refugees needed roads without landmines, basic infrastructure, health and sanitation systems, and, not least importantly, international oversight and monitoring. UNTAC as a whole, and not just the Repatriation Unit of UNTAC, had to respond.

While the peace agreement in El Salvador did not incorporate repatriation timetables, the region-wide peace process (see below on CIREFCA) established a framework for dealing with refugees, returnees, and internally displaced persons. That framework, combined with international involvement in peace negotiations and humanitarian assistance, encouraged rebel leaders to organize return movements that brought people back from exile. The refugees collectively demanded the right to return to rebel held zones, although the Salvadoran government opposed it and would not guarantee security. Given the ongoing conflict and inevitable insecurity, UNHCR was understandably reluctant to organize the collective repatriations. Nevertheless, it did so, and international donors channeled relief and assistance through local and international non-government agencies. For the Salvadoran rebels, the return of civilians to the conflict zone and the related CIREFCA process were the *sine qua non* for negotiating peace.

Another dramatic case in which repatriation formed the centerpiece of an internationally negotiated peace accord was that of Bosnia and Herzegovina. The Dayton Peace Agreement was signed at the end of 1995 and, as in the case of Cambodia, was the product of international involvement at the highest levels. It opened the way to billions of dollars in reconstruction aid and placed governing structures under international authority. In Bosnia and Herzegovina, as much as or more than in Cambodia, successful refugee repatriation and the return of ethnic minorities among the internally displaced persons were considered essential to fulfilling the terms of the peace agreement. Virtually all donors and agencies targeted their assistance projects in some measure toward reintegration efforts (Fagen 2003a: 233–46).

UNHCR assumed joint responsibility with the Office of the High Representative, OHR, for return and reintegration of refugees as well as internally displaced persons, and oversaw humanitarian assistance generally. Ultimately the refugees did not return either in the numbers or at the time they were expected. The complexity and limited success of reintegration efforts in Bosnia and Herzegovina raised questions about the major humanitarian assistance responsibilities that UNHCR and the Office of the High Representative had undertaken, given the inability to provide meaningful protection.

Effecting protection during war to peace transitions

Germany and Croatia withdrew safe haven status for Bosnians almost immediately after the end of the conflict, in 1996. In reality that population still could not safely return to their homes in Serb-controlled areas from which most had originated, so most of those who did come back lived as internally displaced persons in the Federation area of Bosnia. Contrary to the Cambodians who willingly repopulated a country lacking infrastructure, rule of law, and a viable economy, Bosnians resisted returning to areas they knew to be physically insecure and economically depressed. Neither the presence of peacekeepers nor a series of well funded international projects and incentives aimed at luring them back and easing their transition were sufficient to overcome their fears. The fears were well grounded. The Serb and Muslim leaders in Bosnia may have signed the Dayton agreement, but they did not accept the requirement to restore a multi-ethnic society. They stayed in their respective locales, and continued to threaten the wellbeing of returnees of the opposing ethnicity. There could be no meaningful protection until after the enactment of serious sanctions against the nationalist leaders who were continuing to violate the human rights of ethnic minorities.

Although there were continuing repatriations, a protection regime in Afghanistan was untenable before the Taliban fell. After the fall of the Taliban, the refugee host countries no longer were hospitable to them (host country hospitality having already declined owing to continuing outflows and declining international assistance); large-scale repatriation was all but inevitable. Both push and pull factors have led about three million Afghans to return between 2001 and 2004.[4] To date, the Afghan government has not been able to impose national institutions or rule of law throughout the territory. Therefore, the returnees, once in Afghanistan, have been unable to benefit from protection because the population in general has lacked security. Humanitarian workers and international officials are still at risk especially outside cities, and neither UNHCR nor other international agencies have established operations in many regions to which returnees have gone.

Taking a protection role in countries of origin has led UNHCR to contradictions and some anomalies. For example, UNHCR was heavily engaged in protection related activity on behalf of returnees to El Salvador and Guatemala during the 1980s and 1990s. This was made necessary by the fact that the majority of refugees, by their own choice, returned to conflict zones, and the military generally treated them as combatants. While UNHCR had primary responsibility for refugee-returnees, the UN peace mission, ONUSAL and MINUGUA, had major responsibility for the internally displaced populations. The two groups were located in close proximity. The overlapping international jurisdictions led to some very positive results, but also to frequent confusion.

In 1996 Rwandan Hutus were driven from the then Zaire back to Rwanda by that nation's Tutsi security forces. UNHCR established an ambitious assistance program in Rwanda with the intention of easing tensions between Hutus and Tutsis. The agency met housing needs and encouraged reconciliation projects. The Tutsi-led government, however, did not see this as a means of easing tensions and, instead, was far from appreciative at the outset. In its view, UNHCR was giving preference to the aggressors (the Hutu returnees) and withholding benefits from the victims of genocide.

In the past, refugees repatriating to their home countries could expect their governments to respect their rights. Because repatriation increasingly has become the only available option for refugees, the refugees now may be obliged to return to settings where the factors that drove them into exile remain largely in place. Repatriations to war-torn countries bring people back to what are almost inevitably unstable and politically tense situations. Even in the absence of armed hostilities, war-affected populations face contentious issues related to land titles, property loss, personal documentation, ethnic and religious rights, abuse of power, etc. In such settings, UNHCR has little choice but to assume protection responsibilities by defending the repatriates against competing claims or wilful neglect. Because countries engaged in war-to-peace transitions are generally insecure, governments are weak and there are almost always pockets of resistance to authority and violence for which nobody is held accountable. Those governments with a political will to respect returnee rights may lack the capacity to do so. Afghanistan is a clear case in point. Clearly the need for international protection and the ability of international agencies to protect future Palestinian returnees will depend on the legal and political situation in place.

Some particularly worrisome repatriations have taken place during the last decade under UNHCR's watch. These include the return of Rohingyas from Bangladesh to Myanmar in 1993, the forced return of Hutus from Tanzania and Zairian camps in 1996, the return of Somalis from Ethiopia and Sudan, the premature returns of Afghans from Iran and Pakistan, and also Burundians from Tanzania. They are worrisome because individuals and groups were given no option other than returning to inappropriate and dangerous situations, with little or no political support and too few resources to rebuild their lives. Although the outcomes in these places may have been less dire than some were predicting, the returnees' struggles have been enormous.

Returnees in need of protection

Recent and forthcoming large-scale return movements involve significant elements of coercion and risk. As people who have sought refuge or asylum – from wealthy countries as well as from poor countries – are channeled back to their homes, they need an international presence to work for their protection. UNHCR has tried to intensify its protection role in countries of origin despite short-term funding and the obvious fact that its effectiveness is limited by the fact that the international bases for refugee protection do not hold once the people in question have returned and no longer are refugees.

Even when the returnees affirm that they are moving voluntarily and wish to return home, the reintegration process is problematic. Unquestionably voluntary repatriations also pose protection concerns upon arrival in the countries of origin. Some not uncommon examples are:

- An individual decides to bring his family back to the homeland. His wife and children follow him despite the fact that they have fewer rights and less access to education in their countries of origin than in their country of refuge, and are fearful.
- A large group undertakes a massive return, but there are elderly and ill persons amongst them who make the difficult journey with UNHCR

assistance in transport. They are unable to fend for themselves thereafter. Neither host country nor home country – nor often their own families – can provide for their continued protection and assistance.

- Local populations may and frequently have refused to accept repatriate groups or individual repatriates despite prior agreements.
- Likewise, despite prior agreements negotiated with UNHCR, returnees are unable to recover property or to exercise rights.
- Because minefields preclude return to their own land, returnees live as IDPs in temporary arrangements.
- Renewed conflict, drought, corruption, and all the ills that make life miserable for the general population cause particular hardships for the recently returned population, who lack local protection networks and the survival strategies that other groups have established.

UNHCR guidelines cover all such issues, and there is far more sensitivity than in previous times to the potential dangers facing certain categories of people. Nevertheless, the agency does not have adequate numbers of well trained staff and resources to deal with these situations in all its operations. Where the problems are related to widely accepted cultural behaviors, UNHCR cannot easily effect changes once refugees have returned to their own societies. Moreover, protection problems related to reintegration are likely to last, or even to commence, after UNHCR has withdrawn much of its staff.

For these reasons, the language of human rights instead of protection has come to prevail. UNHCR, along with the International Committee of the Red Cross and/or the peacekeepers and human rights monitors in UN missions and other international agencies, has developed strategies for monitoring and protecting people officially under the legal protection of their governments, but vulnerable to abuse. In accepting that UNHCR has a legitimate interest in and responsibility for monitoring returnee human rights, protection officers face the dilemma of defining which of the many rights that may be violated are of primary concern. The conclusions of a "lessons learned" evaluation on the UNHCR operations in Guatemala noted a serious "lack of clarity regarding the scope and duration of UNHCR's protection monitoring role." UNHCR, the report noted, could be drawn into assuming responsibility for a whole spectrum of abuses, ranging from land issues to domestic violence. The challenge was not only to determine which rights were of legitimate concern, but where UNHCR could be more effective than other UN agencies or than the state itself (Jamal 2000: 9).

Linking repatriation assistance programs to broader economic revitalization

After decades of conflict, the countries enjoying the first taste of peace also face overwhelming devastation. In the early 1990s, when peace agreements were signed in Mozambique, Bosnia and Herzegovina/Croatia, El Salvador, Guatemala, and Cambodia, UNHCR was well funded and encouraged to engage more deeply in integration activities. During this period, traditional practices of assuring safe return and short-term relief to returnee families gave way to community-based and rights-based assistance programs.

The basic concept of refugee and returnee aid and development goes back to the 1980s. The African governments complained that they had hosted hundreds of thousands of refugees, yet were unable to provide economic opportunities for their own returning citizens. The call for development aid to be made available to governments receiving returning refugees was a central African concern during the 1980s. At that time, however, UNHCR and donors persisted in viewing refugee problems primarily in legal and political realms while development actors had other priorities.

The change in perspective came only at the end of that decade in Central America, where a regional peace process and donor commitments led to a new and broader approach to reintegration. In the Central American Conference on Refugees, Returnees and Internally Displaced Persons, called CIREFCA, donors pledged to support the region-wide peace process with additional assistance for the war-uprooted populations. The CIREFCA process constituted a coordinated international response that targeted the full range of uprooted people throughout the Central American region. CIREFCA combined relief assistance with development. The plan provided for coordinating the activities of donors, governments, and local and international NGOs, by means of a Joint Secretariat with UNHCR and the United Nations Development Program, UNDP. It was the first time that these two agencies had worked together in a long-term program. In addition, within the CIREFCA framework, UNDP created a parallel program, the Development Program for Refugees, Displaced and Repatriated Persons (PRODERE). In this context, the needs of both refugees and internally displaced persons could be addressed and, in theory at least, the projects initiated as short-term relief could be absorbed into development plans. Most of the assistance was delivered to communities where uprooted people had settled rather than given to individuals. This approach averted the long criticized practice of channeling assistance only to the returned refugees, but leaving the often more destitute IDPs with nothing. Community-based assistance now has become an accepted norm where the two groups live in close proximity.

The quick impact projects, QIPs, became the mechanisms of choice for much of the community-based assistance. QIPs, elaborated in the Central American context during the early 1990s, not only were the hallmarks of UNHCR's reintegration approach, but were utilized globally by numerous agencies. They were taken from Central America to Cambodia, Mozambique, Tajikistan, and other returnee situations and, at the time of this writing, are being implemented in Afghanistan and Angola. QIPs are usually micro projects, (e.g. water systems, schools) requiring a one-time modest donor investment and community involvement. They are made available to communities with high proportions of recent returnees in order to respond to immediate and urgent needs identified by community members. In so doing, they are meant to encourage the sharing of ideas, skills, and resources, thereby relieving local tensions and promoting reconciliation. QIPs are potential bridges to development rather than development projects in the strict sense. QIP projects have attracted donor interest and support and they have been very important for communities lacking resources in the early period following conflict. However, in the absence of donor support beyond the first investment, or government commitment to incorporate QIPs into national development strategies, the actual projects very rarely have proved sustainable (Fagen 1993: 33; Smillie 1998: 1–5; Crisp 2001: 12–14).

The apogee of UNHCR involvement in reintegration activity took place in Mozambique. Between 1993 and 1996 UNHCR assisted in repatriating and/or reintegrating more than 1.5 million people and an estimated twice that number of IDPs. Of the total $108 million spent on the Mozambican operation, only 20 percent was spent on the repatriation itself, while 80 percent went to the activities related to integration (UNHCR 1996: 1). The reintegration program encompassed perhaps four times the number of people that UNHCR had repatriated, as most Mozambican refugees had returned spontaneously. During its tenure in Mozambique, UNHCR oversaw three sub-offices and seventeen field offices, and launched over 1,500 QIPs, affecting every war-impacted department of the country. As in Central America and Cambodia, assistance was community-based, targeted at areas containing large numbers of refugees, internally displaced persons, and former combatants. And, as in Cambodia, UNHCR operated within the general framework of a UN Peace Mission.

The Mozambique operation was well funded, and by all accounts UNHCR's interventions had major impacts in the poorest parts of the country. By the time UNHCR left in 1996, there were schools, wells, health clinics, and access roads dotting the countryside. Previously abandoned communities were repopulated and had come to life. The organization was justly proud of its achievements. Subsequent internal and external assessments, however, found reasons to temper the praise with more critical conclusions. The reintegration strategy was late in being formulated. There was neither adequate information sharing nor collaboration with other agencies, especially UNDP. In the interest of attending to the needs of returnees within an unrealistically short timeframe, UNHCR rarely used local materials if others were more easily obtained, or employed national NGOs if the multiple international NGOs in the country offered greater expertise. The tight time frames precluded adequate research to determine the best location or the most vital of the many needs to support (Fagen 2003b: 217–20).

From the start, the government's ownership of peace and reintegration projects – whether undertaken by UNHCR, another UN agency, or one of the multiple humanitarian NGOs – has been limited. Not surprisingly, in the years that followed, the Mozambican government has been unable to send sufficient health professionals, teachers, or technicians to many of the facilities created with international humanitarian support.

As in the area of human rights, UNHCR accepted a deeper involvement in creating conditions conducive to reintegration, but then faced the difficulty of determining the dimensions of the activities to be undertaken, the composition of the beneficiary population, and the appropriate time frames for assistance. The key to resolving these questions lies in the nature of co-ordination with other agencies and NGOs and national agencies. Ultimately, reintegration projects for refugees and internally displaced persons have to be combined with the broader rebuilding plans of the national government. These dilemmas, very much present in Mozambique, intensified later on as post-conflict situations multiplied and international funding for integration decreased.

The debate over UNHCR's role in reintegration

At the end of the decade of the 1990s, the countries where peace negotiations seemed to be progressing reverted to conflict, e.g. Angola, Liberia, Sri Lanka, Afghanistan, and plans for repatriations had to be shelved.[5] Growing demands for resources to address the old and new complex emergencies taxed donor generosity to non-emergency situations. Donor support for UNHCR across the board diminished decisively between 2000 and 2003, adding to the misery of a large number of refugee populations. Reporting on refugee situations during 2000, Jeff Drumtra of the US Committee for Refugees commented, "The international community's main 'gift' to UNHCR . . . was to starve it of more than $100 million of desperately needed funding and to brow beat the agency into purposely obscuring the real costs needed to meet protection and assistance needs of refugees worldwide" (USCR 2001: 14).

Two themes emerged in debates over how UNHCR should define its role: first, the notion that it was necessary to restore the primacy of protection in the UNHCR mandate, and second, that UNHCR should withdraw from extensive involvement in reintegration programs. Neither proved especially helpful in resolving the problems.

Taking into account the dire situation caused by funding shortfalls at the beginning of the decade, the newly appointed High Commissioner talked of reducing levels of activity in countries of origin in order to return to the UNHCR core mandate of protection. This theme was promoted, as well, among important refugee advocates (see Frelick 1997; Goodwin Gil 1999: 231; Loescher 2003a: 12, 14). Their basic premise was that other agencies could meet material needs for refugees, but only UNHCR could offer protection. The UK's DfID was a leading voice among donors encouraging more bilateral assistance directly to NGOs delivering services rather than to UNHCR, presumably so that UNHCR could emphasize protection.

With regard to post-repatriation integration, donors as well as some senior officials in UNHCR shared the premise that the refugee organization was stretching its mandate by taking a significant role in post-conflict reintegration and reconstruction. According to this view, UNHCR work in countries of origin should be focused, as previously, on legal activities, including documentation and restoration of property and defense of rights. Anything beyond a few short-term QIPs should be left to NGOs and other UN development actors, thereby permitting UNHCR to establish a viable exit strategy.

Attractive as the arguments about UNHCR and its core protection mandate may seem, it is untenable in practice for UNHCR to separate assistance from protection either in refugee or repatriation operations. There is ample evidence that refugee and returnee protection can deteriorate badly when funding for assistance through UNHCR is reduced, and that the effects fall most profoundly on women and children (see UNHCR Children's Evaluation 2002; Women's Commission 2002; Casa Consulting 2003). Although other entities are able to provide services and attend to needs of refugees and repatriates, UNHCR protection has been exercised in large part *through* the assistance it provides and the manner in which it has been provided. As for de-emphasizing returnee programs, when UNHCR cut back its operations, it left some newly returned groups in dire situations, such as Somalis returning from Ethiopia. In some instances UNHCR postponed previously planned individual repatriations because funding could support only life-sustaining activities in the camps (RCK 2003: 8).

On the other hand, there is much validity to the insistence that UNHCR should not engage in reintegration projects that are more appropriately carried out by development actors. Unfortunately for the returning refugees, the donors thus far have not adequately funded development actors to undertake the tasks that UNHCR has relinquished, and the development actors have pursued other priority agendas of their own. New initiatives are now under way to redress the gaps in reintegration efforts, and one hopes these will be available to ease a future Palestinian return/reintegration operation.

A promising alternative to accepting a diminished UNHCR role is striving for greater collaboration between UNHCR and agencies with long-term mandates for development. The first iteration of this concept – the "Brookings Process" – was put forward in 2000 (see Crisp 2001: 14–16). It was a promising proposal from UNHCR, the World Bank, and, later, UNDP for commonly formulated and agreed operational responses to span relief to development transitions. At its heart was to be a trust fund so that coherent planning could be accompanied by coherent funding mechanisms. The proposal was soon abandoned because, while donors were sympathetic to the need for coherent planning, they rejected the funding mechanism. Subsequently, UNHCR has established a framework for durable solutions that is meant to bring together humanitarian and development actors and funds in order to address issues related to development assistance to refugees and returnees (UNHCR Executive Committee 2003). The "4Rs" approach links repatriation, reintegration, rehabilitation, and reconstruction and development through local integration. A September 2003 document explaining the framework underscores the need for comprehensive planning with development partners and, again, funds.

> The aim [of this approach] is that greater resources should be allocated to create a conducive environment inside the countries of origin so as to, not only prevent the recurrence of mass outflows, but also facilitate sustainable repatriation.
> [. . .]
> The aim of working in partnership with the World Bank, bilateral development partners and the United Nations is that such a cross-cutting concern will be seen as a collective task and that sister agencies, the donor and development communities will inscribe this imperative on their agenda.
> (UNHCR Executive Committee 2003: para. 15, 19)

In this model, UNHCR will focus on its traditional strengths, but engage with a range of humanitarian and development partners and donors *from the outset* to strengthen burden sharing, development, and capacity-building components for refugees and other similarly affected populations. While UNHCR takes the lead on repatriation, the other components of the 4Rs – reintegration, rehabilitation, and reconstruction – depend largely on the participation of UNDP and the World Bank partners, along with other UN agencies and NGOs. Full government ownership and effectiveness are essential. The program is being piloted in Eritrea, Sierra Leone, Sri Lanka, and Afghanistan.

To buttress the 4Rs, UNHCR has put forward a related plan, operated by a new unit in the Department of International Protection, called *Convention Plus*. This foresees special agreements with donors and agencies so that it will be possible to manage challenges better and cover needs in specific situations. One of the three objectives of the Convention Plus proposal is targeting development assistance to achieve durable solutions.[6] The durable solutions refer to both local integration and return.

This is a positive and sensible approach, which at the time of writing is beginning to be implemented. Whether the long-term international resources needed to support it will be forthcoming remains to be seen.

Post-conflict returns: present prospects

Once again, and for the first time in many years, large scale refugee repatriation is on the international agenda. In addition to the millions returning to Afghanistan, a major repatriation movement is under way in Africa. UNHCR predicts that the resolution of several African conflicts will allow up to 2 million people to return in the next five years (IRIN: 5/19/04).

Over the past approximately three years, peace agreements or much improved prospects of peace are changing realities in Angola, Burundi, the Democratic Republic of Congo (DRC), Eritrea, Liberia, Rwanda, Sierra Leone, (parts of) Somalia, and Sudan. Responding to the changes, hundreds of thousands of refugees – millions with the returning IDP population – have been returning, sometimes after decades in camps and temporary settlements. If and when the prospects of peace are realized in Burundi, DRC, and Sudan, millions more will follow. (There are 790,000 Burundi refugees in Tanzania alone (IRIN: 5/19/04).)

The consequences of massive repatriations throughout the continent prompted UNHCR in March 2003 to organize a Dialogue on Voluntary Repatriation and Sustainable Reintegration in Africa. The officials assembled from high-level aid groups, donor governments, and African governments were optimistic that many prolonged refugee situations throughout the continent might be on the verge of resolution. Nevertheless, all present acknowledged that the prospect of repatriating millions of persons to countries as yet unable to absorb them is troubling. Like Afghanistan, all of the African countries in question would be facing extremely difficult political and economic prospects. The added burden of integrating hundreds of thousands, or millions, of war-uprooted people could well undermine stability.

At the time of writing, the integration programs that should accompany the repatriations presently under way are inadequately supported. For example, despite a strong international commitment to support the Angolan war-to-peace transition, a recent report describes the shortfalls in food relief, slow landmine clearance, and limited provincial capacities facing newly repatriated Angolans (JRS: 18 May 2004). International appeals for Angola have come up short.

Sierra Leone, where peace has been in place since 2001 and over 270,000 refugees have returned, is one of the pilot countries for the 4Rs approach. There, as in all the post-war countries, reintegration requires a comprehensive multi-agency approach, a long-term commitment, effective resolution of the factors at the root of conflict, and significant improvements in citizen security, socioeconomic conditions, human rights, and good governance. Since August 2003, a UN Transition Team has been operating in the country to assess needs and priorities, to develop strategies and design projects for the transition period. Despite better coordination and planning, the new approach still has not meant that international pledges are filled in a timely manner and, consequently, restoration of infrastructure and basic services lags badly. For these reasons as well as persistent fears of violence, returnees in Sierra Leone have been gravitating to cities rather than rural homes (Kamara 2003). This is not at all unusual in return situations, and is characteristic of the returns also under way in Afghanistan and Angola. Nor is it unusual that international assistance tends to bypass the swelling urban population, going instead to support projects in the rural regions to which donors and international agencies thought refugees would return.

Miscalculations, short funding and inappropriate time frames are likely to affect future reintegration efforts unless international policy makers rethink the premises of their engagement. The major reason for inadequate international resources and commitments seems to be that, when emergencies occur, donor governments neither anticipate nor plan for long-term multi-faceted forms of involvement. It is well understood that international funding alone is insufficient to induce meaningful political, economic, and social reforms or to assure that people who have been uprooted can remake their lives safely and productively. Likewise, aid professionals know that a large and longstanding international presence is almost sure to stifle local initiative. It takes planning, coordination, and careful monitoring to strike the right balance. Progress inevitably occurs more slowly in some sectors than in others. This is the reason for promoting multi-agency integrated planning and transition strategies and for "staying the course" – whether in Africa or the Middle East. Realities on the ground, and not prefabricated projects and previously established time frames, should determine the nature of international interventions and the funding needed for these interventions.

Palestinian residents and returnees – before, during, and after durable solutions have been achieved – will be subject to the political agendas of their own leadership. For reintegration programs to succeed, it is essential that national governments correct serious deficiencies: corruption and cultural and religious obstacles undermine theoretically positive programs. Equally importantly, for integration to be feasible – and here national governments do not control the full deck of cards – economic development must be strong enough to sustain the local population, settlers, and/or returnees. In the multiple places where the formula has not worked well, refugees and IDPs have returned to problematic situations where rule of law is fragile, corruption is high, and economic prospects are dim. In such settings the international protection that can be made available to returnees is unavoidably limited.

The themes elaborated in these pages related to repatriation and integration have a bearing on all groups contemplating return operations. The issues go beyond today's divisive controversies about who will return, to what places, and under what circumstances. Questions still to be resolved include: To what extent will potential returnees be able to choose? If there is a collective or political decision that defines the mechanisms for the majority of Palestinians, will there be alternative options for individuals who disagree? Will international protection monitoring be put in place and, if so, with what terms of reference? Whether Palestinian refugees return to (or settle in) a new state, reside within the boundaries of Israel, or obtain citizen rights within one of the other neighboring countries, will an international body help them to secure firm legal status, gain access to essential state services, and achieve property rights? Will specific projects be introduced for returnees to a new Palestinian state or will they simply be incorporated into the development plans of the state? And how will integration be financed? The international community, the Palestinian leadership, and the refugees themselves can and should insist on a return and integration process that serves not only their immediate interests but also contributes to their long-term security and prosperity.

Notes

1 At some point following a peace agreement and/or change of government, UNHCR may invoke a cessation clause that removes refugee protection on the grounds that the refugees are under the protection of their own national governments or, more problematically, because the circumstances that caused them to be refugees have ceased.
2 The Cambodians here are an exception. A minority were in resettlement camps based in Thailand, but the majority of those who had survived the genocide in their country lived along the Thai border, in camps not recognized by the Thai government as under its control.
3 Support for UNHCR in 2004 seems to be somewhat improved.
4 The major push factors, which are related, have been the sharp decline in financial support for refugees, as donors channeled funding instead for repatriates inside Afghanistan, and the already referenced hostility of host country governments to remaining refugees.
5 At the time of writing there are repatriations under way in Afghanistan, Angola, Liberia, and, despite a still elusive peace accord, Sri Lanka as well.
6 The other two are strategic use of resettlement and clarification of state responsibilities in relation to secondary movements.

References

Casa Consulting (2003) *The community services function in UNHCR: An independent evaluation*, EPAU/2003/02 March, 2003, www.UNHCR.ch

Crisp, Jeff (2001) "Mind the gap. UNHCR humanitarian assistance and the development process", available online at www.UNHCR.ch

Fagen, Patricia Weiss (1993) "Peace in Central America: Transition for the uprooted", in *World Refugee Survey* (Washington, DC: US Committee for Refugees), pp. 30–9.

Fagen, Patricia Weiss (2003a) "The long term challenges of reconstruction and reintegration: Case studies of Haiti and Bosnia Herzegovina", in Edward Newman and Joanne Van Selm (eds.), *Refugees and forced displacement: International security, human vulnerability, and the state* (Tokyo: UN University Press), pp. 221–49.

Fagen, Patricia Weiss (2003b) "Post-conflict reintegration and reconstruction: Doing it right takes a while", in Niklaus Steiner, Mark Gibney, and Gil Loescher (eds.), *Problems of protection: The UNHCR, refugees and human rights* (New York: Routledge), pp. 197–224.

Farah, Randa (2003) "The marginalization of Palestinian refugees", in Niklaus Steiner, Mark Gibney, and Gil Loescher (eds.), *Problems of protection: The UNHCR, refugees and human rights* (New York: Routledge), pp. 155–78.

Frelick, Bill (1997) "Assistance without protection: Feed the hungry, clothe the naked and watch them die", in US Committee for Refugees, *World Refugee Survey 1997* (Washington, DC: US Committee for Refugees).

Goodwin Gil, Guy (1999) "Refugee identity and protection's fading prospect", in Frances Nicholson and Patrick Twomey (eds.), *Refugee rights and realities: Evolving international concepts and regimes* (Cambridge: Cambridge University Press).

Hendrie, Barbara (1995) "The Tigrayan refugee repatriation 1985–7", in Barry Stein,

Fred Cuny and Pat Reed (eds.), *Refugee repatriation during conflict, a new conventional wisdom* (Dallas: Center for the Study of Societies in Crisis), pp. 105–18.

Jamal, Arafat (2000) "Refugee repatriation and reintegration in Guatemala: Lessons learned from UNHCR's experience", UNHCR EPAU/2000/03, September, available online at www.UNHCR.ch

Jesuit Refugee Service (JRS) *Dispatches,* available online at http://www.jrs.net/dispatches/disp.php?lang=en

Kamara, Victor (2003) "Accelerated dynamics of resettlement in emerging from conflict Sierra Leone", Field Report December 2003, Conflict Stability in West Africa Series, Community Action for Refugees, CAP.

Loescher, Gil (2003) *Beyond Charity: International Cooperation and the Global Refugee Crisis.* Oxford University Press.

Ogata, Sadako (1991) speech presented at the University of Notre Dame, 14 September.

Refugee Consortium of Kenya (RCK) (2003) "UNHCR budget cuts, dealing a death sentence to refugees in Africa" (Nairobi: RCK) (information booklet).

Ruiz, Hiram (1993) "Repatriation: Tackling protection and assistance concerns," in *World Refugee Survey* (Washington, DC: US Committee for Refugees), pp. 23–9.

Smillie, Ian (1998) *Relief and development: The struggle for synergy.* Occasional Paper 33 (Providence, RI: Thomas J. Watson Jr. Institute for International Studies, Brown University).

UNHCR (1996) "Mozambique: An account from a lessons learned seminar on reintegration", Geneva, 24–26 June (manuscript).

UNHCR (1995) *The state of the world's refugees: In search of solutions* (Oxford: Oxford University Press).

UNHCR (2000) *The state of the world's refugees: Fifty years of humanitarian action* (Oxford: Oxford University Press).

US Committee for Refugees (2001) *World Refugee Survey 2001* (Washington, DC: USCR).

UNRWA (2004) http://www.un.org/unrwa/overview/qa.html

Valid International (2002) *Meeting the rights and protection needs of refugee children*, available online at http.www.UNHCR.ch

Women's Commission for Refugee Women and Children (2002) *UNHCR policy on refugee women and guidelines on their protection: An assessment of ten years of implementation*, available online at www.womenscommission.org/reports/pdf/UNHCR2002pdf

4 Perspectives on Palestinian repatriation

Rex Brynen

Palestinian refugee repatriation – understood here as repatriation to a future Palestinian state, as opposed to "return" to their original homes within what became Israel[1] – was little studied until the late 1990s. On the Palestinian side, emphasis was placed instead on the "right of return" to 1948 areas. Discussion of repatriation was discouraged, lest it weaken refugee rights. Among Israelis (with the rare exception of Gazit 1995) there was very little policy attention to resolving the refugee issue, other than to reject the idea of any such return. For the international community, the issue was seen as too remote to necessitate much analytical concern. (For a useful overview of Palestinian, Israeli, and other perspectives, see Zureik (1996).)

This situation began to change in the later stages of the Oslo peace process, and especially with the approach of final status talks in 2000–1. As both the Palestinians and Israelis prepared for negotiation, they both began to reflect on how repatriation might occur. At the same time, the PA Ministry of Planning and International Cooperation explored the issue in greater detail, as an intrinsic part of its development planning for a future Palestinian state (Nijem 2003). Within the international community, Canada, the World Bank, European Union, and the United States initiated work on the issue. Starting (somewhat belatedly) in December 2000, an informal "no name" group of interested donors met to discuss their potential role in any refugee agreement.

This chapter will examine the evolution of Israeli, Palestinian, and donor thinking on repatriation issues. In doing so, it will attempt to identify major issues and possible elements of a repatriation and absorption strategy. This will include an analysis of the implications for repatriation of the clauses proposed in the official Taba negotiations in January 2001, as well as the unofficial Geneva Accord of 2003. Finally, the chapter will assess the extent to which the changed political environment of the post-Oslo *intifada* era may alter the possibilities and contours of any future refugee repatriation.

In doing so, this chapter will resist the tendency to identify "Palestinian", "Israeli", and "international" perspectives on the issue. To do so would be to imply an unwarranted degree of consensus within each group, and also obfuscate those areas where some degree of agreement has emerged across lines of national affiliation. Instead, this chapter will focus on several key issues that would need to be addressed in the repatriation of refugees: border controls, repatriation management and relocation assistance, absorption policy for returnees, refugee camps, the future of UNRWA and social service delivery to refugees, and the role of donors.

Key issues

Border controls

A critical first factor shaping any future refugee repatriation will be the nature of any border or population controls imposed on a future Palestinian state. Palestinian analysts and negotiators have always assumed, and worked towards, full Palestinian control over international boundaries, and unrestricted access to Palestine for the Palestinian diaspora. During the Oslo period, however, the initial position of many Israelis was that some sort of border controls were needed on the Palestinian state, whether for security reasons or to control a potentially destabilizing influx of returnees to the new Palestinian state.

Some outside analysts concurred with this view. McCarthy (1996) and Arzt (1997: 85) argued that an influx of Palestinian refugees could destabilize the West Bank and Gaza. A draft report of a major refugee study undertaken by the Institute for Social and Economic Policy in the Middle East at Harvard University (Borjas and Rodrik 1997) expressed similar concerns, and called for a Palestinian state to adopt a points system or influx controls whereby it could limit flows and assign priority to certain groups, such as those facing precarious political or economic situations, or with needed skills. A study commissioned by the EU Refugee Task Force (Tsardanis and Huliaras 1999) also expressed concerns about the limited "absorptive capacity" of the WBG, and suggested a formula linking repatriation to economic and social conditions in the territories.

Of these studies, the Harvard project was wracked by disagreements among participants, and the report was never completed or published. The Tsardanis and Huliaras (1999) report was quickly shelved by the EU on the basis of weak methodology and unsupported findings. To replace it, the EU Refugee Task Force later commissioned a new and larger examination of the issues by the Exeter Refugee Study Team led by Mick Dumper.

The study (Exeter Refugee Study Team 2001) did not propose influx controls. Similarly, work by the World Bank rejected the notion that there was any sort of fixed "absorptive capacity" to the WBG, instead arguing for a far more dynamic linkage between local economic conditions and successful population movements (World Bank 2000a). It also argued, "the developmental challenges of absorption are most easily dealt with if population movements are voluntary and not bureaucratized" (Krafft and Elwan 2003: 1. See also

World Bank 2000a; World Bank 2000b: 28; Brynen 2001a; Brynen 2002; UK FCO 2002; Brynen 2003: 1–5).

In any case, the issue was probably moot: politically, it is hard to imagine a future Palestinian state barring the repatriation of some Palestinians on the basis of economic need, a point that clearly emerged in second track discussions on the refugee issue between Israelis and Palestinians (see, for example, Brynen *et al.* 2003: 15).

By the time of final status negotiations, the notion of border controls was fading – but had not entirely vanished. According to the European Union's internal account of the January 2001 Taba negotiations, "The Palestinian side was confident that Palestinian sovereignty over borders and international crossing points would be recognized in the agreement. The two sides had, however, not yet resolved this issue including the question of monitoring and verification at Palestine's international borders (Israeli or international presence)" (Eldar 2002).

With *intifada* and the intensification of Palestinian–Israeli violence, many Israelis have now revisited this issue and favor border controls. In this regard, the views of Israeli commentator Ehud Ya'ari are fairly typical: "it is unimaginable that any Israeli government . . . would agree to grant the Palestinians a state that has exclusive control over its borders with Jordan and Egypt. It was always stupid to assume that Israel might take such a risk. It would be even more stupid to think that Israel could take such a risk from here on" (Ya'ari 2002).

Under the terms of the May 2003 Quartet "Performance-Based Roadmap to a Permanent Two-State Solution to the Israeli–Palestinian Conflict," the question of a border regime during the interim period of Palestinian quasi-statehood ("independent Palestinian state with provisional borders and attributes of sovereignty") is unclear, although it seems likely that Israel would probably retain full security control. Prime Minister Sharon's disengagement plan, as first outlined to the US, reportedly stated that "Israel will supervise and secure the outer envelope of the geographical land mass, will exclusively control the airspace of the Gaza Strip, and will continue to carry out military operations in the territorial waters of the Gaza Strip." While the plan held out the possibility of an eventual withdrawal from the Philadelphi corridor and the construction of Palestinian air and seaports, this was postponed to some future and unspecified time. The plan further noted that in Gaza, "The existing arrangements at the [border] crossing will remain in place" while in the West Bank "The international crossings between Judea and Samaria and Jordan, the existing arrangements in place at the crossings will continue to be in place" (Sharon 2004). This would appear to be consistent with Sharon's long-term vision of permanent Israeli control over the Jordan Valley as an essential strategic interest.[2]

Were a Palestinian state to be encased in Israeli-controlled borders, it would have major implications for its ability to establish a repatriation strategy – especially if Israel acted, as it did in the case of 1967 displaced persons during the Oslo period, to restrict or prevent the return of refugees.[3] A restricted border would also tend to create a situation where population flows were decoupled from refugee choice and economic opportunities, further complicating the dynamics of refugees. For security and other reasons, Israel might restrict population movements to certain demographic categories (for example, those over a certain age), possibly altering dependency ratios in the territories. Given the extent to which the "demographic threat" of an Arab majority in historic Palestine now figures prominently in Israeli political discourse, repatriation might be prevented altogether.

It is, of course, doubtful that any Palestinian leader would ever agree to a truncated quasi-statehood hemmed in by Israeli-controlled borders. Were a future Palestine to gain control of its international borders, and permit the unrestricted repatriation of refugees, would this precipitate an uncontrolled flood that would overtax and destabilize the nascent state?

There is little reason to believe that this would occur. The vast majority of refugees outside the WBG are, by most measures, socially and economically integrated: they have homes and jobs, and enjoy a standard of living equal to that of the non-Palestinian host population. At present, due to the *intifada*, per capita incomes in the WBG are lower than those in Jordan and Syria, while unemployment and poverty rates are higher. Even were peace to break out, catching up might take years. A majority of Palestinians in Jordan have close relatives living in the WBG, and roughly 1 million once resided there (most as refugees from Israel in 1948). Most refugees in Syria and Lebanon do not have the same linkages, however, and neither state is contiguous to the Palestinian territories. Most Palestinian refugees in Jordan are full Jordanian citizens, while those in Syria enjoy nearly equivalent rights to Syrian citizens.

One non-public World Bank overview of the refugee issue written prior to the Camp David talks suggested that, in the case of Jordan, proximity and preexisting linkages may result in opportunity-led movement to the West Bank, predominately by younger males seeking employment, as well as some movement linked to family reunification and marriage. According to UNRWA, some 1,740,170 refugees were registered in Jordan at the end of 2003 (UNRWA 2003a).[4] If the borders between the Palestinian state were relatively open, the flow of this population would be largely self-governing, determined by relative economic conditions in the two areas (World Bank 2000b).[5] Jordanian government policy changes could affect this, however. On the one hand, Amman could push its non-citizen refugees (in particular, the roughly 100,000 or so Gazans) to repatriate. On the other hand, any hint that Palestinian citizens of Jordan might lose their citizenship, travel documents, or other rights if they took up residency in the WBG would likely slow the pace of repatriation. At the time of the Camp David and Taba negotiations, Jordanian officials had only begun to think about these issues, and had yet to formulate any clear policy positions.[6]

It is in Lebanon – where UNRWA reports some 394,532 refugees registered in December 2003 (UNRWA 2003a), but where the number actually resident is probably half that number – that the strongest "push" factors are likely to be felt in the aftermath of any peace agreement, as a Lebanese government uses harassment and discriminatory measures moves to divest itself of an unwanted Palestinian refugee population. Unfortunately, refugees in Lebanon also have the least capital and educational resources, and might therefore be least well equipped to deal with the challenges of (involuntary) repatriation. According to FAFO studies, some 60 percent of young adults in refugee camps in Lebanon did not finish their basic education, half of all camp households have no family member who has done so, and only 9 percent (compared with 30 percent in Jordan) have a household member who has completed secondary education (Hanssen-Bauer and Jacobsen 2004, 12–13). While the absence of any border between Lebanon and the WBG would preclude efforts by the Lebanese to dump their refugees *en masse* into the new Palestinian state, an intensification of existing state restriction on employment, property ownership, and similar measures might well precipitate a substantial flow of returnees.[7]

By contrast, Syria has treated its refugees (413,827 at year-end 2003, according to UNRWA) relatively well, and any future flow would likely be relatively slow and voluntary, shaped in large part by (limited) family linkages and economic opportunities.

Repatriation management and relocation assistance

In the course of final status negotiations, as well as in analytical work on the issue, two clear models of repatriation management have emerged. The first model – evident in the non-papers under discussion at the January 2001 Taba negotiations – envisages the establishment of an institutional structure to receive and determine application for return, repatriation, and resettlement. This model is also embodied in the informal/unofficial "Geneva Accords" of December 2003. The second model, most clearly associated with the work of the World Bank in 1999–2003, emphasizes that repatriation mechanisms should be facilitative and minimalist rather than large, complex, and organizational.

Specifically, the Israeli Taba "non-paper" of 23 January 2001 outlined five options for refugees: return to Israel (according to a certain limit), repatriation to areas of Israel swapped to a Palestinian state, repatriation to the Palestinian state, settlement in existing host countries, and resettlement in third countries. In the joint draft "refugee mechanism" paper of 25 January 2001, a "return, repatriation, and relocation committee" was proposed, to (among other functions) determine repatriation procedures, ensure that all repatriation is voluntary, "process applications," "repatriate refugees," and provide other assistance (Israel 2001; Israel and PA/PLO 2001). Although it is not clear, the assumption seems to be that such a committee will play a significant organizational role in refugee repatriation.

This approach is further developed in the Geneva Accord (2003). This calls for the establishment of a "permanent place of residence" ("PPR") committee, which will receive applications from refugees regarding which of the five residential options they wish to utilize. The committee is then to determine permanent place of residence of the refugee, taking into account individual preferences and maintenance of family unity. Refugees must apply for an option within two years or lose their refugee status. All return, repatriation, or (re)settlement is to be achieved within five years.

The possible complications of such a PPR committee have been discussed at greater length elsewhere (Brynen 2004). With regard to repatriation in particular, it is not clear why such a committee need accept application for repatriation or why any outside party need be involved. On the assumption that the new Palestinian state legislates some sort of Palestinian "Law of Return," the process of repatriation ought to be as simple as applying for Palestinian travel documents and residency at the nearest Palestinian consulate. There is also little need for organized repatriation, on the model of UNHCR-managed refugee returns in Afghanistan or sub-Saharan Africa. In the Palestinian cases, the distances are short (most refugees live less than 100 km from the West Bank/Gaza) and refugees have more assets and hence are better able to organize their own returns. This would be particularly true if refugees were to receive significant amounts of funds as part of any refugee compensation program. Indeed, the dynamics of any future refugee absorption into a Palestinian state will be heavily influenced by the timing and amount of compensation that refugees might receive as part of a permanent status agreement.

At times, a few Palestinian planners have suggested an even more directive process, in which repatriated refugees would be directed toward residency in particular areas or purpose-built new towns, in a modern echo of Israeli immigrant absorption in "development towns" in the 1950s and mid-1960s. These assigned residential areas would be located to fit the strategic and demographic needs of the new state.[8] Israel's heavily statist and directive immigrant absorption policies of the 1950s and 1960s suffered from a number of shortcomings. By contrast, the more choice-based Israeli absorption programs of the 1980s and 1990s were much more effective (Alterman 2003). Fortunately, the notion of directing returnees to specific residency locations was essentially abandoned as unworkable and counterproductive in later PA planning on refugee absorption.

As previously noted, analytical work undertaken by the World Bank[9] has tended to oppose influx controls and favor policies that might simplify repatriation choices by leaving them largely in the hands of refugee families. The Bank has been particularly wary of creating perverse incentives that could encourage population movements disconnected from local economic realities, or create rent-seeking migration by those seeking benefits. Consequently, while some form of relocation assistance is appropriate, this should be designed to reduce the transaction costs of moving while not creating a net positive incentive to do so. As argued elsewhere (Brynen 2003: 11), such a program might take the form of cash, per capita payments; vouchers, usable towards transportation costs for persons or possessions; organized and/or subsidized transportation; or some combination of these. The relocation assistance basket would also include support for information, outreach, and information resource programs. Drop-in centers for returnees could be established in major urban areas, to provide a one-stop location for gathering information on housing, retraining, programs, and other relevant public and NGO services available to returnees. Similar information centers could also be established in the diaspora, to inform potential returnees and to facilitate their efforts to secure travel and other needed documentation. In cases where relocation might be involuntary, such as refugees "pushed" from Lebanon, there would also be an emergency need to assist individuals and families in securing documentation and making other necessary arrangements.

To the extent that there was discussion of these issues among donors (notably, and perhaps solely, within the Canadian-led "No-Name" group of refugee donors) the World Bank's views on these issues tended to be shared by much of the international community. One paper prepared for MOPIC after the December 2000 No-Name Group meeting summarized donor views in the following terms:

> In the design of refugee development, repatriation, and absorption programs, donors are particularly wary about establishing perverse incentives which may distort population flows. The provision of substantial benefits of certain types to returnees, for example, could encourage refugees to repatriate to a Palestinian state to obtain those benefits – despite the absence of adequate employment and other economic opportunities. If not carefully structured, the result could also be rent-seeking behavior, in which individuals undertake short-term, temporary migration with the sole purposes of obtaining benefits.
>
> Donors are also eager that any developmental initiatives enhance refugee knowledge and choice, empowering individuals to make decisions about migration (and the timing of any such migration) that serve their individual and family interests. For this reason, they generally do not believe that quota planning or any sort of international committee is required to process repatriation applicants from Palestinians wishing to move to the West Bank and Gaza. On the contrary, excessively bureaucratic procedures will invite delays and tend to create a mismatch between population flows and local economic conditions. On the other hand, if movement is simple, unbureaucratized, and informed by individual initiative, it is likely to be self-regulating: as economic opportunity in Palestine increases, repatriation will increase; if substantial population movements begin to raise prices and unemployment in the West Bank and Gaza, the flow of returnees will slow to offset this.
>
> (Brynen 2001b)

Absorption policy for refugees

Analytical work on housing, employment, social service, and other aspects of absorption policy has, in many ways, mirrored the differences over repatriation management. Some (including both some Israeli analysts and some early Palestinian planners) have favored a relatively statist approach, managed by the Palestinians. This would, as noted earlier, involve purpose built public housing for returning refugees. The development of new towns would also be undertaken. Evacuated settlement housing would be used for refugee housing. Refugee camps would be comprehensively rehabilitated, with the inhabitants rehoused in new quarters. Large-scale employment-generation programs would be undertaken with donor support, to create employment opportunities for returnees.

Some analysts – including some associated with the Harvard project (Klinov 1995, Borjas and Rodrik 1997) and the Economic Cooperation Foundation's work on refugees – suggested that refugee compensation ought to be controlled or directed in a certain way, such as through a voucher system to assure that refugees spent their funds on the "right" things. Some echoes of the statist approach were also reflected in policy planning by the US State Department. One internal policy paper on the refugee issue (US 2000), developed by the State Department prior to the Camp David negotiations, envisaged the possible provision of vouchers for housing and education/training as part of a refugee compensation scheme. Some Israeli analysts are also strongly attached to the idea that compensation payments to refugees ought to be structured and delimited in some way, rather than assuming the form of cash payments. Cash payments, they fear, would not be spent on productive investments, but rather "wasted" by refugees on immediate consumption or housing expenditures.[10]

Generally, the World Bank rejected such a statist approach, on grounds of both cost and practicality. Indeed, in order to deflate American, Israeli, and Palestinian enthusiasm for massive donor-financed employment generation for returnees, a working paper was produced casting doubt on the efficacy and utility of such an approach. This argued that "while it might be possible to assist returnees to stabilize or slightly increase household income (through temporary employment in infrastructure projects or through micro loans for income-generating activities), or to gain employment in very small businesses, it is unlikely that these types of programs will create a large number of sustainable jobs" (World Bank 2000c). In another paper, the Bank also came out in favor of cash payments for compensation, arguing that these "are likely to be well-used by recipients . . . and do not necessarily in themselves carry the danger of unproductive use and lack of absorptive capacity" (World Bank 2000a: 2). In the December 2000 "No-Name Group" meeting in Washington, DC, an informal donor discussion of possible costs associated with large-scale public housing programs soon suggested that these costs would be well beyond the likely levels of aid that would be made available.[11]

It is difficult to tell to what degree, within the Palestinian Authority, there was a real debate between different approaches to refugee repatriation, especially as concerned housing and integration policies. As with issues of repatriation management, those most involved in negotiations (notably the Negotiations Support Unit of the PLO) tended to focus on the political and legal aspects of the refugee issue, rather than its developmental challenges. The PLO Department of Refugee Affairs had (and has) limited analytical capacity on the issue. The Ministry of Planning and International Cooperation did have a larger role, both because of its planning mandate and because of the appointment of MOPIC minister Nabil Sha'th as head of the refugee negotiations for most of 2000–1. However, the often severe discontinuities and tensions between MOPC/Gaza and MOPIC/Ramallah inhibited the development of a consensus. While MOPIC/Gaza (and, at times and in some ways, Sha'th) seemed to favor a more statist and directive approach, the planning staff of MOPIC/Ramallah seemed to see the state's role as more of a facilitative one, intended to create appropriate enabling conditions for refugee repatriation. The focus tended to be on physical land use policy, however, and less on the social aspects of (re)integrating returnees.

Most of the main Palestinian line ministries did little or no planning for refugee repatriation, and were out of the loop. Political sensitivity was much of the reason for this: A focus on repatriation seemed to imply a de-emphasis on the Palestinian "right of return" to 1948 areas, something that had long been an ideological lynchpin of the Palestinian nationalist movement. Also, some ministries that might be expected to play a key role in policy reflection – notably the Ministry of Housing – lacked the capacity to do so, and were never engaged.

In the summer of 2001, an external consultant prepared a paper for senior MOPIC staff that outlined the advantages and disadvantages of different approaches to refugee absorption (Brynen 2001a).[12] It is not clear that this had any effect, however. Instead, the inclinations of MOPIC's Ramallah-based planning staff appear to have been far more important. In contrast to some senior planners then in Gaza, they tended to have a more realistic sense of what might be possible in terms of housing and absorption policy. Both independently, and in partnership with the second phase of the World Bank's refugee studies, this group assumed the leading role in planning a possible PA response to the challenges of refugee absorption (for an overview of MOPIC absorption planning, see Nijem 2003).

The World Bank also continued its work up until early 2003, producing more detailed studies of costs and approaches to refugee-related urban redevelopment in the West Bank and Gaza, housing finance options, and lessons to be learned from Israel's own experience in immigrant absorption (for a synthesis and summary, see Krafft and Elwan 2003). Some work has also been produced by other analysts on the repatriation issues, notably the papers produced in 1995–7 for a Harvard University project on the refugees, the work of the Exeter Refugee Study Team (2001), and most recently that by Arnon and Kanafani (2004).[13]

One of the key issues to emerge from both PA and World Bank work is the challenge of maintaining equity in program design. Absorption policies that are seen to unfairly favor one group over another (say refugees over non-refugees, returnees over those staying in the host country, camp dwellers versus non-camp dwellers, or some camps compared with others) are unlikely to be successful, and are likely to generate considerable political backlash. For this reason, much of both the World Bank's and MOPIC's work stressed the need to embed refugee absorption policies within the broader framework of Palestinian development policies and dealing with demographic change – a pressing challenge for Palestine in any case, given the very high rate of natural population increase. Consequently, the task is not so much to develop refugee housing policies, land use strategies, or social welfare initiatives for refugees alone, but overall programs in these areas that address the needs of all poor and vulnerable populations in Palestine.

Refugee camps

In theory, the future of Palestinian refugee camps after a peace agreement is not so much a "repatriation issue" as a "non-repatriation issue" – that is, what happens to camp-dwellers who either remain in host countries or who were already resident in the WBG? Nevertheless, it is such an essential part of any refugee absorption policy in a future Palestinian state is that it deserves some attention herein.

At the time of final status negotiations, a number of Palestinian, Israeli, and Jordanian officials and analysts presumed that resolution of the refugee issue would result in the elimination of the camps. For most Palestinians, providing camp residents with improved housing is a matter of social justice. For Israelis, the refugee camps remain a reminder of the refugee problem, and their eventual disappearance thus has symbolic and political significance. Some Jordanian officials expressed a preference for eliminating the camps and moving residents to new residential areas, most likely as a way of reducing the political challenge to the Hashemite monarchy emanating from concentrations of poor Palestinian refugees.[14]

There are several practical problems with "decamping" refugees en masse. To start with, the task would be enormous, and the costs well beyond the likely resources that would be available.[15] Most camps have developed as vibrant (if generally poor) communities, characterized by a range of amenities, social and family linkages, and rich local history. This social fabric is not simply one that should be torn up by a bulldozer. The provision of some services and utilities (education, health care, water, sewage, electricity) may be better in the camps than in other locales, such as rural villages. In many areas, camps are located near (or in) major urban centers, with good access to employment and services. With the exception of Lebanon (where insecurity has pushed many refugees to camp residence) and to some extent Gaza (where there is limited land for residential use), there is no barrier to people leaving camps. To the extent that they stay, they either lack the financial resources to move or have other reasons for maintaining their current residence. Indeed, some populations with deep local social or economic roots might resist being rehoused in new areas. The camps, in effect, act as a supply of low cost accommodation for the poor. Consequently they represent a set of housing stock that would likely exist in any case in some form or another, whether as camps or low-income districts. This is not to say, of course, that most camps are optimal or desirable places to live. It is to say that the task of dealing with the camps in the aftermath of the agreement is a difficult one (for an excellent examination of the issues, see Razzazz 1997).

The most likely approach is one of camp upgrading, involving improvement of camp conditions and varying degrees of dedensification (that is, relocation of some refugees to new housing areas so as to free up space for improved access, public services, and/or enlarged housing plots). Certainly this appears to be the direction of Palestinian planning assumptions about the future of the camps. Even this can be expensive, however; the World Bank estimated the cost at between $3,077 and $4,830 per person (depending on the density of housing and the degree of upgrading) when construction, land, and public and social infrastructure costs are included.

Such costs would be reduced, of course, if camp populations provided some of the costs of redevelopment themselves, whether through financial or labor ("sweat equity") contributions. Substantial compensation payments to refugees would facilitate this. However, there remains another challenge: that of property ownership. Camp redevelopment would function best if it also involved the privatization of housing, with title passing to refugee families. This, however, is an enormously complicated process. In a few cases (notably in Jordan and Syria), refugee camps are located on privately owned land, which landowners might wish to reclaim. Furthermore, while refugees do not currently "own" their homes, most believe and behave as if they do so, especially if they have made substantial improvements in them over the years. Refugee camp homes are thus bought and sold, despite the absence of legal title. Simply transferring title to refugees could involve substantial inequities: Property near the beach in Gaza at Shati' camp or on the outskirts of Jerusalem at Qalandiya camp would very likely be worth far more than camp homes in Jenin or near Jericho. Finally, improving refugee camp housing and/or relocating some refugees to new housing could generate significant dissatisfaction among non-camp refugees or low-income non-refugees who were not offered housing improvement opportunities of their own.

Future, post-peace changes to refugee camps would also require changes in their administrative status, whether they were incorporated into existing local government units or assigned a new municipal status of their own. This would presumably be accompanied by a wind-down of UNRWA and the assumption of its camp social services by the PA (or host governments) – an issue to be explored in the next section.

All of this again underscores the need to address questions of refugee repatriation and absorption in the broader context of overall development planning for the future Palestinian state. Any redevelopment of refugee camps should be part of a broader housing and land-use strategy, and, as far as possible, programs should be needs- rather than status-based to avoid wasteful and politically costly inequities among client groups.

UNRWA and refugee social services

Refugee repatriation and absorption in a Palestinian state involve two sorts of interrelated social service challenges. The first concerns the future of UNRWA following a peace agreement, including both transitional and supporting roles that UNRWA might assume, as well as the transfer of former UNRWA services to the Palestinian state and host countries. The second issue concerns the broader pressures on Palestinian social service delivery that might be created by substantial refugee repatriation to the WBG.

With regard to UNRWA, the current salience of the Agency in the lives of refugees points to the importance of managing its transitional role in an appropriate manner. In 2002, UNRWA expended some $298 million in all its areas of operation. Approximately 44 percent of all UNRWA expenditures are in the WBG, rising to 56 percent if headquarters costs are included. It also employs some 11,636 staff in the WBG, of whom all but 86 are Palestinian (UNRWA 2003b). Prior to the current *intifada*, UNRWA expenditures were estimated to be equal to around one-seventh of PA recurrent expenditures, and its staff equivalent to around one-sixth of the PA public service. As the World Bank (2000d: 95) noted, "the possible assumption [by Palestine] of UNRWA services in the WBG (representing around 3 percent of Palestinian GDP) would have major fiscal and developmental implications." The report of a February 2000 Palestinian Refugee ResearchNet workshop put the challenge even more starkly:

> in the Palestinian territories, there is absolutely no prospect at all that the Palestinian budget could suddenly absorb the costs of providing former UNRWA health, education, and other social services in the immediate future. Indeed, if one presumes to repatriation of a significant number of Palestinians to the West Bank and Gaza, one estimate presented at the workshop suggested that service costs could rise to 4.4% of GDP before stabilizing. Sustained economic growth, at higher than present levels, would be needed before this level of expenditure would become fiscally sustainable.
>
> (PRRN 2000)

Clearly, in the event of post-agreement termination of UNRWA, there would be the need for some sort of external transitional budget support to Palestine, and indeed possibly to host countries too. Without such support, the benefit to refugees of compensation payments might well be more than offset by the cost to them of lost UNRWA services (Brynen 2000).

Among Palestinian and Israeli officials involved in negotiation on the refugee issue, the question of UNRWA's future was dealt with as a predominately political one: Israel wished to see the agency terminated as soon as possible (so as to hasten the symbolic end of the refugee issue), while the Palestinians favored a long wind-down process. At the Taba negotiations, the initial Palestinian position paper (PA/PLO 2001) proposed that "UNRWA should be maintained until [the refugee article of an agreement] is fully implemented and UNRWA's services are no longer needed. The scope of UNRWA's services should change appropriately as the implementation of this Article proceeds." In response, the Israelis proposed that "The phased termination of UNRWA shall be in accordance with a timetable to be agreed upon between the parties, and shall not exceed five years. The scope of UNRWA's services should change appropriately as the implementation of this agreement proceeds (whereby the first phase shall include the transfer of the service and administrative functions of UNRWA to host governments and modalities for the transfer of relevant functions to the International Commission, as well as the discontinuation of the status of Palestinian refugee camp[s])" (Israel 2001).

More broadly, the EU-commissioned study on the refugee repatriation and absorption undertaken by Mick Dumper and colleagues at the University of Exeter identified an "UNRWA plus" and an "UNRWA minus" approach (Exeter Refugee Study Team 2001: 84–5). The former approach sees UNRWA assuming the role of lead agency in informing refugees, organizing the logistics of reform, and perhaps even undertaking some developmental tasks. The latter approach sees a much more modest role for the agency. This difference was also evident at the Palestinian Refugee ResearchNet workshop on "the future of UNRWA," which outlined two similar perspectives (PRRN 2000). On the plus side:

> UNRWA has shown itself able to flexibly adapt its mandate to changing circumstances; has a substantial capacity for project implementation; has a large skilled staff with vast experience with the refugee issue, who could be quickly reassigned to address new tasks; has a supply of vehicles, offices, and other important institutional infrastructures; and is structured in such a way as to make it profoundly sensitive to refugee concerns. The organizational structure of UNRWA also permits decisive action to be taken from the top.

Conversely, others were more doubtful about UNRWA developing a new, post-agreement repatriation role:

> Other participants were more doubtful about UNRWA's ability to take on tasks outside its present mandate and areas of expertise (health, education, small-scale infrastructure). Some argued that past experience suggested that the Agency's ability to flexibly interpret its mandate had been overstated, and that most changes had been incremental. Some suggested that organizational/managerial weaknesses remained within

the Agency. It was also noted that UNRWA's freedom of action was potentially limited by its intimate relationship with a highly politicized refugee constituency as well as its status as a UN agency reporting to the General Assembly. Donors might be wary about seeing UNRWA – an agency slated to eventually end with the resolution of the refugee issue – effectively placed in managerial control of its own demise in this way. Moreover, excessive reliance on UNRWA might come at the cost of building institutional capacity within host governments.

(PRRN 2000)

Instead, such tasks might be taken on by the new Palestinian state, or by a broad array of host countries, specialized agencies, and NGOs.

(Exeter Refugee Study Team 2001: 84–5)

The PRRN workshop did not reach a consensus on the issue. The Exeter study, however, supported the "UNRWA plus" position, proposing that the EU support efforts to "transform UNRWA into a return programme agency" (ibid.: 96).

In addition to the question of UNRWA and UNRWA service provision, there is the broader question of social service provision to refugees (Babille *et al.* 2003). In this regard, it is important to note that not all refugees live in areas serviced by UNRWA, and not all UNRWA-registered refugees rely on UNRWA services. In Jordan in particular, and in Syria to a lesser degree, host countries also assume a significant share of social service costs – as do, of course, refugees themselves. According to FAFO data, around 40 percent of refugees in Jordan have some sort of non-UNRWA health insurance coverage, and only 25 percent of camp refugees (and 2 percent of non-camp refugees) used UNRWA health services when last ill (Jacobsen, Endresen, and Hasselknippe 2003: 14). In Jordan and Syria, all refugees attend government (not UNRWA) secondary schools.

Very preliminary work by the World Bank (2000e) attempted to gauge the capital and recurrent social services costs associated with the repatriation of 100,000 refugees to the WBG over five years. Capital costs were estimated at between $35.2 million and $61.5 million. Recurrent costs were estimated at between $3.4 billion and $5.4 billion over ten years.[16] In the long term, of course, returnees would become net contributors to the Palestinian economy, as workers, investors, and taxpayers. Indeed, in Jordan in particular, refugees presumably already finance their non-UNRWA social service usage through taxation and their own private payments to service providers. Consequently, these estimates do not really identify the additional fiscal burden on the state, which would be less than the aggregate total presented above, especially in the long term. In the long term, the economic buoyancy of the WBG economy will be the primary determinant of Palestine's capacity to pay for social services. However, the figures do underscore the point, already evident in the narrower context of UNRWA service transfer, that some sort of transitional budgetary support would be required to enable Palestine to address the immediate social service needs of returnees.

This needs to be seen, moreover, in the context of an already high population growth rate in the WBG: approximately 4 percent per annum, one of the highest in the world. This (and the very high dependency ratio that it generates) places an increasing burden on existing health, education, and social welfare services (especially in the context of economic depression and the *intifada*). Even without refugee repatriation, it has been estimated that the Palestinian Authority needs to construct fifty new schools per annum just to keep pace with growing enrollments (World Bank 2000d: 90–1). Clearly, addressing future refugee repatriation needs to be undertaken in the broader context of planning for ongoing Palestinian demographic change.

The role of donors

Donors clearly have a key role to play in any future repatriation of refugees to a Palestinian state, both in financing the process and in helping to design and implement the various efforts that will be required. Several ideas have been proposed as to how this might be structured and organized.

The US State Department (2000), in a confidential internal briefing paper prepared prior to the Camp David negotiations, suggested "an international facility or commission, co-chaired by the World Bank or UN under the direction of a political steering committee." This would be modeled on the existing Ad Hoc Liaison Committee structure for WBG assistance, and would assist in refugee relocation and meet some of the long-term developmental needs of refugees, displaced persons, and host countries. A regional refugee fund, administered by the World Bank, might be created to which donors could contribute and from which specific subfunds would address indemnification, relocation, and development needs. The assistance package would be "front-end loaded" to assure that the bulk of funds flowed quickly, in the first two years of an agreement. An international conference would attempt to raise $20 billion for the regional refugee fund. The US paper also proposed that compensation claims and payments for specific property losses (as opposed to indemnification payments associated with refugee status) be handled by a separate international claims tribunal, consisting of international jurists, facilitated by UNRWA, and with compensation funded by Israel. Several of these ideas subsequently surfaced, in modified form, at the Camp David negotiations – although, in general, little real progress was made at Camp David beyond declaratory statements by the parties.

The World Bank (2000f) also prepared an unpublished paper on donor coordination mechanisms prior to Camp David. This emphasized several key challenges for donors: the need to front-end load much of the assistance, and disburse it quickly; the need to think about long-term developmental challenges; the need to avoid "pledge inflation;"[17] the desirability of flexibility (through, for example, a central fund/facility, and cash payments);

and the need for integrated planning (including joint and parallel financing of multilateral refugee development initiatives). The World Bank also examined a variety of possible refugee donor coordination mechanisms, including a modification of the current (AHLC) structure for WBG aid, the Refugee Working Group of the multilateral negotiations, the United Nations (whether UNRWA, UNHCR, UNDP, UNSCO, or the UN Conciliation Commission for Palestine), and the World Bank. It proposed – much as the US had – the separation of donor coordination and compensation functions, with the former managed by an AHLC-linked refugee secretariat, and the latter overseen by an independent commission, perhaps operating under the auspices of the UN. This view was discussed at the December 2000 donor "No-Name Group" meeting, where it seemed to receive fairly broad, if informal, agreement.

The issue of an international mechanism was explored in considerable detail at the Taba final status negotiation in January 2001, where it was the subject of a joint Israeli–Palestinian working draft. This proposed that an overall international commission for Palestinian refugees be established, consisting of Israel, Palestine, Arab host countries, the UN/UNRWA, and major donors.[18] The commission's board of directors would oversee three technical committees, with responsibility for status determination; return, repatriation, and relocation; and compensation and restitution. An international fund, co-managed by the World Bank and the UN, would finance the activities of the commission, including compensation payments, payments to host countries, and payments to Palestine. It was also suggested that the World Bank might be asked to develop multilateral funding instruments to facilitate the flow of resources. Israel would make a lump-sum contribution to this international fund, against which the value of Israeli fixed assets left behind in the WBG (notably the settlements and associated infrastructure) would be deducted (Israel and PA/PLO 2001).

There was some criticism of the Taba model within the donor community. Some felt that it was overbureaucratic, and presumed a more rational and coordinated donor response than was likely to occur. It seemed doubtful, for example, that donors would be willing to channel most of their funding in cash through an international fund, which could then pay it out again to the Palestinian state and host countries. Instead, donors were likely to want to develop their own bilateral assistance programs. Perhaps most important, the Taba draft seemed to suggest a single integrated mechanism, whereas both the earlier World Bank and State Department papers had tended to favor separating off the compensation mechanism so as to maximize its independence, neutrality, and semi-judicial status.

The unofficial Geneva Accord (2003) closely follows the Taba model. Under these, an international commission would be established, which "shall have full and exclusive responsibility for implementing all aspects of this agreement pertaining to refugees" (article 7.11.i.a). The proposed membership of the commission would be Israel, Palestine, the UN, UNRWA, the US,

Arab host countries, the EU, Switzerland, Canada, Norway, Japan, the World Bank, Russia, and others. No system of voting or decision-making is specified (an issue that was also unresolved in the Taba negotiations).[19] The international commission would form a series of technical committees to deal with determination of refugee; remuneration of host countries; rehabilitation and development of refugee communities; administration of a collective "refugeehood fund" (to be detailed in an as yet unwritten annex). As noted earlier, the Accord also calls for a "permanent place of residence" committee to deal with the refugee's application for return, repatriation, residency in current host countries, and resettlement elsewhere.

Conclusion

It is possible to draw several sorts of conclusions from the discussion presented above. The first concerns what lessons can be drawn from past analytical work on Palestinian refugee repatriation. Elsewhere, this author has highlighted a dozen such lessons (Brynen 2003):

1 Repatriation flows depend on many things, but repatriation decisions should be voluntary.
2 Repatriation and development policies should empower refugee choice, and avoid bureaucratic distortions and perverse incentives.
3 There is no such thing as "absorptive capacity."
4 Refugee absorption ought to be part of a broader strategy of planning for demographic change.
5 The Palestinian state ought not to construct housing for returnees.
6 "Decamping" of refugee camps is not feasible.
7 Evacuated settlements are ill-suited for refugee absorption.
8 Returnees should be assisted in voluntarily relocation in a way that reduces the transaction costs of relocation.
9 Refugee housing policies should form part of a broader national strategy to stimulate housing supply.
10 Housing finance initiatives are a critical element of any refugee absorption strategy.
11 Costs are high, and donor resources are limited.
12 Refugee compensation is a key part of the absorption equation.

A second set of conclusions could be drawn as to where there is a need for additional work.[20] Housing policy is clearly one area, particularly given weak PA capacities in this area. So too is the future utilization of settlement assets, although some analysis in this area is currently being completed by the Foundation for Middle East Peace, as well as by the PA and the World Bank in the context of a possible Gaza withdrawal. A third area is refugee compensation – both the modalities of compensation and its interrelationship to the changes of repatriation and development. A variety of projects are ongoing with regard to the former aspect (most notably a major study now under way by the International Organization for Migration), but very little has been done with regard to the latter. The PA/PLO Refugee Coordination Group (consisting of the Ministry of Planning, PLO Negotiations Support Unit, and PLO Department of Refugee Affairs) has also drawn up a list of research projects that it would like to undertake, so as to increase Palestinian knowledge and analytical capacity on the refugee issues.

A third set of conclusions – particularly relevant for this volume – is how to apply lessons from "best practice" in other cases of refugee repatriation to the Palestinian case. The present paper, implicitly at least, suggests that in doing so it is important to recognize that there are unusual specificities to the Palestinian case, and that some other practices may not be fully applicable.

For a variety of reasons (more settled refugees, physical proximity, higher per capita incomes, higher education levels, and extensive Palestinian experience with economic migration) the physical and logistical aspects of repatriation may be very different than in a Cambodia, Mozambique, East Timor, or Afghanistan. International actors may be called on less to organize than to facilitate – and the very best repatriation process may be one in which the private initiative of refugees plays the most important role.

Substantial compensation payments to refugee families may also substantially alter repatriation dynamics, social conditions, and economic opportunities.

The level of international resources available for development is likely to be both higher than in most post-conflict settings – and, at the same time, much less than what many in the region may expect.

In contrast with other refugee populations, a large proportion of Palestinian refugees have secure residency/citizenship in their present host countries. Roughly 40 percent of all UNRWA-registered refugees, and around two-thirds of all UNRWA refugees outside the WBG, are full citizens of Jordan.

A large proportion of refugees (or, perhaps, internally displaced) are already living in their homeland, and are fully integrated in the WBG. However, their needs will still be an important part of any refugee absorption policy. This group comprises around 38 percent of all UNRWA-registered refugees.

The intense politicization of the refugee issue also needs to be stressed. Such politicization is not an aspect unique to the Palestinian case – on the contrary, it is common to most refugee challenges around the world. However, it too may create important context-specific characteristics to Palestinian refugee repatriation, characteristics that will need to be addressed in repatriation programs and refugee absorption policies.

On the other hand, there are clearly aspects of Palestinian refugee repatriation that can be informed by experience elsewhere, especially perhaps in cases of either the return of long-term refugees (in areas like Afghanistan, Cambodia, or Rwanda) or relatively high-income refugees (such as in the Balkans, in contrast to much of Africa). The former cases point to the challenges of social integration where "insider" and "diaspora" cultures have developed. The latter cases point to the pressing need to have appropriate regulatory environments in place with regard to housing policy, land registration, real estate markets, housing finance, and similar issues. They also point to possible linkages between repatriation and diaspora investment, as well as the extent that, in an era of globalization, repatriation need not be a binary state of "returned" and "not returned". Refugees may choose to return as periodic visitors, to maintain dual residence, or to live in one area and invest in the other. Families may consist of individuals with different citizenship status, and residing both in the homeland and abroad.

Finally, how might the current political climate affect future repatriation efforts? Here, several preliminary observations can be suggested.

The time frame for resolving the refugee issue has been postponed substantially. This author does not expect a meaningful return to final status negotiations within the decade. With this, questions can be raised about the utility of undertaking additional work on repatriation at the current juncture. Indeed, there is the risk that current knowledge may be lost, and current capacities atrophy because of the continued failures of the peace process.

It will be much more difficult than before to secure Israeli agreement to allow the return of even token numbers of refugees to 1948 areas. It will also be even more difficult, post 9/11, to generate significant numbers of slots for third country resettlement. Consequently, the repatriation option will increase in importance.

Israel is likely to press for some form of border controls in future final status talks.

The current deteriorating socio-economic conditions in the WBG – a consequence of violence and occupation – will pose a constraining legacy for future refugee absorption. Even were the Palestinian economy to grow by 5 percent per year, it would now take approximately two decades to return to the real level of per capita income that Palestinians in the West Bank and Gaza enjoyed before the *intifada*.

In the meantime, UNRWA will find itself increasingly overstretched as it seeks to cope with a growing refugee population on a limited budget.

While none of this suggests that it is inappropriate to focus on refugees, it does suggest that equal or greater analytical attention be devoted to how refugees, the PA, and UNRWA will cope with the very difficult challenges of the status quo.

Notes

1 There are several reasons for focusing this chapter on refugee repatriation to a

future Palestinian state in the West Bank and Gaza, and not on refugee return to 1948 areas. The numbers involved in refugee repatriation to the WBG will be much larger than those returning to Israel. This, coupled with resource constraints, will pose serious developmental challenges to a future Palestinian state. Despite the legal rights and moral claims of the refugees, this author believes that very few refugees with be able to exercise any sort of right of return to 1948 areas under any likely future peace agreement. Those who do not share this political assessment are welcome to consult the works of Salman Abu Sitta (1999), who has done extensive work on large-scale refugee return to Israel. On the opposite side, of course, are those Israelis who oppose any sort of refugee return to either Israel *or* the West Bank/Gaza. This, in my view, is an equally unlikely outcome of future peace negotiations.

2 Sharon has previously argued that giving up control of the Jordan Valley would pose "a concrete danger to [Israel's] existence," and has pledged to retain control over fully 58 percent of the West Bank and Gaza (Shavit 2001). Admittedly, in the same interview Sharon also rejected the notion of withdrawing from the Gaza settlements, something he now favors. However, it seems fair to argue that he sees the West Bank as the far more important strategic and nationalist objective.

3 Under the terms of the Oslo Accord (1993), Israel agreed to "decide by agreement on the modalities of admission of persons displaced from the West Bank and Gaza Strip in 1967, together with necessary measures to prevent disruption and disorder." In practice it dragged its feet on the issue, and no 1967 displaced persons ever returned to the WBG under the specific terms of this agreement (although others did return in other ways).

4 Not all the UNRWA refugees registered in Jordan actually reside there, however – and not all the Palestinians in Jordan are registered refugees. FAFO estimates around 1.5 million (1948) refugees in Jordan as of 2003 (Hanssen-Bauer and Jacobsen 2004). The total number of 1948 refugees and 1967 displaced persons in Jordan is probably around 2.1 million.

5 According to a 2003 poll of refugee attitudes conducted by the Palestinian Center for Policy and Survey Research (PSR), 27 percent of Palestinians in Jordan would wish to take up residency in the WBG, and a further 10 percent would wish to live in previously Israeli territory swapped to the Palestinian state. These figures, however, are meaningless in the absence of contextual details (employment rates, relative standards of living, Jordanian government policy, etc.). See PSR 2003.

6 Jordan is not likely to develop clear positions on many aspects of the refugee issue prior to a final status agreement, since it is an enormously sensitive issue in Jordan, and the safest course of action is to avoid clear or controversial positions until forced to do otherwise by events.

7 For this reason, the Taba negotiations agreed on prioritizing refugees in Lebanon for return and repatriations, and preliminary informal international discussions on limited third country resettlement also tended to focus on the problem of refugees in Lebanon.

8 Conversations with officials from the PA Ministry of Planning and International Cooperation, Gaza, 2001.

9 There is not a formal "World Bank" position on many of these issues – instead, the positions outlined in this chapter reflect the author's sense of consensus positions that developed among Bank staff and consultants working on the refugee issue in 2000–3.

10 This view has been expressed to me by several Israeli analysts. Quite apart from the debate over the flexibility of cash compensation payments versus the desire

to influence how refugees spend money most productively, there is an enormous moral argument against limiting refugee choice: By what right is it that refugees, having spent over a half century as refugees, can be told that they must spend compensation monies in the ways that some economists think are best for long-term growth, rather than on improving the immediate living conditions of themselves and their families?

11 Based on very preliminary data from the World Bank, one participant estimated the costs of full refugee camp redevelopment and limited public housing at $17 billion.

12 This paper noted several problems associated with a statist approach: State housing/rehousing would be too expensive; Palestine had no successful experience with public housing programs; such programs could be vulnerable to corruption and patronage; a statist approach might limit refugee choice and distort residential choices; redevelopment of camps (including dedensification) might be preferable to complete "decamping"; expanding existing urban areas might be preferable to new towns; and settlement housing might be inappropriate to refugee needs. The paper also highlighted the political costs of unmet expectations, patronage, or corruption that could arise from a heavily statist approach.

13 Arnon and Kanafani (2004) conclude (in keeping with the general thrust of MOPIC and World Bank studies, which they do not address) "the role of the public sector in absorption and reconstruction will need to be significant, especially under the current conditions of the Palestinian economy. However, it is important to emphasize that the government should not take upon itself direct involvement in spheres where the private sector can do better. An indirect approach, via financial arrangements to support private initiatives, would probably be more appropriate. We envisage, in particular, a set of financial arrangements which would answer the basic needs of the impoverished population, including the returnees, for a limited period of time. A comprehensive system of subsidized mortgage credit should be put in place, to be partly financed perhaps from the proceeds of selling the houses in the settlements. A parallel system of easy credit to support small and medium size enterprises and to provide liquidity for entrepreneurs and real estate developers will also be needed. Along with providing and improving the basic infrastructure in the existing camps and in the WBGS in general, the public sector should be ready to step in to ease any bottlenecks in the process, especially with regard to large scale investment for upgrading human capital and vocational education and training." The earlier Harvard study group (of which Arnon was a part) also favored a leading role for the private sector.

14 Discussions with various Palestinian, Israeli, and Jordanian officials, 2000–2.

15 According to UNRWA (2003a), over 1.3 million refugees currently reside in 59 camps in Gaza (484,563), the West Bank (179,541), Jordan (307,785), Syria (120,865), and Lebanon (223,956).

16 Some of these costs would have been previously borne by UNRWA and others by host governments and refugees themselves.

17 This may have been aimed at the American tendency, in the run-up to Camp David, to exaggerate the level of funding that might be available for the refugee issue by including non-cash contributions and general development assistance. US statements to the parties of "$20 billion" for the refugee issue, for example, included the imputed costs of third country resettlement of up to 200,000 refugees.

18 The US, EU, Canada, Norway, and Japan were mentioned in the draft.

19 Some Israeli commentators (Susser 2003) have expressed concern at what they see as the power and membership of the commission.

20 See also the forthcoming report of the IDRC Stocktaking II Conference on Palestinian Refugee Research, Ottawa, 17–20 June 2003.

References

Abu Sitta, Salman (1999) *Palestinian right to return: Sacred, legal, possible* (London: Palestinian Return Centre).

Alterman, Rachelle (2003) "Land and housing strategies for immigrant absorption: Learning from the Israeli experience", IDRC Stocktaking II Conference on Palestinian Refugee Research, Ottawa, 17–20 June.

Arnon, Arie, and Kanafani, Nu'man (2004) *Absorbing returnees in a viable Palestinian state: A forward-looking macroeconomic perspective,* Discussion Paper 04–01, February (Be'er Sheva: Monaster Center for Economic Research, Ben-Gurion University of the Negev). Available online at http://www.jcpa.org/jl/vp491.htm

Arzt, Donna (1997) *Refugees into citizens: Palestinians and the end of the Arab–Israeli conflict* (New York: Council on Foreign Relations Press).

Babille, Marzio, Barney, Ian, Brynen, Rex, Jacobsen, Laurie Blome, Endresen, Lena, and Hasselknippe, Gro (2003) *Finding means: UNRWA's financial situation and the living conditions of Palestinian refugees, Volume 3: Social service delivery to Palestinian refugee – UNRWA and other providers, UNRWA financial and donor environment.* FAFO Report 415 (Oslo: FAFO).

Borjas, George, and Rodrik, Dani (1997) "Harvard project on refugees: Draft summary report". Unpublished. August.

Brynen, Rex (2000) "The future of UNRWA: An agenda for policy research", Workshop on the Future of UNRWA, Minster Lovell (UK), 19–20 February. Available online at http://www.arts.mcgill.ca/MEPP/PRRN/papers/future.html

Brynen, Rex (2001a) "Planning for demographic change: A discussion paper", draft prepared for the Ministry of Planning and International Cooperation, Palestinian Authority. June.

Brynen, Rex (2001b) "General donor perspectives on the developmental aspects of the refugee issue", draft prepared for the Ministry of Planning and International Cooperation, Palestinian Authority. February.

Brynen, Rex (2002) "The Palestinian–Israeli conflict: A non-paper on political scenarios and refugee implications", non-paper prepared for the refugee donor "No-Name Group". February.

Brynen, Rex (2003) "Refugees, repatriation, and development: Some lessons from recent work", IDRC Stocktaking II Conference on Palestinian Refugee Research, Ottawa, 17–20 June.

Brynen, Rex (2004) "The Geneva Accord and the Palestinian refugee issue", 29 February. Available online at http://upload.mcgill.ca/icames/genevarefugees.pdf

Brynen, Rex, Alma, Eileen, Peters, Joel, and Tansley, Jill (2003) "The Ottawa process: An examination of Canada's track two involvement in the Palestinian refugee issue", IDRC Stocktaking II Conference on Palestinian Refugee Research, Ottawa, 17–20 June.

Eldar, Akiva (2002) "The 'Moratinos Document' – The peace that nearly was at Taba", *Ha'aretz,* 14 February.

Exeter Refugee Study Team (2001) "Study of policy and financial instruments for the return and integration of Palestinian displaced persons in the West Bank and Gaza Strip". Unpublished study prepared for the EU Refugee Task Force.

Gazit, Shlomo (1995) *The Palestinian refugee problem* (Tel Aviv: Jaffee Center for Strategic Studies, Tel Aviv University).

Geneva Accord (2003), available online at http://www.heskem.org.il/Heskem_en.asp

Hanssen-Bauer, Jon, and Jacobsen, Laurie Blome (2004) "Living in provisional normality: The living conditions of Palestinian refugees in the host countries of the Middle East" (FAFO), based on an earlier paper presented at the Stocktaking II Conference on Palestinian Refugee Research, Ottawa, June 2003.

Israel (2001) "Non-Paper", Taba, 23 January.

Israel and Palestine Authority/Palestine Liberation Organization (2001) "Refugee Mechanism" draft II, Taba, 25 January.

Jacobsen, Laurie Blome, Endresen, Lena, and Hasselknippe, Gro (2003) "Health Services", in Marzio Babille, Ian Barney, Rex Brynen, Laurie Blome Jacobsen, Lena Endresen, and Gro Hasselknippe, *Finding means: UNRWA's financial situation and the living conditions of Palestinian refugees, Volume 3: Social service delivery to Palestinian refugee – UNRWA and other providers, UNRWA financial and donor environment.* FAFO Report 415 (Oslo: FAFO).

Klinov, Ruth (1995) "Reparations and rehabilitation of refugees." Unpublished draft paper prepared for the refugee project of the Institute for Social and Economic Policy in the Middle East, Harvard University. July.

Krafft, Nick, and Elwan, Ann (2003) "Housing and infrastructure scenarios for refugees and displaced persons", IDRC Stocktaking II Conference on Palestinian Refugee Research, Ottawa, 17–20 June.

McCarthy, Kevin (1996) *The Palestinian refugee issue: One perspective* (Santa Monica: RAND).

Nijem, Khalil (2003) "Planning in support of negotiations: The refugee issue", IDRC Stocktaking II Conference on Palestinian Refugee Research, Ottawa, 17–20 June.

Oslo Accord (1993) *Declaration of principles on interim self-government arrangements.*

Palestinian Authority/Palestine Liberation Organization (PA/PLO) (2001) "Palestinian Statement on Refugees", Taba, 22 January.

Palestinian Center for Policy and Survey Research (PSR) (2003) *Results of PSR refugees' polls in the West Bank/Gaza Strip, Jordan and Lebanon on refugees' preferences and behavior in a Palestinian–Israeli permanent refugee agreement*, January–June. Available online at http://www.pcpsr.org/survey/polls/2003/refugeesjune03.html

Palestinian Refugee ResearchNet (PRRN) (2000) "Workshop report", Workshop on the Future of UNRWA, Minster Lovell (UK), 19–20 February. Available online at http://www.arts.mcgill.ca/MEPP/PRRN/prunrwa3.html

Razzazz, Omar (1997) "From refugees to citizens: Upgrading Palestinian refugee camps". Unpublished paper prepared for the refugee project of the Institute for Social and Economic Policy in the Middle East, Harvard University. July.

Sharon, Ariel (2004) "Prime Minister Sharon's plan for unilateral disengagement." Text in *Jerusalem Post*, 16 April.

Shavit, Ari (2001) "Sharon is Sharon is Sharon", *Ha'aretz*, 13 April.

Susser, Asher (2003) "A shaky foundation", *Ha'aretz*, 15 December.

Tsardanis, Charalambos, and Huliaras, Asteris (1999) "The economic and social absorptive capacity of the West Bank and Gaza Strip" (Athens: Institute of International Economic Relations). Unpublished study prepared for the EU Refugee Task Force.

United Kingdom, Foreign and Commonwealth Office (2002) "UK comments on Canadian non-paper". February.

United Nations Relief and Works Agency (2003a) *UNRWA in figures*, 31 December.

United Nations Relief and Works Agency (2003b) *Report of the Commissioner-General of the United Nations Relief and Works Agency for Palestine Refugees in the Near East, 1 July 2002–30 June 2003.* United Nations General Assembly, 58th Session, Supplement No. 13, 10 October (A/58/13).

United States, Department of State (2000) "Proposed initiative on Palestinian displaced persons and refugees". Unpublished draft, *c.* May.

World Bank (2000a) "Palestinian refugees: An overview". Unpublished draft, *c.* July.

World Bank (2000b) "Assessment of the absorptive capacity of the West Bank and Gaza in integrating returnees and associated costs: A concept note". Unpublished draft, *c.* July.

World Bank (2000c) "Income and employment generation". Unpublished draft, *c.* July.

World Bank (with Japan) (2000d) *Aid effectiveness in the West Bank and Gaza.* Report prepared at the request of the Ad Hoc Liaison Committee, June.

World Bank (2000e) "Social infrastructure: Education, health, social welfare". Unpublished draft, *c.* July.

World Bank (2000f) "Donor coordination and implementation". Unpublished draft, *c.* July.

Ya'ari, Ehud (2002) "Arafat is Arafat", *Jerusalem Report*, 28 January.

Zureik, Elia (1996.) *Palestinian refugees and the peace process* (Washington DC: Institute for Palestine Studies).

5 The Palestinian refugees of 1948

Models of allowed and denied return

Menachem Klein

The resolution of the plight of the Palestinian refugees of 1948 is a highly charged issue. It touches the rawest nerves of both Israelis and Palestinians and is a fundamental element of the formative myth of each of the two nations. From the Palestinian point of view, the refugees are the indigenous inhabitants of their land, driven out by a foreign colonial invader. Israel views the Jews as the original inhabitants of Palestine, legitimately returning to their ancestral land. The Palestinian refugees, in the Israeli view, have deliberately been kept indigent and stateless by Arab leaders intent on destroying the Jewish state.

The need to find a solution for the refugee problem was acknowledged by both sides after the 1948 war. But the positions of each side, determined by its narrative, were diametrically opposed. For Palestinians, the solution was simple: repatriation of the refugees to their former homes. From the Israeli point of view, it was obvious that the refugees should be resettled in other Arab countries.

Serious discussions of how to solve the refugee problem did not begin until the late 1980s, when Israel and the leadership of the Palestine Liberation Organization (PLO) commenced unofficial contacts. To date, the issue has been addressed at length in many non-formal Israeli–Palestinian interactions.

These discussions took place for the most part in "track two" meetings – unauthorized contacts conducted alongside the official Israeli–Palestinian negotiations, or pursued at times when official talks have been stalled. These meetings can occur in a variety of formats. They can be professional academic forums. They can also be preparatory discussions among lower-level officials not delegated by decision makers, prior to official negotiations, or conducted to resolve deadlocks that kept the official track one talks from progressing. (Recent publications on track two diplomacy are Davis and Kaufman (2002) and Agha *et al.* (2003). The topic has also come up in People to People meetings. On People to People, see Israel/Palestine Center for Research and Information (2002).)

Track two talks have been especially important in the context of Israeli–Palestinian negotiations because such a charged subject could not be addressed in an official, publicized forum where leaders and decision makers are afraid of being seen by their publics to compromise on sacred and fundamental principles. This article seeks to trace the importance of track two talks for producing ideas for the resolution of the Palestinian refugee problem. (For summaries of track two meetings on the refugee issue see Brynen (1998) and Cahana (1996).)

Although I was a participant in some of these talks, I can hardly claim to be acquainted with all the material from every channel. Since there were any number of track two channels, I am certainly not aware of all the track two channels that discussed the refugee issue, and some such talks were in any case not documented, making a comprehensive picture impossible. However, from the information now available, I believe it is safe to work on the assumption that the models that emerged in the documented talks are not fundamentally different from the ones in these other unofficial meetings (Klein 2003: 44, 70, 122–5, 142, 201–2, 209–12; Pressman 2003: 5–43; Klein forthcoming). The refugee issue was eventually discussed in the official talks on the final status agreement of 2000–2001, but they reached no resolution.

In this article I will focus on one specific parameter of the 1948 refugee issue: the distinction that track two discussions made between ways in which Palestinian refugees could be permitted to return to live in their former locales and ways in which such return would be forbidden. First I will describe and analyze how this distinction was made in track two meetings. Subsequently, I will examine the impact these distinctions had on the official talks and their participants.

The problem in context

The question of whether the Palestinian refugees of 1948 and their descendants should be allowed to return to their original places of residence is central to all attempts to solve the refugee problem. Reports and proposals from track two talks address a large range of subsidiary issues and problems, but all of them depend on a resolution of the Palestinian claim to a "right of return." The question has its legal aspects, such as whether the refugees' rights are held collectively or individually, and whether and how they are to be compensated for lost property and assets. Another important aspect is historical. Some track two contacts have put much effort into formulating historical narratives that can be accepted by both sides. Such narratives seek to resolve or at least create an "agreement to disagree" regarding questions such as who is responsible for the creation of the refugee problem and whether Israel should apologize for its role. These two contradicting historical narratives relate to different foundation myths, concepts of historical justice or injustice, and to the collective identity of each of the two nations.

The issue has also a political and moral dimension. Correcting the injustice done to the refugees by permitting all of them to return to their original homes might cause further injustice. The influx of so many Palestinians would radically affect Israel's demographic composition and would almost certainly mean that Israel would lose its Jewish majority, its Jewish character, and its definition of itself as a Jewish state. Is this a desirable goal? And what would be the psychological and sociological effects of any given repatriation on Israeli and Palestinian collective identity and self-determination?

Resolution of the refugee problem also requires discussion of technical and practical issues. For example, track two forums sought to draft formulas to determine what financial compensation refugees would receive. They debated what criteria should be used. Would it be better, and more in keeping with legal standards, to seek to estimate the property loss and financial damage suffered by each refugee, or should the standard of compensation be what means individual refugees need to rehabilitate their lives? The latter requires a mechanism for determining the cost of the refugee rehabilitation in whatever location it is to occur – is it to be in their present location or elsewhere? Financial damage was incurred not only by individuals but also by the countries they fled to and resided in, and the issue of compensation for these losses was also broached in track two talks.

Other questions that track two talks discussed were: who is a refugee and what records are there of refugees' status and property? If refugees return to what is now Israel, where exactly will they return to – to their original homes and villages? Do these still exist? If they do, what happens to their current Israeli inhabitants? If the original home or community no longer exists, can and should the refugees be given homes elsewhere in Israel? How would they be absorbed in either case? Are there other countries willing to absorb the refugees of 1948? Who is going to determine which refugees are to return or not? What will be the general rubric under which the repatriation will take place – "right of return," as the Palestinians want, or "family unification," as some Israelis have suggested? How many refugees will in fact return to what is now Israel? Will it suffice to return to Israel only symbolically?

Besides tackling concrete problems like these, the initiators of track two discussions aimed to bypass fundamental differences on the core problem. A pragmatic approach and problem-solving strategies served as tools to promote understanding and bridge over contradictory Israeli and Palestinian positions and historical narratives. (For discussions of some of these issues see Benvenisti and Zamir (1995); Tamari (1996); Ginat and Perkins (2001); Kelman (2001). See also a list of publications at http://www.arts.mcgill. ca/mepp/new_prrn/research/research_papers.html and at http://prrn.org.) Some relevant issues were not, however, addressed in track two talks. Among these were how Palestinian establishment, institutional, and bureaucratic interests played a role in the formation of Palestinian negotiating positions, tactics, and final positions, how to inform the geographically and politically divided refugee communities on the negotiations and the options under discussion, and how to rehabilitate refugees on the individual, family, and community level after repatriation becomes possible under a peace agreement.

Point of origin

Since the mid-1970s, the right of return has been, for the Palestinian national movement, a sacred principle no less than the right to self-determination and a Palestinian state. The individual right of return, formulated immediately after the 1948 war, made way for a claim to a collective right of return. In practical terms, this meant that the PLO focused on the right of return as a principle rather than on the practical, physical issue of whether and how the refugees could return to their erstwhile homes. The mechanics of refugee repatriation were considered by the PLO leadership to be the consequences of overriding theoretical axioms and moral values, and were no substitute for the principle itself. In other words, recognition of the right determines the obligation of full and automatic execution, regardless of any practical obstacles (Klein 1998: 1–19). This understanding of the right of return as a principle equal to the right to self-determination delineated the boundaries of Palestinian public debate which was consequently governed by a national rights rather than a pragmatic discourse. When, in the late 1980s, the PLO achieved international recognition of the Palestinian right to self determination and independence, and when official talks on a final status agreement commenced in 2000, the PLO leadership once more raised the issues of individual rights, financial compensation, and other practical consequences of the abstract, collective right. Some of their Israeli interlocutors proposed to the Palestinians that they exchange the individual right to return to Israel for a collective return embodied in the establishment of a state that could absorb those refugees who wished to relocate there, but the latter refused to consider this. The PLO's official negotiators insisted that each individual refugee had to have the right to decide if he or she wished to realize his or her right to return to the territory that is now Israel.

The classical Israeli position was also one of fundamental principle. From independence onward, Israel denied responsibility for the refugee problem, and refused to recognize any Palestinian collective right to return to the territory of the new Jewish state. It also refused to allow individual Palestinians to return to their homes. Unlike the Palestinians, who viewed the refugee issue as a national issue, Israel viewed it as a humanitarian problem that could be resolved by improving the lot of the individuals involved. Israel advocated the resettlement and rehabilitation of the refugees in their host countries, and accepted that the refugees had a right to receive compensation. When the Arab host states refused to rehabilitate and naturalize the refugees, Israel accused them of deliberately seeking to prolong Palestinian suffering. The Palestinian leadership made the same charge against Israel.

Israeli public opinion began changing in the 1980s. Israelis who favored accommodation and compromise with the Palestinians accepted a Palestinian right of self-determination. These doves believed that the Palestinian state, when established, could absorb Palestinian refugees just as Israel had absorbed Jewish refugees. The Palestinians could view this as a limited right of return – to a sovereign Palestinian state, if not to their original homes and communities. Israel should, in the doves' view, welcome such a solution since it would resolve the refugee issue without requiring Israel to absorb any refugees. Israeli hawks, however, rejected this idea on the grounds that a refugee return to a state of Palestine would be a destabilizing factor in any peace agreement. They argued that the refugees would continue to demand to return to their original homes in Israel. Therefore the refugees should be settled outside the Palestinian territories or even outside the Middle East altogether. Furthermore, they maintained, should refugees be permitted to enter the Palestinian territory, Israel should maintain oversight and control of the number of entrees (Alpher and Shikaki 1999).

Notice that an inversion occurred between the Israeli dove position and that of the PLO. Up until the year 2000, the PLO for the most part focused on the collective right of return. From October 1967 through the Intifada that began in 1987, the PLO resisted accepting UN Security Council Resolution 242, which calls for a resolution of the refugee problem. At this time, the PLO claimed that the Palestinian problem was not a refugee problem, but rather a problem of self-determination and national liberation. The return was not perceived as the return of individuals but rather as a collective return (Klein 1998: 1–19). During this same period, most Israeli doves did not accept the Palestinian demand for a state and sought to strike a deal with Jordan, which would receive control of part of the occupied territories. The first Intifada brought about a change in the thinking of many Israelis who sought accommodation with the Palestinians. They came to accept a Palestinian right to self-determination, and this new thinking was codified in the Oslo Accords of 1993. Most Israeli doves now support the de facto collective return of the Palestinian people to the Palestinian territories, rather than an individual right of return.

However, these Israelis still disavowed responsibility for the creation of the refugee problem and were unwilling to commit Israel to make an official statement of apology. In response to this, the PLO shifted the nature of its claim and, instead of stressing a collective right of return, it began to demand an individual right. This gap between the sides persisted throughout the final status talks and no resolution was reached.

Many Israeli doves have trouble accepting the right of return. Acceptance of this Palestinian demand and symbol will not end the conflict but rather entrench it, they believe. Instead of a final agreement that would bring to an end the issue of the 1948 refugees, it would keep the contention over their future alive. Furthermore, they reasoned that Israeli acceptance of an absolute "right" of refugee return would leave a door open to Palestinian demands for full realization of that right in the future – even after a compromise agreement ostensibly resolving the issue had been signed and carried out.

The Palestinians faced a different problem. The PLO leadership demanded a collective right of return, but the memories of the refugees and their descendents were personal and concrete. So long as the moment of decision was not at hand there was no contradiction between the two and they could exist in parallel. During the interim period of Palestinian self-government that followed the signing of the Oslo Accords, the Palestinian Authority neglected the rehabilitation of the refugee camps under its control in the West Bank and Gaza Strip. Unrest grew in the camps and led to the growth of a new internal opposition to the established Palestinian leadership. The Palestinian leadership found itself in a dilemma. It had difficulty accepting the Israel demand that it abjure any right to return to the State of Israel itself, and sought to transfer at least part of the burden of deciding this to the individuals themselves (Klein 2003: 97–100, 152–64).

Track two models on Palestinian return

The most common position taken by Israelis who seek accommodation and compromise with the Palestinian leadership is an acceptance of the right of return in principle so long as its practical execution is accomplished within the boundaries of the Palestinian state. There would be no, or strictly limited, repatriation to Israel. This approach was proposed by several Palestinian track two negotiators, sometimes with an Israeli co-sponsor and sometimes alone. Mark Heller suggested this option in 1983, as did Faisal Husseini in 1989, Abu Iyad in 1990, Mark Heller and Sari Nuseeibeh in 1991, Shlomo Gazit in 1995, Yossi Beilin and Abu-Mazin in their joint draft paper of 1995, and Sari Nusseibeh and Ami Ayalon in their joint statement of guiding principles for a peace agreement, which they published in 2002 (Cahana 1996: 30–1, 60–2; Brynen 1998; Klein 1998).

A similar distinction between a return to the Palestinian homeland and a return to the Palestinian state was made in 1989 by an Israeli Professor of international law, Gideon Gottlib (Cahana 1996: 31). At this time, most Israeli doves still advocated an agreement with Jordan rather than with the PLO, so Gottlib framed his idea in the context of letting the Palestinians bear two passports, Palestinian and Jordanian, in the framework of a confederation of three states, Israel, Palestine, and Jordan. This proposal for a confederation was rendered moot when Israel's doves came to accept the establishment of an independent Palestinian state.

The proposal that Palestinian refugees would be absorbed by a Palestinian state comprising all or part of the West Bank and Gaza Strip was generally presented as part of a compromise. Israel would agree to the Palestinian demand that it recognize the right of return in principle, in exchange for Palestinian consent that refugees would not actually return to Israel, or would do so in only limited numbers. For example, in the preamble of the Ayalon–Nusseibeh document of 2002, each side recognizes the other's historic rights to the entire territory of Israel/Palestine. The section on the right of return states: "Recognizing the suffering and the plight of the Palestinian refugees, the international community, Israel, and the Palestinian State will initiate and contribute to an international fund to compensate them. Palestinian refugees will return only to the State of Palestine; Jews will return only to the State of Israel. The international community will offer to compensate toward bettering the lot of those refugees willing to remain in their present country of residence, or who wish to immigrate to third-party countries" (http://www. mifkad.org.il/Eng/PrinciplesAgreement.asp). Israelis who rejected any form of the right of return were forced to offer the refugees a way to return to Israel but under a different title and procedure. Absorption in Israel of a limited number of refugees as part of a process of family reunification was proposed by Mark Heller (1991), Shlomo Gazit (1995) (Brynen 1998), Ziad Abu Zayad (1994) (Cahana 1996: 53–4), and in the Beilin–Abu-Mazin proposal (1995, see below). Two Palestinian track two negotiators, both of them from the Palestinian diaspora, sought to formulate a proposal for a limited right of return. Rashid Khalidi (1992, 1995) made Israeli recognition of the injustice it inflicted on the 1948 refugees his point of departure, while Elia Zureik (1994) began with United Nations General Assembly Resolution 194, passed by the international body in 1949, which calls for the return of Palestinian refugees to Israel. Both Khalidi and Zureik expected Israel to recognise the right in principle of each individual refugee to return to his or her original home. They acknowledged, however, that in most cases it would be impossible to actualize the right either because the physical house no longer exists or because Israel would refuse to allow the refugees to take possession of it. To this distinction between the abstract right and actual return Khalidi added the distinction between return and family reunification. Refugees would return to the state of Palestine. But wherever it was possible physically and socially for Palestinian refugees to resettle in Israel as full citizens, they would be allowed to do so under the rubric of family reunification. All others would have to choose between rehabilitation in their Arab host countries or emigration to countries outside the region.

Elia Zureik preferred a geographical criterion instead of the family reunification formula. His major concern was the Palestinian refugees in Lebanon – some 300,000 people who have no chance of obtaining Lebanese citizenship. Lebanese government and society are based on a delicate balance between different confessional and ethnic communities, and absorbing Palestinian refugees would throw this system out of kilter. Zureik thus maintained that these refugees must leave Lebanon and return to Israel. Likewise, Zureik believed it necessary to guarantee the resettlement in their current host countries of those refugees who do not actualize their return (Khalidi 1992; Zureik 1994; Khalidi 1995).

A similar package was suggested by Ziad Abu Zayad in 2002. In his draft of final status principals, Abu Zayad suggested that the 1948 refugee problem should be addressed in accordance with Resolution 194, but with limited implementation. The right of return would be realized in the state of Palestine. However, Abu Zayad left a door open for a Palestinian claim to return to Israel by giving both sides a veto power over the issue. In his view, any solution or settlement must be negotiated and agreed upon by the two sides.

In his package Abu Zayad also demanded that Israel recognize its moral responsibility for the Palestinian refugee problem, and set up an international fund to compensate the 1948 refugees. The international community would contribute to this fund, offer any possible assistance to facilitate the implementation of the agreement, and provide the needed guarantees for its provisions (Eldar 2002a).

Limited success on track two: four case studies

In-depth and comprehensive track two meetings dealing with all final status issues created the possibility of increasing the opportunities for trade-offs when they dealt with the specific issue of the right of return. Chips could be traded not only within the discussion of the refugee problem but also among a large range of other issues on the agenda. Theoretically, this should have made it easier to reach an understanding, but the actual effect was quite limited.

The following four case studies demonstrate that representatives of the two sides were able to reach agreement on practical and technical issues, but not on principles, titles, and a joint historical narrative.

The Harvard forum

The Israeli–Palestinian working group at Harvard University met during 1994–5 and attempted to draft general principles for a comprehensive final Israeli–Palestinian agreement. It was unable to reach a compromise solution on the refugee problem. Instead, each side published its own paper. The Palestinian compromise offer was not based on achieving justice as the Palestinians see it. Instead, it laid out what the Palestinian participants argued was acceptable and honorable resolution of the issue, accommodating realities on the ground and Israeli security needs. Under this proposal, Israel would have to acknowledge the refugees' moral right to return to their homes and property, and would have to accept the responsibility for creating the refugee problem. In exchange, only a limited number of refugees would actually return to their original homes in Israel. These would be refugees who chose not to move to the new Palestinian state or to accept resettlement in any of the hosting countries, and whose property still exists in Israel. In other words, the actual exercise of the right of return will be mostly in the state of Palestine. The tradeoff that the Palestinian group offered also included a requirement that Israel withdraw to its 1967 borders, in order that the Palestinian state have maximum absorptive capacity for the refugees.

The Israeli proposal was very careful in its wording. With regard to responsibility, the maximum the Israeli team was ready to acknowledge was that Israel shares, to some extent, practical responsibility, together with other parties, for the plight and suffering of the refugees who lost their homes in the 1948 war. The Israelis would not, however, accept moral responsibility.

The Israeli team also accepted that the Palestinian refugees had a right of return that could be realized in the Palestinian state, but not in Israel proper. Israel could accept the repatriation of some tens of thousands of Palestinian refugees as part of a family reunification program, the Israeli participants suggested. However, Israel would also demand direct physical control over the flow of refugees into the Palestinian state. Thus, for example, if Palestine were to take in refugees beyond its absorptive capacity then Israel could curtail its financial compensation obligations. While the Israeli team suggested a few formulations aimed at creating a consensual Israeli–Palestinian narrative of the events of 1948, none of them met the Palestinians' minimum demands (Alpher and Shikaki 1999). As Kelman wrote: "for Israelis to acknowledge anything more than shared practical responsibility for the refugee problem, and for Palestinians to accept anything less than an Israeli acknowledgment of moral responsibility, would undermine their respective narratives and most members of the group were not prepared to go that far" (Kelman 2001: 206). On the practical level, however, the two sides found some common ground. They agreed on the following basic parameters: the return of some defined and limited number of refugees to the state of Israel; the resettlement of a large number of refugees in the state of Palestine, this constituting the primarily realization of the Palestinian right of return; absorption of other refugees in their host countries; and financial compensation (ibid.).

Beilin–Abu-Mazin

At the same time that the Harvard group was meeting, another track two channel was discussing the same issues. In this case, the teams were led by senior officials on each side – Israel's minister of justice, Yossi Beilin, and the Palestinian Mahmud 'Abas, known by his *nom de guerre*, Abu-Mazin. Unlike the Harvard forum, the Beilin–Abu-Mazin talks succeeded in producing a joint document outlining specific proposals for a permanent settlement agreement in many areas. However, the two sides reached no consensus on the refugee issue fundamentals. The document's refugee chapter thus opens with each side's acknowledgment instead of a joint narrative.

The Palestinian side stated that the right of its refugees to return to their homes was enshrined in international law and natural justice. But it recognized that the practical requirements of a peace agreement and realities on the ground had rendered the implementation of the right impractical. The Palestinians involved in the Beilin–Abu-Mazin channel therefore declared that they were prepared to accept and implement policies and measures that would ensure the welfare and well-being of the refugees.

The Israeli side acknowledged the moral and material suffering the Palestinian people had suffered as a result of the 1948 war. It further acknowledged the Palestinian right of return to the Palestinian state and their right to compensation and rehabilitation for moral and material losses. Israel would undertake to facilitate family reunification and would absorb Palestinian refugees in specific cases, as established by an International Commission for Palestinian Refugees to be established jointly by the two parties. The Palestinian side would enact a program to encourage the rehabilitation and resettlement of those Palestinian refugees presently residing in the West Bank and Gaza Strip within these areas, instead of demanding their return to their original homes. The PLO would consider the implementation of the above measures a full and final settlement of the refugee issue in all its dimensions. (The Beilin–Abu-Mazin document was published in *Newsweek* on 17 September 2000.)

The Madrid paper

The Madrid track two unpublished paper (1999) goes beyond the above-mentioned documents on three points. First, both sides agreed on Israel's shared responsibility for the creation of the Palestinian refugee problem. Second, for the first time in any track two paper, it includes in the Israeli–Palestinian bilateral deal the issue of Jewish refugees who fled from Arab countries in the period following the 1948 war. The paper contains a clause on seeking the Arab states' acknowledgement of the need to compensate Jews for lost property in the 1948 war. At all other track two meetings, the Palestinians had objected to this Israeli claim, arguing that it was not the Palestinians who forced the Jews to leave Arab states. Furthermore, they had argued, they were not prepared to serve as Israel's agent in its future talks with each of the relevant Arab states.

Third, the Madrid negotiators agreed that a just solution of the Palestinian refugee problem is vital to the resolution of the Palestinian–Israeli conflict. In previous track two talks, the Israelis would not agree to use the word "just," offering instead other formulations. In exchange for this concession, the document limits Israel's obligation by requiring the solution to be based on "realistic justice." The Madrid understanding defines the standard of "realistic justice" as the following four measures:

1 The creation of a Palestinian state in the West Bank and Gaza Strip. Palestinian refugees currently residing in these areas will be rehabilitated and settle there permanently, as will other refugees who may resettle in the state.
2 The resettlement of refugees in the Arab countries that currently host them. The document emphasises the need to involve other partners in this project, in particular the host countries themselves.
3 The absorption of some refugees in Israel, on the basis of reunification with family already living there. This would be done on an individual, humanitarian basis, in the framework of an understanding to be reached by the two parties.

4 Israeli cooperation in an international effort aimed to mobilize the financial resources necessary to implement collective and individual financial compensation.

The Geneva Model Accord (2003)

The Geneva Model Accord is the most detailed document to emerge from track two negotiations. The participants in this channel sought to bring to a conclusion the final status talks that took place at Taba, January 2001. The document is formulated as a legal contract and was signed by more than twenty people from each side. Each group of negotiators and signers includes veteran track two professional negotiators and active politicians. (The text of the Geneva document and the signers' list is at http://www.heskem.org.il/Heskem_en.asp. On the agreement, see Klein (2004).) The Geneva Model Accord's Article 7 addresses the refugee issue. The provisions are based on United Nations Security Council Resolution 242, on United Nations General Assembly Resolution 194, and on article 2.ii. of the Arab Peace Initiative of 2002. This latter article emphasizes that, while Resolution 194 is the basis for the solution of the refugee problem, the solution also has to be agreed on by both sides. This is an important qualification, since it means that the Arab states signed on the 2002 initiative accept that Resolution 194 does not compel Israel to accept the return of the refugees, as the PLO has argued. It recognizes that Israel's consent is an essential part of the solution offered by Resolution 194. This view of 194 provides a ladder for the Palestinians to climb down by reasserting the centrality of the United Nations resolution but obviating the Palestinians' previous insistence on imposing the return of the refugees on Israel. In doing so, it allows Israel to accept the resolution by providing assurances that no Palestinian refugees will be imposed on the Jewish state without its consent.

The Geneva Model Accord does not contain even a partial Israeli apology for its role in the creation of the 1948 refugee problem or an Israeli acknowledgment of its shared responsibility. Due to the inability of previous frameworks, both track one and track two, to reach an agreement on these issues, the Geneva understandings leave this task to the two civil societies, under the leadership of their respective governments. This strategy is based on the presumption that a diplomatic accord cannot suddenly change deeply rooted memories, or modify national and historical myths overnight. Reconciliation and openness toward the narrative of one's fellow human being are the result of long-term processes that take place within civil society. Diplomatic mechanisms can promote reconciliation processes but not dictate them.

The Israeli partners to the Geneva Accord did not present their Palestinian counterparts with an unequivocal demand that they renounce the right of return to areas within the State of Israel. In effect, the accord leaves this to the conscience of each individual Palestinian refugee. He or she can make a claim to exercise the right of return. But each such individual will have to go through the formal process of immigrating to Israel. Israel thus maintains formal control over whether refugees can, in fact, return.

The Geneva Model Accord avoids the charged terms "right of return" and "return." Instead, the two sides preferred to use technical term "choosing permanent place of residence." Knowing that the surest way to prevent an agreement was to claim that Israel must recognize the right of return as a basic principle and must leave it to each individual refugee to choose whether or not to exercise this right, the Palestinian side agreed to mechanisms that would limit the implementation of the return to Israel.

According to the Geneva document, every Palestinian refugee may choose to make his or her home in the State of Palestine by virtue of being Palestinian. Permanent residence in the State of Israel can, however, be granted by Israel only. In other words, the refugee is free to believe that he or she has a right to return to the territory that is now Israel, but the accord offers him or her no legal or institutional backing nor means to achieve this objective. According to the Geneva Accord, Israel is no more and no less than a country to which the Palestinian refugee may immigrate. All of the mechanisms extant since 1948 for dealing with the refugee problem will cease to exist, and the legal status of "Palestinian refugee" will be terminated. Refugees who reject the accord and nevertheless demand the right of return in the classical sense will find no institution that supports their claim and will have no legal standing. The determination of refugees' permanent place of residence will not be made by them alone but by a technical committee to be established by the international commission appointed to oversee the implementation of the accord. The commission will include an Israeli representative who will submit to the committee the number of refugees Israel is willing to accept. In determining this number, Israel will take into consideration the average number of refugees who will immigrate to countries outside the region.

The permanent status talks

The positions of the two sides on the refugee issue remained starkly irreconcilable whenever there were contacts on a permanent status agreement during the interim period that followed the Oslo accords. The issue was not resolved in the Stockholm secret talks of spring 2000, nor in Camp David a few months later. Indeed, at Camp David, both sides simply reiterated the positions they had submitted in Stockholm. Israel refused to recognise Resolution 194 and to accept responsibility for the creation of the 1948 Palestinian refugee problem. At most, Israel was prepared to express its regret for the suffering the Palestinians endured during and after the 1948 war. Israel's negotiators refused in principle to accept any form of the right of return. Instead, Israel offered to take part in an international effort to provide the refugees with financial compensation, to rehabilitate their camps, and to help resettle refugees either in their host countries or in other countries. Israeli negotiators said they were willing to allow a few thousand refugees to immigrate to Israel under the rubric of family reunification, or of special humanitarian cases. But they emphasized that such immigration of Palestinians would be the result of a sovereign Israeli decision, and would under no circumstances be an application or acknowledgement of a Palestinian right of return. From the Israeli point of view, the Palestinians were free to repatriate refugees to their new state and to call that "return," but Israel would not acknowledge that the right existed (Klein 2003: 44; Sher 2001: 104–5; Klein forthcoming).

At Camp David, Israel also rejected a Palestinian proposal to establish, after Israeli acceptance in principle of a right of return, a mechanism that would channel refugees towards more attractive resettlement possibilities than a return to the State of Israel. According to the Palestinian offer, the return of Palestinian refugees from Lebanon would serve as a pilot program for examining how the system would work and where the refugees would prefer to realize their right. It expressed a willingness to absorb a maximum of 2,000 refugees per year over a five- to six-year period. This meant a total of 10,000–12,000 refugees, all in the framework of family reunification and as a humanitarian gesture only. Israel proposed dismantling UNWRA, the United Nations agency that oversees the Palestinian refugee camps, within a ten-year period and establishing in its place a new body that would oversee the rehabilitation and resettlement of the refugees. The gap between the positions of the two sides was so great that, for all practical purposes, no negotiations on the 1948 refugee issue took place at Camp David. At most of the encounters where the subject was raised there were only exchanges of accusations and myths and unproductive arguments (Haniyyeh 2000; Sher 2001: 199, 213–14, 216, 430–432; Abu Mazin to *al-Ayyam*, 29 July 2001; Klein 2003: 70).

The sides debated the issue again in December, on the eve of the publication of President Clinton's bridging proposals and immediately thereafter. The president accepted the concept of the right of return but differentiated between the actual return to a sovereign Palestinian territorial and political entity, and return to the periphery outside the state of Palestine yet within the historical homeland (www.jmcc.org/documents/clintonprop.htm and Klein 2003: 199–203). Before the president tabled his parameters, each side tried to draw him to its side. The Israelis and Palestinians also drew red lines that they told Clinton not to cross. After publication, each side tried to see its own point of view in the American proposal, or to convince the other side to abandon Clinton's parameters in favour of a bilateral agreement. In both rounds of debate Israel rejected, categorically and unsurprisingly, the right of return, Resolution 194, and the Palestinian demand to take responsibility and apologize for the refugee problem. Israel reiterated its willingness to ab-sorb few thousands of refugees over a long period of time, as a humanitarian gesture (Ben Ami 2004: 367–73, 378).The Clinton parameters were a problem for Israel. Despite this, Israel decided not to break with the Americans. Israel's government immediately accepted the parameters and presented its serious reservations later. The Palestinians did the opposite. Because of their deep disappointment and lack of confidence in the US's ability to be an honest broker, the Palestinian Authority took its time before making an official response. It in the end accepted the Clinton parameters, but included a significant reservation that allowed Israel to argue that the Palestinian leadership had in fact rejected Clinton guidelines (Pressman 2003: 20).

The Israeli reservations stressed that it would not accept the right of return, and that it refused to allow any refugees to return to its territory as realization of such a right (Sher 2001: 373–4, 383–4; Ben Ami 2004: 369–72, 378, 383–5). For their part, the Palestinians complained that the American proposal reflected a wholesale adoption of the Israeli position that the implementation of the right of return be subject entirely to Israel's discretion. In response, the Palestinians formulated a counter-principle stating that the essence of the right of return is choice: Palestinians should be given the option to choose where they wish to settle, including return to the homes from which they were driven. Recognition of the right of return and the provision of choice to refugees was, they insisted, a prerequisite for ending the conflict. They insisted the solution contained in the permanent settlement be in accordance with UN Resolution 194, and that the Palestinian refugees in Lebanon be given priority in resettlement. The Palestinians said, however, that they were prepared to think flexibly and creatively about the mechanisms for implementing the right of return (http://www.jmcc.org/documents/clintonprop2.htm; http://www.jmcc.org/documents/clintonprop3.htm). Once again the sides reached a dead end.

The Taba talks of January 2001 were convened as a last-ditch effort to save the Oslo process, following the failure of Camp David and the resumption of hostilities. For the first time, the two sides conducted serious negotiations about the 1948 refugees. However, they reached no understanding about the foundation of the 1948 refugee problem. The Palestinians demanded that Israel recognize its moral and legal responsibility for displacing civilians during the 1948 war and preventing their return thereafter. They also demanded acceptance, in accordance with UN Resolution 194, of the right of each 1948 refugee, his or her spouse, and their offspring and descendants to return to their former home in Israel. According to the Palestinians, the right of return of each refugee would not expire until he or she exercised it, in accordance with the agreement. There would be no time limit (Eldar 2002b; Israeli Private Response 2002; Klein 2003: 122–6).

In its private response to the Palestinian proposal, Israel used the term "the right of return" only once, and then in quotation marks, referring to it as a Palestinian yearning. The Israeli paper did not contain an explicit acceptance of UN Resolution 194, which calls for the return of 1948 refugees to their homes on an individual and voluntary basis. Instead, it referred to the implementation of this resolution in a manner consistent with the existence of the State of Israel as the homeland of the Jewish people. The two Palestinian principles of the right of return and Resolution 194 were put in the Israeli paper in connection with Palestinian demands that Israel had already accepted: the establishment of an independent Palestinian state and UN Resolution 242. Israel suggested a joint narrative in which it was prepared to accept a certain measure of responsibility for the creation of the refugee problem and was prepared to express its regret. But Israel would not accept legal responsibility. Under the circumstances, the two sides agreed that each would maintain its own narrative about the circumstances under which the problem of the 1948 refugees came into being. They also ratified their commitment to a solution based on two national ethnic states, meaning that the solution to the refugee problem would have to respect Israel's existence as the state of the Jewish people. Israel suggested a "return basket" made up of five options: rehabilitation and citizenship in the refugee's current location; absorption in the Palestinian state; settlement in territories that Israel would transfer to Palestinian sovereignty in the framework of territorial exchange; emigration to a country outside the region; emigration to Israel. The refugees in Lebanon would have priority in choosing among the options. The options would not have equal status. Incentives and financial aid would be used to encourage refugees to waive their right to return to Israel. But the Palestinian negotiators stressed that the refugees had to retain the individual freedom of choice among the options and that agreement to a range of options would not prejudice their right to return to their homes.

In keeping with President Clinton's ideas from December 2000, it was understood by both sides that Israel's immigration quotas for Palestinian refugees would be low relative to the quotas for immigration into other destinations. No numbers were agreed upon but unofficially Israel referred to 25,000 in the first three years of a 15-year absorption program and 40,000 in the first five years. The Palestinian paper stated that all refugees residing in Lebanon should be allowed in principle to return to Israel, in addition to some unstated number of those residing in other countries. Both sides concluded that Israel would also have the sovereign power to decide which refugees had the right to return to its territory and which did not, this subject to criteria agreed on by both sides. Another agreement reached at Taba was that each refugee would have to give up his refugee status and accept full and equal citizenship in his new place of residence. His choice of residence would be his final location as a refugee. Both parties agreed that during this five-year period an international commission, replacing UNRWA, would be established as a mechanism for dealing with compensation and to administer the rehabilitation of the refugees (Beilin 2001: 204–8, 214–16; Eldar 2001; Klein 2003; Matz 2003; Moratinos non-paper, in Klein 2003: 204–14; Pressman 2003).

Summary

The track two talks introduced the following distinctions into the Israeli–Palestinian diplomatic discourse:

1 The right of return in principle as opposed to return in actual practice.
2 Return as opposed to family unification – whether the term "family reunification" is merely a more acceptable label for the right of return, or whether it should indeed be limited in practice to actual cases of split families.
3 The right of return as an unfulfilled principle on the one hand and compensation on the other hand (i.e. financial, territorial, and symbolic optional Israeli compensations including an official apology for the wrongs it committed during the war).
4 Return to Israeli territory versus return to Palestinian sovereign land.
5 Return to an area under Israeli sovereignty versus an immigration process that governs the practical arrangements of changing the refugee's permanent place of residence. Placing the refugees' return under the category of immigration to Israel gives Israel the authority not to let the refugee in, even though it is theoretically supposed to do so under the right of return.

These distinctions do not necessarily exclude one another. Mostly attempts have been made to introduce several of them simultaneously in order to maximize the Palestinian compensation for not permitting all the refugees to exercise their right to return. These distinctions were discussed on both track two and track one, but the discussions rarely ended with an agreement.

The discussions on these issues on both official talks and track two followed the following lines. First, there was a constant shift in position from collective to individual rights. Whereas the collective discussion is about state formation and international principles, the discourse on individual return is mainly pragmatic, technical, and aimed to meet humanitarian aid needs. Second, in many cases the discourse did not end with a signed agreement or mutually agreed conclusion. Rather the discussion went in a circle. On the one hand the participants were future-oriented. They sought rehabilitation, restitution, reconstruction, and repatriation of the Palestinian refugees and their physical living conditions. On the other hand, because for both sides 1948 is a foundation myth, their discourse is heavily oriented towards the past. What for Israel was a war of independence was for the Palestinian national movement the catastrophe that justifies their national goals and their right to demand a just solution to the Palestinian problem. Thus, for the Palestinian national movement 1948 is not only about the past. It has to guarantee their future. The same is true of Israel. Israel is afraid to lose the Jewish majority and character that it achieved in the 1948 war. Both sides are caught between past and future, traumatic memories and fears. It seems that there is no better way to reduce the burden of this complexity and defuse its destructive potential than to formulate a package deal that will move the sides from debating the 1948 refugee issue on its own and lead them to make practical tradeoffs.

The critique of refugee studies is that refugees are referred to as victims without addressing political identity. In the Palestinian case there is no base for such criticism since the PLO combines the right of return of 1948 and 1967 refugees with Palestinian self determination and struggle. In their ethos PLO leaders, most of them first and second generation 1948 refugees, succeeded in minimizing victimhood approaches and channeling them toward political action, armed struggle, and organization formation. These created the following advantages for the Palestinian case:

The PLO succeeded in forming representative institutions, politicizing the Palestinian refugees, maintaining their identity, developing collective memory, achieving international legitimacy, launching top-down process in dealing with the refugee issue, and linking between refugee repatriation and comprehensive peace treaty.

As shown in other cases, the return of Palestinian refugees needs a political agreement and involves rebuilding social institutions and agencies, as well as national planning so that resources do not compartmentalize refugees. The PLO began working on this direction, yet did not achieve enough progress.

The Bosnia-Herzegovina lesson is that certain circumstances can limit the number of returnees. Only 50 percent returned to their original places in Bosnia and Herzegovina; they did not want to go back to the countryside and the insecurity that they faced there once they had fled to urban areas where their economic opportunities seemed better, and more options were open to those with dual citizenship, especially Croatians. Theoretically these circumstances are applicable to the Palestinian case where the physical and social conditions in the places of origin are totally different than 57 years ago, and many 1948 refugees are integrated into their host countries, first and foremost in Jordan.

Yet the same process created also the following disadvantages.

Lessons learned from other cases show the need to include more effectively the Palestinian refugees in the process. But the main concern of the Palestinian political elite is preserving its own power, therefore it excludes the refugee grassroots organizations from the political negotiation. Moreover, the refugee communities do not get a great deal of attention or reliable information from PLO leaders. In response, refugee organizations challenge PLO representation on their issues.

Since the PLO and Israel were occupied mainly in defining models of allowed and denied return, which is a typical top-down/state-driven issue, they neglected issues coming from the opposite direction, from a bottom-up approach. In other words, there is a need to connect ideas on return with reality. As also shown in other cases, return is linked with development and conditions at original homes that the refugees left behind and target homes as well. Palestinian refugees need to get information on what happened to their original homes, property, villages, and towns. What are the real return options available? How would the return be made in actual terms? What would happen to the people once they had returned and were living in totally different surroundings than they had left? What are the expected integration problems for the returnees and for the absorptive society as well? Can the return improve their standard of living and make them happy citizens? In what context will the return happen? And what may be the long-term effects of their return? Confronting the dream of return with reality is the duty of a responsible leadership, and such a dramatic act calls for the inclusion of the refugee grassroots organizations in the settlement and repatriation process.

Return is permanent and secure and involves a high level of international guarantees and coordination with the relevant governments. The very fact that the settlement of the Palestinian refugee problem is discussed in the context of final status agreement helps in meeting these needs. On the other hand, in cases where there is a weak central government as in Bosnia, return has resulted in cantonization. In order to prevent that while the Palestinian central authority is still weak, strong international umbrella supervision is needed to protect the process of repatriation.

Linkage between return and justice is strong in the PLO political discourse in general and in the refugees' rhetoric in particular. Their argument is based on international resolutions that may help them in forwarding their return. The international community has usually opted for repatriation to countries of origin, as shown clearly in Bosnia. But this alone is not enough to solve the Palestinian refugee case. More than 50 years have passed since UNGAR 194 and scores of other international resolutions have followed, yet 1948 refugees have not returned. This makes the Palestinian case unique.

The linkage of return to justice in its juridical and political meanings will determine whether conflict is resolved or prolonged, as will the linkage of reconciliation to accepting responsibility for the plight of the refugees. In order to achieve reconciliation there is a need to deal with the question of who is responsible for the creation of the 1948 refugee problem. A Palestinian precondition for reconciliation is Israeli acknowledgment of responsibility for the wrongs it did to the Palestinian refugees. However, as the German case shows, restitution and reconciliation are not the result of a formal declaration but long-term processes linked to personal emotions and collective memoirs. No formal act can do more than open the door for a long-term change process. The gradual change takes place mainly after the formal agreement on technical issues signed between the governments.

References

Agha, Hussein, Feldman, Shai, Khalidi, Ahmad, and Schiff, Zeev (2003) *Track II diplomacy: Lessons from the Middle East* (Cambridge, MA: MIT).
Alpher, Joseph, and Shikaki, Khalil (1999) "Concept paper: The Palestinian refugee problem and the right of return", *Middle East Policy* 6 (3), 167–89.
Beilin, Yossi (2001) *Guide for a wounded dove* (Hebrew) (Tel Aviv: Yedioth Aharonoth).

Ben Ami, Shlomo (2004) *A front without a rearguard: A voyage to the boundaries of the peace process* (Hebrew) (Tel Aviv: Yedioth Aharonoth).

Benvenisti, Eyal, and Zamir, Eyal (1995) "Private claims to property rights in the future Israeli–Palestinian settlement", *American Journal of International Law* 89 (2), 295–340.

Brynen, Rex (1998) "Palestinian refugees and the Middle East peace process", available online at www.arts.mcgill.ca/mepp/mepp.html or www.prrn.org

Cahana, Shamay (1996) *Differing and converging views on solving the Palestinian refugees' problem* (Jerusalem: Hebrew University, Leonard Davis Institute for International Relations).

Davis, John, and Kaufman, Edward (eds.) (2002) *Second track/citizens' diplomacy: Concepts and techniques for conflict transformation* (London: Rowman and Littlefield).

Eldar, Akiva (2001) "The monster of the right of return", *Ha'aretz,* 31 May.

Eldar, Akiva (2002a) "Ziad Abu Zayad's statement of principles", *Ha'aretz,* 23 July.

Eldar, Akiva (2002b) "The peace that nearly was at Taba", *Ha'aretz,* 15 February.

Ginat, Joseph, and Perkins, Edward J. (eds.) (2001) *The Palestinian refugees: Old problems – new solutions* (Brighton: Sussex Academic Press).

Haniyyeh, Akram (2000) "Camp David diary" (Arabic), *Al Ayyam,* 29 July–10 August.

Israel/Palestine Center for Research and Information (December 2002). *Yes PM: Years of experience in strategies for peace making: Looking at Israeli–Palestinian people to people activities 1993–2002* (Jerusalem: Israel/Palestine Center for Research and Information).

Israeli Private Response to Palestinian Refugee Proposal (2002) *Journal of Palestinian Studies* 123: 145–50.

Kelman, Herbert C. (2001) "The role of national identity in conflict resolution: Experience from Israeli–Palestinian problem-solving workshops", in R. D. Ashmore, L. Jussin and D. Wilder (eds.), *Social identity, intergroup conflict and conflict reduction* (Oxford: Oxford University Press), pp. 187–212.

Khalidi, Rashid (1992) "Observations on the right of return", *Journal of Palestine Studies* 21, pp. 29–40.

Khalidi, Rashid (1995) "The Palestinian refugee problem: A possible solution", *Palestine–Israel Journal* 2, 72–8.

Klein, Menachem (1998) "Between right and realization: The PLO dialectics of 'the right of return'", *Journal of Refugee Studies* 11 (1), 1–19.

Klein, Menachem (2003) *The Jerusalem problem: The struggle for permanent status* (Gainesville: University Press of Florida).

Klein, Menachem (2004) "The logic of Geneva agreement", *Logos* 3 (1), available online at http://www.logosjournal.com/klein.htm

Klein, Menachem (forthcoming) "The negotiations for settlement of the 1948 refugees", in Eyal Benvenisti and Sari Hanafi (eds.), *Israel and the Palestinian refugees problem* (Heidelberg: Max Planck Institute for Comparative Public and International Law).

Matz, David (2003) "Trying to understand the Taba talks", *Palestine–Israel Journal* 10 (3), 96–105, (4), 92–8.

Palestinian Proposal on Palestinian Refugees of 22 January 2001, non-paper, draft 2 (2002) *Journal of Palestinian Studies* 123: 145–50.

Pressman, Jeremy (2003) "Visions in collision: What happened in Camp David and Taba", *International Security* 28 (2), 5–43.

Sher, Gilad (2001) *Just beyond reach: The Israeli–Palestinian peace negotiations 1999–2001* (Hebrew) (Tel Aviv: Yedioth Aharonoth).

Tamari, Salim (1996) *Return, resettlement, repatriation: The future of Palestinian refugees in the peace negotiations* (Beirut: Institute for Palestine Studies).

Zureik, Elia (1994) "Palestinian refugees problem", *Journal of Palestine Studies* 24 (1), 5–17.

Part II
Case studies

6 'Sustainable returns'?

State, politics and mobile livelihoods – the Guatemalan case

Finn Stepputat

Based on research on the Guatemalan process of return and repatriation, this chapter will address the three themes of the workshop, but will also emphasize the necessity of analyzing cases of return and repatriation in a longer-term perspective than implied by the suggested topics. Apart from providing a background to the Guatemalan case, the chapter will analyze the official accords, the institutional frameworks – including the dynamic of refugee organization – and the choices and options that have been available to the refugees. The chapter presents some ideas regarding the state-building effect of the Guatemalan return process and looks at the fate of one of the return settlements set up in the 1990s. Against this background, it is suggested that the refugees' mobile livelihood strategies be considered when return and repatriation are analysed and planned. In the concluding section, similarities, differences and lessons learned are discussed in relation to the Palestinian case.

The conflict in historical perspective

Lasting 35 years, the armed conflict in Guatemala became one of the most enduring of the hot Cold War conflicts in Latin America. Apart from 1981–3, military confrontations were of low intensity and took place in geographically limited areas. However, the institutionalization of a counterinsurgency state from the late 1960s onward had a profound impact on the entire Guatemalan society, which was the first in the continent to experience death squads and forced disappearances.[1] The transformation of this system has been a long and difficult process in which the return of refugees has played an important and much debated part.

One may interpret the Guatemalan conflict as a conflict over social order, related to the rapid process of modernization in a conservative and highly unequal agricultural society, and fuelled by the geopolitical interests of the Cold War. But the fact that the Guatemalan state was never able to resolve the national question and incorporate the indigenous population into civil institutions is the fundamental key to understanding the spread of the violent conflict and the militarization of the Guatemalan state (Smith 1990). The Maya speaking population makes up half of the population in Guatemala.[2]

Two different moments in the Guatemalan history are important to understand. One is the late nineteenth-century liberal land reforms which provided the basis for 1) the production of a large group of poor, mostly Mayan peasants whose livelihood depended on seasonal migration to the export-oriented plantations, and 2) the exclusion of Mayans from effective citizenship. The state apparatus that evolved around the plantation economy was firmly controlled by a small land-based oligarchy, and at the local level in the highlands a class of (explicitly non-Indian) *ladinos* achieved a privileged position as middlemen between the Indian population on the one side and the plantations and the state apparatus on the other (McCreery 1994). In practice – but not by law – a quasi-apartheid regime was produced through the segregation of Mayans and *ladinos*. These local relations of power in the highlands conditioned the emergence of a rural reform movement which, in the late 1970s, came to support the basically non-Mayan guerilla organizations.

The second decisive moment in the history of Guatemala is 1954, when a CIA-organized coup brought an end to ten years of modernizing reforms and, according to James Dunkerley, to the faith of one generation of radicals in peaceful and legal means of change (Dunkerley 1988). In the early 1960s, after the Cuban revolution, a group of officers from the reform period formed a leftist guerilla movement in an attempt to replicate the Cuban experience in Guatemala. The existence of the guerillas legitimized the strengthening of the hitherto small and ineffective army as well as the institutionalization of its control over the civil administration. Rather than replacing the oligarchy, the army eventually came to form part of the ruling elite in Guatemala.

The guerillas were defeated in 1971, but survivors formed the kernels of new guerilla movements which emerged during the 1970s with a reformulated political and military strategy. The guerrillas of the 1970s, and in particular the EGP (the Guerilla Army of the Poor), turned to the western highlands with a long-term strategy of silently building up political and logistical support among the Mayan population, who were expected to become a new revolutionary subject (Le Bot 1995: 118).

At the new agricultural frontiers in the forested lowlands as well as in the highlands, the armed guerillas encountered a multifaceted Indian movement for change including Catholic catechists, cooperatives, peasant unions and groups of peasants organized for the titling and purchase of land. Population growth in the highlands and an extreme expansion of cattle ranches at the agricultural frontier in the northern lowlands increased the pressure on land considerably during the 1960s and 1970s and made land reform a crucial issue.

The encounter between the guerillas, who were mainly involved in national politics, and the modernizing factions of the rural population engaged in local struggles over power, proved to be a forceful combination. At the height of the conflict, the guerillas had 6,000 full time combatants – unified from 1982 in the URNG, la Unidad Revolucionario Nacional de Guatemala – while an estimated 250,000 persons made up the base of support for the guerillas (Le Bot 1995: 195). By then, the army had launched its counterinsurgency programme intended to remove 'the water from the fish', i.e. eradicate or alienate the social base of the guerilla. But the programme was also intended to prepare the ground for a civilian government through a development-oriented approach to counterinsurgency (Schirmer 1996). As explained elsewhere, the army succeeded in controlling the guerillas through massive displacements and massacres and had sufficient control to concede formal power to a civilian government in 1986. Shortly after, negotiations on repatriation started (Stepputat 1999a).

Dynamics of displacement

The insurgency and in particular the army's counterinsurgency programs left a balance of more than 400 villages destroyed, maybe 150,000 killed, 45,000 disappeared, up to 1 million internally displaced (some 20 per cent of the population) and several hundreds of thousands externally displaced in Belize (10,000–25,000), Mexico (100,000–150,000) and the USA (100,000–200,000).[3] Many returned shortly after, filtering back or passing through army camps for displaced people. In the regions of conflict, mobility was tightly controlled, and the army was in charge of reception and resettlement of displaced persons. They applied the strategy of 'security and development' (or 'guns and beans' in the popular version) which devised the incorporation of all males into the newly formed Civil Defense Patrols (comprising 900,000 males at its peak in the 1980s) and the resettlement of the rural population in model villages, clustered in 'development poles', where state institutions would support their integrated development. Because of scarce resources, difficult conditions and limited commitments, the development efforts undertaken by the army remained rudimentary during the 1980s.

Other displaced people stayed away and led an anonymous existence in the major cities and in the plantation zone at the south coast. Given the dangers of visibility and collective organization, these groups received minimal attention and assistance. However, in spite of the dangers, displaced persons formed the Council for Displaced Persons in Guatemala, CONDEG, in 1989, which, following the peace accord on displaced populations (see below), achieved some assistance for resettlement.

In Mexico, only 46,000 of 100,000–150,000 fleeing Guatemalans were recognized as refugees by UNHCR and assisted through the Mexican Commission for Refugees, COMAR. The 'other refugees', those who were neither assisted nor recognized, filtered back into Guatemala or melted into a region of Mexico where Guatemalans have traditionally been engaged in seasonal labour (Salvadó 1988). The 'filtering back' mode of return gave rise to the notion of 'silent returnees', the refugees who went back one by one to the south coast or the cities of Guatemala, thus slowly establishing a base for one or more households. The Catholic Church and a few NGOs have been involved in discreet support to these small groups within Guatemala.

The refugees who were recognized as such by UNHCR lived in more than 100 camps along the border. The Mexican government never gave them refugee status, and security and political considerations limited their options for livelihood. In 1984, following numerous incursions by the Guatemalan army, the Mexican government decided to relocate the refugees from the camps along the border in Chiapas to the peninsula of Yucatán. Half of the refugees resisted relocation. Although these continued to receive limited, individual assistance, the relocated refugees received 0.2–1 hectares of land each and became integrated in an ambitious programme for self-sufficiency, while individual assistance was cut back gradually.

As for the rest of the displaced population, the refugees were mainly poor peasants, either subsistence farmers with access to communal, national or private land, or members of cooperatives. Many had an embryonic cash crop production. Most of the refugees were Mayans, and many of them, in particular the women, were monolingual. In Mexico, at least nine of Guatemala's 24 ethnic groups were represented. Demographically, the refugee population had the same characteristics as the rural population in Guatemala in general, testifying to the indiscriminate violence which lead to the flight (Stepputat 1989). The refugees came from regions, close to the border, which were under guerilla control when the army launched the counterinsurgency programme in 1982. Segments of the refugee population maintained political relations with the URNG, while others were in opposition to the guerilla movement.

For the refugees, the stay in Mexico meant a rapid process of modernization, nurtured by a number of factors: the mixture of different ethnic groups in the camps, the improved access to education and frequent recurrence to wage labour in the construction and tourist industry (often without due documents), as well as domestic labour for the women, increased the usage of Spanish as the common language. The youth in particular adopted attitudes and consumption patterns common to urban Mexicans.

At the same time, however, the refugees developed a nationalist but anti-statist discourse, underpinned by an effective organization within and among the camps in Mexico. Whereas identity in indigenous Guatemala has traditionally been defined in terms of the local township, the refugees began to identify themselves as 'Guatemalans' as well. Given their experience with state violence and the ongoing dialogue with URNG and popular organizations, the dominant discourse among refugee leaders cultivated anti-statist attitudes. Thus, while the discourse discouraged further integration into the Mexican society and urged people to 'wait and see', a politically informed project for return to Guatemala took form during the late 1980s in response to the first repatriation agreement from 1987 (Stepputat 1992; 1994).

Frameworks of return

Over time, the institutional frameworks for return to Guatemala varied a great deal, with the effect that refugees returned under very different conditions (Table 6.1). From 1984, refugees could return under different amnesty laws where they would be interrogated by the army and resettled in armed villages with minimal relief provisions from the National Reconstruction Commission, CNR.

The development of a framework for repatriation proper (i.e. the return of recognized refugees from Mexico) started in 1986 when a civilian president had been elected. From the Guatemalan perspective, the policy on repatriation was characterized by a schism between opposed interests and sectors, between the persistent perception of refugees as guerrillas or guerrilla supporters and the attempts to break the international isolation of Guatemala and remove the country from the class of pariah states (alongside Chile and South Africa) to which it had been relegated. Furthermore, the improvement of the Guatemalan image was supposed to deflate international support for URNG.

The bilateral negotiations between Mexico and Guatemala constituted one element of the international recognition of Guatemala, which led to a tripartite agreement (UNHCR, GoG and GoM) in February 1987 in support of voluntary repatriation and to the creation of a Special Commission for Assistance to Repatriates, Refugees and Internally Displaced Persons (CEAR). UNHCR supported CEAR with funds and managed to open an office in Guatemala. At this moment the Central American peace process had achieved a fruitful dynamic, culminating in 1987, when five Central American presi-

Table 6.1 Frameworks of return

	Framework	Agencies	Benefits	Numbers[a]
1983–6	Amnesty laws	The army/S-5, CNR	Minimal relief Building material in armed villages No const. guarantees	(only 1,276 registered by UNHCR)
1987–92	Tripartite repatriation agreement	CEAR, UNHCR	WFP food (9–12 months) Tools and building materials No constuction guarantees	7,052 (+4,068 from 1993 to 1999)
1993–9	October 1992 agreement (1996 Peace agreement)	CEAR, FORELAP, FONATIERRA, UNHCR, NGOs	Food for 12 months, etc. plus credits for land projects (rehabilitation/reconstruction) Construction guarantees	31,200

Note
a Numbers based on Worby (1999).

dents signed the Esquipulas II agreements on peace and democracy in the region.

The regional peace process and the following efforts to manage the problems of displacement in the region (including Mexico) took place under very special circumstances and may be difficult to duplicate elsewhere. There were both left- and right-leaning governments in the region, but they all hosted refugees and they were all reluctant to give in to USA pressures to create a military alliance against the Sandinistas. This situation opened a space for mutual commitments between the governments. The process was very much in the interests of the Guatemalan government, and the army, which had its relatively limited forces fully occupied in the internal conflict (AVANCSO 1989).

The issue of massive displacements drew much attention and was included in the Esquipulas agenda. When UNDP, in support of the Esquipulas II process, prepared the UN Special Programme for Economic Assistance to Central America, refugees, returnees and displaced had top priority. Next step was the 1989 'International Conference on Central American Refugees' (CIREFCA), which was designed to commit governments, international organizations and NGOs to the development of programmes for refugees, returnees and displaced persons in the region.

The CIREFCA Plan of Action followed more or less the UNDP guidelines on this issue, 1) adopting a critical distance from the national security-based approach to displaced populations, 2) including internally displaced persons in the programmes, and 3) adopting an integrated approach to assistance emphasizing the integration of programmes for displaced populations in national development plans and including 'local' (not displaced) communities in the programmes (Zinzer 1992).

Although the CIREFCA process had a positive impact in terms of focusing attention and developing governmental capacities in the field of displaced populations, CIREFCA had a limited direct impact in the case of Guatemala. The government (supported by UNDP and UNHCR) presented several programmes to CIREFCA in 1989 and 1990, but obtained only minimal funding since the international donors favoured NGOs as implementing institutions. One of the achievements of CIREFCA, according to UNHCR,[4] was the recognition of international and regional NGOs as players in the process. However, in Guatemala the relationship between NGOs and the government was marred by a complete lack of mutual confidence. The government never consulted the national NGOs, whom it regarded as active supporters of the guerrilla movement, and hardly any of the national NGOs wanted to work with the government.

Meanwhile, repatriation took place on a limited scale. In 1987, official representatives of the Guatemalan government visited the refugee settlements in Mexico in order to promote repatriation, but the majority of the refugees rejected the idea. Rather, the invitation to repatriate under the official programme sparked off a process of organization which resulted in the election of the 'Permanent Commission' (CCPP), the standing committee of the Guatemalan refugees in southern Mexico, who voiced a politically informed, nationalist project for return to Guatemala.

The CCPP was given the mandate to undertake negotiations with the Guatemalan government in order to establish conditions for an 'organized and collective return'. Their demands included guarantees of getting access to land, guarantees of their security, recognition of their rights to return collectively (i.e. in large groups), to settle, organize and move freely, as well as the right to international accompaniment in the process of return. The registration of refugees' land possessions in Guatemala and the promises to recover their land or receive compensation were the main reasons for the widespread support of the CCPP (Stepputat 1992).

From 1989, the CCPP, together with other civil sectors, participated in the 'National Dialogue' within the framework of the Esquipulas II agreements, and from 1990 direct relations were established between the Guatemalan government (CEAR) and CCPP. A 'Mediating Instance' was established with UNHCR, the Catholic Church, the Guatemalan Human Rights Committee (residing in exile) and the Human Rights Ombudsman, and a donor sponsored 'technical team' in Mexico City supported the work of the Permanent Commission. UNHCR facilitated and accompanied the visits of the refugee representatives in Guatemala. In the beginning their relations with CEAR representatives were hostile, but after some time 'we became like good friends', as one of the refugee representatives put it.

In 1991, negotiations accelerated. The Mediating Instance developed into an international support group, GRICAR, the International Group for Consultancy and Support to the Return comprising the embassies of Mexico, Sweden, Canada and France, a representative of the International Committee of Voluntary Agencies, ICVA, and later a member of the World Council of Churches. The government and UNHCR signed a pathbreaking Letter of Understanding relative to the 'voluntary repatriation' of the Guatemalan refugees, which among other points granted the right of the refugees to return to their land and to deny participation in the Civil Patrols. Moreover the Guatemalan government recognized the role of NGOs in the return process and promised to facilitate their activities. The letter of understanding prepared the ground for the final agreement between CCPP and the government, which was signed in October 1992. This agreement entailed an elaborate framework for mediation, supervision and verification, and defined obligations and rights of the parties (see box).

In the peace negotiations between the government and the guerrilla movement URNG, one of the first accords to be signed (in 1994) was the accord on uprooted people, for which the October 1992 accord served as a model, now extended to other groups of displaced people, such as the dispersed refugees in Chiapas and the IDPs in Guatemala. The Guatemalan government announced the end of programmes of support for return and repatriation in 1998, allowing for the last refuges to return with support in 1999.

Content of the October 8th Accords negotiated between Guatemalan refugees and the Guatemala government in 1992

Many of the specific guarantees mentioned in the October 8th Accords are constitutional rights, regardless of the problems in enforcing them.* Nevertheless, the visibility of the agreement and the fact that the refugees had to pressure the government to guarantee what was already theirs by right, helped create a context for international monitoring of government compliance. On the other hand, new and specific advantages were offered for returning refugees under the Accords:

Explicit mention that all rights and benefits in the Accords apply equally to men and women returnees.

The Guatemalan authorities would recognise all formal and informal education and training for the purposes of continued studies and employment.

A three-year exemption from military service for all returnees legally subject to being drafted (argued on economic grounds due to the duress of reintegration activities).

National and international organisations could provide 'accompaniment' and be present during the return and reintegration phases.

Specific efforts would be made by the government to help refugees recover land to which they had claim in the event that these were occupied by others.

New land would be purchased for land-less families through a "credit" that would be repaid by the community into its own development fund.

A mediation mechanism (via the Mediation Group described above) would continue to function given potential disputes related to the Accords implementation. A three-member national/international Verification Group was created with the powers to assess compliance by the signatory parties.

* The rights to organise, free expression and freedom of movement are explicitly mentioned in the October 8th Accords as are the rights to life and property. Specific mention is made of the right to not participate in civilian militias, as guaranteed in the Guatemalan Constitution.

(Worby 1999: 3)

The institutional set-up(s)

The institutional framework for the return involved a range of governmental and non-governmental, national and international institutions, as well as organizations representing the refugees and repatriates.

International institutions

Among the international organizations, UNDP had a longstanding presence in Guatemala and was the UN lead agency in the country, but apart from one programme (PRODERE) UNDP did not have any field presence beyond the capital, where planning, policy-making, and coaching of government institutions were undertaken. UNHCR, responsible for coordinating repatriation operations and monitoring the conditions of returning populations, emphasized its presence in the areas of return through field offices. Until the peace accords in 1996 and the establishment of the Technical Commission for the Resettlement of Populations Displaced by the Armed Conflict, CTEAR, coordination between UNHCR and UNDP was limited;[5] but in CTEAR, UNDP, together with the EU and seconded by UNHCR, became the international representative on the Committee where representatives of the government and the displaced had seats.

UNHCR worked closely together with WFP and the Habitat programme, and when the peace accord on human rights in 1994 gave a mandate for the presence of a human rights verification mission, MINUGUA, this entity and UNHCR became close operational partners because of their presence in the conflict areas and related interests in protection and human rights. During the initial phase, MINUGUA drew upon the extensive UNHCR experience in the conflict areas, and many of the (c. 300) international employees of MINUGUA had past experience from UNHCR missions in Mexico and Central America.

National government institutions

In the government, CEAR was the immediate counterpart of UNHCR, and formally responsible for repatriation operations. UNHCR supported operating costs but not salaries, and the relationship was often strained because of CEAR's limited operational and strategic capacity and its dependence on the army. CEAR was mainly occupied with logistics related to relief items and until 1994 for the provision of documents which was later contracted by UNHCR to (Church-related) NGOs.

Of other government institutions, FONAPAZ, the National Peace Fund, was responsible from 1991 for support to 'the population most affected by the armed confrontation', and in particular for the reinsertion of the uprooted population in the former conflict areas ('the Peace Zone'). FONAPAZ channelled national and international funds into projects and programmes, which were carried out by NGOs, local authorities or other government institutions. It is worth noting that FONAPAZ reported directly to the President. For many donors, FONAPAZ represented a comparatively flexible and fast channel of funds whereby they could bypass the line ministries, renowned for bureaucratic complexities.

In 1992, FONAPAZ, in collaboration with CEAR and the International Organization for Migration, IOM, created a special 'fund for the productive insertion of repatriates and returnees', FORELAP, as well as a land fund, FONATIERRA. The function of FONATIERRA was to provide credits for land purchase while FORELAP funded productive projects. For groups of fewer than 50 households credits were to be reimbursed in cash, whereas larger groups reimbursed credits to a communal fund for the social and productive development of the community in question. The institution drew upon a land fund which in 1992 received US$30 million from Taiwan. Other donors were reluctant to finance land purchases because it soon became obvious that landowners inflated prices knowing that there were political pressures and time constraints on the government. Prices per beneficiary family varied from US$1,000 to 20,000 with an average of US$6,000 per family (Worby 1999: 25). Given the low productivity and marginal position of much land, it was totally unrealistic that the returnees could reimburse these funds, and for the collective returns, the rotating community funds did not function well, among other factors because of lack of technical support.

Other institutions and organizations

Upon the return of the repatriates, UNHCR left operational responsibilities to NGOs, community organizations and the government, and concentrated on monitoring, some coordination, and troubleshooting related to conflicts within returnee communities or between these and neighbours, government institutions or others. UNHCR facilitated and participated actively in conflict resolution, but usually only by incorporating the Human Rights Ombudsman, the Church, Minugua and others in negotiations.

In support of the reinsertion of repatriates and returnees, UNHCR created a fund for the so-called QIPs, Quick Impact Projects. Given previous experience from Nicaragua and the cumbersome UN procedures, it was decided to leave the administration of the fund to the Canadian development NGO, CECI. In total some US$10 million were invested in QIPs which presumably benefited returnees and their neighbouring communities equally (more than 250,000 beneficiaries officially), although this was not always the impression of the neighbours who saw the returnees as receiving preferential treatment. CECI worked with national or local NGOs that flourished during the peace-process aid boom in the mid-1990s, or directly with community organizations.

In addition to the organizational set-up related to the UN system, a number of bilateral (e.g. Norway, Sweden and Spain) and multilateral donors (mainly the EU) funded reconstruction and reintegration projects for the returning refugees and the former conflict areas. These projects were often solicited, defined and monitored by European or North American NGOs and implemented by Guatemalan NGOs. Also labour unions funded projects, and solidarity organizations of volunteers from 16 countries accompanied the process of return and reinsertion from 1993 onwards with the idea of fending off aggressions from the army, civil patrols or others through their physical presence in the return sites. Although the seriousness of the *'solidarios'* and the experience of the accompaniment varied somewhat, the overall impression of the value of the system was positive (Worby 1999).

While the UN system had its own channels of communication and coordination, other inter-institutional fora were established in support of the return process. The NGO sector formed the 'Coordination of NGOs and Cooperatives for the accompaniment of the population affected by the internal armed conflict', which on the other hand formed part of the 'Forum for accompaniment' together with the Catholic Church, a group of Protestant churches and the sector of 'popular (social) movements'. These actors were usually in opposition to the Government and many were also very sceptical of the UNHCR, considered as being closer to governments than to the refugees and their organizations. At the beginning of the process, very few national NGOs were prepared to coordinate with Government institutions and they even sought to bypass local administrations as much as possible.

This highly complex organization and high level of mobilization was at its highest at the time of the negotiations and preparations for the first 'organized and collective return' of some 2,500 refugees, which took place in January 1993. Given the tense situation in Guatemala, the international community gave ample attention to the return process. Peace negotiations had not gained momentum yet, and sectors in Guatemala were very hostile to the return of the refugees. Hence, every step in the return process was an occasion for political demonstrations and positioning between the government on one side, and the refugees and their national and international backing on the other. After the self-coup of President Serrano, who dismissed the Parliament in 1993 before he himself was expelled from the country, the process stopped for a while, but from 1994–5 returns became increasingly routinized. Donor attention continued until the end of the 1990s, but after the peace accords in 1996 the returnees were no longer a predominant focus of attention as they were in the beginning, when they were seen as the spearheads of the peace process and an occasion for international engagement.

The refugee organizations

Until the 1992 agreement, return to Guatemala was not considered a politically correct or recommendable solution by the majority. Among the small family-based groups who enlisted themselves for repatriation, affiliates of different Evangelical churches were overrepresented, a fact which can be related to the political signification of different churches in the conflict areas (Stepputat 1992). Here, the Catholic Church had been associated with the organizational work which preceded the armed insurrection, while Evangelical groups that proliferated in the conflict areas after counterinsurgency were associated with the army.

The conditions of repatriation, in particular the forced participation in the Civil Patrols and the political and military control of the villages, induced the idea of returning in large groups, not necessarily to the 'place of origin',[6] where the returnees would have to confront neighbours who had made other choices during the conflict, but to segregated return settlements. The return of Salvadoran refugees from Honduras to the settlements of 'Segundo Montes' in the former FMLN controlled area of Morazán (MacDonald and Gatehouse 1993) served as a model for the CCPP; but in El Salvador there were no prior accords between the refugees and the government.

When the Permanent Commissions were formed and they propagated the proposal for a negotiated, organized and collective return, it generated some opposition in the more than 100 refugee settlements spread out across three provinces. Many refugees were reluctant to be associated with anything 'organized' because 'organization' during the counterinsurgency became synonymous with the guerrilla organizations during the violence. With regard to the 'collective' aspect of the return, some settlements had experimented with collective forms of production and organization during the first years of exile, an experiment which was rejected by many refugees, in particular the ones who had no prior experience of cooperative enterprises. Still, however, a majority held that 'organization' was the way forward, the means *per se* of development.

After the accord, CCPP was in charge of the process of forming return groups around different possible return sites. These 'return blocks' undertook negotiations directly with representatives of the Guatemalan government (CEAR and FORELAP) regarding the purchase of land, visited possible sites and had technical reports produced. The different return groups were accompanied in these efforts by one or more NGOs, often in direct competition with each other for the contracts for reintegration assistance. The NGOs needed the support of the return groups in question in order to have their project proposals approved by the donors, and the refugees were not unaware of their power to make decisions and choose among different proposals. Unfortunately some of the NGOs had little experience in the field and had somewhat unrealistic and idealist expectations regarding the capacity of the returnees and their willingness to share and collaborate with each other after the first phase of reinsertion. One NGO sought to develop a brick factory where the returnees would produce their own building materials, but it never really worked, and the returnees preferred 'formal bricks' anyway. Also many returnees gave priority to individual livelihood strategies rather than to the collective or cooperative enterprises suggested by the NGOs.

The whole issue of return and repatriation achieved a political dynamic of its own as different political interests were played out around the decision to return and the way in which return would be orchestrated. As mentioned, the first repatriation agreement and modus generated the oppositional movement for the CCPP return. However, in response to the stipulations of the 1992 accord which favoured collective returns of groups of more than 50 families, CEAR and FORELAP developed a third mode of repatriation, 'the organized, individual repatriation' (ROI) which seems to suggest a third way between individual repatriation and collective returns, a proposal that had significant political undertones. Several groups which splintered from CCPP over different disagreements took advantage of the ROI proposal which, unlike the CCPP schemes, entailed a more active presence of government institutions in the return settlements.

Political disagreements and competition over the control of resources generated several conflicts and splits among the refugees. The CCPP split into three geographically defined subgroupings (*vertientes*) which more or less corresponded to the constituent organizations of the guerrilla organization, URNG. To complete the picture, alternative organizations were set up in the hope of attracting support for organizations of different political and practical orientations, such as CODAIC, the Coordinator for Integrated Communitarian Development. CODAIC was formed in 1994 in Chiapas by mainly Pop'ti speaking refugees who represented themselves as a non-political alternative to the CCPP, with the purpose of uniting rather than dividing the refugees in their efforts to find support for a 'technologically sound and culturally based development' in Guatemala.[7] But the group never found substantial backing from the UNHCR or economic support for their project. At this point the field had become saturated.

Choices and options

Until 1996, repatriation was officially the only durable solution open for rural Guatemalan refugees in Mexico. Resettlement programmes existed on a limited scale (for Canada) but rural refugees were not eligible for these resettlements. Local integration was not considered an option by the Mexican government, which extended temporary visas to the refugees in the settlements, to be renewed every 6 or 12 months. The government actively discouraged local integration by restricting mobility and employment of the refugees and prohibiting ownership to land. Legally, the refugees could only engage in agricultural labour schemes in the provinces of settlement, officially mediated by the Mexican Refugee Commission, COMAR. Children born in Mexico were on the other hand eligible for Mexican citizenship.

The expectation that the presence of refugees in Mexico would be of a temporary nature was shared between the GoM and the refugee organizations. COMAR supported the training of Guatemalan education (and health) promoters and the development of a special curriculum for the Guatemalan children so as to reproduce the 'Guatemalan culture'. Likewise, the refugee leadership discouraged attempts at integrating in Mexican society, which was regarded as an unpatriotic and selfish thing to do. The young men who left for wage labour in the cities or tourist hubs were regarded as being in danger of moral corruption. In the 1980s, COMAR, UNHCR and the leadership sought to develop a locally based plan for achieving self-sufficiency in which access to land (in Quintana Roo and Campeche) and to labour-intensive projects for public benefit in Chiapas played a major role.

In practical terms, however, the refugees were increasingly being integrated, socially and economically as well as culturally, and in 1996, when the return process was up and running, the Mexican government encouraged programmes actively promoting the integration and naturalization of the refugees. As of 2001, some 23,000 refugees remained in Mexico (half of them born in exile), of whom 9,000 had become naturalized, while the rest had permanent residency (FM2) or were in the process of becoming naturalized (USCR 2004). Apart from these, however, a large number of Guatemalans – migrants or non-recognized refugees – reside in southern Mexico without due documents and with their access to social services severely limited.

As mentioned, the option of repatriation developed considerably over the years. Before 1992, access to land was highly conditional upon local conditions and power relations – much of the refugees' land had been reoccupied or resold to internally displaced families or others, applying a law according to which the occupants of communal, national or cooperative land lost their right after one year of absence. The 1992 accords stipulated a series of steps for the refugees' recovery of their land, be it communal, national, cooperative or private. Basically the accord stated their right to return, and the duty of the authorities to help make the land available, by resettling the occupants or by helping the refugees get land elsewhere.

Considering the practical problems of recuperating occupied land, the returnees typically opted for return to one of the segregated return settlements where they received land on soft credits (to be reimbursed through labour in communal projects), while those who had land before flight pursued recovery through negotiation upon return. These negotiations have been a very long process in which they have had little support from the authorities. I have no data on the number of refugees who owned land before flight, and how many of these have been able to recover the land.

When choosing between the different options, the refugees considered a number of variables, such as:

Access to land: Given the limited access to own land in Mexico, and in particular in troubled Chiapas, the return to their land was an obsession for the older generation of refugees in Mexico: 'Here we always have to change our attitude [because of the unstable conditions]. To live on one's own land is different.' 'Outside your home, a long way from your country, one has no rights. In Guatemala, wherever you go, no one can say that you're a stranger.' 'We are floating in the air, we have no land. We have to think about the future so the children will not be lost when we die. We have to position our family in our own land (tierra).'[8] In studies on the Guatemalan refugees, their attach-ment to their ancestral land and the importance of corn production for their identity have frequently been highlighted as the reasons why they fought so bravely for their return (e.g. Hanlon 1999). Many leaflets on the Guatema-lan refugees and their return represent them as culturally bound to return, 'culture' being depicted as the traditional attachment to the land. But, as the above statements indicate, the will to return had as much, or even more, to do with the question of how to provide the political conditions for their livelihood. Thus, for them, livelihood encompassed the right to move, the right to own land and to settle freely, and the security of a place to stay until you yourself decide to move: in short, mobile livelihoods with rights. Further-more, while land may be important as linking people to the ancestors, the connection with the future seemed to preoccupy the older generation as well: 'Here in Mexico life is happy, there is food, there is work, but we cannot make progress: you cannot plant even the smallest tree because here we are *posados* [lodged on the land of others].' Planting trees is not only a long-term strat-egy for diversifying livelihoods by investing in, for example, fruit and coffee production and hence for 'making progress'; it is also an important symbol of land ownership as opposed to the conditions on the private estates, where tenants were not allowed to 'plant things with roots'. This was, however, an imagination that was specific to the older generation. The younger genera-tion was in general not keen to pursue agriculture as their main activity.

Access to communal resources, such as water and firewood, which, as they expe-rienced in Mexico, could be very expensive.

The quality and location of land, a question often linked to where the land was located in high ('cold') or low ('hot') lands. While the men were more inter-ested in the productivity of the land, regarded as higher in the lowlands, the women were often concerned about the health conditions in the lowlands.

Social networks: Refugees considered whether to return to the municipali-ties of their lineages in the highland, or to return together with people they had come to know in the cooperatives or in exile.

Security was probably the most important single variable considered, where violent incidents or tense political situations stopped the process of return. The 'going back together' option was on one side seen as a way of creating more secure conditions of return, but on the other hand, the association be-tween 'organization' and the guerrilla movement also represented a threat to the refugees.

'Development', that is the access to 'projects' of support to communal ser-vices and productive support, which tended to put the CCPP returns in a more favourable light as they had the best connections.

Speed, timing and organization: These considerations tended to turn people against the CCPP returns because of the cumbersome process of forming and maintaining the groups and negotiating for the land, a process which took several years in many cases. The problems associated with the 'collective organization' were also mentioned since this, although viewed positively as a principle, was also associated with destructive interpersonal conflicts.

Access to markets and wage labour: This variable tended to be regarded as being much more favourable in Mexico than in Guatemala, and most young people who had become highly mobile and well integrated into the labour market would opt for staying and integrating.

As it was, a total of 43,600 refugees opted for returning to Guatemala (about two-thirds of the recognized refugees and their offspring). Of these, 12,400 repatriated 'individually', and 31,200 returned 'organized' to a total of 50 settlements in rural Guatemala.

Return, reintegration and mobile livelihoods

Without going into details of the reintegration of returning refugees and the relief–development linkages, I think it is important to raise some questions about the common perceptions of successful return and sustainable reintegration. These hold that the sign of sustainable reintegration is that returning families stay in the place to which they have returned and develop their livelihoods in this place. Rather, considering that the areas of return are often characterized by being marginal in terms of potential for productive development, I would suggest that the engagement of returnees in systems of national or transnational migration could be seen as a form of sustainable reintegration and adaptation to local conditions. The following serve as an example of the dynamics of reintegration in the case of Guatemala.

When, in 1994, 200 returnee families took over the former cattle ranch of Chaculá, close to the Mexican border, they discussed what name to give

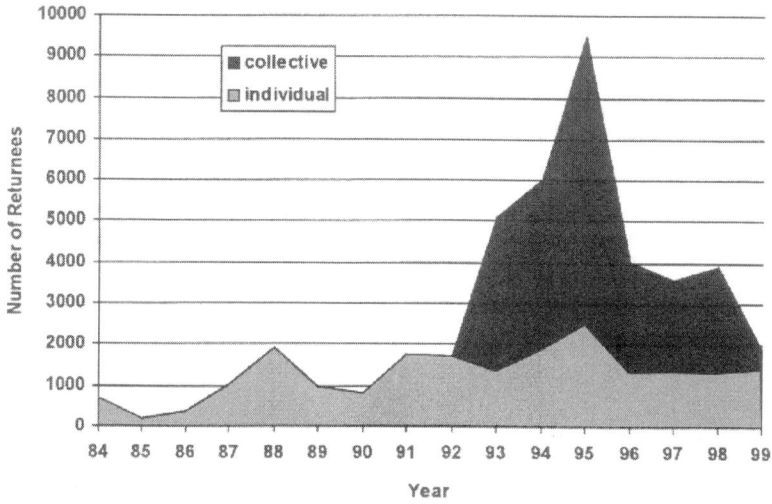

Figure 6.1   Proportion of collective vs. individual returnees to Guatemala by year (until June 1999). Source: Worby (1999: 10).

their new home. Colonia Nueva Esperanza was agreed upon, since it symbolized the utopian enterprise of the collective return. The Mexican word for an urban neighbourhood, *colonia*, signalled the inclusive, multi-ethnic, urban character of the new settlement, and distinguished it from the mono-ethnic and rural 'village' community or *aldea* in the surrounding area. The vision was to found a 'peasant settlement' with an urban layout, but with more space between the houses, for intensive agricultural use. Production-wise, the idea was to construct an industrialized 'peasant enterprise' for the cooperative exploitation of the land, the cattle and the forest. At the local level, the settlement was supposed to be a model of alternative modernity, with an autonomous governing body, new forms of production and organization, promotion of human rights in a militarized area, and initiatives for regional organization for improvements at the level of infrastructure and services. A secondary (board) school, the first one outside the municipal capital, was planned, and leaders envisioned the founding of a 'peasant university' in the settlement.

The intricate organization of the cooperative and the settlement, the centralized control of the common property, the generous (but short-lived) international funding and the technical support were intended to enable the returnees to make a living without having to engage in labour migration. Migration was considered by the leadership, their advisors and the aid agencies to be inimical to the welfare of the population. While resonating with the older generation's 'peasant utopia', which developed in reaction to a century of enforced migrant labour on the lowland plantations, the younger generation had different ambitions and connections. In particular the young men were keen to explore possibilities in Mexico and the US.

Several years later, the common name of the settlement was still Chaculá, and the 'new hope' had faded considerably. The cooperative enterprise was in deep trouble, not least because many members actively resisted the cooperative. After two years, 20 per cent of the households had left the settlement for good, most of them returning to their former villages in nearby municipalities. Their places were taken by the next generation of adolescent men who otherwise had no independent access to land and rights as members of the cooperative. Unpaid labour obligations had been reduced, and high degrees of absenteeism were forcing many aid projects – construction works, reforestation, shops, herding etc. – to hire on the basis of salaries. The 'private' land that had been granted by the cooperative to individual households had grudgingly been extended from 0.4 to 2.8 hectares. This reduced the possibilities for large-scale collective enterprises, but individual households were eagerly pursuing individual corn and coffee production. Those who were able to recover their access to communal land in their former village community shared their labour between Chaculá and these villages. As relief provisions dwindled and coffee prices soared, many men returned to Mexico for temporary work, and by 2000, close to one-third of the adult males had left for labour in the US (Ackerman 2002).

Thus, while the returnees had hoped to establish a diversified production with industrialization of agricultural products and forestry as an example of development for the area, they ended up being in a somewhat similar situation to their neighbours who always had been engaged in seasonal migration and impoverished subsistence farming. Adopting 'local' livelihood strategies, the returnees became in a sense well integrated into the regional economy, although their experience, contacts and better education from abroad gave them some advantages in migration compared with their neighbours who had not been in exile.

It should be mentioned, however, that for many of the members of the Chaculá return group the location close to the border between Mexico and Guatemala was an important reason for opting for this site. Apart from the access to land for corn production, the proximity of the border, which was seen as the single most valuable asset in the area, was expected to allow them to engage in trade and other cross-border activities. And so it happened.

Refugee return and state- and peace-building

Although the return settlements in most cases did not become flourishing and innovative centres of new forms of production, they nevertheless can be interpreted as having had an effect in terms of the reconstruction of the state after the armed conflict. As has been mentioned, the return and reintegration of refugees has a legitimizing effect on the state, at least from the point of view of the international community, and the very event of resettlement after uprooting may be seen as an important symbolic marker of the transition from conflict to peace in generally sedentary societies (Stepputat 1999b; Helton 2002; Petrin 2002).

Regarding the local level, I have previously suggested that the return and reinsertion of refugees may have the effect of helping the civil state territorialize at the margins of its range of influence (Stepputat 1999). In the case at hand, the army was the first representative of the state to have a more or less permanent presence in the villages of marginal municipalities. In this area of anticipated return, the establishment of a field office of UNHCR in 1992 constituted an umbrella for other national and international organizations, in particular NGOs, which otherwise feared repression from the army. With the event of the return, many relief, development and human rights institutions arrived in the area because of the funding and because the former conflict area had been 'opened up' to civil actors, thus providing an alternative for the village population in search of assistance.

But the returnees themselves also contributed to state reconstruction by constituting a relatively well informed 'civil society'. Paradoxically as it were, the preoccupation with state-building of many donors has found a focus in the will to construct a civil society that can produce checks and balances *vis-à-vis* the state and in this way, through demands on the state, contribute to its reinforcement. Thanks to their experience from exile, the refugees were very well versed in the linguistic repertoires of state (and international) representatives, and they were inclined to solve problems by directing themselves to authorities and pleading their rights or otherwise making appeals to government institutions or NGOs (ibid.). In this sense, the return settlement became more a bridgehead of the civil state than of the leftist revolutionary movement as expected.

At a more general level it has been argued that the return process, and in particular the negotiations that preceded it, were helping bringing about the final peace accord. When the peace accord was signed in 1996, almost 80 per cent of the refugees that wanted to return had returned. Worby suggests that while the incipient peace negotiations provided a fertile context for the negotiations of return, the latter represented a blueprint for the way in which the partial accords could be formulated through mixed commissions with government, civil society and international participation (Worby 1999). Also the widely publicized return of the first large group brought an alternative vision and memory of the armed conflict to the fore in Guatemalan society where this version had been effectively silenced for a decade.

Conclusion

To what extent is the Guatemalan experience of return and repatriation relevant for the Palestinian case? Without being an expert on the Palestinian refugee situation, I would suggest 1) that the contexts are too different to make strong parallels and 2) that many of the 'lessons learned' in Guatemala coincide with what has been incorporated in the general body of knowledge in the international organizations during the last couple of years: the need for coordination between relief and development agencies, the need for transitional categories of funding between relief and development budget lines, the benefits of regionally based solutions in regional conflict complexes, the need to broaden the group of beneficiaries to include the neighbours of the repatriates, the use of a group of international agencies and interested governments as bystanders and mediators in the process of repatriation, the need to avoid building parallel systems of service and administration etc.

Nevertheless, a few points of comparison deserve mention. The case of Guatemala is often described as a unique example of a negotiated return agreement where the refugees themselves were protagonists, engaging in long-lasting negotiations as well as fierce confrontations with national and international institutions. But the refugees could count on ample political and economic backing from the international community for a number of reasons: the refugees were identified with cultural (Mayan) markers in a period when the question of indigenous people had reached the international agenda; and they demonstrated well developed skills for organization and for engaging international representatives at a moment when Guatemala was the only remaining – but also the most enduring and complicated – conflict in Central America.

These features elicited comparatively generous support from donors and agencies, which has to be included in the final assessment of the experience. In addition to the US$30 million Taiwanese support for the land fund, UNHCR alone spent US$50 million on the return and reinsertion of the refugees (Worby 1999), which means that the expenditure per returnee was at least US$2,000. Compared with African repatriation operations, the return of Guatemalan refugees was a very costly affair. Being a popular target of international aid can, however, also be a mixed blessing for the refugees at the receiving end, who may experience a 'burden of solidarity' when numerous donors, NGOs and international agencies rush to help in the hot spots of international media attention. In some of the early return settlements the number of construction works, projects and visits within a short time span were extremely taxing and surpassed the capacity of the returnees to live up to all the diverse expectations of peace-, community- and state-building at the same time as they had to establish their individual livelihoods. Only the experienced refugee leaders were aware that the support would be a very short-lived phenomenon. Although these potential burdens of solidarity may be difficult to avoid in a highly media-exposed conflict like the Israel–Palestine conflict, donors should give priority to long-term commitments.

Another point of comparison between the Guatemalan and the Palestinian cases is the importance of an 'imagined return community' (Stepputat 1994; Bowker 2003), an abstract, nationalist community which is formed around a set of 'quasi-sacred foundations' (Bowker 2003: 226), that is a mythology of loss and exodus and the struggle for return to the places of origin. As Bisharat has mentioned in the case of the Palestinian refugees, the imagination of the places of origin becomes more and more abstract and associated with ideas of homelands and symbolic sites of utopian imaginations of the good life (Bisharat 1997). In the Guatemalan case, most of the refugees connected to the Permanent Commissions opted, for a host of reasons, for return to newly purchased farms for cooperative agricultural schemes. This kind of return movement can be very efficient for the mobilization, struggle and preparations for return as well as during the 'emergency phase' upon arrival. However, expectations of the new life 'back home' were highly unrealistic – both among the returnees themselves and among many of the accompanying organizations – and the process of reintegration was a shock to most of the returnees, who had a tough time adapting to conditions in marginal areas of rural Guatemala. In many cases, the tight, centralized organization of future peasant enterprises was slow in producing viable livelihoods, and was challenged and gradually undermined by the individual tactics of the families engaged in the daily struggle to reestablish livelihoods.

One effect was the lack of sustainability of the high level of organization that was achieved in exile, where such activities were in part subsidized through different forms of support. The problem of sustainability was particularly marked in the field of gender relations since it seems that, although women groups were very popular, active and powerful in exile (e.g.

Mama Maquín), they tended to disintegrate upon return, when the women experienced pressure from their families and from the tough conditions of survival to concentrate on reproductive and productive tasks in and around the household (Ackerman 2002). Another effect was the (re-)engagement in US- and Mexico-bound labour migration which, on the other hand, may be seen as an adaptation to conditions in rural Guatemala, where labour migration has become an important and generalized element of rural and urban livelihood strategies.

Thus, while the process of collective return was politically successful, it was less successful in terms of the productive reintegration of the returnees, at least if we are to judge from the expectations of returnees and agencies. The point is not that the refugee and return organizations should not be crucially involved in the process, but rather that the grandiose and spectacular mass return or repatriation operations may not be the optimal way of organizing return and reintegration. This modality was chosen for reasons of security and a politics of changing public perceptions of the conflict history in a war-torn society. But for more practical, organizational and livelihood-related purposes, return operations should incorporate common ways in which households and extended families usually establish new sites of (mobile) livelihoods: these tend to be much more gradual, flexible, processual and iterative, and hence adapted to the actual and changing conditions for developing livelihoods across areas of exile and return. As Rex Brynen (2004) argues, there are no logistical reasons for organizing repatriation to the Palestine territories as one or more grand moves. However, if a return to the 1948 areas ever happens, it may well be difficult politically to avoid the public spectacles of return.

The last two points to bring out from the Guatemalan experience are: 1) it is important that the refugees have an actual choice of place of residence;[9] for the Guatemalan refugees, this only happened towards the end of the peace process when Mexico offered naturalization as an alternative to repatriation; and 2) support for the local administrations (the municipalities) is essential since they have to bear the largest burdens of reintegration. In the Guatemalan case, the peace process and the general trend towards decentralization of state budgets and administration coincided with the collective return of refugees, which gave a certain political dynamic that the returnees could tap into. Whereas local administrations have often been bypassed by relief and development agencies, the development of their funds and capacities are urgently needed when they are to respond to the challenges of returning refugees.

Notes

1 As James Dunkerley (1988) mentions, the mutual support group of family members to disappeared persons, GAM (Grupo de Apoyo Mutuo), was created in 1967, a decade before similar organizations appeared in the South Cone.

2 In 1981 Guatemala had a population of 8 million. Current estimates come close to 12 million inhabitants.
3 Numbers vary significantly (see for example AVANCSO 1990, COINDE 1991 and UNHCR 2000).
4 Worby (1999), who also mentions the Forum for Refugee Women (FoReFem) as a significant step in the development of gender-based approaches to permanent solutions.
5 They both participated in the CIREFCA support unit, but in practical terms UNHCR looked more towards national and local counterparts and undertook only limited publicity of its role in reintegration programs (Worby 1999: 44).
6 The place of origin for many families was a village in the poor highlands, but among the population that took refuge in Mexico, many had migrated to the tropical lowlands close to the Mexican border where they had formed cooperatives under the guidance of the church or the government.
7 Interview with a CODAIC representative in the Cocalito camp in Frontera Comalapa, Chiapas.
8 Excerpts from interviews undertaken in Chiapas in 1994.
9 As argued by Takkenberg (1998) in the Palestinian case.

References

Ackerman, Lizanne (2002) *Violence, exile and recovery. Reintegration of Guatemalan refugees in the 1990s – a biographical approach*. PhD dissertation. School of Geography and the Environment, University of Oxford.

AVANCSO (1989) *Politica exterior y estabilidad estatal*. Cuadernos de Investigación, 5 (Guatemala: AVANCSO).

AVANCSO (1990) *Assistance and control. Policies towards internally displaced populations in Guatemala* (Washington, DC: Hemispheric Migration Project, Georgetown University).

Bisharat, George E. (1997) "Exile to compatriot: Transformations in the social identity of Palestinian refugees in the West Bank", in Akhil Gupta and James Ferguson (eds.), *Culture, power, place. Explorations in critical anthropology* (Durham, NC: Duke University Press).

Bowker, Robert (2003) *Palestinian refugees. Mythology, identity, and the search for peace* (Boulder, CO: Lynne Rienner Publishers).

Consejo de Instituciones de Desarollo (COINDE) (1991) *Diagnostico sobre refugiados, retornados y desplazados de Guatemala* (Guatemala: Mimeo).

Dunkerley, James (1988) *Power in the Isthmus. A political history of modern Central America* (London: Verso).

Hanlon, C. Nolin (1999) "Guatemalan refugees and returnees: place and Maya identity", in L. L. North and A. B. Simmons (eds.), *Journeys of fear: Refugee return and national transformation in Guatemala* (Montreal: McGill-Queen's University).

Helton, Arthur C. (2002) *The price of indifference: Refugees and humanitarian action in the new century* (Oxford: Oxford University Press).

Le Bot, Yvon (1995 [1992]) *La guerra en tierras mayas. Cominidad, violencia y modernidad en Guatemala (1970–1992)* (Mexico: Fondo de Cultura Económica).

MacDonald, Mandy, and Gatehouse, Mike (1993) *In the mountains of Morazan* (London: Latin American Bureau).

McCreery, David (1994) *Rural Guatemala 1760–1940* (Stanford: Stanford University Press).

Petrin, Sarah (2002) "Refugee return and state reconstruction: A comparative analysis", in *New Issues in Refugee Research. Working Paper* 66 (Geneva: UNHCR).

Salvadó, L. R. (1988) *The other refugees: A study of nonrecognized Guatemalan refugees in Chiapas, Mexico* (Washington, DC: CIPRA, Georgetown University).

Schirmer, Jennifer (1996) "The looting of democratic discourse by the Guatemalan military: Implications for human rights", in E. Jelin and E. Hershberg (eds.), *Constructing democracy. Human rights, citizenship, and society in Latin America* (Boulder, CO: Westview Press).

Smith, Carol A. (ed.) (1990) *Guatemalan indians and the state, 1540–1988* (Austin: University of Texas Press).

Stepputat, Finn (1989) "Self-sufficiency and exile in Mexico", *Discussion Paper* 9 (Geneva: UNRISD).

Stepputat, Finn (1992) *Beyond relief? Life in a Guatemalan refugee settlement in Mexico*. PhD dissertation. University of Copenhagen.

Stepputat, Finn (1994) "Repatriation and the politics of space: The case of the Mayan diaspora and return movement", *Journal of Refugee Studies* 7 (2–3), 175–85.

Stepputat, Finn (1999a) "Politics of displacement in Guatemala", *Journal of Historical Sociology* 12 (1), 54–80.

Stepputat, Finn (1999b) "Repatriation and everyday forms of state formation in Guatemala", in R. Black and K. Khoser (eds.), *The end of the refugee circle? Repatriation and reconstruction* (Oxford: Berghahn Books).

Takkenberg, Lex (1998) *The status of Palestinian refugees in international law* (Oxford: Clarendon Press).

UNHCR (2000) *The state of the world's refugees: Fifty years of humanitarian action* (Oxford: Oxford University Press).

USCR (2004) Country report: Mexico. Accessed online at http://www.refugees.org/world/countryrpt/amer_carib/mexico.htm on 22 May 2004.

Worby, Paula (1999) *Lessons learned from UNHCR's involvement in the Guatemala refugee repatriation and reintegration programme (1987–1999)* (Geneva: UNHCR).

Zinser, Adolfo Aguilar (1992) *The International Conference on Central American Refugees: Promises, realities and perspectives* (Washington, DC: Hemispheric Migration Project, Georgetown University).

7 What does "adequate assistance" mean in the context of promoting viable return and appropriate compensation?

Lessons from the Horn of Africa

Laura Hammond

In the Horn of Africa, as in many other regions, the promotion of solutions for protracted refugee situations has been hampered by poor planning and a lack of understanding about conditions in the areas of return. Decisions about the amount and type of assistance are often based on calculations of either the minimum level of assistance that will induce refugees to return, or the availability of resources. Seldom are they based on a realistic picture of the opportunities and constraints of post-return life. Prospects for post-return life are principally influenced by returnees' ability to become integrated into the local economy. This is the key to establishing themselves socially and politically within wider community, ethnic, regional, or national networks – and to self-sufficiency.

In this chapter I argue that in order to promote viable livelihoods in a post-repatriation/return context, program assistance must be based on solid empirical research. Specifically, it must cover issues such as: availability of employment, market dynamics, agricultural or pastoral production, and availability of essential social services. Prior to return, there is a need for socio-economic research to determine: a) What is the cost of living in the area of return? b) What will be the likely impact of mass return on the economies of host communities? c) By what criteria should self-sufficiency (or viability) be measured, and with what mechanisms (i.e. attainment of a certain income, employment rate, level of satisfaction, etc.)?

Too often assistance packages to promote return are based on generic approaches that are defined more by organizational mandates and fiscal schedules of aid agencies (for instance, integration and/or self reliance is expected to be achieved within one calendar year following return) than by an appreciation of the local economic and social realities in the area of return/settlement.[1]

Based on research conducted in Ethiopia with refugees repatriating from Sudan (1993–present) and participants in a massive government-sponsored resettlement programme (2003–present), and in Somalia (1998) with returnees from Ethiopia, I argue that assistance packages for returnees and settlers have not been designed to reflect local conditions in areas of return/settlement. Such information is essential to determine the type and duration of assistance provided, and to mitigate the potential for conflict between returnees/settlers and hosts. Ultimately, most social integration is carried out by returnees themselves, through their own ingenuity. However, appropriately planned assistance can facilitate this process, rather than derail it.

It might seem that lessons learned from repatriation and resettlement in the Horn of Africa have few parallels with the Palestinian context. Indeed, the economic condition of Palestinian refugees, as desperate as it is, is much different from that of refugees in the Horn of Africa where starvation is a constant threat and basic survival even in the absence of war is a major preoccupation. However, I propose that the methods used to determine what is meant by successful reintegration in the Horn are in fact transferable to Palestine.

Using household food economy analysis and anthropological research methods, my work examines seasonal fluctuations in income (which in the Palestinian context might also be correlated to changing security conditions and their impact on employment opportunities), economic decision-making at the household level, strategies for risk minimization and resource maximization, renegotiation of kinship networks, and improvization of relationships between individuals, families, communities, and political organizations. Many of the lessons learned from repatriation planning in the Horn of Africa may be applicable to thinking about refugee repatriation and compensation in the Palestinian Territories.

The dream and the reality of return

The goal of repatriation assistance is generally considered by those who provide it as being the integration of returnees. This seems a straightforward enough concept. In a perfect repatriation model, refugees expressing a desire to return to their country of origin sign a voluntary repatriation form, are assisted to return to their "home" country, receive a minimum level of individual and community-based assistance to help facilitate their integration process, and then, within one year, they are integrated to the point that they no longer require external assistance. This kind of thinking guided UNHCR's Decade of Repatriation during the 1990s and continues to be the dominant paradigm in repatriation planning.

Analysts of repatriation have been – throughout that past decade – pointing out the reasons that this line of thinking is inadequate and unrealistic. Assistance tends to be based on virtually arbitrary estimates of what constitutes self-sufficiency and conflicting definitions of what constitutes integration. The costs (both economic and social) of returning are often not fully recognized, which leads to the erroneous assumption that people can emerge from dependency on external assistance, and can build economically and socially viable livelihoods within a single year after return. Integration assistance has in many cases been suspended after only one year, with disastrous consequences.

Despite the preference for cookie-cutter-like approaches that seek to provide a single model for facilitating return for all groups in all contexts, and the pursuit of "integration" as the goal of repatriation assistance, there is remarkable ambiguity about how exactly integration should be defined. In this chapter, I suggest five different definitions for integration, all of which are operational (some are applied at the same time in the same place), but none of which necessarily takes into account the real criteria (that is, as defined by returnees themselves) for success of an assisted integration program. I argue that, rather than being based on an ad hoc definition of integration, assistance packages should be formulated based on a thorough consideration of what the requirements for post-return life are. Such assistance should go beyond the basic necessities for maintaining life, and should reflect an understanding of the criteria that people use to define their own requirements for successful return and integration. Integration assistance will vary from one case or geographic area (and perhaps even one historical period) to another. Yet all variations will certainly include provision of assistance that helps people to attain economic productivity. It may also include elements that help people to consolidate and promote the fragile peace and to constitute social networks out of new and old kin, neighbor, and community relationships in ways that provide social safety nets for returnees.

UNHCR's mandate with respect to return

Some of the confusion about how repatriation assistance should be given stems from UNHCR's own mandate. The organization describes its role vis-à-vis post-return assistance in various ways. Repatriation assistance, according to UNHCR, is intended as a durable solution:

> to release [returnees] from a sense of dependency and help restore their self-respect ... provide opportunities for [them] to make a new start following the trauma that has accompanied the act of seeking refuge outside their homeland ... [and to] reduce the burden on the international community and relieve the burden on local communities when refugees who join them become economically independent and socially integrated.
>
> (UNHCR 2003: Section 1.2, p. 10)

> to help refugees overcome practical difficulties in repatriating to their home country ... assistance in the initial phase of reintegration [entails] the provision of basic needs and measures for rehabilitation
>
> (ibid.: Section 2.1, p. 39)

> to assist returnees to integrate, as rapidly as possible, into the economic

and social life of their country of origin, which will once again assume
responsibility for their protection.

(ibid.: Section 1.2, p. 10)

to ensure the durability of the voluntary repatriation. It entails a range
of measures that vary according to local circumstances and needs.

(ibid.: Section 1.3, p. 22)

These different ways of describing the enterprise of providing assistance to
returnees raise several questions: What does integration mean? How should
social and economic integration be measured? How much assistance is to be
considered "enough" to facilitate integration? Over how long a period should
assistance be maintained to ensure that integration is achieved without encouraging dependency?

Lessons from the Horn of Africa

In the Horn of Africa, where I have been working for the last 12 years, political
upheavals over the last 30 years have led to massive population movements
and returns. Analysis of repatriation assistance in several of these cases helps
to show the approaches and thinking behind assistance packages, and raises
issues important in considering repatriation in other parts of the world,
including Palestine.

The civil war that raged in Ethiopia from 1974 to 1991 (and between
Eritrea and Ethiopia from 1960 to 1991) resulted in an estimated 600,000
Ethiopian and Eritrean refugees fleeing to Sudan. Following the overthrow
of the Derg government in 1991, refugee repatriation was initiated in 1993.
From 1993 to 1995, I lived in a returnee settlement near the Ethiopian town
of Humera, close to the borders of Eritrea and Sudan. Twenty-five thousand
refugees returned to Ethiopia during that period. I have been continuing my
research with periodic visits to the settlement since then, most recently in
2002.

The repatriation experience has been used as a model for planning other
types of organized population movements in Ethiopia, including a program
of voluntary resettlement that the Government of Ethiopia has been implementing at a massive rate since early 2003. In an effort to move people from
over-populated and degraded farmland to larger, more fertile plots close to
commercial farms where they might find employment as daily labourers, the
government has embarked on an ambitious program to move as many as 2.2
million people from the central highlands to the western lowlands by 2006.
I have been studying this operation for the past year, and have found that
many of the issues that arise from not having a clear idea of what constitutes
integration are appearing once again. Morbidity and mortality rates for both
adults and children are many times the standard defining emergency condi-

tions. Rather than making significant strides towards self-sufficiency, many settlers have become even more destitute than they were before joining the resettlement campaign. It appears in fact that the resettlement programme itself is the cause of a spiraling humanitarian crisis (Hammond and Dessalegn 2003; Hammond 2003).

Yet another example from the Horn of Africa that I will refer to in this chapter involves the return of refugees from Ethiopia to Somaliland in the late 1990s. In the late 1980s and early 1990s, an estimated 500,000 refugees from Somalia fled to neighbouring Ethiopia. Establishment of a government administration in the self-declared independent territory of Somaliland (northwest Somalia) created the conditions enabling return for Somalilanders living in the camps.[2] In 1998, I spent the year working for UNDP in Somaliland, attempting to develop a strategy for UNDP and UNHCR to cooperate on repatriation and social integration.

In all of these cases, the goals and means of achieving post-return integration have been considered in similar ways. The same mistakes have been made, which have produced many negative results closely resembling one another. In addition, there is ample evidence to show that some approaches are more effective than others and might be considered useful in defining "best practices" for future repatriation and integration planning.

In these three cases, there are five different conceptual models for thinking about and measuring integration, which have all at one point or another been operative in the planning and implementation of assistance programs. These may be summarized by the following assumptions:

*   Returnees should be able to regain the same standard of living that they had *before they became refugees*.
*   Returnees should enjoy at a minimum the same level of assistance that they had *while living as refugees*.
*   Returnees should enjoy the *same standard of living as those living in return areas* who did not migrate.
*   Return should be seen as a *development opportunity*, whereby the standard of living of both returnees and local communities should be raised.

Conditions of life should be at least at the level of:

*   *international standards* (e.g. Sphere guidelines, WHO/UNICEF/WFP standards, etc.);
*   *national or regional standards* in the country of return.

I will consider each of these notions separately.

Restoration of pre-exile conditions

Recent literature on return argues against the position, still maintained by many assistance providers, that displacement amounts to an uprooting or deterritorialization of individual and collective identity. Malkki observes that botanical and "territorialising metaphors of identity – roots, soils, trees, seeds – are washed away in human floodtides, waves, flows, streams, and rivers" (Malkki 1995, 15–16, emphasis added). For the sedentarist scholar, policy-maker, or aid worker, refugees represent matter out of place, and the experience of displacement is thought to strip people of their identity, culture, and history. With such dire descriptions of the experience of displacement, it is no wonder that repatriation is thought of as the most desirable durable solution, as opposed to resettlement or local integration, both of which seek to promote refugees' construction of a new viable home outside their country of origin.

Such sedentarist thinking gives preference to the notions not only that return is the best option, but that, in keeping with what UNHCR calls a vital condition for return, it is right that, "as far as possible, returnees should be allowed to return to their place of former residence" (UNHCR 2003: Section 1.2, p. 10). In being restored to their previous homes, returnees should regain that which they lost as a result of the displacement. If restitution of lost assets is not possible, then compensation should be considered to help restore the returnees' standard of living to a level that they enjoyed prior to becoming refugees.

There are several problems with this line of thinking, particularly in cases of return after prolonged periods of exile. First, it may not be possible for people to return to the communities they left. Others may have laid claim to their land, homes, and other property, such that restoring one group's assets may disenfranchise another group, leading to further displacement or conflict. This is certainly the case for many Palestinians, whose homes have been appropriated, demolished, or made inaccessible during the years since they were displaced. Second, the quality of life in the area of origin may have changed over time so that even those who did not migrate out of the area may have experienced a decline in their standard of living. Returnees may not be willing to return if they feel that they would have to accept a poorer standard of living than they had before they left or while they were living in exile. Finally, refugees' experiences in exile may have altered their expectations of what a reasonable standard of living is. Refugees who have a nostalgic vision of what return to the area of origin will be like are often discouraged when they return to find that many of the social and community services they became accustomed to in refugee camps or exile sites are not available. For many, particularly younger adults, the difficulty of return to the area of origin is so great that they may choose to remain in, or return to, exile, or else to resettle somewhere else where the economic opportunities are greater. Again, the application of this line of thinking to the Palestinian context is clear: People who have been living in exile or as displaced persons for more than 50 years may not find return to be a practical solution for them. However, the "right to return," as I will discuss, signifies more than merely a logistical possibility – it also amounts to a recognition of the suffering that Palestinian refugees have endured over the last half decade. In such cases, compensation might be considered a more appropriate solution than restitution of the actual property that was lost.

Tigrayan refugees returning to Ethiopia from Sudan in the mid-1990s were given the option of returning to their areas of origin in the central and eastern highlands of Tigray Region, but were told that, if they did so, they would not be allocated land. Landholdings in the highlands were already too small to maintain the average household size, and while they had been living as refugees their land had been taken over by others who remained behind, including young adults who had formed their own first households in the intervening years. Conditions in the central and eastern highlands were and still are desperate – in most years between one quarter and one third of the population of Tigray is dependent upon externally provided food aid. Integration of returnees to the standard of living of people living in the area of origin, even if land had been available close to their areas of origin, would have left them vulnerable to the same famine conditions that had played such a major part in displacing them in the first place.

Instead, returnees were given land in the lowland areas of Western Tigray, close to the Ethiopia/Sudan/Eritrea borders. The crops that they would grow (sorghum and sesame) were very different from those they had grown in the highlands (where wheat, teff, and barley were the main crops). As cash crop producers and wage laborers on commercial farms, returnees were tied to international and local markets in very different ways from their relatives in the highlands. Thus, replication of highland living conditions in the lowland returnee settlements would have been impossible even if it had been desirable. Returnees had to adapt to a new environment with unfamiliar challenges and opportunities – successful integration had to be defined based on local conditions.

Similar obstacles faced returnees to urban centres of Somaliland (particularly Hargeysa, Gabiley, Dilla, and Boroma). The refugees had been displaced to Ethiopia (and to a lesser extent Kenya) during the civil war being fought between the Somali National Movement (SNM) and Somalia President Siad Barre's regime between 1988 and 1991. Repatriation was initiated with the support of UNHCR in 1997 and has continued to the present day. Most returnees to these cities could not reclaim their lost property – most had found that their houses had been destroyed by a devastating series of aerial attacks launched by government forces from the Hargeysa airport, as well as by sustained street fighting. While some returnees camped outside the rubble of their stone houses, hoping to be able to reconstruct the dwellings, others joined "returnees" and other internally displaced persons who had come from rural areas but could no longer support themselves as pastoralists. They established shanty towns on the outskirts of the cities. These settlements were dangerously crowded, had no safe water supply and no social services, and afforded very few income-generating opportunities.

In Somaliland, as in other war-torn countries, the challenge of repatriating refugees intersects with the needs of integrating or returning the internally displaced, helping demobilized soldiers and war veterans find meaningful work, and rehabilitating other vulnerable groups such as the disabled and war orphans. The challenge has become one of taking on all of these tasks at once, relaxing distinctions and definitions between the groups and helping all people to build a new, stronger post-war society. The result has been one that in many ways does not resemble pre-war, pre-exile life.

Refugees should enjoy the same standard of living that they had when they were in exile

In extremely poor societies, conditions in refugee camps once the emergency phase has passed may actually be better than conditions in the areas of origin. Tigrayans returning to Ethiopia told me repeatedly that the standard of living in the camps in Sudan was far better than it had been either prior to displacement or after return. Some lamented that they would never again have access to the kinds of services that they had had in the camps.

Critics of the position that the standard of living in camps or in exile should be maintained following return often argue that these kinds of remarks are indicative of dependency, and that refugees have in fact been "spoiled" by years of care and maintenance from UNHCR, WFP, NGOs, and the host government. They tend to overlook the fact that refugees have typically lived without recourse to legal employment, land title, or other means of self-support. Far from being spoiled, refugees do what anyone would do – they make the most of the resources that are made available to them. Refugees living in camps for several years, with access to services that they did not have in their areas of origin, become accustomed to the conditions of life in the camp, and feel entitled to, for instance, free health care, primary education for their children, and food distributions.

This sense of entitlement is often mixed with an acute awareness of the precariousness of their situation. In the face of unreliable delivery of aid resources, many people cheat the system by obtaining multiple ration cards, misrepresenting their household size, or purchasing, bartering, or bribing officials for resources. In 1998, a re-registration exercise was conducted in the Somali refugee camps in Ethiopia; UNHCR and WFP were convinced, and rightly so, that the number of refugees was much smaller than the number of rations that were being delivered to the camps. An EU official observing the registration process told me that he had heard a household head shouting in Somali at the Ethiopian government officials. When he asked a Somali-speaking colleague what was being said, he was told that the man was urging the officials to hurry up because he had taken some extra children from a nearby town and they needed to be returned early since they had to attend school the next day. I prefer to think of these activities as not different from other resource maximization strategies (rather than as cheating, or as coping mechanisms or survival strategies). People take advantage of whatever opportunities are available to them, whether they are "legal" or not. As Kibreab has shown, such abuse of the system is often a reaction to limited access and rights to resources that could provide more sustainable support and could promote self-help, such as access to farm or grazing land or access to employment.

There may be nothing wrong with returnees wanting to maintain the standard of living that they enjoyed while living in the camps – who can blame them after all? No one likes to have their income cut or their services taken away. However, maintaining such services is usually not sustainable. Returnees settle in areas that have been devastated by war, in which local governance structures and budgets are too weak to be able to meet even the most basic needs of the population, let alone a standard that the rest of their local population does not enjoy. Whereas those who are vulnerable should be assisted to help regain their potential to be economically productive, returnees should not be given special treatment in return areas just because they are returnees – to do so would be to invite conflict with local "stayee" communities.

Such preference has been seen in the current resettlement program in Ethiopia. While many observers (donors, UN agencies, and NGOs) have argued that settlers are being almost literally "dumped" in settlement sites without adequate services or assistance, what little assistance there is is being targeted at returnees and not at local communities. In some cases, local communities reported to me in 2003 that they were no longer able to use the clinic or water point that they had previously been using, but had to travel long distances to get these resources since the nearby facilities had been reserved for settlers. This has resulted in tensions and even open conflict between settlers and local communities.

Returnees should enjoy the same standard of living as those who did not migrate

This position is one of the most common, as it seeks to establish parity between returnees and the local communities (whether the area of return is the same as that from which people migrated or is a new area). However much this approach may make sense, it is fraught with difficulties, since it is a rare case in which the standard of living of the local population is ever fully understood prior to the settling of newcomers. Without clear standards to define exactly what is the standard of living of the local population, it is impossible to monitor how well-integrated returnees become.

In 2003 and 2004, I conducted a series of projects for the United States Agency for International Development (USAID) looking into the Government of Ethiopia's (GoE) voluntary resettlement program.[3] The GoE intends to resettle up to 2.2 million people by 2005 from food-insecure and degraded parts of the highlands to more fertile and less densely populated lowland areas in the west of the country. In 2003, an estimated 170,000 people were relocated. In 2004, it appears that as many as 500,000 people may have been resettled despite repeated expressions of concern from the international community that inadequate planning and assistance were contributing to the development of a humanitarian crisis in settlement sites, as well as doubts about the overall effectiveness of resettlement as a tool for fighting food insecurity.[4] Settlers were given a basic ration that looked very much like what returning refugees received ten years earlier (in fact, some of the government officials implementing the project told me that they had learned how to do this when they were involved in the refugee repatriation operations then) – nine months' food, one hectare of land, seed and ploughing on credit, a box of kitchen utensils, and housing materials. It was assumed that people would be self-sufficient as soon as the first harvest was ready. Calculations about how much money a settler farmer could make in the first year were based on Ministry of Agriculture estimates of the maximum possible yield under optimal conditions. They were not based on careful assessments of the kinds of yields, and the annual incomes of local people who had been living in the area for 20 years or more. My interviews with these farmers revealed that the maximum expectable income (from agricultural production, waged labor on commercial farms, trade, and other sources) was only a fourth of what the government had estimated. Moreover, settlers had arrived with only the clothes on their backs, with no furniture, few tools, no livestock assets, and no cash. They would need to sell much of their first harvest to cover these costs. They also faced the unfamiliar threats of malaria, leishmaniasis, and, due to split households and economic vulnerability, increased exposure to HIV/Aids and other sexually transmitted diseases. Whereas the government had planned for settlers to become self-sufficient at the end of their first year in their new farms, several observers estimate that it will take at least two, and probably three years for self-sufficiency to be reached under the best circumstances (Hammond and Pankhurst 2004).

Return should be seen as a development opportunity

Where return takes place in a context of emergence from a period of prolonged conflict, or where returnees are settled in areas that suffer from extreme poverty, repatriation can be seen as an opportunity to improve the quality of life not only of returnees, but also of the local community, including IDPs, stayees, demobilized soldiers, and other vulnerable groups such as female headed households and the disabled.

Unlike the first three options presented here, which seek to preserve the status quo of one group or another, the developmental approach seeks to take advantage of available aid resources to promote economic and social activities that help to blur the distinctions between groups. Tensions between returnees and stayees, IDPs and demobilized soldiers are minimized by the promotion of the welfare of all. In this way, groups are not as likely to compete for or fight over resources, since the presence of each group serves as catalyst for the provision of assistance that helps the others.

While the developmental approach appears to be the most attractive of the options presented here – after all, who would argue with the idea of raising everyone's standard of living and avoiding conflict in the process? – it is the road taken the least often. Except in a few notable instances (Central America in the 1980s, parts of the former Yugoslavia in the mid-1990s), UNHCR has adamantly stuck to its insistence that it is not a development agency, and that it lacks the resources to provide such comprehensive assistance, particularly when the beneficiaries include people who are not, and never have been, refugees. In Somaliland during 1998, UNDP tried to work with UNHCR to develop a strategy for promoting developmental assistance to all vulnerable groups including returnees once UNHCR had provided start-up assistance and basic infrastructural support in the form of dozens of Quick Impact Projects (QIPs). However, lack of donor faith in UNDP's capacity to provide development support outside the policy arena, and institutional infighting between the two UN agencies derailed the effort and little came of the attempt to work in a cross-mandate fashion.

Developmental approaches to integration are attractive to governments in countries of origin, but they are difficult to execute given that many countries lack the resources to make these efforts sustainable. Somaliland is littered with mother–child health clinics, TB hospitals, and schools that were created through QIPs but stand empty because the Somaliland Administration, facing both the challenges of establishing a taxation system and a long-term loss of revenue from a ban imposed by the Gulf countries on sale of livestock from the Horn of Africa, lacks the financial resources to provide the staffing, equipment, and other running costs for the facilities.

In the Palestinian context, finding a solution to the question over the right of return could usefully be considered as a development opportunity. Whether people return to their areas of origin or accept compensation settlements, they will probably be committed to ensuring the long-term viability of the lives of themselves and their families in Palestine. Thus, resources are likely to be reinvested into Palestinian society in ways that will help to promote social and economic development.

Adherence to international, national, or regional standards

Given the difficulty of determining whether the objective of post-return assistance should be to restore pre-exile conditions, establish parity with local communities, preserve conditions found in refugee camps, or promote development of return areas, many assistance providers have sought instead to identify basic minimum standards to be observed. The Sphere Guidelines for Humanitarian Operations (2004) provide some guidelines for such assistance, and are widely cited as the threshold for repatriation assistance. However, many developing countries, including those in the Horn of Africa, are unable to ensure that these conditions are able to be guaranteed even in areas that have not been affected by displacement, famine, or conflict. In Ethiopia, for instance, the average amount of water available in many rural areas does not exceed 7 liters per person per day, whereas the international standard is for 17 liters per person per day. Such minimum standards are too high for extremely poor countries to be able to maintain without external support.

As a compromise between too-high international standards and too-low local conditions, some agencies have focused on national or regional standards. These are at least standards that have been identified by the government in the country of origin as basic requirements that are achievable. In many cases, however, these standards are framed more as targets than as minimum standards. Thus, they may be too high to be able to maintain in the long term. Ethiopia's voluntary resettlement program is guided by its Programme Implementation Manual, which identifies regional standards as the indicators for program success. Monitoring carried out by donors, NGOs, UN agencies, and the government itself have found that these standards have not been upheld. Despite this, the Prime Minister declared the 2004 repatriation operation a success.

In the Palestinian context, where the standard of living is not as low as it is in the Horn of Africa, international standards are probably appropriate indicators for ensuring that basic conditions are met. Moreover, adherence to international standards will provide some level of protection for Palestinian people against those who might argue that some lower benchmarks of well-being may be appropriate.

Measuring self-sufficiency through household economy analysis

Model A: parity with local communities

In all of the cases described here, there are real challenges to defining integration, and thus to developing a strategy for promoting sustainable return. Disputes about which definition should be used are not idle academic banter. When different agencies have different views about what the integration or assistance operation's goals are, it becomes nearly impossible to plan the operation, to monitor its effectiveness, to hold those responsible for implementing it accountable, or to make recommendations or conditions for future improvements to the program that may be needed. Such is the case in Ethiopia right now, where donors, NGOs, UN agencies, and the government all have different ideas about what the objectives of resettlement should be, and thus each measures success differently. Although some government officials insist that the resettlement program has been a success because people have more land than they did before, they overlook the fact that those who have moved face the additional health risks of exposure to malaria and leishmaniasis (kalazar) endemic in lowland areas, as well as heightened vulnerability to HIV/Aids and other sexually transmitted diseases due to family separations and economic marginalization of single women. They also overlook the fact that settler households often have much less land than their neighbours who have lived in the area for many years.

In an environment in which people are to be settled amongst a local population (as opposed to one in which they are settled in areas where there is no local population, as I will discuss in model B), the best way to measure success of integration processes is to consider the perspective of both potential returnees and locals living in return areas. How do or would they each measure success? At a very bare minimum, returnees and locals tend to measure their well-being against that of others living around them. If returnees feel that they are not able to achieve the same standard of living as those amongst whom they are settled, they will not be satisfied, even if they are better off than they were in their area of origin or area of exile. If locals feel that services and resources have been taken away from them to be given to settlers, then they will feel that the operation has not been a success, and will come to resent the newcomers. Obviously, there are other considerations to be made with regard to settler/local relations that may influence their ability to live together peacefully, such as religious, ethnic, or political differences, but the focus of this analysis is on economic integration.

There are, of course, important caveats to the notion that parity with local hosts should be the objective of integration assistance. If, for instance, the entire community lives under conditions that are life-threatening or unsustainable (for instance, if the local community is also dependent upon external assistance for survival, or if there is a basic lack of services such that the settlement of large numbers of additional people in the area would endanger the livelihoods of everyone living in the area), then assistance must be aimed at raising the general conditions of those living in the area above a minimum threshold.

But what should this threshold be? How are we to know whether the livelihoods of those living in the area of return are viable, vulnerable, or endangered? For this, household economy analysis (HEA, also known as food economy analysis, or FEA) is a very useful tool.

Household economy analysis was developed first by Save the Children UK in the early 1990s as a way of tracking resource flows inside households and communities (Save the Children UK 2002). By recording resource flows in and out of a household, discussing wealth differentials with groups of people, and identifying the relative impact of potential shocks to the system, household economy analysis can provide a reasonable picture of the cost of living in a given area. Once a baseline food security profile is compiled, HEA can also quantify the impact of likely or actual shocks, whether crop failure, market price fluctuations, conflict-related instability, loss of income due to restrictions on movement, loss of land or access to land, escalating HIV/Aids rates, or further displacement. By conducting HEA with local communities in areas of return, one can arrive at a fairly accurate estimation of the average cost of living in that area, as well as the range of income levels that exist. These figures can then be used as a benchmark for identifying the requirements for sustainable return or integration, and can identify many of the potential hazards or shocks that returnees may face following their arrival. Put another way, HEA analysis can define the minimum requirements for integration and can serve as a tool for guiding decisions about the type and amount of assistance to be given in a return context.

Much of the initial work done to develop the Household Economy methodology was done in the Ethiopian highlands (Holt and Lawrence 1993; Webb and von Braun 1994). Thus, there is relatively good information on the sending areas for resettlement. However, very little is known about the economies of lowland areas in of the country. Generally located in remote areas close to Ethiopia's borders, and dependent upon a mix of both food and cash crops, lowland economies cannot easily be compared to highland economies. They tend to be more dependent upon market activity, and their welfare is more directly tied to fluctuations in national and global prices of cash crops such as sesame, cotton, and coffee. In the lowlands of northwestern Ethiopia, the local economy has been severely impacted by the fact that the border between Ethiopia and Eritrea has been closed since 1998, when the two countries went to war. Local sesame and sorghum prices have plummeted as a result of the loss of an export corridor through Eritrean ports for the former and an inability to sell the latter to Eritrean markets.[5]

In 2003, I conducted very basic preliminary research in Ethiopian resettlement areas with local communities to try to get a sense of the local cost of living.[6] Local officials had planned that, with assistance for the first year after their arrival, resettled households would be able to achieve self-sufficiency following the first harvest. Discussions with regional and local government officials revealed that these calculations were based on the assumption that households would achieve the maximum possible agricultural productive output from the single hectare that they had been allocated, that they would sell these crops for the maximum price available during the year (which comes approximately 4–5 months after the harvest), that they would work the maximum number of days on commercial farms, and that the wage rate, despite the arrival of thousands of workers in the area, would remain constant (i.e. high).

Given the work that I had done in lowland returnee settlements during the mid-1990s (many of the resettlement sites are located close to refugee return sites), these predictions seemed to be unrealistic, so I gathered information from local residents who had been living in the area for at least 20 years (many had taken part in the 1980s forced resettlement program implemented by the former Ethiopian government), local traders, and local markets to try to determine how realistic the government's calculations were. Table 7.1 shows that, with data obtained from these sources, the estimate of the income-generating potential of the local population was as little as half what the local government officials were expecting settlers to achieve in the first year after they had settled.

Wage labor, both on local commercial farms as well as large mechanized and irrigated farms, is expected to be a major source of income for new settlers. Workers are contracted for clearing land (men only), weeding (both men and women) and harvesting (generally only men unless there is a shortage of labor). Whereas sorghum and sesame harvests are completed by January, cotton harvesting can continue into March. Regional estimates of the daily wage rate, however, appear to be double the prevailing rate reported by local residents, and the estimate of days is double the amount that locals say they work. Thus, the expectation of being able to earn 1,200 birr in a year from wage labor is certainly a massive overestimate. A more realistic figure, as indicated in Table 7.1, is 300 birr. Even this figure would require each household to have one member working for at least two months per year, a figure that is probably the upper limit of what is feasible.

Based on the estimates given in Table 7.1, with the average consumption needs for a household of five people estimated at 10 quintals, the average household would be able to produce 80 percent of its total cereal consumption requirements, and would need to purchase 2 quintals. Assuming that the household purchased grain a few months after the harvest, when prices had risen to 160 birr per quintal, this would leave the average household with a budget of 580 birr per year (equal to approximately US$70) with which to purchase complementary food items such as pulses, oil, sugar, salt, spices, and coffee. Other essential items that must be paid for from this source include clothing, farm inputs, school fees and materials, taxes, medical care, and milling.

The government's expectation of the income that a smallholder family can achieve is exceedingly optimistic, at approximately 8,000 birr per year. Table 7.2 shows the breakdown in expected components of this income profile. The figure includes income from harvesting of gum arabic, beekeeping, and poultry production, industries that have yet to be developed in the resettlement sites. Local residents expressed disbelief in the possibility of earning this much money from these activities.

Thirty percent of the total amount that the government expects settlers to have access to is expected to come from farm production. The other 70 percent is expected to be derived from non-farm sources. These calculations appear to have been made by calculating maximum potential yields and cash values, rather than actual yields and incomes of local residents. Most households are expected to reach their maximum earning potential within three years.

The woreda and regional estimates of crop production achievable from a single hectare of land are only slightly lower than local farmers' own estimates of their yields. However, whereas the average landholding size of local residents is 5–6 hectares, that of settlers is only 1 hectare. The justification given for the smaller size of land given to settlers is that in the first year they

Table 7.1 Expected yields of a settler household, Metemma area, Amhara region

Crop	Area to cultivate	Expected yield	Woreda estimate of value/quintal	Woreda estimate of total value	Estimated actual unit/quintal	Estimated actual total value
Sesame	0.25 ha	100 kg (1 Q)	500 birr	500 birr	240 birr	240 birr[a]
Sorghum	0.50 ha	800 kg (8 Q)	160 birr	1,280 birr	100–160 birr	800–1,280 birr[b]
Cotton	0.25 ha	200 kg (2 Q)	300 birr	600 birr	200 birr	400 birr
Total farm income	1 ha	11 Q	960 birr	2,380 birr	540–600 birr	1,440–1,920 birr
Income from other sources						
Wage labor	60 days/year		20 birr/day × 60 days	1,200 birr	10 birr/day × 30 days[c]	300 birr/year
Total expected income/year				3,580 birr		1,740–2,220 birr

Source: Metemma Woreda Office of Agriculture.

Notes

a The region estimates the value of a quintal of sesame to be 500 birr (US$1 = approximately 8 birr). However, most small farmers must sell sesame immediately after the harvest to pay off debts and purchase essential items. Therefore, the actual selling price is usually much lower. The market price of sesame increases dramatically in the four months following the harvest.

b Price varies depending on when the farmer sells or purchases grain; grain is cheapest immediately after the harvest and rises steadily in price until the next harvest period.

c Amhara region estimates a daily rate of 20 birr/day. We found that 10 birr is currently the maximum daily rate being paid to workers. Locals said that they preferred not to work on commercial farms, but that when they did, they did not have time for more than thirty days of work per year given their other work responsibilities on their own farms.

Table 7.2   Woreda estimate of potential income for settler households

Activity	Expected income (birr)
Incense harvesting:	3,600
Wage labor	1,200
Livestock	811
Crop production	2,380
Total	7,991

will not be able to adequately clear and farm it. While this may be true, no land use assessment has been done to identify where, or whether, additional land is available that might eventually be given to local settler farmers so that they might have the same access to farmland as the local farmers.

In addition to considering income sources, an analysis of the local economy should consider the kinds and levels of expenses that a household regularly faces. This will include startup costs for the household – materials for house-building, furniture, tools, kitchen implements, etc. – prices of food and other essential items from local markets, the cost of repaying credit (settlers must borrow money from the government for seeds and plough animals), school fees, taxes, and other costs. What might seem like an attractive income to a farmer who has come from an area that is primarily a subsistence agriculture-based economy may, upon analysis of the costs of living there, turn out to signal a net drop in the individual's or household's standard of living.

Finally, for the Household Economy Analysis to be complete, one would need to consider the potential shocks that could take place within the resettlement area that might have an adverse impact on the household economy. This might include increased health risks (both the cost of treatment and the loss of productivity caused by one or more family members becoming ill), interruption of the supply or demand market for one or more commodities, policies of discrimination that block settlers from being able to access markets as effectively as locals, and even the eruption of conflict between locals and incomers or from external sources.

Using Household Economy Analysis to determine the cost of living in a local community can be useful in planning post-return integration. It can identify the type of activities that settlers are likely to become involved in, the relative significance of each income source to the overall household economy, and the impact of shocks. This information should form the basis for designing assistance programs, both in selecting the type of interventions that are most appropriate and in designating the window of time, or even better the conditions under which assistance should be provided, before true integration can be expected to be achieved.

Model B: integration in the absence of a local community

In some situations returnees may be settled in areas where there is no sizable local community. This may be desirable from the point of view of avoiding the emergence of conflict over resources or mitigating ethnic tensions. Such settlements may also have a greater natural resource base to support the establishment of the returnee community. However, it becomes difficult in such a situation to determine the cost of living, and the expected window of time that it might take returnee households to achieve economic viability.

Such was the case in northwest Ethiopia, where refugees were repatriated from Sudan. As they had been settled into what was literally an empty field (farmed by large commercial farms, but seized by the government for the purposes of settling the returnees), the nearest permanent local community was 20 kilometers away. Thus, settlers did not have to compete much with locals for access to water or social services.[7] In such a situation, Household Economy Analysis can also be used to determine basic minimum costs of living and to identify appropriate types and amounts of assistance to facilitate integration.[8]

In 1993, when I began my research in Ada Bai, the largest of the returnee settlements in the Humera area, no one had any idea of what the cost of living was in the area. It was assumed that returnees could be settled in the area, given land, and loaned traction animals or access to mechanized ploughing services, and within a year they would become self-sufficient. Yet during the first year after the returnees and I arrived, it was clear that most people were not making ends meet. In the first half of 1994, many children and several adults died of malnutrition (though exact figures are not available, to those of us living in the community it was clear that conditions were deteriorating).

Government and aid agencies' ideas of how much food and cash were required to support a household, and where these assets came from if not from aid, were based on rough guestimation. Even less clear were the means by which households interacted with one another, through exchange of cash, food, labor, and other forms of mutual assistance in their efforts to provide for their own basic needs. With such a shortage of accurate information, government and aid agencies could argue that their assistance was not needed. Without this information, however, it was impossible to monitor returnees' progress in achieving self sufficiency and economic integration.

While many people were struggling to feed their families, others appeared to be doing better, though no households could be said to be thriving. To try to determine what differentiated the poorest households from those that were better off, I conducted an assessment of resource flows into and out of a small sample of ten households over a four month period. I chose not to use a large sample size, because I was interested in learning more about how households made economic decisions, rather than arriving at a figure of average household income. I wanted to know what prompted people, for instance to sell off a sheep, or to purchase a quintal of grain at one time over another. The small sample size allowed me to follow up with households to discuss their decision-making with them. The survey tracked the households from the harvest period through to the "lean" or dry season, when grain prices were at their highest and household food and cash stocks were at their lowest.

The survey found that household incomes expanded and contracted significantly during the year. During the agricultural season, people borrowed seeds, plough animals, tractor services, money to pay laborers (or paid them on credit), and money to transport their product out of the fields. These debts had to be paid off as soon as the harvest was brought in. Thus, people had to sell their products for the lowest possible price. By the lean season, they had exhausted most of their cash and food reserves. Those households who were labor rich were able to send one or more members to the mechanized farms in Sudan, or to work elsewhere, to bring wages into the household. Others sold livestock or other assets. Still others began the cycle of borrowing all over again. The poorest households changed their consumption patterns, eliminating a meal a day or subtracting one of the components from their diets (for instance, meat was never eaten, pulses were eaten less frequently, and the main diet consisted of bread with spicy paste or salt spread over it).

The survey revealed that households that were labor or livestock rich had greater resilience than those who did not. This put female headed and younger households at a particular disadvantage, as they lacked the human capital to access wage labor markets. One of the most significant findings of the survey was that the range of incomes between the poorest and the "wealthiest" households was extremely narrow.

Over time, as people became more established in their new homes, they were able to increase their harvest and herd sizes such that they did not need to borrow as much money. In the ten years since I first began research in this community, household resilience has increased markedly. None of the households is now dependent upon external food aid, and most have been able to construct new, improved homes, pay for their children to go to school, and purchase things like donkey carts and other equipment to help improve their productivity. Although there still are not many people whom I would consider to be wealthy, the community is self-sufficient (those individual households that are not are supported by others in the community who have enough to share) and the community has grown into the second largest town in the woreda. An indication of its viability was shown during the war with Eritrea, when people opted to remain in the community even though it was vulnerable to attack rather than be evacuated to a safer, more remote area. People told me that they had spent too long making this place work for them to give it away so easily. Nearly everyone remained in Ada Bai throughout the war.

Although I did not do a full food economy analysis while I was in Ada Bai, my research on the dynamics of the household economy during the year was useful in showing the relative importance of different sources of income, and some of the potential shocks that could spell the difference between self-sufficiency and dependency. The results showed the reasons that integration was a longer, more drawn-out process than the government, UNHCR, or other aid agencies had thought it would be. For households to emerge from destitution to a plateau of self-sufficiency took two, and in some cases three years. Assistance to returnees dried up after only one year – thus, the achievements made by the people of Ada Bai in reaching relative security came as a result of their own efforts and not those of an external assistance provider. Although their resilience is impressive, it should not obscure the fact that aid agencies failed to appreciate the dynamics of return, and to fashion their assistance programs in ways that could support that process. What may be considered a success on the part of returnees to integrate may be considered a failure on the part of aid agencies, whose lack of understanding made integration a more distant goal for returnees, and who were unable to prevent the suffering and needless deaths of many people in the first two years following repatriation.

Conclusion: implications for Palestine

Of the many ways of evaluating integration from the perspective of what kinds of assistance might be required, I suggest that the best way is to consider how potential returnees might answer the following questions. What criteria will they use to determine whether or not their return has been successful? How will they determine whether assistance provided is adequate? If return is not possible or desirable, how will people define what adequate compensation might be? If aid agencies choose indicators other than those that the returnees themselves choose, it is likely that not many people will choose to participate in the organized return. The answer to which of the five possible ways of considering integration that I have given should be followed depends very much on the conditions of a particular return environment. Even within Ethiopia, the same strategy would not have worked in both of the cases that I have explored here.

How then should return to Palestine be considered? I am convinced that Household Economy Analysis can be a useful tool both in selecting the parameters of assistance in a return context, and in identifying a reasonable level of self-sufficiency that aid agencies might work towards in their efforts to promote integration. Although I have discussed its use in Ethiopia, where the economic profile of the population is much poorer than that of most Palestinians, the same framework can be applied to any country no matter how wealthy or poor its people may be, and regardless of the nature of their income base and the kind of shocks they might face.

One might be tempted to steer away from household economy analysis in the Palestinian context because, despite the many challenges that Palestinians face in returning, including continued security threats, compensation for lost property, and community formation in a return setting, food insecurity is not (for most) a paramount concern. It is true that Household Economy Analysis has previously been used primarily to consider groups where food shortages are rife, and basic survival is threatened by lack of access to food.

However, there is nothing to say that such analysis cannot be used to define benchmarks of acceptable living conditions in societies where other concerns than food present economic challenges. Because the definition of basic household well-being is defined by communities themselves, and because the components of that profile will change markedly from one society to another, there is every reason to believe that this approach would be a useful tool in identifying requirements for sustainable return to Palestine.

An approach to considering the household economies in this context would consist of first establishing a baseline profile of household economies living in areas of return (assuming that people will be returning to established communities). If the basic standard of living in these communities is inadequate, the deficiency should be identified (this can serve as a strategy for improving conditions for local populations as well). Following identification of the potential range of possible income sources and the likely constraints to returnees seeking self-sufficiency, strategies for providing necessary resources to promote productivity and integration may be designed. These benchmarks can also be used to measure returnees' progress along the way to economic integration, and the factors that may enhance or impede their progress.

Economic integration is surely not the only (and some might argue it is not the most important) indicator of successful return. However, it is a necessary condition of sustainable return. Given this, it is remarkable that more careful planning is not done to ensure that assistance given to promote integration is well targeted and effective. Without clearly defined targets and an understanding of the dynamics of the economic universe into which returnees enter, there can be no way of knowing whether the assistance provided is achieving its goals.

Notes

1 In this chapter, "settlement" is used to refer to the largely voluntary relocation of people to areas that offer the prospect of better agricultural land. I realize that in the Palestinian context, "settlement" has a very different connotation, whereby Israeli settlers are occupying Palestinian territory. Readers should be aware that the use of the term "settlement" is not intended to imply that Ethiopian settlers are occupying land claimed by others in the same way that Israeli settlers are. Indeed, there are disputes arising between Ethiopian settlers and local communities over land claims, but the primary reason for movement is not to assert a right over the land in the settlement areas.

2 Many refugees living in the camps were from southern Somalia, and are unable to return to their country of origin due to continued violence and the absence of administrative structures. Most refugees from Somaliland have been repatriated from Ethiopia and Djibouti.

3 The work has been carried out with the assistance of Bezaiet Dessalegn, and part of it in collaboration with Dr. Alula Pankhurst of Addis Ababa University. See References.

4 The international community has been reluctant to support the program in part because of fears that the program might ultimately become forced. People remember the involuntary resettlement program of 1984–86, in which 600,000 people were moved against their will. Death rates were extremely high in settle-

ment sites and humanitarian organizations that did not condemn the program early enough were accused of being complicit in it.

5 Despite the signing of a Cessation of Hostilities Agreement in June 2000 and a Comprehensive Peace Agreement in December 2000, relations between the two countries remain extremely tense and neither border trade nor cross-border communication has been opened up. A border demarcation process, facilitated by the United Nations Mission in Ethiopia and Eritrea, and arbitrated by a Border Demarcation Commission, has been stalled by Ethiopia's refusal to accept the BDC's findings. For further information about the impact of border closure on local economies in both Ethiopia and Eritrea, see Hammond (2003).

6 For the full assessment of the 2003 resettlement programme, see Hammond and Dessalegn (2003).

7 There had been a local population of approximately 100 agro-pastoralists who stayed in the area seasonally, but given that no services had been available before the arrival of the returnees these locals welcomed the arrival of the newcomers. Only rarely did disputes over access to water arise. In Humera town (the administrative center of the woreda), conflicts sometimes arose over access to health care since returnees were able to get free health care while townspeople had to pay for that service.

8 For a more detailed analysis of the food economy in Ada Bai, see Chapter 4 of Hammond (2004).

References

Hammond, Laura (2003) "Obstacles to regional trade in the Horn of Africa: Borders, markets and production". Report for USAID/OFDA (Washington, DC: USAID/OFDA). Available at http://www.usaid.gov/locations/sub-saharan_africa/publications/eg.html

—— (2004) *This place will become home: Refugee repatriation to Ethiopia* (Ithaca, NY: Cornell University Press).

Hammond, Laura, and Dessalegn, Bezaiet (2003) "Safara: An assessment of current and future resettlement in Ethiopia", Report for USAID/Ethiopia (Addis Ababa).

Hammond, Laura, and Pankhurst, Alula (2004) "Framework for Monitoring and Evaluation of the Government of the Federal Republic of Ethiopia's Voluntary Resettlement Programme". Report commissioned by USAID/OFDA Washington for the Multi-Agency Task Force on Resettlement (Addis Ababa).

Holt, Julius, and Lawrence, Mark (1993) "Making ends meet: A survey of the food economy of the Ethiopian north-east highlands". Report published by Save the Children UK (London: Save the Children).

Malkki, Liisa H. (1995) *Purity and exile: Violence, memory and national cosmology among Hutu refugees in Tanzania* (Chicago: University of Chicago Press).

Save the Children UK (2002) *The household economy approach: A resource manual for practitioners* (London: Save the Children).

Sphere Humanitarian Charter and Minimum Standards in Disaster Response (2004) (Geneva: Sphere Project). Available at www.sphereproject.org

United Nations High Commissioner for Refugees (2003) "UNHCR's Mandate", in *An Operations Management Handbook for UNHCR's Partners* (Geneva: UNHCR).

Webb, Patrick, and von Braun, Joachim (1994) *Famine and food security in Ethiopia: Lessons for Africa* (London: John Wiley and Sons).

8 Linking return and reintegration to complex forced migration emergencies

Diversities of conflict, patterns of displacement and humanitarian responses – a comparative analysis

Christopher McDowell and Nicholas Van Hear

The systematic failure of mass organised returns to provide durable solutions to refugees' needs, and the needs of communities that play host to them, throws into serious question the premises on which repatriation is promoted and undertaken. Return programmes in the highly complex context of UN-managed state-building, and internationally managed transitions from conflict to post-conflict democracies, present both political and conceptual problems. The political agendas informing repatriation as the favoured solution today are largely a response to increasing numbers of refugees, relief budget constraints and the growing antagonism of host countries. In almost all cases repatriation is intricately tied to the fate of peace agreements and successful return is vital in legitimising new democratic regimes that are of great strategic importance to the UN, donors and many Western states (McDowell and Eastmond 2002). The accelerated return of refugees is politically significant because it signals to the world the end of conflict and the beginning of national reconstruction; further, high profile return programmes are seen to legitimise the activities and policies of the UN in managing global and local conflict. Frequently, in this context, repatriation appears to address 'the refugee problem', i.e. the political and institutional challenges that the refugees pose, rather than the *refugees' problems*, that is, the struggles of refugees to create a secure life for themselves, whether that be in the country of origin or elsewhere (Harrell-Bond 1989; Wilson and Nunes 1994).

This chapter explores these issues through an examination of return and reintegration programmes in five diverse complex forced migration emergencies: East Timor, Sri Lanka, Georgia, Colombia and Burundi. These cases indicate the range of protracted, ongoing, frozen, suspended and part-resolved conflicts that characterise such complex forced migration emergencies. The chapter takes on the challenge to refugee research posed by Koser and Black

(1999) to explore the linkages and interrelationships between refugee repatriation and the wider political, economic and institutional context in which initial displacement occurs and the humanitarian and post-conflict responses are shaped. Specifically, the comparative analysis of repatriation seeks to address two sets of issues. First, it examines the extent to which repatriation programmes, and the policy contexts in which they take place, should be considered as an extension or continuation of the management of forced migration emergencies in the conflict, pre-peace and post-conflict phases. And if so, what are the continuities and the consequences of this for post-conflict return and reconstruction? Second, it considers whether in fact current trends in repatriation signal a new approach to post-conflict transformation in which the return and repatriation of refugees is an integral element of wider political and economic policies to shape post-conflict societies in a neoliberal mould. And again, what are the implications of this?

In examining these two sets of issues, the chapter draws on five case studies prepared by teams of researchers contributing to a programme of research funded by the MacArthur Foundation which examines options for the reform of the international humanitarian regime. Led jointly by Georgetown University in Washington, DC, and the Refugee Studies Centre in Oxford, research teams comprising international and local scholars undertook field visits and interviewed officials in international and non-governmental humanitarian agencies, human rights organisations, journalists and members of displaced communities in East Timor, Sri Lanka, Burundi, Georgia and Colombia. Extended case studies of these complex forced migration emergencies and the response of the humanitarian regime feature in a volume entitled *Catching fire: Containing complex forced migration in a volatile world* (Lexington, 2004) edited by the authors of this chapter. Specific country information and analysis drawn on in this chapter was prepared by Christopher McDowell (East Timor); Patricia Weiss Fagen, Amelia Fernandez Juan, Finn Stepputat and Roberto Vidal López (Colombia); Susan Martin and Trish Hiddleston (Burundi); Matthew Karania (Georgia); and Nicholas Van Hear and Darini Rajasingham-Senanayake (Sri Lanka). The interpretation of that material, however, is the responsibility of the authors of this chapter.

The chapter is concerned with the response of the humanitarian regime to different types of conflicts and different forced migration emergencies. It explores how and why responses change over time, what internal and external pressures are brought to bear, and the implications of those changes for addressing protection and assistance needs of the displaced, for peace processes, and in relation to longer-term post-conflict development. In so doing the chapter provides analysis of the institutional, political and humanitarian context in which return, repatriation and reintegration programmes are conducted. It is argued that such an exercise is necessary in order to better understand the continuities, opportunities and potential obstacles that exist for comprehensive, durable and sustainable post-conflict return.

The diversity of conflict and shifting patterns of displacement

Complex forced migration emergencies create humanitarian needs largely around physical protection and assistance in the form of addressing basic needs such as health, shelter, food and clean water. International responses, through UN diplomacy or coalition-type military interventions, contributions to peacekeeping or Consolidated Appeal pledges, define individual governments and the UN's perceived responsibility for and engagement with a particular conflict situation. International responses to forced migration emergencies vary from conflict to conflict, and change over time depending on a number of factors. In recent years the international humanitarian regime has generated a range of responses from, at one end of the scale, an almost unequivocal generosity and political unanimity in the case of East Timor, to one of continuing neglect in the case of Burundi or Sudan. The availability of resources and political commitment is clearly a significant factor in determining the size, scope and effectiveness of any response. Efficiency in the use of resources and agency coordination is also a critical factor. Within specific emergencies, responses are shaped and reshaped by political assessments to do with the public demand for continued involvement, historical responsibility, concerns about threats to regional or global security, or economic national self-interest in the short and longer term. In addition, perceptions about a particular conflict influence levels of commitment to a humanitarian response. For example, conflict situations are continually reassessed and redefined as being somewhere on a point in the transition from conflict, through stability, to pre-peace, peace and the post-conflict development stage. The political and institutional response to a particular emergency situation, and the ways it changes over time, determine assistance and protection programmes for refugees and displaced people who remain within the borders of their countries but unable to return home, and as we shall see that response influences significantly the scope and content of post-conflict repatriation initiatives.

Since the early 1990s forced displacement has increasingly defined conflicts, and the ability to control populations has become a decisive component of military strategy. Return and reintegration programmes are conducted in the context of those emergencies and at various stages in their transition or transformation. While a given conflict may be resolved or in abeyance the political, social, economic and cultural impacts of forced displacement will still be felt and humanitarian needs associated with them will remain. In the following brief accounts of diverse conflicts and shifting patterns of displacement, the humanitarian response and repatriation efforts that followed, the continuities and discontinuities in the institutional and political responses are described. Within these transitions, changes in the priorities of host governments, international agencies and civil societies are explored, and the changing institutional structure and funding arrangements are examined. Shifts in the discourse of assistance are also considered.

Sri Lanka

Sri Lanka has experienced complex forms of migration within and outside the country over the last three decades (McDowell 1996; Fuglerud 1999; Rotberg 1999). A combination of ethnic, nationalist, socio-economic and religious tensions contributed to the armed conflict which took off in the early 1980s between the Sri Lankan military and the separatist Liberation Tigers of Tamil Eelam (LTTE). A large outflow of asylum-seekers, mainly Tamils, has taken place, largely from the north and east of the island where the conflict has been waged; there have been intense periods of fighting in 1983–7, in 1990–4 and from 1995 until 2001. Much of this refugee movement was initially to Tamil Nadu in southern India, but many Sri Lankan Tamils have sought asylum further afield, adding to the diaspora of Sri Lankan migrants who left for work, education or to take up professional positions abroad in Europe, North America and elsewhere. During interludes or lulls in the fighting, notably in the late 1980s and early 1990s, large-scale repatriations from Tamil Nadu have taken place; but the resumption of fighting has rendered these return movements short-lived. In 2000 there were around 110,000 Sri Lankan Tamil refugees in southern India, of whom about 60,000 lived in camps, and some 200,000–300,000 in Europe and North America, who joined other Sri Lankan migrants. In addition to movements outside the island, there has been large-scale displacement within the country. Depending on the intensity of the conflict, between 500,000 and 1 million people have been displaced within Sri Lanka at any one time in recent years (US Committee for Refugees 2001). Some individuals and households have been displaced many times, and members of a single household may be dispersed in different parts of the country or in different countries abroad. The conflict has thus produced a complex range of forcibly displaced and war-affected populations that poses difficult challenges to the regime charged with providing protection and assistance.

A full review of displacement, its consequences and the response of the humanitarian regime would have to take account of those who have sought safety in India and further afield, since those abroad both shape and are an integral part of Sri Lanka's 'forced migration complex'. Within the country the situation is extremely complex and diverse, with a wide range of local and regional contexts of internal displacement arising from nearly two decades of armed conflict. To give just a few examples:

The 1983 pogrom that is usually taken as marking the start of the conflict entailed the internal and external displacement of minority Tamils from the south, principally the capital city of Colombo and the central hill country. Members of the small local Sinhalese minority in Jaffna were also displaced south in retaliatory attacks.

In 1990 Muslim and Sinhalese minorities were displaced by the LTTE from the northern Jaffna peninsula and Mannar district. Some 75,000 Muslims ended up on the west coast of the island in Puttalam district.

Large numbers have been displaced since what is termed the third Eelam War started in 1995. One of the major displacements was the entire population of Jaffna when the Sri Lankan military recaptured the northern city.

Substantial numbers of people have been caught in the crossfire between the combatants in the north and east, some of whom have been repeatedly displaced along the 'border areas' of the conflict.

In the east, attacks on Muslims and Sinhalese villages have led to the creation of mono-ethnic enclaves, with Muslims moving to Muslim majority areas and Sinhalese moving to Sinhalese majority areas. Tamil civilians who have been subject to harassment, intimidation and retaliatory attacks by the military have also fled their homes.

The humanitarian challenge posed by this diversity of displacement is explored later in this chapter and compared to the situation in the other countries. The implications in terms of return and reintegration are addressed later.

East Timor

The humanitarian crisis in East Timor, triggered by pro-Jakarta militia violence and assisted by the Indonesian military, followed the UN-backed independence referendum in August 1999 and led to almost two-thirds of the territory's population of 750,000 people being displaced. This sudden mass displacement of such a large proportion of the population was only the latest in a series of forced migration crises in East Timor. From 1976, the Indonesian military undertook a massive programme of forced resettlement for political and strategic reasons. The processes and repercussions of past and more recent forced migration and involuntary resettlement should be part of any analysis which seeks to understand contemporary political and social dynamics in East Timor. The post-referendum East Timor emergency, compared with other crises addressed in this chapter, was relatively short-term. That is not to say, however, that the impacts of forced displacement which occurred immediately following the UN-backed 1999 referendum on independence from Indonesia are not still felt in East Timor, and will be for some time. Almost 80 per cent of the housing stock was destroyed in a scorched earth retreat by the pro-Jakarta militia intent on denying the newly independent nation access to vital infrastructure and inflicting as much damage as possible to the economy. This mass upheaval and dispersal of so many people in such a short space of time posed a challenge for the international community as it assumed sovereignty over the territory and embarked on an ambitious state-creation exercise, and those challenges clearly extended to refugee return and IDP reintegration.

The forced migration issues in East Timor relate to the response to the initial emergency phase as well as refugee movements and post-conflict return. The diversity of displacement included mass movement out of urban centres, Dili in particular, which were considered too dangerous by thousands of internal refugees; thus urban streets remained eerily quiet for many weeks following the post-referendum violence. Thousands sought refuge for varying periods of time in rural, often mountainous areas above the island's main towns, waiting until the militia had passed through their villages. For those prepared to risk their lives by returning to put out fires and reclaim their lands and the remnants of their property, flight and refuge were relatively short-lived. Many, on the other hand, elected to remain in their forest hide-outs for weeks, confident to re-emerge only when the international peace-keepers had arrived. For some 240,000 people, displacement took the form of a swift and sometimes brutal eviction across the border into camps in West Timor. For those refugees, the experience of displacement turned into a form of captivity that lasted for several months or even years, in extremely dangerous circumstances and with only minimal assistance from international agencies.

Burundi

Burundi's history since gaining independence from Belgium in 1962 has been one of rivalry and conflict betweens its two largest ethnic groups, the Hutu majority and the Tutsi minority which has traditionally formed the ruling class. Despite a shared language, religion and culture, the smallest of differences have been manipulated to rigidify this categorisation of Burundi's populations and promote the politics of separation pursued through violence. Including the massacres of 1972, this has resulted in the deaths of over half a million people and the displacement of several hundred thousand more. Broadly, three categories of IDPs, with some movement between the categories, are referred to in Burundi: the *displaced* in IDP camps, the *regrouped* in regroupment or former regroupment camps and the *dispersed* who do not live in camps but rather live in the forests and marshes or have sought refuge with relatives or friends. The terminology employed can lead to confusion. For instance, references to IDPs or displaced persons can sometimes refer only to those in IDP camps.

Many Burundians fled abroad and many more were displaced, some temporarily and some more long-term. There are currently some 750,000 Burundian refugees living in Tanzania – most of these since 1972 – in refugee camps, villages and communities along the border with Burundi. Another 281,000 internally displaced persons (IDPs) reside in camps in Burundi, while approximately 100,000 other men, women, adolescents and children are otherwise dispersed in the country. The number of refugees and IDPs combined thus amounts to more than 17 per cent of the total Burundian population. Damage to the infrastructure inside the country due to the conflict has been devastating and the conditions and quality of life have deteriorated severely because of the crisis.

In 1998, negotiations for peace were initiated. The Arusha Peace and Reconciliation Agreement for Burundi (subsequently Peace Agreement) was signed by most, but significantly not all, of the parties to the conflict on 28 August 2000. No ceasefire was agreed upon. The agreement remains fragile and could collapse at any time. In fact, fighting intensified following the signing of the Peace Agreement, primarily between extremist Hutu rebel factions and the Burundian armed forces. Refugee flows to Tanzania, which had been decreasing steadily between January and July 2000, consequently increased. Civilians continue to be caught in the middle and the numbers of deaths continue to rise. Both rebel forces and extremists within the Burundi military are implicated in attacks against civilians and humanitarian aid organisations. Regional instability and conflict further complicate prospects for peace in Burundi.

Georgia

Inter-ethnic conflict dominated the internal politics of Georgia throughout the first half of the 1990s, causing massive displacement of the population from conflict zones, and in the case of ethnic Ossetians from outside the South Ossetian region as well.

On the collapse of the Soviet Union, the Abkhaz constituted approximately 18 per cent of the total population of Abkhazia, whereas Georgians made up approximately 46 per cent. Conflict in Abkhazia erupted in 1992 after the Abkhaz members of the region's supreme soviet voted for independence. Georgian troops entered Abkhazia but suffered a comprehensive defeat in the following year. The war led to the displacement of over 300,000 persons, most of them Georgians, and the devastation of the once thriving agricultural and tourist destination. In 1994 the Georgian and Abkhaz sides, under the auspices of the United Nations and with facilitation by the Russian Federation, signed the Moscow Agreement on the Separation of Forces, bringing two years of fighting to a halt. However, relations have continued to be tense, leading to resumption of hostilities, most dramatically in May 1998 when fighting broke out in Gali District, causing the renewed displacement of approximately 30,000–40,000 persons, many of whom were returnees receiving assistance from international organizations who were now displaced for the second time. During those events, many homes and communal facilities built or rehabilitated by UNHCR to support returnees were destroyed. Despite protracted efforts by the international community, the peace process remains in a deadlock.

During the Soviet era the South Ossetian Autonomous Region was relatively prosperous; its mines, factories, and farms supplied raw materials to markets across the Soviet Union, and the mountainous regions of Java were dotted with tourist resorts. Following the collapse of the Soviet Union in 1989, the South Ossetian Supreme Soviet declared its intention to raise its status to that of an autonomous republic within Georgia. The Georgian authorities annulled this decision and further revoked South Ossetia's status as an autonomous region. A violent conflict ensued during 1989–92.

As a direct consequence of the Georgian–Ossetian conflict, South Ossetia and adjoining regions of Georgia proper suffered substantial material damage, and over 60,000 individuals, mainly ethnic Ossetians, were displaced from their homes. Some 40,000 of them crossed into North Ossetia in the Russian Federation and became refugees. At the same time several violent earthquakes and aftershocks struck the region, causing significant damage. As early as the summer of 1992, an attempt was made to seek an amicable solution to the conflict. A ceasefire agreement was signed, leaving the authorities of the former region in control of Tskhinvali, Java, Znauri and parts of Akhalgori, and the central government in control of Akhalgori and several isolated ethnic Georgian villages. A peacekeeping force was deployed, consisting of Russian, Ossetian and Georgian troops and known as the Joint Peacekeeping Force or JPKF.

In November 2001, local presidential elections, unrecognised by the international community, were held in South Ossetia. This resulted in the defeat of the incumbent and a relatively peaceful transfer of power to the new *de facto* president and administration. Despite passing tensions in negotiations and security repercussions on the ground, the Georgian–South Ossetian conflict settlement process continued with regular meetings in 2002 and 2003. As a result, some agreements were reached on important issues related to security matters, economic rehabilitation and IDPs/refugees.

Taken together, the conflict in South Ossetia in 1991 and the events in Abkhazia in 1992–93 resulted in mass displacement. According to UNHCR data as of 31 December 2003, Georgia has currently 12,821 IDPs from Ossetia and 247,394 from Abkhazia. Together they comprise 6 per cent of Georgia's population (4.4 million according to the General Population Census 2000). This is not taking into account Ossetians displaced from parts of Georgia other than South Ossetia who have moved there, including those who have recently left the Pankisi Gorge for Tskhinvali because of insecurity. Statistics provided by UNHCR show a total male IDP population of 116,274 (45 per cent) and a total female population of 143,941 (55 per cent); among the adult population of 188,980, roughly 57 per cent (108,629) are women and roughly 43 per cent (80,351) are men.

The concentration of IDPs and hence their pressure on the local situation differ widely in different parts of Georgia. The majority of IDPs (100,750 persons) live in Samegrelo, a region bordering Abkhazia, and Imereti (29,916 persons). However, the number of IDPs residing in the capital Tbilisi has been steadily growing, amounting to 95,044 persons as of 31 December 2003. IDPs are moving from rural to urban areas, especially to the capital, in search of better employment, better living conditions and better education opportunities for their children.

Colombia

Colombia has experienced conflicts and displacement for over 40 years. The conflicts reflect the complicated political alignments in contemporary Colombia, and all the armed groups engaged in these conflicts have either deliberately or indirectly caused displacement.

During the 1980s and early 1990s, the paramilitary forces confronted the civilian population primarily in the areas where sympathy for the guerrillas was known to be high. The guerrillas, in fact, were protecting peasants in 'areas of colonization', i.e. in places where the latter had settled on unoccupied land, formally claimed – but not used – by large owners and to which they had no titles. The paramilitary/AUC forces displaced them in the name of preserving private property for the formal owners and in order to eliminate support for guerrillas. After 1994, as noted, drug traffickers expanded operations in Colombia and the guerrillas spread beyond their earlier bases in the poorer departments of the country. The consolidated paramilitary and AUC forces amassed wealth and power, and successfully contested guerrilla control in the latter's previous strongholds. As the armed groups compete in their quests for land, all concerned have profited – save the peasants who continue to be killed and forcibly displaced, and the Colombian state. Violence and displacement today encompass regions of commercial agriculture, large agricultural and cattle ranching holdings, and are on the rise in oil producing sites.

While displacement follows as conflict expands, relatively few among the present population of displaced persons have left simply to flee armed clashes. The majority of the displaced since 1995 attribute their flight to fear, threats, massacres, direct attacks on themselves, and extreme pressures to enter the ranks of the armed parties.

Nor is forced displacement solely the result of violence. The area around Putumayo was wrested from guerrilla influence by the paramilitaries, and is a major site of coca fumigation, supported by US funds. With the initiation of fumigation in 2000, there were predictions of significant increases both in internal displacement and cross-border flight. In reality, the fumigation zones have seen increasing levels of violence since the breakdown of the peace talks in early 2002, and massive displacement has been occurring for combined reasons. Among those most affected by the recent displacements have been indigenous groups.

In the early 1990s poor rural Colombians moved on a continuing basis but in small numbers to towns and cities in search of better socio-economic opportunities and social services. Most remained in their region of origin, but gradually more individuals and families found their way to the larger cities. This typical form of rural–urban migration was transformed by the end of the decade, and by 2001 some 70 per cent of the internal movement was directed at major urban centres. At the same time, political violence rather than poverty became the principal cause of internal migration. Since 2002 there has been a significant increase in cross-border movements (people crossing into the neighbouring countries of Ecuador, Venezuela and Panama) and migration further afield to the US and Europe as well as internal displacement.

The typical pattern of displacement migration begins either with threats or attacks made against residents of a rural community or an armed confrontation. The press, human rights reports and international missions have confirmed dozens – if not hundreds – of such peasant dislocations. The guerrillas, for their part, increasingly attack peasant families believed to have had dealings with the paramilitary forces and forcibly recruit youth, especially in indigenous communities. They demand active support from the peasant population, and expel those who deny such support (personal interviews with some of those displaced). The FARC has directly targeted civilians where they have sought refuge and, in addition, have been increasingly attacking urban areas. In 2003, the FARC increasingly launched its attacks in heavily populated major urban centres.

Humanitarian challenges and constraints on assistance

Despite wide variations in the circumstances of displacement, in the complex forced migration emergencies just described, the humanitarian challenges are similar, as are the constraints on success in relation to the delivery of assistance and the provision of protection. In such crises it is clear that many factors constrain humanitarian effectiveness and some of the key findings from the case studies are outlined below. Those same constraints impact on refugee repatriation and IDP return programmes and they will be discussed in the following section.

Relief and security

A wide range of security problems form perhaps the greatest current challenge to the international community's capacity to provide humanitarian relief, not only in the conflict situations described in this chapter, but throughout the world. It has been the focus of the UN Secretary General's attention in reports to the Security Council and the General Assembly. While recognizing that the ultimate responsibility for security rests with the host government in which the humanitarian operation takes place, the UN has put into place measures to increase the safety of its personnel and other humanitarian workers. The daily realities for all those working in conflict situations include the unpredictable flaring up of violence resulting in official and unofficial restrictions on travel, staff evacuations and the cancellation of relief programmes. Humanitarian workers are at considerable risk during fighting and are frequently directly targeted in the course of their work. In Burundi, for example, in 2000 an Italian priest was ambushed and killed by soldiers; shortly after, an Italian nun was killed by armed men. Some observers have suggested that these killings were intended to create panic and instability. In the same year three UNHCR personnel were murdered close to refugee camps in West Timor. Those killings had a profound effect on the UN and its perceptions of its work in West Timor and the management of its operations. Following the attacks, what limited access to the camps the international community had secured was further restricted and this had the impact of increasing the demand for an accelerated return programme and the closure of the camps.

It raised also the complex issue of organised criminality in conflict situations and the added dangers this presents for international staff. The West Timor camps were established by militia gangs in part to enable smuggling and other activities to flourish in the chaos of post-referendum East Timor. The coming together of political and criminal extremism similarly presented heightened security dangers in the Balkans in the 1990s. This targeting of humanitarian workers and its implications for humanitarian relief have been another tragic feature of the Iraq occupation.

Insecurity and the unpredictability of violence inevitably affect the quality and amount of humanitarian assistance that can be provided. The inability to predict whether peace will be established in the short term, or when it will come about, and what will happen in the meantime, makes forward planning and programming extremely difficult. Humanitarian workers can easily become demoralised in these circumstances and many humanitarian organisations and agencies are stretched to, or beyond, their capacity to react and are often forced to resort to employing inexperienced, albeit well-meaning staff. However, in all of the emergencies studied, but perhaps exceptionally so in East Timor, where staff refused evacuation, preferring instead to remain behind with their East Timor workers as the militia attacked the capital Dili, the commitment of UN and other agency staff is exemplary and pivotal in guaranteeing essential assistance.

Circumstances of displacement and the provision of relief

Any humanitarian response must adapt to the fluidity of population movements and the range of challenges these present. For example, the duration of displacement, whether long- or short-term, shapes which relief-development interventions are feasible. Further the security situation in the region of displacement, whether the displaced find themselves within or outside conflict areas, shapes the protection challenge. Similarly the residence of the displaced, whether resident in or outside camps or with relatives, shapes both protection and relief-development measures. And finally, the conditions of resettlement or relocation are critical in the type and duration of relief-development interventions. It was evident in all the emergencies studied for this chapter, that the categories attached to displaced people, whether 'displaced', 'internally displaced people', 'dispersed' or even 'regrouped' cover a great range of experiences that profoundly influence the form and provision of assistance. Humanitarian regimes require highly sophisticated structures of coordination if they are to be effective in such diversities of displacement. But it is evident in all of the case studies that there are glaring disparities in the treatment and coverage of displaced and war-affected people.

In the case of Sri Lanka, the living conditions and life chances of displaced people varied greatly according to the geographical area in which they found themselves, the reach of the humanitarian regime and the duration of displacement. The outcome of the combination of these various factors, circumstances and entitlements was a range of experiences of displacement. The following could be distinguished:

- *Refugees* still in exile.
- *Returnees,* mainly from Tamil Nadu in India, living in transit or welfare camps, or with friends or relatives.
- *Internally displaced people* in transit camps or welfare centres, or living with friends or relatives; these might be locally displaced within their own districts or displaced over greater distances.
- *Resettled* people: those who had returned to their homes.
- *Relocated* people: those who had found or been found new homes, usually in their own districts.

Each of these categories could be further divided according to whether they were in areas held or controlled by the government or by the LTTE (which determines access to assistance); the distance and duration of displacement; the number of times they had been displaced; conditions (such as changed ethnic composition) in the area from which they had been displaced, and therefore the possibility or likelihood of return; and the time elapsed since they had been displaced, resettled or relocated.

In Colombia, being labelled as an IDP has strongly negative consequences. The displaced persons themselves are all but 'invisible' in terms of their perceived importance in national policies and geopolitics. Insofar as they are visible, it is in being perceived as collective blights on society. The displaced are blamed for crime, for environmental degradation, and for lowering the living standards of the local populations in the places where they settle. Regardless of how they characterise themselves, they are assumed to have links with one of the armed groups. In Colombia the government is criticised for its failure to adequately address displacement, but it is fair to say the problem has become an issue of national debate not because of humanitarian concern so much as because the IDPs are seen to exacerbate local problems and demand services the state cannot provide.

Broadly, three categories of IDPs, with some movement between the categories, are referred to in Burundi: the *displaced* in IDP camps, the *regrouped* in regroupment or former regroupment camps and the *dispersed* who do not live in camps but rather live in the forests and marshes or have sought refuge with relatives or friends. Treatment and conditions inside the IDP camps were generally better than the regroupment camps although poor conditions and suffering have been features of both. Conditions inside the camps were for the most part appalling and some of the camps were inaccessible to humanitarian agencies. Women and children in particular were vulnerable when food was short. They were often sidelined at food distributions, sometimes despite the efforts of distribution agencies. There also were reports of the rape and sexual abuse of women and young girls in the camps (Human Rights Watch 2000: 18–20).

Similarly in East Timor, those forcibly evacuated into refugee camps in West Timor confronted intolerable conditions and were by and large beyond the reach of the humanitarian regime established to deal with the crisis. From the case studies therefore it is clear that relief and assistance interventions are far from uniform and consistent, and that the experiences of displacement, the circumstances of displacement and attitudes towards the displaced impact the quality and quantity of assistance that conflict-affected populations are able to access.

Declining aid budgets

Humanitarian budgets globally are stretched and this affects both the overall amounts of aid committed to specific emergencies and commitments within those emergencies. The humanitarian aid dollar follows high-profile and strategically important conflicts (such as Afghanistan and Iraq) while neglecting others (Sudan and the African Great Lakes region). The civil war in Abkhazia, for example, led to mass displacement and economic collapse, which severely impoverished much of the population. While international humanitarian agencies continue to provide aid, targeting the most acute food and medical needs among the most vulnerable segments of the population, international aid has been steadily decreasing since 1998. During this time the humanitarian situation has not significantly improved and, according to most humanitarian organisations present in the region, has been aggravated for many people.

It was certainly the case in East Timor and Georgia and to a lesser extent in Sri Lanka that, despite a proven case that humanitarian aid was still required for vulnerable groups, it became a commonly shared view of the international community active in those countries that the provision of emergency relief should give way to development aid designed to address the underlying causes of humanitarian needs more proactively. In Colombia emergency assistance made available through government and non-government sources fell far short of meeting the humanitarian challenges posed by so large a number of uprooted people.

As attention shifts from low-level rehabilitation activities and the improvement of basic living conditions to more structural and adjustment type support, emergency-related needs are in many cases neglected. This is extremely important in relation to return and reintegration programmes, because for those populations their situation on return resembles in many ways an emergency type situation. Returnees from West Timor, for example, found on their return to East Timor that their homes had been destroyed and they urgently required shelter kits. However, humanitarian agencies had previously deemed that emergency shelter requirements had been met and no further orders had been placed for tarpaulin or wooden poles, leaving returnees seeking shelter in schools and hospitals.

Incoherence in coordination

In each of the case study countries, perhaps with the exception of East Timor, there was an acknowledgement on the part of the main humanitarian players of the overly fragmented nature of relief provision. Research in all countries found that better institutional coordination was crucial to improving effectiveness of relief, reconstruction, reconciliation and, importantly, repatriation and reintegration. Poor coordination was seen to result in the duplication of effort, a lack of prioritisation, and uncertainties about leadership or planning systems in any given response. Such institutional incoherence not only hinders efforts at tackling immediate and underlying problems but presents a poor image to the international community, sometimes resulting in a failure to attract international donations. The case of Burundi was perhaps the most extreme example of institutional failure contributing significantly to an overall humanitarian failure, and this occurred largely because of the unwillingness of any of the principal actors to address seriously the humanitarian needs of the civilian population. Many agencies including the Burundian Government were responsible for this lack of attention. For example, the UN significantly pulled back its presence, withdrawing all non-essential international staff following the murder of two of its officials. The killings shocked the humanitarian community, especially the UN, and their impact can still be felt today. Following this attack, coordination among UN agencies and between the UN and national and international NGOs deteriorated. The UN mostly stays in urban areas, restricting the movement of its staff because of continued security threats. The impact of this on attempts to repatriate refugees, particularly from Tanzania, is described below.

In Colombia, despite relatively sophisticated coordination and response mechanisms, assistance was insufficient and failed to reach beneficiaries months after their displacement, and displaced persons, for the most part, lost whatever health and education benefits they had in their communities of origin. In their new places of residence, numerous bureaucratic obstacles prevent them accessing these services even though they were mandated by law.

Refugee repatriation, IDP return, and reintegration

We have addressed the features of complex forced migration emergencies and the shortcomings of humanitarian action within them in some detail in previous sections because, to state the obvious, understanding of the conditions of forced displacement, of exile, and of the role of the humanitarian regime is crucial to an understanding of the dynamics of return.

The conditions outlined in the previous two sections – divided populations with very different experiences of conflict and displacement, poor security, institutional fragmentation and incoherence, funding shortfalls and so on – affect the return of the displaced and of course provide the context for repatriation programmes.

Conceptually, then, return and repatriation programmes need to be understood not as 'new chapter' events signalling a clear shift from conflict to post-conflict nation-building. Rather they must be understood in the context of the type of conflict, the forced migration dynamic and the nature of the humanitarian response. It is this context that will shape return programmes and to a large extent determine the success or failure of them. Some of the most salient contextual factors are as follows:

Conflict often does not have a clear 'end', but is ongoing, often at a local level and perhaps not very visibly, but in a way that directly affects returnees, and may lead to increased tensions between returnees and hosts. For example, where, as is often the case, land disputes were a strong element underlying conflict, return can revisit and re-elevate tensions.

Security issues and the protection of displacees and returnees are not seen as a priority when the focus shifts from emergency to development, leaving a protection gap for returnees.

Humanitarian failings impact on the displaced and returnees in ways that limit their capacity to rebuild livelihoods. For example, there is often a failure to address displacement-related humanitarian needs in the post-conflict phase (such as shelter, health and education) on the assumption that the emergency has passed.

The nature of the humanitarian regime, the institutional setup, the attitudes towards displacement and the attitudes towards the country's transition all shape the type of response. The urgency to move beyond the emergency phase leads to switches in budgets and expertise away from forced displacement issues: in this line of thinking the UNHCR is often under pressure to wind down its operations and withdraw, often prematurely.

Policy and practice are evolving in which World Bank and others see post-conflict conditions as an opportunity for reforms and adjustment in line with neo-liberal agendas. Apart from the general critique as to whether such an approach is intrinsically desirable, this process may well severely limit humanitarian space and lead to co-optation of humanitarian agencies before their work is finished.

It follows that return needs to be re-linked with conflict, displacement and the humanitarian response. This in turn means that elementary, immediate needs must not be overlooked by the international community and governments in devising policies and programmes around return. Problematic issues around return and repatriation, protection, land, humanitarian and anti-poverty action and so on must all be part and parcel of ongoing humanitarian relief and other assistance efforts, and should not be left unaddressed until people begin drifting back homewards. They must rather be planned for and programmed in. In conventional terminology, emergency relief should co-exist with aid for reconstruction and development. Some of these issues as they have arisen in the cases studied are amplified in what follows.

Repatriation and protection gaps

Security and protection are clearly major constraints on the successful delivery of humanitarian assistance in conflict settings, and remain obstacles in the way of refugee and IDP return, often making the whole undertaking of homecoming extremely uncertain. Sometimes the modalities of return can in themselves exacerbate insecurity and increase the vulnerability of returnees. West Timor returns for example were in part conducted through the very militia leaders who in the first place forcibly removed refugees across the border into camps. Investing the militia with the ability to continue to control the lives of returnees saw them re-establishing the relationships of dependency created in the camps (including prostitution and illegal trading) on return to home villages.

Too frequently in repatriation operations, neither international military nor police presences are tasked with guaranteeing the protection of returnees. Again in East Timor, the levels of available protection were woefully insufficient to guarantee security in a context in which tensions between returnees and hosts, particularly where returnees were thought to have been involved in the post-referendum violence, were very high. An Amnesty International (AI) report criticised the UN for 'failing in its primary task of ensuring that the new state of East Timor has protection and promotion of human rights at its core' (AI 2000, 2001). AI assessed that with independence 'the new judicial system was only partially functioning and was fragile and vulnerable to interference'. Judicial officials, AI argued, lacked the necessary support and training to make up for their lack of experience and had been subjected to threats and intimidation. Among East Timorese in general, but on the part of returnees in particular, there was little confidence in the formal judicial procedures, and concern that accelerated repatriation without necessary safeguards was placing refugees at potential risk. Returnees were far more vulnerable than others in the population because of their genuinely pro-Indonesian and anti-independence views; however, mechanisms necessary to monitor and act on potential protection problems once people had returned to their villages were not in place. What 'reactive monitoring' was in place was very limited in scope, and there was no arrangement for UNHCR to hand over returnee protection monitoring to the new Ministry of Justice. There was no guarantee that the ad hoc arrangement with CIVPOL to receive complaints would continue or that there was an acceptance that returnees constituted a particularly vulnerable population.

As McDowell and Eastmond have previously discussed (2002), in many repatriation programmes there is an assumption that refugees are returning to rural communities with a social fabric that is effectively unchanged by previous violence, and that existing community structures and institutions will serve to return the community to the status quo that existed before the violence. But research referred to in this chapter suggests such optimism is unfounded. Returnees pose a whole series of difficulties and, fundamentally, their reappearance in towns and villages alters social relations and places an additional strain on available resources. The genuine fears of returnees about their personal security, the manner of their return tied, as it was in the East Timor case, to an amnesty for former militia, and the complexities of reconciliation at the village level in coming to terms with past acts, together mean that return is fragile and the outcome uncertain.

This is certainly the case in Colombia, where, despite having in place one of the most comprehensive structures in the world for managing and responding to internal displacement, continuing violence and insecurity has meant that neither international nor national programmes have been able to contribute in a meaningful way to enabling the voluntary return and reintegration of the victims of displacement. The absence of any entity guaranteeing the security of returning groups, or any regular monitoring of conditions in places of return, means that very few programmes were or are in place to facilitate economic reintegration; consequently, resettlement projects have been few in number and rarely successful.

The complex issue of land

In all the return programmes reviewed for this chapter, a key recurring issue is whether a returning refugee or IDP can recover the family land. In Colombia, authorities organising return movements have been unable to resolve the legal issues entailed in land and property restoration. UNHCR has taken on this task to a small degree, and the administration has been promoting a programme of land and property registration in places vulnerable to displacement. In Colombia, as elsewhere, returnees' land, if not taken over by parties to a conflict, is likely to be occupied by someone else, in which case the original owners may have to pay rent for access to their own plots. A major gap in many repatriation operations is the failure to provide reparations for losses related to displacement. Considerable research has been conducted on livelihood reconstruction in relation to development-created displacement and comparing this type of involuntary resettlement with refugee return and the economic, social and cultural risks that return entails (Cernea and McDowell 2000). The general conclusion is that in the right enabling environment, with extensive and consultative planning, adequate resources and a long-term commitment, sustainable livelihoods can be rebuilt on return but the development challenge is immense. Secure legal access to adequate, productive and appropriate land is essential. Land ownership alone, however, will not guarantee livelihood re-establishment. Other significant risks including social disarticulation, food insecurity, declining health standards, poor housing, marginalisation and the risk of joblessness also have to be successfully addressed in a comprehensive compensation and development-assistance programme.

The situation in Sri Lanka appears particularly acute in this regard where returnees' attempts to reclaim land and other property – essential for the reconstruction of their livelihoods – are likely to generate tensions where, as is often the case, land and property has been occupied or taken over by others. Such issues are particularly acute in Jaffna and Mannar districts; in the latter there is the further complication of the prospect of the return of tens of thousands of refugees currently in India, also seeking to reclaim their land. This will make for a heady cocktail of locally displaced people, internally displaced people returning from other districts, and returning refugees from India – all looking to occupy or recover land for housing and cultivation.

Where return to original homes and land is not feasible, resettlement in another location is one of few alternatives. Where this has been tried in Colombia, for example, resettlement agricultural land has been provided in relatively safe areas but the projects themselves have tended to fail. First, it became clear that there are very few plots of land that the state controls that can be turned over to returnees. Consequently, resettlers find themselves on privately owned and long uncultivated properties for which they are obliged to pay rent before they can produce anything and while they are clearing, preparing and planting the private land. This generally presents an unsustainable financial hardship, since the displaced returnees have already suffered the loss of personal property, and have usually exhausted their resources in the course of migration. Second, a large number of owners reportedly demanded the return of their land after the first crop was harvested, leaving the resettlers again without a means of livelihood. And lastly, in these examples, very little planning went into either the compatibility of the proposed residents, or the economic viability of the proposed productive activity.

It was the case with Cambodian repatriation in the 1990s that refugees faced considerable hardship on return (see McDowell and Eastmond 2002) and failings were related both to the strategy adopted by the UN and to external factors which increased the vulnerability of returnees. Those external factors included the introduction of new adjustment policies such as the privatisation of land which had a direct impact on returnees inability to secure land; similar issues may now be emerging in Sri Lanka.

Political expediency and unrealistic timeframes

At the outset of this chapter it was suggested that repatriation operations are driven by political rather than humanitarian agendas. Many such operations are intricately tied to the fate of peace agreements and seen as pieces in a jigsaw aimed at legitimising new democratic regimes and therefore of enormous strategic importance to the UN, donors and many Western states. As such, return operations demand the swift and effective movement of large numbers of people in time for elections. In such large-scale organised operations, standardised solutions and tight control are the key to 'operational success' but rarely result in a positive outcome for returnees or their long-term prospects.

External political pressure may include a change in attitude on the part of refugee host countries. In Burundi,[1] it could be argued that recent refugee return from Tanzania – which saw 50,000 returnees in 2003 – was to a large extent driven by the Tanzanian government's impatience with its Burundian refugee population. In 2003 the UNHCR was in the position of having to resist pressure for accelerated return across border areas which it considered – and certainly the refugees themselves considered – unsafe for return. Cuts in food rations to refugees in the Tanzanian camps (to 50 per cent of the daily recommended minimum in 2003) and their sporadic reinstatement were interpreted by the refugees as a sign of imminent forced or encouraged repatriation, and though short of *refoulement* constituted indirect pressure to return.

In East Timor there were pressing political reasons to kick-start a faltering return programme. The so-called 'residual' refugee population had become an obstacle in the path of improving relations between Dili and Jakarta, and indeed between the government of Indonesia and the UN. The UN were applying pressure on Jakarta to take back control of the camps from the local West Timor authorities and the TNI, and in turn to reduce the influence of the militia. Despite the setting up of a refugee 'Task Force' to be headed by senior military and other government officials in Jakarta, the West Timor authorities proved resiliently autonomous and retained their influence over the camps. By claiming an allowance from Jakarta for each of the refugees under its care, the West Timor authorities were inclined to over-estimate the numbers of refugees in the camps, and because they directly benefited from their continued presence, may not have been entirely reliable partners in the UN-sponsored return initiative.

In East Timor itself, the timetable for the handover of responsibility for the main functions of government from UNTAET to the East Timor government-in-waiting influenced the evolving repatriation policy. The UN was seeking a resolution to what was rapidly becoming a refugee crisis at a crucial time in East Timor's transition from a UN-Administered Non-Self-Governing Territory to a fully independent nation-state.[2] The transfer of power was generally known as *Timorisation* and it represented a new and important departure for the UN. Promoted as a showcase example of the UN's 'new approach' to the administration of territories in transition, *Timorisation* represented a form of administration which from the outset claimed to promote *consultation with the people of East Timor, permitted their views to take precedence*, and *encouraged the progressive delegation of authority* to the East Timorese people. The repatriation programme of refugees from West Timor should, therefore, be seen in the context of UNTAET's Administration-through-Partnership approach and its overall stated objective to secure democracy in East Timor, underpinned by formal justice processes (particularly for serious crimes) and human rights, and achieved through consultation. These objectives were contained in a series of Security Council Resolutions, which set out UNTAET's mandate and obligations.

With elections to appoint ministers to the important Council of Ministers held in August 2001, and presidential elections scheduled for May 2003 which would signal the end of UNTAET's mission in East Timor, the UN were anxious to bring about the closure of the camps and the return of refugees. The continued presence on the border presented a security threat and an ever present concern that former militia, intent on resuming their pro-Indonesia campaign, would use the cover of the camps to launch border incursions, and recruit from the remaining refugee population. Such a threat would necessitate the continued presence of a Peacekeeping Force which had already cost in excess of US\$3 billion (up to October 2001) and the UN had experienced problems since September 11 maintaining such a large presence as troops were required to be committed elsewhere.

Return and humanitarian failure

That return and repatriation programmes are in most cases undertaken in the institutional context that shaped the humanitarian response is an obvious point, but bears repeating. Budgets and lines of responsibility may have shifted from a primary emergency focus to one that pursues state-building and medium-term development. However, the culture of the humanitarian regime remains imprinted through an institutional landscape, personnel on the ground, and established working relationships between agencies and the national government. The same problems that were a feature of the humanitarian response are carried over and provide the context in which repatriation operations are conducted. In Colombia, for example, where the system was grossly under-financed and understaffed, responsibilities were vaguely defined and officials rarely if ever held accountable, and only one-third of the approximately 2 million internally displaced received assistance from either the government or international humanitarian agencies (UNICEF 2002), complex repatriation programmes were most unlikely to be successful.

Humanitarian failure impacts on refugee repatriation in complex ways. For example, a series of reviews of the international humanitarian response to the East Timor emergency criticised the shelter programme and the shortfalls in the provision of replacement housing. The UNHCR and NGO programmes, which distributed 50,000 shelter kits (not targeted at former IDPs or returnees) out of an estimated need of 80,000 units, ended in March 2001 and no further kits were available to those returning from the West Timor camps. The World Bank estimated that 15,000 returnee families would be in need of shelter (McDowell and Ariyaratne 2001). The focus of UNTAET in East Timor had shifted from an emergency response to a development response in early 2001 and a previously planned second Consolidated Appeal (CAP) was cancelled, and neither the budget nor the mechanisms were in place to respond in an adequate and timely way to the housing needs of re-turnees. This led to a situation in Aileu District, for example, where more than 100 of 600 returnees who returned to the Sub-District of Lequidoe were forced to find refuge in school buildings, unable to return to their villages.

The lack of preparedness and the lack of attention to returnees' needs had serious implications for the health of returnees and the communities that were expected to absorb them. In 2001 there were a number of cases where returnees with serious health problems were being returned to areas which did not have the means to care for them. There were reports of TB sufferers being returned to areas that were formerly TB free, thus placing healthy populations at risk. Children suffering malnutrition were returned to subsistence economy areas where food productivity had not recovered to its pre-1999 levels, and host families did not have the means to support new households.

Poor planning and insufficient knowledge

Planning for refugee return must be done carefully to avoid an impression of forced repatriation and should specifically involve consultations with all refugees and include them as decision-makers. At present, and the evidence from East Timor and Burundi certainly bears this out, most planning is conducted between UNHCR and government officials from the refugee sending and refugee receiving countries in some rather closed tripartite arrangement charged with overseeing repatriation. Rarely are these discussions broadened to include key sectors of civil society. Sri Lanka would seem to be an exception, where consultative projects were carried out by Oxfam and SCF (UK) (Oxfam and SCF 1998; Harris 2000). Called 'Listening to the displaced', three surveys were conducted between 1996 and 1998. The project's scope, methodology and specific areas of inquiry evolved over time, but there were four basic objectives, focusing on the opinions and perspectives of those people directly affected by the conflict: 'to assess changes in the concerns, needs and capacities of people affected by conflict; to evaluate humanitarian and development inputs from a constituency perspective; to identify issues on which international NGOs could provide improved support to their constituents; and to enable the voices of conflict-affected people to be heard by humanitarian agencies and key parties to the conflict' (Harris 2000: 20). Nearly 2,500 people from 25 displaced communities in the Vanni region and more than 800 returnees to Jaffna participated in the Listening programme in 1998. Such initiatives could be extended to refugees in camps and other displaced populations in preparations for their return.

Repatriation, new humanitarianism and neo-liberal reforms

Post-conflict situations are always fragile and present a new set of opportunities and challenges. The opportunities are principally the reconstruction of normal life; the possibility of return for those who have been displaced from their homes within the country or internationally; and more widely a 'peace dividend' for the whole country.

However, the challenges are many. Two are highlighted here that emerge from the Sri Lanka case but have wider application. The first relates directly to return, and the reality that the return of refugees and other displaced people generates social instability, tension and friction. In the case of Sri Lanka, the return of Tamils, Muslims and Sinhalese to their districts of origin may well upset the ethnic composition that has obtained in those districts during the conflict, with potentially destabilizing political impact. As previously discussed, returnees' attempts to reclaim land and other property – essential for the reconstruction of their livelihoods – will generate tensions where, as is often the case, that land and property has been occupied or taken over by others.

The second challenge is organizational and to some extent conceptual. While there is still great room for improvement, the organizational structures of the humanitarian regime, including the government, have functioned fairly well in Sri Lanka (as in Colombia). If these organizational structures are backed by donor funding, lasting peace in the coming years could be secured. In the short term, however, the emergence of the peace process has led to the proliferation of task forces, working groups and subcommittees within the relief and aid system. Coordination has almost become an end in itself. The relief and reconstruction system has become even more complicated now that joint bodies involving the government and the LTTE are being formed on many different issues. In common with many 'post-conflict' societies, 'post-conflict, pre-peace' Sri Lanka has seen a proliferation of organizations and policies with the prefix 're-' in their description: 'rehabilitation', 'resettlement', 'recovery', 'reconstruction', 're-awakening'. As Hammond (1999: 230–4) and others have pointed out, the use of 're-' words implies a return to the status quo ante, when in fact what is going on is construction of a new society and political economy. In fact, another kind of 're-' process is under way: the 're-casting' of the society and economy, with international and local fractions of capital seeking to shape it for their purposes.

This hints that the real challenges lie not in technocratic organisational change, still less in more 'coordination', but in the local, regional and international political economy. As they have done elsewhere in post-conflict societies (Moore 2000), the World Bank and other international financial institutions will attempt to co-opt the humanitarian industry to shape post-conflict Sri Lanka in a neo-liberal mould. Donor assistance for immediate reconstruction needs is already being made conditional on such moulding – through reform of the legal system and of property rights, for example. The leverage that IFIs and donors will have as a result of Sri Lanka's burgeoning debt (largely military) in coming years will also be substantial. While some such 'adjustment' may be warranted, humanitarians will need to be wary of co-optation and be ready to contest the excesses of such leverage if the transition to peace is to be consolidated.

That this tendency needs careful attention is again borne out by recent experience in Sri Lanka. In recent parliamentary elections (2004) the incumbent party, which had been pursuing peace negotiations with the LTTE, was somewhat surprisingly thrown out of office. Some interpreted this as a protest against the peace process itself, and a manifestation of the perception by the Sinhalese majority that too many concessions were being made to the LTTE. An alternative explanation has been suggested to lie in the donor-led neo-liberal reforms that have been enacted in recent years and which, it has been claimed, have generated unrest in the shape of strikes and other actions by urban workers, as well as disgruntlement in the rural areas: quite a number of pieces of legislation aimed at reforming the land tenure system, the judiciary and other key areas in a neo-liberal direction have gone though parliament since the ceasefire was signed in February 2002. The election result was less against the peace process, it is argued, than against the tenor of neo-liberal reforms driven by the donors who currently hold sway over the Sri Lankan government.

Conclusion

Repatriation programmes have always been political in nature but that politicisation is becoming more overt. The tidying up of the world's displaced, the regrouping and return of those scattered by conflict is presented symbolically as a triumph of global conflict and migration management, and a legitimisation of models of post-conflict transition and societal renewal. The return of East Timorese imprisoned in the militias' West Timor bases, the Burundians of whom the Tanzanian Government has become intolerant, the 'invisible' displaced Colombians who are scapegoats for all the country's current woes, or the internally displaced 'security risks' in Sri Lanka's grim 'welfare centres' are episodes that are seen to close the old chapter on conflict and emergency relief while opening the new chapter on normality, renewal and development. The range of international players involved in post-conflict reconstruction is growing and powerful international financing institutions such as the World Bank working in partnership with bilateral and other multilateral donors and the private sector are directing adjustment programmes which seek a neo-liberal reform agenda. Return and repatriation programmes are being undertaken in this new political and economic context informed by global rather than local priorities or needs.

There are potential dangers in this situation for return and repatriation programmes and for the security and well-being of returnees. As argued above in relation to Sri Lanka, there is the danger that humanitarian agencies will be co-opted into this new reconstruction effort and an already diminishing humanitarian space will be further eroded. When this occurs, humanitarian needs which are always a feature of refugee and IDP return are likely to be further overlooked. Budget lines that have switched from emergency-related needs to longer-term economic development and state-building now under-fund essential shelter and health requirements of both returnees and the communities that play host to them. In a bid to promote the image of post-conflict normality on which longer-term development depends, insecurity and new threats that are directly associated with return are not addressed in peace arrangements or the deployment of peacekeeping forces. Newly establishing governments are as keen as the international community to shake off the label of conflict society or failed state and the realities of residual, simmering and local level conflict are denied.

The forced migration emergencies studied for the MacArthur project and drawn on in this chapter suggest that return and repatriation programmes do not constitute a new phase, a turning of the corner; nor should they necessarily be seen as an indicator of a recovery of democratic norms. Rather it is the planned movement of people itself, the act of repatriating, the footage of people crossing the border that is performative, and suggestive of positive change. But underlying this is a larger and more immediate human drama. We have seen in the case of East Timor that international legal obligations to establish formal procedures to try suspected war criminals are negotiable when they obstruct timely repatriation. Although useful in terms of achieving a bureaucratic solution, the consequences for the displaced were in this case continued vulnerability to exploitation. Elsewhere it is described how rushed repatriation presents direct threats to the well-being of returnees and their hosts by increasing resource demands on communities that cannot absorb newcomers, and introducing health risks.

Evidence presented here suggests, therefore, that the success or failure of return and repatriation programmes will depend to a large extent on the success or failure of the humanitarian regime's response to conflicts in all stages of transition; and in how it responds to conflicts as ongoing, potentially open-ended, complex forced migration emergencies. Complex displacement-related humanitarian challenges do not end with the signing of a peace agreement or the relinquishing of temporary UN sovereignty to a remodelled new government. Those problems continue and they demand sustained, ongoing intervention and support. However, evidence is not strong that the international community, in general, or the United Nations, in particular, has the capacity or the resources to respond to these pressing needs. This of course is a short-sighted view, for neglecting such concerns will most likely help to sustain the conditions that will lead to resurgent complex forced migration emergencies in the future.

Notes

1 In September 2003, UNHCR reported that 95 per cent of Burundi's 500,000 refugees resided in Tanzania. In March 2003, however, UNOCHA reported more than 800,000 Burundian refugees scattered throughout the region. The majority of these lived in 12 refugee camps along Tanzania's western border. An estimated 51 per cent are women, and 56 percent are children[?]. Most are ethnic Hutu who fled between 1993 and 1996, after violence erupted following the murder of President Ndadaye, although there has been a continuous albeit less dramatic

flight in each of the intervening years, mainly to Tanzania. More than half of all Burundian refugees in recent years have originated from four provinces and by far the majority is from provinces bordering Tanzania. (These provinces are Muyinga and Kirundo in the north, Ruyigi in the east, and Makamba in the south.) Most new refugees in 1999 fled from Makamba, Gitega and Kirundo provinces.

In addition to those refugees living in camps, an estimated 170,000–200,000 Burundians (mostly Hutu) live in Tanzanian settlements, some since 1972. Some of these were born in Tanzania, have lived all their lives there, and may speak little or no Kirundi. It is unlikely that substantial numbers of this group will return in the initial stages of repatriation. A further 300,000 Burundians are estimated by the Tanzanian government to be spontaneously settled in Tanzanian villages along the border with Burundi. UNHCR places the figure closer to 470,000. There is no available information on their exact location or their profile.

More than 200,000 refugees returned to Burundi between 1996 and 1999, but many of these fled again when they found the situation in Burundi not conducive enough to retain them. In 1999, there were 64,200 spontaneous new refugees from Burundi, mostly to Tanzania, and 12,200 repatriations. Arrivals from Burundi had been decreasing steadily, UNHCR reported, between the beginning of 2000 and July 2000, after which increased insecurity led to the influx of 7,800 arrivals in Tanzania in August alone. Following the signing of the Arusha Peace Agreement, an additional 78,524 refugees returned from Tanzania to Burundi between 2001 and 2002. UNHCR reported at the end of 2003 that another 81,201 refugees had returned to Burundi during the course of the year, and 44,964 of these were spontaneous returnees.

2 East Timor has never been under UN Trusteeship within the meaning of Chapter XII of the United Nations Charter, which was a system established after the Second World War, applicable to a small number of territories under mandate, territories detached from enemy States as a result of the Second World War, and territories voluntarily placed under the system by States responsible for their administration. The UN Transitional Administration in East Timor was established under a Security Council Resolution which provided its mandate.

References

Amnesty International (2000) *East Timor: Building a new country based on human rights.* ASA 57/05/00.

Amnesty International (2001) *East Timor: Justice past, present and future.* ASA 57/0001/2001.

Cernea, M. M., and McDowell, C. (2000) *Risks and reconstruction* (Washington, DC: World Bank Publications).

Fuglerud, O. (1999) *Life on the outside: The Tamil diaspora and long distance nationalism* (London: Pluto Press).

Hammond, L. (1999) "Examining the discourse of repatriation: Towards a more proactive theory of return migration", in R. Black and K. Koser (eds.), *The End of the refugee cycle: Refugee repatriation and reconstruction* (Oxford: Berghahn Books), pp. 227–44.

Harrell-Bond, B. E. (1989) "Repatriation: Under what conditions is it the most desirable solution for refugees? An agenda for research", *African Studies Review* 32 (1), 41–69.

Harris, S. (2000) "Listening to the displaced: Analysis, accountability and advocacy in action", *Forced Migration Review* 8 (August).

Koser, K., and Black, R. (1999) "The end of the refugee cycle?", in R. Black and K. Koser (eds.), *The end of the refugee cycle: Refugee repatriation and reconstruction* (Oxford: Berghahn Books).

McDowell, C. (1996) *A Tamil asylum diaspora: Sri Lanka migration, politics and settlement in Switzerland* (Oxford: Berghahn Books), pp. 2–17.

McDowell, C., and Ariyaratne, R.A. (2001) *Complex forced migration emergencies: East Timor case study* (Oxford: Option for the Reform of the International Humanitarian Regime Project, University of Oxford, Refugee Studies Centre), 54 pp.

McDowell, C., and Eastmond, M. (2002) "Transitions, state-building and the 'residual' refugee problem: The East Timor and Cambodian repatriation experience", *Australian Journal of Human Rights* 8 (1), 7–27.

Moore, D. (2000) "Levelling the playing fields and embedding illusions: 'Post-conflict' discourse and neo-liberal 'development' in war-torn Africa", *Review of African Political Economy* 83.

Oxfam/SCF (1998) *Listening to the displaced and listening to the returned. A community study. Summary report* (Colombo: Oxfam GB, Save the Children UK).

Rotberg, R. (ed.) (1999) *Creating peace in Sri Lanka: Civil war and reconciliation* (Washington, DC: Brookings Institution Press and the World Peace Foundation).

UNICEF (2002) Press conference, Manuel Manrique, reported by EFE, 5 June. Available at www.efe.com

US Committee for Refugees (2001) *World refugee survey 2001*, Washington DC: USCR.

Wilson, K. B. and Nunes, J. (1994) "Repatriation to Mozambique", in Allen, T. and Morsink, H. (eds.) *When refugees go home* (Geneva: UNRISD), pp. 167–236.

9 Refugee return in Bosnia and Herzegovina

Paul Prettitore

In 1992, war erupted in Bosnia and Herzegovina (B&H) following the break-up of the Federal Republic of Yugoslavia. For the next three and a half years, violence, much of it aimed at displacement of different ethnic/religious groups, created over 1.2 million refugees and 1 million displaced persons out of a population of roughly 4.3 million. Some individuals fled active fighting, while others were forcibly evicted and displaced through the policies of "ethnic cleansing." Roughly 412,000 housing units were damaged or destroyed during the course of the conflict, accounting for almost one-third of the housing stock. In many cases housing was destroyed as a deliberate measure to prevent the return of minorities. Housing that was not destroyed was normally allocated to other individuals on a temporary basis. Much of such housing was occupied by refugees and displaced persons who themselves had lost property elsewhere. However, in many cases individuals who had not been displaced moved to larger and better-situated properties, normally through political connections. This problem was particularly prevalent in urban areas.

The allocation of "abandoned" property during and immediately after the war was extensive. Like the systematic destruction of housing, the allocation of abandoned property was an important tool in the pursuit of ethnic cleansing. During the conflict each group – Bosniaks, Serbs, and Croats – established their own administrations that, among other things, administered "abandoned" property.[1] Legislation was enacted in all areas of B&H that deprived individuals of their property and allocated such property to other individuals on either a temporary or a permanent basis. In the Republic of Bosnia and Herzegovina, both the Law on Temporarily Abandoned Real Property Owned by Citizens[2] and the Law on Abandoned Apartments[3] provided authorities with the ability to allocate property declared abandoned. In the Republic of Herceg-Bosna the Decree on the Use of Abandoned Apartments[4] was enacted. The authorities of the Republika Srpska adopted the Law on the Use of Abandoned Property of the Republika Srpska[5] only in 1996. Prior to this property had been allocated by municipal authorities pursuant to the Decree on Accommodation of Refugees and Other Persons in the Territory of the Republika Srpska,[6] which covered allocation of abandoned property, and the Decree on Accommodation of Refugees,[7] which covered the rationalization of space and forced certain property owners to allow refugees and displaced persons to reside with them. Abandoned property legislation covered not only residential dwellings, but also agricultural land and business premises.[8]

The General Framework Agreement for Peace, otherwise known as the Dayton Peace Agreement (DPA), was signed in Paris on 14 December 1995 and ended the conflict by establishing the state of Bosnia and Herzegovina (B&H) consisting of two entities, the Federation of Bosnia and Herzegovina (Federation of B&H) and the Republika Srpska (RS). The DPA contains 11 annexes governing both civilian and military matters, with the Office of the High Representative taking the lead role of monitoring and fostering all aspects of civilian implementation.[9] Of particular importance to the issue of repossession of property restitution[10] are the Constitution of B&H (Annex 4), the Agreement on Human Rights (Annex 6), the Agreement on Refugees and Displaced Persons (Annex 7), and the Agreement on Civilian Implementation (Annex 10). Annex 7, in particular, includes the right of refugees and displaced persons to return to their prewar places of residence and repossess their prewar property.

Immediately after the signing of the DPA, a Peace Implementation Conference was held in London to mobilize support for the agreement. This conference resulted in the establishment of the Peace Implementation Council (PIC), which consists of 55 countries and international organizations that sponsor and direct the peace implementation process.[11] The PIC provides political guidance to OHR, and has met periodically as the PIC Steering Board to elaborate on OHR's mandate through the issuance of communiqués on aspects of implementation of the civilian aspects of the DPA. A number of these communiqués have addressed the issues of return of refugees and displaced persons and property repossession.

There are a number of similarities between refugee return in B&H and the situation regarding Palestinian refugees. In both cases a large number of civilians were displaced by conflict and abandoned property laws were put into effect to confiscate property of refugees and displaced persons. For these reasons the post-conflict returns process in B&H can offer some useful lessons. However, there are some considerable differences between the situations that should be kept in mind. First and foremost is the extent to which the lengthy duration of displacement in the Palestinian context will infringe on the rights of Palestinian refugees and displaced persons. This is particularly important in relation to rights to restitution of property. After this length of time displaced Palestinians may be more reluctant to return for practical reasons, and so more resources may need to be dedicated to resettlement and compensation. Another major difference will be the extent of enforcement mechanisms. The strong position of international organizations in the administration of B&H allowed for considerable enforcement mechanisms. Alternative enforcement mechanisms will need to be developed for any return process involving displaced Palestinians.

The rights of refugees and displaced persons

The issue of return of refugees and displaced persons was addressed in several ways prior to the end of the conflict. During the course of the conflict a number of UN Security Council resolutions were adopted concerning B&H. Of importance to restitution of property are UN Security Council Resolutions 752 (15 May 1992) and 820 (17 April 1993). In Resolution 752, the Security Council expressed full support for all efforts to assist in the return of displaced persons to their homes. It also called upon all parties concerned to ensure the cessation of forcible expulsions. Resolution 820 expressed Security Council insistence that displaced persons be allowed to return to their former homes, and reaffirmed that any commitments made under duress regarding land and property were null and void. This was especially important as many individuals were forced to exchange property or renounce all rights to property as they were forced to leave their homes.

In March 1994, the Confederation Agreement between the Bosnian Government and Bosnian Croats was signed in Washington, DC.[12] This agreement effectively stopped the conflict between Bosniaks and Croats, and provided for the establishment of the Federation of B&H, one of the postwar entities. This agreement contained a number of provisions regarding the form and function of the Federation, and included specific language on the rights of refugees and displaced persons.[13] In particular, it provided that all refugees and displaced persons had the right to return to their homes of origin, and to repossess, or be compensated for, property lost during the conflict. It also provided that all commitments made under duress regarding property were made null and void. This language set the precedent for the rights included in Annex 7 of the DPA.

The rights established in Annex 7 of the DPA are individual rights, in that each refugee and displaced person is free to exercise any of the rights guaranteed. The first paragraph of Annex 7 states:

> All refugees and displaced persons have the right freely to return to their homes of origin. They shall have the right to have restored to them property of which they were deprived in the course of hostilities since 1991 and to be compensated for any property that cannot be restored to them.[14]

Annex 7 establishes not only individual rights for refugees and displaced persons, but also includes certain obligations on the Parties to ensure the return of refugees and displaced persons.[15] Article I (1) states that "the early return of refugees and displaced persons is an important objective of the settlement of the conflict" and obliges the Parties to accept the return of such persons. In subsequent paragraphs the Parties undertake to ensure that refugees and displaced persons can return without risk of discrimination[16] and agree not to interfere with choice of destination.[17] Article I (3) obliges the Parties to, among other things, take the necessary steps to prevent any activities which would impede safe return of refugees and displaced persons. And of particular importance to the restitution of property, this article specifically obliges the Parties to undertake "the repeal of domestic legislation and administrative practices with discriminatory intent or effect."[18] This provision was used as a basis to adopt post-conflict laws that annulled legislation used to deprive refugees and displaced persons of their property during the conflict.

The right to restitution of property or compensation is also elevated to a constitutional right. Article II of the Constitution of B&H, which is included in the DPA as Annex 4, contains provisions relating to human rights and fundamental freedoms. This article provides:

> All refugees and displaced persons have the right freely to return to their homes of origin. They have the right, in accordance with Annex 7 of the General Framework Agreement, to have restored to them property of which they were deprived in the course of hostilities since 1991 and to be compensated for any such property that cannot be restored to them. Any commitments or statements relating to such property made under duress are null and void.[19]

This provision regarding wartime exchanges of property served as a basis for later legislation that annulled wartime exchanges of property under the assumption they had been completed under duress. Additionally, the Constitution, along with Annex 6 of the DPA (Agreement on Human Rights),[20] obliges the state of B&H and both entities to "ensure the highest level of internationally recognized human rights and fundamental freedoms" and established a Human Rights Commission, composed of the Human Rights Chamber and the Office of the Ombudsman, to ensure compliance.[21] It also established the European Convention for the Protection of Human Rights and Fundamental Freedoms (European Convention on Human Rights – ECHR) and its Protocols as the highest law of B&H,[22] and includes an annex of human rights treaties that are directly enforceable in B&H.[23] Of particular importance to refugees and displaced persons, the ECHR includes the right to home and family life under Article 8, as well as a guarantee of peaceful enjoyment of possessions under Article 1 of Protocol 1. Both of these articles proved important in the exercise of property rights before both the Human Rights Chamber and the Office of the Ombudsman. In addition, both the Constitution and Annex 6 include non-discrimination clauses.[24]

The DPA created a number of special bodies to foster and monitor implementation. In order to facilitate and coordinate the activities under the DPA, the parties agreed under Annex 10 to the designation of a High Representative to be appointed by the Peace Implementation Council (PIC) and endorsed by the United Nations Security Council. The primary responsibilities of the High Representative are to coordinate the activities of civilian organizations and agencies in B&H, and to facilitate as necessary the resolution of any difficulties arising from implementation of the civilian aspects of the DPA. As such, the High Representative is designated as the final authority in B&H regarding interpretation of the civilian aspects of the DPA. In order to provide adequate staff to these issues, the Office of the High Representative (OHR) was established. Since implementation of this mandate proved more difficult than envisioned, the High Representative was accorded increased authority, including the right to impose legislation and dismiss elected and appointed officials.[25] This power has been key to the enactment of adequate legislation concerning the right to repossess property, as after the signing of the DPA none of the Parties were willing or able to enact legislation ensuring the right of return and repossession of property. In addition, the High Representative has dismissed a number of officials for failure to adequately implement property legislation.

Under Annex 6 of the DPA the Commission on Human Rights, consisting of the Human Rights Chamber and the Office of the Ombudsman, was established to assist the Parties in guaranteeing the rights elaborated in the DPA.[26] Both bodies have issued a number of decisions reinforcing property rights. The Office of the Ombudsman is empowered to investigate, on its own initiative or upon request by any Party or person, claims of alleged violations of human rights.[27] The Human Rights Chamber can receive claims referred by the Ombudsman, or on behalf of any Party or person claiming to be the victim of a human rights violation by a Party or acting on behalf of alleged victims who are missing or deceased.[28] Whereas decisions issued by the offices of the Ombudsman institution are advisory in nature, decisions of the Human Rights Chamber are final and binding. Both of these bodies have acted as monitors of the domestic legislature, judiciary, and administration. And since B&H joined the Council of Europe in July 2002, property owners can now file claims to the European Court of Human Rights.

The return of refugees and displaced persons

The return of refugees and displaced persons in B&H has taken two forms: return to reconstructed housing and return to occupied housing. Return in Bosnia began mostly with refugees and displaced persons returning to destroyed housing that had been reconstructed by the international community. The pace of return was in many ways dictated by the amount of available funding. This property was located primarily in rural areas or on the outskirts of urban areas. Return to occupied property was initially slow primarily because the rights of temporary occupants had not yet been addressed. In general, cases of occupied property tended to be located in urban centres. Return to contested space was wholly dependent on implementation of legislation enacted to allow for the repossession of property by refugees and displaced persons. In most cases local authorities were reluctant to evict temporary occupants, most of whom were of the same ethnicity, to return properties to minorities. The primary obstructions to the removal of temporary occupants were political, including official propaganda and intervention by war veterans' groups and organizations promoting resettlement. Housing offices commonly rejected submission of claims or charged illegal fees. The institutional capacity of housing offices was left deliberately weak, primarily through the hiring of unqualified personnel and the lack of resources. In order to address these issues, the international community devised a number of strategies, which met with varying levels of success.

Return programs

Early observations of the Return and Reconstruction Task Force

Throughout the return process a number of return programs were initiated or supported by the international community. Most of these were coordinated by the Reconstruction and Return Task Force (RRTF). The conclusions of the London Peace Implementation Conference established the RRTF with the mandate of coordinating an integrated approach to the return of refugees and displaced persons. It was expected that in 1997 roughly 200,000 refugees and displaced persons would return. The Office of the High Representative took chairmanship of the RRTF, and the other participating institutions included UNHCR, the European Commission, the World Bank, the International Management Group, and the Commission for Real Property Claims. OHR reported that in 1996 roughly 90 percent of returns were spontaneous in nature and followed no organized process.[29] It was also pointed out that in order for safe and orderly return to take root it was necessary for the establishment of the rule of law and certain political conditions, including positive conditionality for the return of minorities.

The basis for the 1997 RRTF plan was for the return to "cluster areas," selected by the following criteria: a) projected numbers of returns; b) present and pre-war population; c) level of damage; d) political climate; e) potential impact of investment upon return; f) the grouping of target areas into regional clusters and hubs.[30] The RRTF report of July 1997 highlighted the fact that many refugees and displaced persons were returning to areas near their prewar homes, but were prevented from returning to their actual homes. In this respect, the RRTF called for a breakthrough on minority returns. In order to make its recommendations more effective on the ground, the RRTF established four Regional RRTFs covering the whole of B&H. The RRTF Report of December 1997 reiterated support of the "cluster areas," while introducing two more tracks to this three-track approach: (i) the need to broker minority returns to strategically important areas and (ii) the provision of flexible funding to support spontaneous returns.[31] The RRTF plan for

1998 focused on four pillars: political environment and security; economic revival and employment; housing; and local infrastructure.[32] Mechanisms for progress on these pillars included conditioning donor assistance on the acceptance of minority returns and matching reconstruction assistance to areas of spontaneous returns.

UNHCR's "Open Cities" Initiative

During this time, UNHCR launched the first return program in B&H – the "Open Cities" Initiative. The aim of this initiative was to encourage municipalities to publicly declare their willingness to support the return of minorities. If a municipality requested recognition as an Open City, UNHCR and other international organizations would make an assessment based on a set of criteria, which focused on a demonstrated willingness to support the return and reintegration of minorities, particularly in the exercise of basic human rights and access to employment and education.[33] This program was originally backed by US$5 million dollars from the US Department of State, which was followed by funding from other international donors.

However, the "Open Cities" Initiative met with little success.[34] Monitoring of municipalities declared open cities was weak, and no set criteria were maintained to ensure progress beyond the designation of "open" status. Another problem was that most donors had their own funding priorities. Often donors prioritized areas that were not declared "open cities", and were not interested in allocating considerable funds to municipalities that were declared open. This was the case not only in relation to the "Open Cities" Initiative, but also affected RRTF attempts to coordinate reconstruction projects. Some European countries preferred to allocate funding to areas that were the prewar homes of refugees they were currently hosting. Other donors chose locations for political reasons. For instance, much assistance of the US Government was focused on Brcko and Central Bosnia at the start of the returns process. The Open Cities initiative demonstrated that the international community would have to play a serious role in monitoring all aspects of the return process if it were to be successful. It also highlighted the fact that sustainability issues, primarily employment, were an integral part of the returns process.

Empty political promises – the Sarajevo Declaration and the Banja Luka Regional Return Conference

The first serious attempt at political support on the part of B&H officials for return came in the form of the Sarajevo Declaration.[35] As the capital of B&H and a model of co-existence, Sarajevo was expected to set the pace for the return of refugees and displaced persons. To lead by example, officials of Sarajevo Canton and the Federation of B&H agreed to enable the return of at least 20,000 minorities residents during the course of 1998. To achieve this a number of issues needed to be addressed: legislative; housing; education; employment; and security. Legislative issues included implementation of property legislation and the Federation of B&H Amnesty Law, and ensuring access to documents necessary for reintegration. Sarajevo authorities agreed to improve management of available housing to support returns, and established the Sarajevo Housing Committee, which monitored housing issues. On the education front steps were to be taken to reintegrate minority students including the reform of text books and curricula. Authorities also agreed to adopt and implement fair labor standards and provide a secure environment for returnees. The Banja Luka Conference, attended by officials of B&H, Croatia, and Yugoslavia, covered many of the same issues.[36] Recommendations were made that B&H officials would adopt and implement legislation consistent with Annex 7. Other steps were to be taken to promote return and reintegration, including the hiring of minority police officers and promotion of the freedom of movement.

In general, neither the Sarajevo Declaration nor the Banja Luka Conference resulted in considerable returns. This was due primarily to the lack of political will. Implementation of the Sarajevo Declaration was severely undermined by the lack of an adequate legal framework to support restitution of property. What legislation did exist was implemented in a discriminatory manner. In particular, Sarajevo officials were reluctant to address the issue of individuals residing in occupied property who had access to other properties – known as "double occupants." On the practical side, Sarajevo also encountered problems creating space for returns because it hosted many displaced persons from the eastern Republika Srpska, an area where very few returns were taking place. Implementation of the recommendations from the Banja Luka Conference also remained inadequate, primarily because of political obstruction.

However, a number of lessons were learned from these political exercises. In regard to the Sarajevo Declaration, the international community put into practice the policy of conditionality. When necessary given the poor performance of Sarajevo and Federation of B&H Officials, the international community would place sanctions on assistance, such as reconstruction of housing and infrastructure, in Sarajevo Canton. This proved an effective measure to further implementation. These political exercises also demonstrated that, because of the nature of displacement, return would have to take place throughout the region at the same time and under the same conditions if there was truly to be a breakthrough on minority returns. In many cases obstruction to return in a certain area would create a logjam in overall return initiatives. Lastly, it became apparent that political agreements on their own would not lead to considerable returns. Such agreements made the ability to return subject to political whims and objectives. Not only was this an inefficient way to support returns, but it was also contrary to the guarantee of individual rights of refugees and displaced persons enshrined in the DPA and the B&H Constitution.

The international community gets serious – the RRTF 1999 Action Plan

The RRTF 1999 Action Plan was a major step forward in the return process, as it adopted a fully comprehensive and integrative approach to the return of refugees and displaced persons.[37] While explicitly stating that the responsibility for the slow rate of return thus far rested with B&H officials, it also outlined the tools available to the international community to overcome these obstructions by forcing a breakthrough in minority returns. Up until this time only a small number of returnees were minorities. The primary obstacles to minority return were political, including obstruction in the adoption of adequate property laws; failure to provide security to returnees; and lack of access to employment, healthcare, pensions, and education. Recognizing that political interventions and economic conditionality could achieve results, what the 1999 Action Plan asked of the international community was the following: greater political will and acceptance of minority return as the key activity; more focused and coordinated activities; a redirection of donor assistance to support returns; and acceptance that the Plan would have to be driven, and the financial resources and management authority necessary to do so would be provided.

The 1999 Action Plan focused on three factors necessary for a breakthrough in minority returns: space, security, and sustainability. The problem of space was due mainly to the fact that most housing belonging to refugees and displaced persons was either destroyed or occupied, and in order for return to take place space would have to be generated. Space could be generated in a number of ways. One of the easiest ways to generate space, at least politically, was the reconstruction of destroyed housing by international donors focusing on RRTF's priority axis. However, the amount of space that could be generated in this way was dependent on the amount of funding available.[38] It also became dependent on the willingness of local officials to ensure beneficiaries of housing reconstruction in turn vacated any property they were occupying. Another mechanism for generating space was the elimination of illegal and double occupancy through improved mechanisms for housing management. Double occupancy refers to individuals who came to occupy more than one property during the course of the war.[39] This mechanism was wholly dependent on the willingness of B&H officials to develop and implement adequate property laws, and the willingness of the international community to monitor this process strictly. The RRTF also recommended a number of other ways to generate space: the construction of buffer accommodation; accelerated return of Croatian Serbs to Croatia; resettlement through the managed allocation of land plots, although no foreign assistance would be granted; and reform of the B&H property market to support sale and exchanges of property.[40]

Security was a key factor in the decision-making process of potential returnees. In order to ensure adequate security, a number of measures were recommended and implemented. These included the recruitment of minority police officers, working with receiving communities on prevention measures, and ensuring adequate patrolling by SFOR. Sustainability concerns were also frequently cited by potential returnees. The most key factors affecting sustainability are employment, education, and access to health and social services. To this end RRTF recommended a number of measures, including assessments and the establishment of working groups to make further recommendations on certain issues.

The problem of occupied property

Birth of the Property Law Implementation Plan

While return to destroyed housing progressed in relation to the amount of funding made available by the international community,[41] return to occupied property was stalled by political obstructions. Throughout this process, the implementation of decisions proved the most difficult task, primarily because in many instances implementation was dependent on the forcible eviction of the current occupant. In most instances local officials were hoping considerable delays in the process would force individuals to give up on claims and instead resettle in ethnically homogeneous areas. During the early stages of the process, local officials would allow the return of property in rural areas while preventing repossession of property in city centers in an attempt to keep minority populations marginalized. The obstructions to the process were primarily political, and included the failure to accept claims; charging of illegal fees for the filing of claims; the failure to implement forced evictions of temporary occupants; and deliberately keeping housing offices understaffed and without adequate resources, such as electricity, computers, and telephones.

Under Annex 7 of the DPA, the parties to the agreement were obligated to revoke domestic legislation that denied displaced persons the right to repossess their property.[42] However, despite continued promises of cooperation, local authorities were unwilling to adopt adequate legislation despite having been provided draft legislation by the international community in May 1997 (Hastings 2001). Following this the PIC requested that the appropriate legislation be adopted and recommended that international assistance for reconstruction of housing be conditional on the necessary changes being made.[43] Only after extensive negotiations with the international community did the Federation in April 1998 adopt property legislation geared towards returning property lost during the conflict. Three laws were enacted: the Law on Cessation of the Application of the Law on Temporarily Abandoned Real Property Owned by Citizens, the Law on Cessation of Application of the Law on Abandoned Apartments, and the Law on Taking Over the Law on Housing Relations.[44] The Republika Srpska (RS) followed by enacting the Law on Cessation of Application of the Law on Use of Abandoned Property in December of 1998.[45] However, these laws still had a number of problematic provisions.

In particular, there was no mechanism provided for forcible evictions, appeals against decisions granting repossession could delay implementation of the decisions, and prewar owners could repossess property only if the current occupant residing in the property was able to repossess their property at the same time (Hastings 2001: 230).

Given the reluctance of B&H officials to adopt adequate legislation, the High Representative was forced in 1999 to impose considerable amendments to legislation in each of the two entities,[46] pursuant to his powers granted by the PIC in Bonn. This imposition established the legal framework for ensuring the right to repossess property and mostly harmonized the property repossession process in both entities. Further amendments were made over the next several years, with considerable amendments imposed by the High Representative in December 2001.

Key aspects of the laws on cessation[47]

The claims process follows an administrative, rather than a judicial process.[48] A large number of claims for repossession of property would have overwhelmed B&H's judicial system, and claimants would have been forced to wait for years for resolution of their cases. In addition, the B&H court system at the end of the conflict was viewed as ethnically biased, in particular as some refugees and displaced persons had been deprived of their property through court proceedings. In total, refugees and displaced persons have filed more than 216,000 claims for the repossession of habitable property.[49]

First and foremost, the Laws on Cessation cancelled the further application of wartime legislation on abandoned property. They also obliged the competent authorities to issue decisions on both the rights of owners to repossess the property, and the rights of temporary occupants. The temporary occupant is entitled to remain in the property under the applicable legal conditions until a decision has been issued on the claim filed by the prewar owner or an authorized proxy. In order to process the claims, Bosnian authorities established housing offices in every municipality in B&H.[50] Owners could submit claims for private property to either the municipal housing office or the Commission for Real Property Claims (CRPC). Claims for socially owned property[51] were to be made to the municipal housing office, but CRPC would also accept claims if the claimant could demonstrate the municipal housing office did not accept the claim or did not issue a decision within the legally prescribed time period. There is no deadline for the filing of claims for private property.[52]

Upon receipt of the claim, the administrative body is under an obligation to issue a decision within 30 days.[53] However, in practice decisions were rarely issued within 30 days, thanks to a combination of political obstruction and lack of resources allocated to the housing offices. Claims are supposed to be resolved in chronological order based on the date the claim was filed. Decisions also contained an explicit warning against looting of the property. Decisions can be appealed to the competent second instance body within fifteen days by either the claimant or current user. However, appeals do not suspend the implementation of the decision.[54] Either party can also appeal from the second instance administrative body and then through the domestic court system. The deadline for the current user to vacate the property depends on his/her housing needs. The deadline is 15 days in cases where the housing needs of the temporary user are otherwise met. If the housing needs of the temporary user are not otherwise met, a decision is given with a 90-day period to vacate the property.[55]

If a temporary occupant does not vacate the property within the specified deadline, the claimant must request enforcement of the decision. At this time, the local housing office must schedule a forcible eviction and secure participation by the local police office.[56] The repossession of the property by the owner is supposed to be recorded in minutes, including the current state of the premises and movable objects by the competent authorities. If minutes are not available from the time the property was declared abandoned, the competent authority is obliged to conduct an inspection at the time the decision on repossession is issued.[57] These measures are necessary to prevent, as far as possible, looting and damage to the property by the temporary occupant. Authorities are also obliged, pursuant to the relevant entity criminal codes, to initiate prosecutions for looting or deliberate destruction by the temporary occupant. It is important to note that there is no legal obligation to physically return in order to repossess or exert ownership of private property.

International vs. domestic decision-making bodies

Since there were concerns as to the ability of local officials to fully implement the right to repossession of property, an international body was created to assist. Chapter II, Article VII of Annex 7, established the Commission for Displaced Persons and Refugees. This Commission was created as the Commission for Real Property Claims (CRPC). Municipal housing bodies were poorly organized and resourced, and many were staffed by political hardliners bent on preventing the return of properties. The judiciary was viewed as biased and ill-equipped to handle a large number of new cases. The original mandate of CRPC under the DPA was to last for five years, but the mandate was extended for an additional three years given the backlog of claims that developed. CRPC ceased operations on 31 December 2003. The mandate of CRPC was to receive and decide claims for real property, whether the claim was for return of the property or for compensation.[58] CRPC consisted of three international and six national commissioners and a number of international and national staff involved in collection of claims and drafting of decisions. Its decisions were final and binding, and only CRPC could alter its decisions upon a request for reconsideration of the decision by either the claimant or the temporary occupant. A CRPC decision could be appealed to the local judiciary on the grounds that the property was legally transferred after April 1992. When issuing decisions CRPC was permitted to disregard any domestic legislation viewed as contrary to the DPA. Through its mobile teams and offices in countries of asylum, CRPC created an easier environment for many refugees and displaced persons to file claims.

However, CRPC decisions addressed only the right of the claimant. Decisions made no determination as to the subsequent rights of the current user. Its decisions confirmed whether the claimant was the owner or occupancy right holder at the start of the conflict. CRPC investigated claims primarily through access to official land records, as there were no oral hearings. After individual claims were investigated decisions were adopted en masse by the Commissioners at regular plenary sessions. A claimant in possession of a CRPC decision must file a request for enforcement with local housing officials. The basis for the implementation of CRPC decisions was pursuant to both the RS and Federation of B&H Laws on Implementation of the Decisions of the Commission for Real Property Claims of Displaced Persons and Refugees, imposed by the High Representative in October 1999 and amended several times thereafter.[59]

The comparative advantage of an international organization such as CRPC was the ability to issue mass decisions confirming prewar ownership or possession. At routine plenary sessions, CRPC Commissioners would adopt tens of thousands of decisions that had been prepared by CRPC lawyers. However, the primary obstacle in the process of repossession of property in B&H proved not to be the determination of rightful owners and possessors, but determining the rights of temporary occupants. In fact, fewer than 7 percent of claims were actually rejected.[60] Given that displacement lasted a relatively short period of time and that property was allocated only on a temporary basis, there were few disputes about the actual owner of the property. Yet CRPC was ill-suited for the role of determining the rights of temporary occupants since there were no procedures for oral hearings. In addition, CRPC could not effectively resolve cases where the legality of wartime property exchanges was in question, especially regarding cases involving duress. For this reason the Laws on Implementation of the Decisions of the Commission for Real Property Claims of Displaced Persons and Refugees was amended to provide judicial proceedings in such cases.[61]

Another weakness of CRPC was that its decisions were not immediately enforceable. An individual who received a CRPC decision in his or her favor must submit the decision along with a request for enforcement to the housing office in the municipality where the property was located and file a request for enforcement with B&H authorities, otherwise housing office officials were under no obligation to act under a CRPC decision. Housing officials were under an obligation to issue a conclusion on enforcement of the CRPC decision within thirty days. Once the request for enforcement was made, housing officials must make a determination as to the rights of the temporary occupant, and issue the appropriate decision pursuant to the

Laws on Cessation. Therefore the value of a CRPC decision became solely dependent on the functioning of the domestic housing office system.

In practice, many officials in housing offices refused to implement CRPC decisions, and instead issued their own decisions that were later implemented. In this respect CRPC served as a parallel mechanism to the system of housing offices, especially since many individuals filed claims with both. The end result was that CRPC and domestic housing bodies ended up issuing decisions on the same cases, since many individuals filed claims to both bodies. However, CRPC was advantageous in issuing decisions in politically sensitive cases, such as those involving elected officials, judges, military officials, and police officers, so that the local housing office could stand behind the CRPC decision as opposed to issuing one themselves and opening themselves up to threats. CRPC also issued decisions for destroyed property, which was a prerequisite for securing reconstruction assistance from international donors.

The rights of temporary occupants

Considerable thought was given to the rights of current occupants, many of whom were displaced persons themselves. Some early legislative provisions allowed for the weighing of interests between the prewar and current occupants in cases involving socially owned property. However, later legislation ensured that the rights of the prewar owners or occupants remained paramount.[62] The deadline for the vacation of property subject to a claim for repossession under the Laws on Cessation depends on the housing needs of the temporary occupant. Such a determination was necessary for a number of reasons. Since a number of temporary occupants were not vulnerable persons, there was no reason to provide them with alternative accommodation. In most cases such individuals could merely return to their prewar property. In addition, as a result of damage caused by the conflict and the fact that little new housing was constructed during this period, there was a housing shortage in most parts of B&H. This housing shortage was exaggerated in most cases by housing officials as an excuse not to return abandoned property. However, the lack of space meant that available housing had to be reserved for truly vulnerable persons.

In cases where the housing needs of the temporary occupant are otherwise met, the deadline for vacation of the property in the decision is 15 days. Housing needs can be considered otherwise met for a number of reasons, including the fact the temporary occupant is a "multiple" or "double" occupant. In general, the housing needs of the current occupant would be considered otherwise met if s/he had access to his/her prewar property or had the means to provide for his/her own accommodation.[63] If the housing needs of the temporary occupant are not otherwise met, a decision is given with a 90-day period to vacate the property.[64] In such cases the current user is entitled to alternative accommodation to be provided by housing authorities, but the burden of proof of demonstrating eligibility is on the temporary occupant. Such accommodation is supposed to be provided within 90 days, but this has rarely been the case. It is not supposed to be housing of comparable size and quality to the property being vacated or the prewar property of the temporary occupant, but only accommodation meeting basic housing needs.[65] Basically it amounts to one or more rooms that provide shelter from adverse weather conditions.[66] Alternative accommodation is meant as a temporary housing solution for only the most vulnerable temporary occupants. For these reasons, housing authorities are obligated to periodically review whether individuals granted alternative accommodation still meet the legal criteria.[67]

In practice, the rights of temporary occupants became the primary obstruction to implementation of the Laws on Cessation in B&H. In general, housing authorities issued decisions granting the right to alternative accommodation to temporary occupants without any real investigation into whether their housing needs were otherwise met. At the same time, housing officials did little to secure space to serve as alternative accommodation. Possible sources of alternative accommodation include unclaimed housing and state-owned hotels, schools, and army barracks. However, the primary source of alternative accommodation should have been unclaimed socially owned apartments.[68] This combination led to an incredible strain on the overall system, such that decisions obliging the temporary occupant to vacate the property within 90 days were almost never enforced within the 90-day period. In some cases temporary occupants with decisions to vacate the property within 90 days remained in the property for several years.

Owing to these obstructions, it was necessary to amend the provisions of the Laws on Cessation relating to alternative accommodation several times. Most importantly, the right to alternative accommodation was further restricted to ensure space would be available for the most vulnerable individuals. A provision was added that provided for the eviction of the temporary occupant at the end of the 90-day period even if housing authorities fail to secure alternative accommodation.[69] Such a provision was necessary given that housing authorities did little to provide alternative accommodation in hopes that doing so would slow or halt the process of repossession. The failure of housing officials to take adequate steps to secure housing space for use as alternative accommodation is also evident in the fact that no municipality has been able to take advantage of a provision that would have allowed for the extension of the 90-day period. This period could be extended to up to one year if housing officials could provide detailed documentation that steps were taken to secure space but none could be obtained, and that this circumstance was verified by OHR.[70] Temporary occupants were also obliged to demonstrate to housing officials that they met the criteria for entitlement to alternative accommodation to offset the problem of housing officials failing to adequately investigate whether housing needs were otherwise met.[71]

The Property Law Implementation Plan

A number of international organizations were strongly involved in property issues, as it was recognized that unresolved property disputes could be a source of tension between formerly warring groups in the future. These included the Organization for Security and Cooperation in Europe (OSCE), the United Nations High Commissioner for Refugees (UNHCR), and the United Nations Mission in B&H, which, together with OHR, adopted the Property Law Implementation Plan (PLIP) in 2001. This plan more clearly defined the role of the international community, as well as the role of each organization, in the property restitution, particularly in regard to monitoring the more than 140 municipalities of B&H. The PLIP strategy adopted a rule of law process for full implementation of the property laws, as opposed to progress via political agreements. This meant that claims were to be resolved in a regular manner regardless of the location of the property. This approach best fitted with the individual rights approach enshrined in the DPA. At the time the PLIP strategy was developed, only 15 percent of claims for repossession of property had been resolved. At this time the rate of implementation of the property laws was so slow that it was estimated that full resolution of all claims would have taken at least 30 years, a time period unacceptable to the international community.

In order to cover the wide range of property-related issues and activities into a more comprehensive mechanism to ensure implementation of the property laws, the PLIP mechanism included administrative reform; capacity-building of local administrative and judicial bodies; de-politicization of the property issues; and establishment of the rule of law. Prior to this attention on property rights was focused on repealing wartime legislation on abandoned property. This campaign was met by intense resistance by local officials, many of who had benefited from the abandoned property laws. Such an approach was also successful in combating the severe regional variations in implementation of property legislation. Until then, many municipalities primarily issued decisions for repossession of property that had been destroyed during the conflict, with fewer decisions issued for the repossession of occupied housing in urban centers. To measure implementation, monthly statistics were produced by monitors detailing the number of claims, decisions, and implemented decisions in each municipality. These statistics have been highly publicized, and for a time the full statistics list was published in local newspapers. One lesson from the PLIP project is that the process became truly effective when it moved from a political process driven by political forces to a rule of law process based on individual rights.

To further strengthen the PLIP process, the same agencies adopted the New Strategic Direction in September of 2002.[72] The strategy built on that of PLIP, but focused more on the chronological processing of claims rather than the creation of special categories of refugees and displaced persons for prioritization of claims.[73] This is in contrast to the prior PLIP policy prioritizing the identification and resolution of cases of multiple occupancy. Chronological processing of claims was necessary to provide more fair and transparent procedures, as opposed to the old system that left more discretion to local authorities and was therefore open to corruption and political interference. It also protected housing officials from political pressure to address, or not address, certain cases, and provided claimants with clearer insight to when their specific claims would be resolved. Providing a "rule of law" approach was important at this stage as the disengagement of the international community had already begun, marked by decreases in funding and personnel.

The PLIP process was also able to capitalize on the policy of conditionality in regard to compliance with the DPA in a number of ways. B&H remains heavily dependant on international assistance, which provided strong leverage to the international community. B&H's entry into the Council of Europe was conditional on progress on the return of refugees and displaced persons in general and on implementation of property restitution laws in particular. Progress on returns has also been a prerequisite for discussions on any future movement towards membership of the European Union. The implementation of restitution laws, measured monthly through PLIP statistics, provided an easy benchmark for donors and others in developing conditionality. International donors were requested to focus funds on municipalities with the highest rates of implementation. Prior to this, international donors withheld funding on several occasions when B&H officials failed to execute their responsibilities, which did have a large effect on forcing them back into compliance (Hastings 2001: 229).

Alternatives to return – compensation and resettlement

Compensation

The RRTF long maintained the policy that scant donor resources should not be spent on support of resettlement activities. This is one reason the right to compensation for property lost during the conflict is one issue that has never been fully clarified. Under both the B&H Constitution and Annex 7 of the DPA, refugees and displaced persons have the right to be compensated for any property of which they were deprived in the course of hostilities that cannot be restored to them.[74] In particular, the phrase "to be compensated for any property that cannot be restored to them" has never been elaborated. Thus there has been no determination as to whether a refugee or displaced person could freely request compensation, or whether compensation could be paid only in cases where the property could not be physically returned to the prewar owner, most likely due to the fact it was destroyed. Annex 7 does provide mechanisms for compensation through the establishment of the Refugees and Displaced Persons Fund to settle claims for compensation.[75] This Fund was to be established in the Central Bank of Bosnia and administered by CRPC. Resources for the Fund were to be provided through the purchase, sale, lease, and mortgage of real property that had been claimed before CRPC.[76] Funds could also be provided through direct payments by the Parties to Annex 7 or from contributions from international donors.

While both the right to, and a mechanism for, compensation were established under the DPA, in practice compensation did not materialize as envisioned. When submitting a claim to CRPC, a claimant could request compensation in lieu of return of the property. But in practice, preferences for compensation were used only for statistical purposes, and no compensation has ever been paid. The Fund was never established because no resources were made available (Garlick 2000). This was the case for a number of reasons, the most important being that the political preference was for the return of refugees and displaced persons in order to create a unified, multi-ethnic state. For that reason most international donors, the biggest being the European Commission and the US Government, directed resources to the reconstruction of destroyed housing and other related activities that promoted return. No part of the B&H government made any resources available. In addition, immediately following the conflict the security situation remained somewhat unstable, and there was concern that at that time refugees and displaced persons would choose compensation because of their concerns regarding return. In that sense, international organizations wanted more time to create an atmosphere to promote return.[77] Another complication is determining the rate of compensation, especially as regards destroyed or damaged properties.

For these reasons, CRPC never undertook any activities regarding purchase, sale, lease, and mortgage of property. Instead, it focused its activities on issuing decisions on claims for repossession of properties – even in cases where applicants had stated a preference for compensation. Yet given the post-conflict emergence of a large and viable market for the sale and exchange of properties, CRPC could have engaged in the sale and lease of properties in order to generate funds for further compensation. But it could be argued that the right to compensation has been partially fulfilled by allowing refugees and displaced persons to repossess and subsequently sell their property because in general there have been no restrictions on the sale of property.[78] In such cases the property owners probably received a fairer price, and more quickly, than they would through a compensation scheme. However, individuals whose property was destroyed remain disadvantaged.[79]

Resettlement

Although the political focus of the international community in B&H has consistently remained on the return of refugees and displaced persons, the issue of resettlement was also addressed in a number of ways. However, the lack of international support for resettlement meant that any programs would have to be funded by domestic bodies. The primary mechanism for resettlement in B&H was the allocation of land and building materials to displaced persons to resettle in their areas of displacement. This took place to a much greater extent in Serb- and Croat-controlled areas. These programs served the goal of "ethnic consolidation" by maintaining the ethnic majority achieved during the conflict.

Many resettlement projects were conducted in such a way that prevented return of refugees and displaced persons. In many instances land that had been used for agricultural or social purposes by refugees and displaced persons has been allocated for resettlement projects. To counter this OHR imposed legislation that restricted the right of authorities to allocate public land for resettlement purposes.[80] This legislation even nullified transactions that had taken place during the war. In most cases authorities would have to seek a waiver from OHR by demonstrating the project would not be carried out in a discriminatory manner. This policy was later solidified in legislation that prevented local authorities from prioritizing certain ethnicities for allocation of land.

In addition to allocation of land, local officials also provided funds for construction or purchase of housing for refugees and displaced persons. In the Republika Srpska, a Housing Fund was established to provide credits to war invalids, families of fallen soldiers, displaced persons, and persons whose housing was destroyed. Such categories ensured that most, if not all funds, went to ethnic Serbs. In the Federation of B&H similar measures were taken, in that proceeds from the privatization process were directed to construction of housing for war veterans, demobilized soldiers, and refugees and displaced persons.

Progress on return

According to the United Nations High Commissioner for Refugees (UNHCR), as of 31 May 2004 439,631 refugees and 555,644 displaced persons have returned to their prewar homes.[81] However, only 441,970 of these returns are considered "minority" returns. The accuracy of these numbers is of course debatable. It is no easy task to accurately count the number of returnees for a number of reasons. In B&H, many returnees kept a presence in both their prewar homes and their areas of displacement. Others remained in displacement but registered in their prewar municipalities in order to receive increased social benefits or reconstruction assistance. Anecdotal evidence shows that many beneficiaries of housing reconstruction subsequently sold their housing and resettled elsewhere. The same can be said of individuals who repossessed their property through the property law framework. Perhaps the best way to ascertain the level of returns is through a nationwide census. Although there has been no formal census in B&H since 1991, and a new census was due several years ago, there has yet to be a post-conflict census. Some members of the international community actively suppressed the census out of concern that the results would confirm the consolidation of ethnic cleansing. Others feared the results could actively work against return by dissuading potential returnees who might fear their status as a relatively small minority in their prewar municipalities. This was of particular concern early in the returns process. In the absence of a census return figures will remain only a rough estimate.

Although there was a concerted effort on the part of the international community to support the return of refugees and displaced persons, there were also a number of factors working against returns. Political pressure from Serb and Croat leaders encouraged many ethnic Serbs and Croats to resettle in Serb- and Croat-controlled areas rather than return. The poor economic environment also had a considerable impact on returns. High rates of un-employment throughout many parts of the country discouraged movements. So did concerns over education, healthcare, and pensions. The international community has often been criticized for placing considerable resources in the reconstruction or return of property as opposed to improving the economic environment. However, efforts have been made to improve social services in recent years. There has also been a general reluctance of refugees to return when given the option of permanent status in third countries.

Return numbers are not the only measure of success in B&H. Probably far too much emphasis has been placed on numbers, primarily for political reasons. After all, return and restitution of property were just two of the options available to refugees and displaced persons. Regardless of whether refugees or displaced persons actually did return in the end, an extremely important factor in the post-conflict reconciliation in B&H is that they had the right to choose whether or not to return and repossess property. The fact that this right became enforceable through legal mechanisms and political pressure played a serious role in reducing tension in B&H, especially in light of the fact such a large percentage of the population was displaced. Access to prewar properties was particularly important in regard to durable solutions since such properties may have been one of the few tangible assets from which refugees and displaced persons could derive some economic benefit.

Conclusion

The development of the rights of refugees and displaced persons in recent decades should be taken into account in any post-conflict situation. These developments are contained in international treaties, UN resolutions, and peace agreements. As one of the most comprehensive peace agreements in terms of refugee rights, the DPA may provide some lessons for subsequent post-conflict situations. In this respect, one question is whether the recognition of rights, and the establishment of enforcement mechanisms, pursuant to the DPA serve as a new standard for refugee rights, or an exception to the rule.

There are a number of issues in the B&H context that may prove useful in addressing the Palestinian refugee problem. Rights to return and restitution of property need to be recognized. In B&H, recognition of those rights began with several UN resolutions, and these rights were elaborated in the Dayton Peace Agreement. Refugee rights have also been addressed in a number of other peace agreements, including those in Cambodia,[82] Guatemala,[83] Rwanda,[84] Mozambique,[85] and Somalia.[86] The rights included in these agreements are consistent with General Assembly resolution 35/124, which reaffirmed refugees and displaced persons have the right to return to their homes in the homelands.[87] The rights of Palestinian refugees and displaced persons have already been addressed by the UN. Resolution 51/126 (Palestine/Israel) reaffirms the rights of those displaced by hostilities commencing in June 1967 and afterwards to return to their homes or former places of residence. Resolution 194 (III) (Palestine) provides that refugees wishing to return to their homes should be permitted to do so at the earliest possible date, and compensation should be paid for those choosing not to return and for damage to property. This resolution goes further to create a body, the Conciliation Commission, to facilitate return and compensation. The question is to what degree these rights will be derogated from in final status negotiations, and the extent of enforcement mechanisms put into place.

A comprehensive framework of legislation is necessary to ensure refugees and displaced persons can exercise their full rights. It is best if such legislation is grounded in international human rights law, in particular providing for some type of regional complaints mechanism, although this may prove difficult in the Palestinian context. Any legal framework ensuring rights in the Palestinian context would need to address rights to restitution and compensation; reversal of the effects of abandoned property laws; mechanisms for the enforcement of rights; and the rights of beneficiaries of abandoned property and *bona fide* third parties. In B&H legislation established administrative rather than judicial procedures to more effectively implement the right to repossess property. In addition, in B&H, the Ombudsman and Human Rights Chamber were mandated with this responsibility, and B&H is now under the jurisdiction of the European Court of Human Rights.

In B&H, a number of return mechanisms were established, with differing results. Return was dependent on construction of destroyed housing and on freeing occupied property. Construction assistance would be important for Palestinians where villages remain vacant. However, occupied property would be much more complex in the Palestinian context because of the long period of displacement. In B&H, property was allocated on a temporary basis, and the period of displacement was relatively short. In the Palestinian context, the rights of current occupants of land, and bona fide third parties, would have to be considered carefully because of the length of time of displacement of the original owners and take into account investments made in the property. Reconstruction and return of property does not automatically lead to return. A number of other factors are also important. Once refugees and displaced persons were able to return, problems regarding sustainability of return, such as employment, health care, education, and pensions, need to be resolved.

Experience in B&H demonstrates that return and repossession of property should be grounded in the rule of law. In the early phases of return, numerous political agreements were made setting out specific arrangements for numbers of returns to certain areas. However, such agreements resulted in little progress. Only when the international community encouraged a system for return and repossession grounded in the rule of law, and not subject to political agreements, did serious progress ensue. The DPA does provide individual rights, and the rule of law approach is the best to ensure they are enforced.

Alternatives to return and restitution, such as resettlement and compensation, should also be addressed more comprehensively than they were in B&H. Under both Annex 7 of the DPA and the B&H Constitution, refugees and displaced persons were given the right to compensation in cases where they chose not to, or could not, repossess property. However, no comprehensive actions were taken in B&H to implement measures for resettlement or compensation. Although a Refugees and Displaced Persons Fund was to be established in the Central Bank of B&H and funded by direct payments by the parties to the DPA, such a fund was never established. In addition, no international donors were willing to fund compensation. Instead, individuals who did not wish to return could simply repossess their property and sell it. In many instances they probably received a fairer price and were able to do so in a quicker manner than through a pure compensation mechanism. Given the length of displacement of Palestinian refugees, it is likely many will choose to resettle and to receive compensation as opposed to physical restitution of property. For that reason, resettlement and compensation activities should be comprehensively addressed.

Notes

1 During the conflict, the Bosniaks established the Republic of Bosnia and Herzegovina, the Serbs the Republika Srpska, and the Croats the Republic of Herceg-Bosna.
2 *RBH Official Gazette* 11/13.
3 *RBH Official Gazette* 6/92; 8/92; 16/92; 13/94; 9/95; 3/95.
4 *Official Gazette of the Republic of Herceg-Bosna* 13/93, § 249, Article 1 (1993).
5 *Official Gazette of the Republika Srpska* 3/96 (1996). Article 58 of the *Law on the Use of Abandoned Property of the Republika Srpska* invalidated both Decrees, while Article 48 obliged the Ministry for Refugees and Displaced Persons to review all previous decisions on allocation and abandonment and annul any decision that did not meet the criteria under this Law.
6 *Official Gazette of the Republika Srpska* 27/93 (1993).
7 *Official Gazette of the Republika Srpska* 19/95 (1995). Article 2 of the *Decree* provided that abandoned property would be allocated by the war presidencies of municipalities as opposed to municipal commissions. Article 4 provided that the property of owners who failed to regulate their military service or work obligations would be declared abandoned.
8 Article 3 of the *RB&H Law on Temporarily Abandoned Real Property Owned by Citizens*

(hereinafter *RB&H Law on Abandoned Property*) and Article 2 of the *Law on the Use of Abandoned Property of the Republika Srpska*.

9   The Parties to the Dayton Peace Agreement are the Republic of Bosnia and Herzegovina and its two entities – the Federation of Bosnia and Herzegovina and the Republika Srpska.

10   In this article the term "restitution" refers only to the repossession of property lost during the most recent conflict. While there are claims for restitution of property nationalized between World War II and the recent conflict, no legal mechanism has yet been established to address such claims. Although the process is in fact restitution, the concept of restitution in Former Yugoslavia refers to the return of properties nationalized by governmental officials in the period after World War II but prior to the recent conflict. This type of restitution has not been addressed pursuant to the Dayton Peace Agreement.

11   PIC members include, among others, Germany, France, the United Kingdom, the United Sates, Russia, Italy, Belgium, the Netherlands, Japan, Turkey, the European Commission, the Council of Europe, the International Committee of the Red Cross, the International Monetary Fund, NATO, the Organization for Security and Cooperation in Europe, the UN High Commissioner for Human Rights, the UN High Commissioner for Refugees, and the World Bank.

12   See the *Confederation Agreement Between the Bosnian Government and Bosnian Croats*, Washington, DC (1 March 1994), also known as the Washington Agreement, available online at www.usip.org.

13   Ibid., Article V: Human Rights.

14   The General Framework Agreement for Peace (*hereinafter* Dayton Peace Agreement) Chapter One, Article I (1) of Annex 7.

15   The Parties to Annex 7 are the Republic of Bosnia and Herzegovina, the Federation of Bosnia and Herzegovina, and the Republika Srpska.

16   The Dayton Peace Agreement, Annex 7, Chapter One, Article I (2).

17   Ibid., Article I (4).

18   Ibid., Article I (3) (a).

19   Ibid., Annex 4, Article II (5).

20   Ibid., Annex 6, Article I.

21   Ibid., Article II (1).

22   Ibid., Article II (2).

23   Ibid., Annex I to Annex 4. This list includes the International Convention on the Elimination of All Forms of Racial Discrimination; the International Covenant on Civil and Political Rights and the 1966 and 1989 Optional Protocols thereto; the Covenant on Economic, Social, and Cultural Rights; and the Framework Convention for the Protection of National Minorities.

24   See Article II (4) of the B&H Constitution and Annex 6, Article I (14), of the Dayton Peace Agreement. Both include non-discrimination clauses that protect against discrimination on the grounds of sex, race, color, language, religion, political or other opinion, national or social origin, association with a national minority, property, birth, or other status.

25   Bonn Peace Implementation Conference 1997: Bosnia and Herzegovina 1998: Self-Sustaining Structures (December 10, 1997), Article XI, available online at www.ohr.int. In this communiqué the PIC welcomed the High Representative's intention to use his final authority regarding implementation of the civilian aspects of the Dayton Peace Agreement. In particular, the High Representative received support for adopting interim measures when the Parties to the Dayton Peace Agreement were unable to do so, and to take actions against officials deemed by the High Representative to be in violation of the Dayton Peace Agreement or the terms of its implementation. As an added disincentive to obstruct implementation of the Dayton Peace Agreement, decisions by the

High Representative on dismissal of B&H officials included a provision barring the dismissed official from holding appointed or elected positions in the future.

26 Dayton Peace Agreement, Annex 6, Article II (1). Any individual can submit applications to either body of the Commission on Human Rights, in regards to alleged violations of the rights covered by the European Convention for the Protection of Human Rights and Fundamental Freedoms and subsequent protocols, as well as alleged discrimination on any ground such as sex, race, color, language, religion, political or other opinion, national or social origin, association with a national minority, property, birth, or other status regarding the rights provided for in the other human rights agreements annexed to the Dayton Peace Agreement. The Ombudsman issues reports and recommendations to government bodies, and can forward such reports to the Human Rights Chamber for further action. The Human Rights Chamber issues decisions on whether the parties have breached their obligations under the Dayton Peace Agreement and what steps must be taken by the party to remedy such a breach, including orders to cease and desist, monetary relief, and provisional measures. In terms of decisions affecting property rights, both institutions have used the right to family and home (Article 8) and the right to peaceful enjoyment of possessions (Article 1 of Protocol 1) of the European Convention on Human Rights to enforce property rights. A number of decisions have also centered on claims of discrimination.

27 Ibid., Article V (2).

28 Ibid., Article VII (1).

29 See *OHR RRTF Report of April 1997*, available online at www.ohr.int. Cluster areas were chosen either for their political importance or because of the potential for a large number of returns.

30 The areas chosen as "cluster areas" were Sarajevo/Gorazde, Una Sana, Posavina, Doboj, and the Anvil areas.

31 See *OHR RRTF Report of December 1997*, available at www.ohr.int.

32 See *OHR RRTF Report of March 1998*, available at www.ohr.int.

33 See Annex 7, UNHCR's "Open Cities" Initiative, in *OHR RRTF Report July 1997*, www.ohr.int.

34 For an in-depth discussion of some of the problems inherent in the "Open Cities" Initiative, see the International Crisis Group, *The Konjic conundrum: Why minorities have failed to return to a model open city*, ICG Bosnia Project – Report 35 (19 June 1998).

35 *Sarajevo Declaration* (3 February 1998), available online at www.ohr.int.

36 See Chairmen's Concluding Statement, the *Banja Luka Regional Return Conference* (28 April 1998), available online at www.ohr.int.

37 *Return and Reconstruction Task Force Action Plan 1999*, available online at www.ohr.int.

38 To maximize resources, many donors restricted reconstruction to only the minimum necessary to allow for return, usually several rooms, a bathroom, and kitchen as opposed to full reconstruction of the previous structure. It was thought that in time the beneficiaries would be able to repair the remainder of the structure themselves. Other donors experimented with "self-help" projects involving the provision of only building materials. However, such projects met with varying success.

39 Double, or multiple, occupancy refers to individuals who managed to attain additional properties during the war despite the fact they had not been displaced themselves. Double occupancy was a considerable problem, especially in urban areas. In many cases individuals with political connections were able to move to larger or better-situated properties – referred to as "upgrading." Elected officials, police and military members, judges, and other prominent citizens were normally able to upgrade. However, at the start of the property law implementation

process double occupants were the natural first targets of forcible evictions, since they required no further housing assistance and there was no public outcry at the evictions of individuals seen to have benefited from the war.

40 However, few of these possibilities resulted in the generation of considerable space. Construction of buffer accommodation became problematic because without adequate monitoring of beneficiaries it could not be assured that those in actual need received accommodation, nor could it be assured that those who initially demonstrated a need vacated the accommodation when they no longer met the criteria for allocation. Some donors were also concerned that once the refugees and displaced persons moved into the buffer accommodation they would lose their desire to return. The return of Croatian Serbs to Croatia remained difficult due to continued obstruction by the government of Croatia. And although the distribution of land plots for resettlement purposes was somewhat widespread, especially in Serb- and Croat-controlled areas, lists of beneficiaries were difficult to obtain so cases of double occupancy were not often identified. While a full-fledged property market is still in the process of developing in B&H, the sale and exchange of properties, particularly by refugees and displaced persons, is widespread.

41 It became quickly apparent, however, that reconstruction of destroyed or damaged housing was not enough to guarantee return. Despite being beneficiaries of housing reconstruction, many refugees and displaced persons did not actually return because of concerns over lack of employment, education, healthcare, and other social benefits.

42 Dayton Peace Agreement, Annex 7, Article I (3) (a).

43 Ministerial Meeting of the Steering Board of the PIC, Sintra, 30 May 1997. Available online at the website of the Office of the High Representative: www.ohr.int

44 *Law on Cessation of the Application of the Law on Temporarily Abandoned Real Property Owned by Citizens* (*Official Gazette of the Federation of B&H* 11/98, 29/98, 27/99, 43/99, 37/01, and 56/01), *Law on Cessation of Application of the Law on Abandoned Apartments* (*Official Gazette of the Federation of B&H* 11/98, 38/98, 12/99, 18/99, 27/99, 43/99, and 56/01), and *Law on Taking Over the Law on Housing Relations* (*Official Gazette* 11/98, § 78).

45 *Official Gazette of the Republika Srpska* 38/98, 12/99, 31/99, and 65/01.

46 In October 1999, the High Representative imposed the Law on the Cessation of Application of the Law on Use of Abandoned Property in the Republika Srpska, and imposed amendments to the Law on the Cessation of the Application of the Law on Abandoned Apartments and the Law on the Cessation of the Application of the Law on Temporarily Abandoned Real Property Owned by Citizens in the Federation of B&H.

47 In this section, citations will refer to the *Law on Temporarily Abandoned Real Property Owned by Citizens* in the Federation of B&H. The RS and Federation laws concerning private property are vastly similar. Notes regarding the RS legislation will be made where it differs from Federation legislation.

48 See Article 17 of the Federation of B&H *Law on Cessation of the Application of the Law on Temporarily Abandoned Real Property Owned by Citizens*. Prior to the adoption of the relevant property laws, property owners could file claims for repossession of property with municipal courts. However, once the property laws went into effect, claims had to be filed with the administrative body responsible for housing issues in the respective municipality or canton. Owners who had filed claims with the courts prior to the passage of the property laws could proceed with the judicial proceedings. However, court decisions on repossession of property covered only the right of the owners to be reinstated. Court decisions did not address the rights of the current users, which created problems when evictions were ordered based on judicial decisions and the current users were in need of,

but not provided with, alternative accommodation. This resulted in a number of cases where genuine vulnerable persons faced forcible eviction without any type of further housing assistance yet secured. An administrative process provided several advantages over judicial proceedings.

49 Claims for repossession of destroyed properties have not been included in statistics on return of properties. This policy decision was made because at the start of the repossession process many municipal officials issued decisions for repossession of destroyed properties only, which did not result in actual return of refugees and displaced persons. The initial aim of the statistics was to assess concrete progress towards the return of refugees and displaced persons. According to later legislation, decisions for destroyed properties could be issued rather easily since there were was no need to assess rights of current occupants. For full information on restitution-related statistics, see Property Law Implementation Plan Statistics, which can be found at www.UNHCR.ba

50 In the Federation of B&H, property issues were handled at the municipal and canton level, primarily by Municipal Housing Offices. The RS adopted a centralized model, where housing offices were established in each municipality under the authority of the RS Ministry for Refugees and Displaced Persons. Both the decentralized and centralized models had their strengths and faults. It is difficult to state which, in the end, proved more effective. In general, progress on implementation of the Laws on Cessation varied drastically by regions, even within the entities themselves.

51 Prior to the war there were two types of property in B&H: private property and socially owned property. Socially owned property consisted primarily of apartments owned by companies or governmental bodies that allocated such apartments to their workers through the issuance of "occupancy rights." While such property did share some aspects of private property, there were certain restrictions on its use, including prohibitions on renting or prolonged absences from the property, and the limited ability to transfer the apartments.

52 Articles 4 and 10 of the *Law on Temporarily Abandoned Real Property Owned by Citizens* in the Federation of B&H.

53 Ibid., Article 12.

54 Ibid., Article 13. Such a provision was necessary as second instance administrative bodies would delay decisions on appeals in order to stall repossession. Article 13 provides that, if an appeal against a positive decision is not resolved within the time period specified in the relevant laws governing administrative procedures, the decision of the first instance body, and thus the right of the claimant to the property, is deemed confirmed. In the case of 15-day decisions, housing officials are responsible for scheduling an eviction at the expiry of the time period and do not have to wait for a request from the claimant to enforce the decision.

55 Ibid., Article 12a.

56 Ibid., Article 16.

57 Ibid., Article 15.

58 Dayton Peace Agreement, Annex 7, Article XI. Originally the mandate of CRPC extended only to private property. However, its competence was extended to receive and decide claims for socially owned property as well since the process administered by domestic housing offices was fraught with considerable obstructions. In such cases a claimant would have to demonstrate that s/he first tried to file a claim with the competent domestic housing office but either was prevented from filing a claim or filed a claim that was not resolved within the deadlines contained in the Laws on Cessation. The effect of this change in policy resulted in many applicants filing claims for the same property to both CRPC and domestic housing offices.

59 See Federation of B&H *Law on Implementation of the Decisions of the Commission for*

Real Property Claims of Displaced Persons and Refugees and the RS *Law on Implementa-tion of the Decisions of the Commission for Real Property Claims of Displaced Persons and Refugees,* available at www.ohr.int

60 Property Law Implementation Statistics, available at www.UNHCR.ba

61 See Articles 7 and 13 of the *Law on Implementation of the Decisions of the Commission for Real Property Claims of Displaced Persons and Refugees (Official Gazette of the FB&H* 43/99 and 51/00). When there is a question as to voluntary transfers of property by the owner after 1 April 1992, housing officials must refer the case to the ap-propriate municipal court to determine whether the transfer was voluntary. The request for enforcement of the CRPC decision will not be acted upon until the court issues a verdict. If the transfer took place between 1 April 1992 and 14 December 1995 the burden of proof is on the party claiming to have acquired rights to the property to prove the transfer was voluntary.

62 For cases involving socially owned property, the Council of Europe issued an opinion that given the special circumstances around the displacement in B&H a presumption in favor of the prewar occupant was required under Article 1 of Protocol 1 and Articles 8 and 14 of the ECHR in order to prevent discrimination against a particularly vulnerable group (Hastings 2001: 237).

63 See Article 16a of the Federation of B&H *Law on the Cessation of the Application of the Law on Temporarily Abandoned Real Property Owned by Citizens*. The housing needs of the temporary occupant will be considered otherwise met if s/he sold his/her prewar property; exchanged his/her prewar property and remains in possession of the property exchanged and transferred it to a third party; refuses alternative accommodation or reconstruction assistance for destroyed housing; was a prewar subtenant; has sufficient disposable income; is offered alternative accommoda-tion, or funds for it, for a period of six months by the owner; withdrew his/her claim for repossession; was allocated a land plot; or received housing credits or building assistance. A multiple occupant is someone who has access to his/her prewar property, which is habitable; a prewar family household with access to their prewar or other property, which is habitable; who has been provided alter-native accommodation; who has a legal right to repossess his/her prewar prop-erty; or whose accommodation needs are otherwise met. See Article 16 of the Federation of B&H *Law on the Cessation of the Application of the Law on Temporarily Abandoned Real Property Owned by Citizens.*

64 Ibid., Article 12a.

65 The fact that alternative accommodation was at best only basic housing had the added effect of encouraging temporary occupants to secure accommodation for themselves. Anecdotal evidence from field officers working with international organizations showed that the majority of individuals offered alternative accom-modation rejected it and found housing for themselves.

66 Article 8 of the Federation of B&H *Law on the Cessation of the Application of the Law on Temporarily abandoned Real Property Owned by Citizens*.

67 Ibid.

68 Socially owned apartments that were not claimed prior to the legal deadlines or upon which claims for repossession were rejected were to be used as alternative accommodation until all claims for the repossession of property in that particular municipality are resolved. See Articles 13 and 18d of the FB&H *Law on Cessation of the Application of the Law on Abandoned Apartments*. In practice, housing officials were slow to allocate such property to those in need of alternative accommoda-tion, instead allowing temporary occupants that did not meet the criteria for alternative accommodation to remain in the property.

69 Article 7 of the Federation of B&H *Law on the Cessation of the Application of the Law on Temporarily Abandoned Real Property Owned by Citizens*.

70 Ibid., Article 12A.

71 Ibid., Article 12.

72 *A New Strategic Direction: Proposed ways ahead for property law implementation in a time of decreasing international community resources, Property Law Implementation Plan*, Sarajevo, 12 September 2002, as adopted by OHR, OSCE, UNHCR, UNMiBH, and CRPC.

73 Pursuant to High Representative decisions, certain categories remained prioritized. The *Decision on the Use of Collective Center Space in Bosnia and Herzegovina to Promote the Phased and Orderly Return of Refugees and Displaced Persons* (1 August 2002) provided for the prioritized return of property for claimants living in collective centers in B&H, Croatia, and the Federal Republic of Yugoslavia. This process was coordinated by UNHCR, and although there was a preliminary deadline of five months, the decision was extended by a subsequent decision of the High Representative on 1 January 2003 for an additional six months. This policy was adopted on the grounds that individuals residing in collective centers were the most socially vulnerable category of refugees and displaced persons. An exception was also made for minority police officers pursuant to the High Representative *Decision Prioritizing, as an Exception to the Chronological Order Rule, the Repossession of Property by Returning Police Officers* (30 April 2002). This decision allowed for the prioritization of claims, for a period of eight months, made by minority police officers on the condition that they would serve on the police force in their prewar municipality of residence. This process was coordinated by UNMiBH, and its basis was the security concerns of refugees and displaced persons in regards to the fact there were no, or few, police officers of their ethnicity currently serving. Many refugees and displaced persons considered the presence of minority police officers as a prerequisite for return.

74 Constitution of Bosnia and Herzegovina, Article II (5) and the Dayton Peace Agreement, Annex 7, Article I (1).

75 Ibid., Article XIV (1).

76 Ibid.

77 This policy was most evident in the Federation of B&H Law on the Sale of Apartments with an Occupancy Right, which forbade the privatization and sale of repossessed apartments in the Federation of B&H until the prewar occupancy right holder physically returned and remained in the apartment for two years. However, this provision was largely abused. Local officials either turned a blind eye to the sales or used the provision to harass returnees through constant checks on their whereabouts in an attempt to cancel the occupancy right, according to the Law on Housing Relations. This provision was eventually annulled by the High Representative. An additional reason behind such a provision was to prevent returnees from the Republika Srpska from repossessing and selling apartments in the Federation of B&H and returning to live in claimed property in the RS, because at the time implementation of the Laws on Cessation was well behind that of the Federation of B&H.

78 In some cases, owners of private property sold their property before actually repossessing it, at times with the temporary occupant still residing in it. Some international donors had property owners sign agreements stating the property would not be sold for a certain period of time after the donation of reconstruction assistance. Nevertheless many sales did take place, with little prospect for international donors recovering the amount of the donation.

79 The European Court of Human Rights has dealt with the issue of destroyed housing in several cases. In *Akdivar and others v. Turkey*, European Court of Human Rights, Reports 1996-IV (16 September 1996), the Court concluded that the deliberate burning of the Kurdish applicant's homes and contents by Turkish forces constituted a serious interference with the right to family life and home under Article 8 as well as the peaceful enjoyment of possessions under Article

1 of Protocol 1. In *Selcuk and Asker v. Turkey*, European Court of Human Rights, Reports 1998-II (24 April 1998) the Court found that the burning of houses constituted inhuman treatment and awarded pecuniary and non-pecuniary damages to compensate for destruction to property, loss of income, and reimbursement for alternative accommodation.

80 Office of the High Representative, Decision Suspending the Power of Local Authorities in the Federation and the RS to Re-Allocate Socially Owned Land in Cases Where the Land Was Used on 6 April 1992 for Residential, Religious, Cultural, Private Agricultural or Private Business Activities, 26 May 1999, available at www.ohr.int

81 For full information on refugee returns, *see* the United Nations High Commissioner for Refugees' (UNHCR) mission to B&H website at www.UNHCR.ba

82 Agreements on a Comprehensive Political Settlement of the Cambodia Conflict, 23 October 1991. See Part V: Refugees and Displaced Persons, Articles 19 and 20, and Annex 4: Repatriation of Cambodian Refugees and Displaced Persons. It provides that efforts should be made to create the necessary conditions for voluntary return and integration, and offers protection for the right to property. It also sets out that the rights included in the Universal Declaration of Human Rights and other relevant international human rights instruments are guaranteed to all persons in Cambodia, including refugees and displaced persons.

83 Agreement on Resettlement of the Population Groups Uprooted by the Armed Conflict (Guatemala), 17 June 1994, UN Doc. A/48/954-S/1994/751 (1994). Displaced persons are provided the right to return or resettle in the place of their choice. In addition, the government is obliged to revise legal provisions to ensure prior abandonment of property is not considered voluntary, and ensure the inalienable nature of land ownership rights. In this respect it is obliged to promote the return of land to original owners and/or seek adequate compensation.

84 Arusha Peace Agreement, 4 August 1993, Article 4. The Agreement contains a provision that prevents the repossession of property by refugees who fled the country more than ten years prior to the agreement if the property is currently occupied. Instead, the Government is obliged to compensate them with other land and resettlement assistance.

85 General Peace Agreement for Mozambique, Protocol III (IV. Return of Mozambican refugees and displaced persons and their social reintegration), March 1992. Refugees and displaced persons are guaranteed restitution of property in cases where in the property remains in existence, and are entitled to initiate legal proceedings against the current possessors.

86 Addis Ababa Agreement concluded at the first session of the Conference on National Reconciliation in Somalia: III. Restoration of property and settlement of disputes, 27 March 1993. Somali refugees and displaced persons are entitled to return of all properties that were illegally confiscated, robbed, stolen, seized, embezzled, or taken by other fraudulent means.

87 UN Doc.A/RES/35/124 (1980).

References

Garlick, M. (2000) "Protection for property rights: A partial solution? The Commission for Real Property Claims of Displaced Persons and Refugees (CRPC) in Bosnia and Herzegovina", *Refugee Survey Quarterly* 19 (3).

Hastings, L. (2001) "Implementation of the property legislation in Bosnia Herzegovina", *Stanford Journal of International Law* 37.

10 Re-approaching voluntary repatriation within a reconciliation framework

A proposal drawn from the Cambodian return process

Ana García Rodicio

Re-approaching voluntary repatriation within a reconciliation framework

Existing approaches: trends, challenges, frameworks and limitations on voluntary repatriation approaches since the 1990s

Challenges are pending for international law and politics to address important issues regarding voluntary repatriation, especially considering that the promotion of voluntary repatriation, the trend in policies and actions by UNHCR and the international community, has become a current evolving reality. The existing framework focuses on the legal status and the socio-economic reintegration of returnees whereas, at the same time, reconciliation is not considered an intrinsic pillar of the framework. Voluntary repatriation should be understood as an integral part of the reconciliation process in the country of origin of refugees. The relevance of the framework on voluntary repatriation to the Palestinian refugee issue is manifest, given that the implementation of the right to return of the Palestinian refugees is legally and politically central to any feasible and long-lasting peace process. Although the uniqueness of the Palestinian case makes references and comparison with other cases a very complex exercise, there are important lessons to be drawn from the analysis of the existing approaches and practices regarding voluntary repatriation since the 1990s.

Upon the end of the Cold War and with the consequent changes in relation to the geopolitics of forced migration, trends in addressing refugee issues and durable solutions to refugee crises have evolved and continue to do so. While consideration is still given to local reintegration of refugees in countries of asylum as well as to resettlement in third host countries, the shifting focus has been an evolving emphasis on voluntary repatriation as the 'panacea' among the options of durable solutions for refugee crises.

UNHCR as well as the international community considered the 1990s 'the decade of voluntary repatriation'. Large-scale and complex operations took place all around the world in countries such as Cambodia, Mozambique, Rwanda, Bosnia and Herzegovina, Guatemala and others. These operations challenged existing approaches on voluntary repatriation, and questions are still pending surrounding mandates, responsibilities, monitoring of return-ees, reintegration of returnees, clear legal and political criteria applicable to those operations etc. Analysis and evaluation of return processes from a medium- and long-term perspective are needed in order to properly address the issues that have arisen. At present, in Africa alone there are seven ongo-ing processes of large scale voluntary repatriation operations and UNHCR has designated this year as the 'return year' with the main topic as 'returning back home'.

Given this evolution and the fact that the 1990s were a milestone both in terms of political changes in international relations and forced migration policies and, more specifically, in terms of voluntary repatriation, it is impor-tant to outline the development in theory and practice regarding the issue in question. Developments in international politics have affected the way in which voluntary repatriation has been addressed since the end of the Cold War. Uncertainty characterizes the present situation of international rela-tions and, specifically, the politics of 'intervention' (both on humanitarian and non-humanitarian grounds). Given this situation, it is too early to make an adequate analysis on whether there are 'new directions' on how volun-tary repatriation is approached. Nevertheless, trends and policies since the 1990s offer sufficient clues for critical analysis with solid conclusions for the current debate. Those clues are interdependent and should be considered in a holistic manner. They include, among others, political factors at both the international and national levels related to the countries involved; an evolving understanding of legal frameworks on refugee protection schemes; specific social and cultural dynamics in the countries affected by forced mi-gration movements and refugee flows; and interests of the different actors and specific characteristics of the conflicts at the core of the refugee crises. It would be naive to think that voluntary repatriation operations focus only on refugee well-being and rights and it is necessary to take into account the complexity of the interrelation among the aforementioned clues in order to place the debate into the 'real politics' arena rather than in the 'absolute rights' discourses. If analysis is to be action-oriented, it is necessary to find the right balance among those frameworks without compromising refugee rights. In this way

> it is precisely the possibility of a gap between the principle of voluntary repatriation and fundamental rights, which may lead to protection prob-lems. . . . In the present international context, faced with pressures from donors and a general lack of political will to find alternative solutions, UNHCR is in many cases obliged to promote return . . . . This gap is often filled by measures to promote or encourage repatriation.
>
> (Boswell 1997: 5)

Firstly, it is necessary to have an overview on the existing and developing legal framework applicable to voluntary repatriation. The core principle in refugee law is the non-*refoulement* principle enshrined by the 1951 Geneva Convention relating to the Status of Refugees in its article 33.1: 'No Contracting State shall expel or return [*refouler*] a refugee in any manner whatsoever to the frontiers of territories where his life or freedom would be threatened on account of his race, religion, nationality, membership of a particular social group or political opinion.' Along with this principle, and specifically relevant in voluntary repatriation, is the 'right to return' enshrined by article 13.2 of the 1948 Universal Declaration of Human Rights: 'Everyone has the right to leave any country, including his own, and to return to his country.'[1] It is on these grounds that the condition of 'voluntariness' plays a key role in voluntary repatriation. Nevertheless, an integral approach makes it necessary to point out that it is precisely this condition of 'voluntariness', together with the question of the responsibilities of the different actors in these operations, which make the area of actions related to voluntary repatriation more vague. Criteria and standards vary depending on the cases and politics involved. Clear legal and conceptual frameworks are lacking, with the result that the operationalization of those principles depends so much on the context that overarching coherence has been, and still is, absent.

An added problem relates to the fact that voluntariness, unlike refugee status, has not been regulated in international refugee law.[2] With the exception of the previously outlined two binding principles that are applicable, voluntary repatriation of refugees has only been referred to in 'soft law' instruments. The main instruments are the UNHCR Executive Committee Conclusions 18 (1980) and 40 (1985), both reaffirmed by Conclusion 74 (1994).

Given these legal binding and non-binding (but generally accepted by States) normative frameworks and in the need to address in a practical way voluntary repatriation operations, UNHCR presented a manual in 1996, called *Voluntary Repatriation: International Protection*. This book, meant to be used as the principal instrument of reference in voluntary repatriation operations, lacks clear concepts and omits key issues. It does not offer proper details regarding, for example, the meaning and extent of monitoring of returnees in their countries of origin as part of UNHCR's mandate, proper conceptualization of returnee reintegration and basic questions like responsibilities regarding recovering of national protection by refugees once they go back to their countries of origin. Aware of these problems, 'UNHCR is planning to update this Handbook to ensure it addresses new legal standards, issues, as well as returnee monitoring, capacity-building and reconciliation' (UNHCR 2002a: 13).

The international community and UNHCR have been conscious of the previously outlined problems from an action-oriented perspective and the evolution of international politics. It has been on these grounds that UNHCR, under its mandate,[3] has promoted debate and reflection on the issue of voluntary repatriation, which are still ongoing and which have not reached clear and rigorous answers so far. UNHCR set up in 2000 the so-called Global Consultations on International Protection. Those consultations led to the

Agenda for Protection in 2002, which in Goal 5, 'Redoubling the search for durable solutions', included specific references to voluntary repatriation in order to operationalize applicable principles and to develop further the existing legal framework applicable in those operations. The fourth meeting of the Global Consultations on International Protection specifically addressed the voluntary repatriation scheme stating that 'from UNHCR's perspective, the core voluntary repatriation is return in and to conditions of physical, legal and material safety, with full restoration of national protection the end product' (ibid.: 15). The so-called 'core elements' in a voluntary repatriation process are:

- the importance of providing necessary information to refugees about conditions in their country of origin to facilitate decision-making;
- where appropriate, 'go and see' visits without loss of refugee status;
- formal guarantees of the safety of returning refugees;
- UNHCR's returnee monitoring function, including UNHCR's direct and unhindered access to returnees at all stages;
- the provision of necessary documentation and the restoration of citizenship;
- the need for reception arrangements and the provision of reintegration assistance by UNHCR and other UN agencies;
- the promotion of dialogue between the main actors;
- the establishment of consultative and tripartite agreements;
- UNHCR's leading role in promoting, facilitating and co-coordinating voluntary repatriation;
- state's primary responsibility in creating conditions conducive to voluntary repatriation as a solution to refugee problems (ibid.: 12).

It is important to note that the precedent texts do not state responsibilities in relation to those core elements. It is a fact that different actors with different interests intervene in a return process. In many cases tripartite agreements establish the framework for a specific operation and its development by the three actors involved in the agreement (UNHCR, country of asylum, country of origin). Nevertheless there are vacuums and, as in the Cambodian case, it is not clear who is 'de facto' responsible for the 'full restoration of national protection' and how responsibilities are shared in relation to voluntary repatriation operations and, more broadly, with regard to return processes of refugees. In this context,

> it could be argued whether returnees have a status different than that of refugee and citizen. This discussion arose in trying to answer the initial question on when returnees are no longer returnees, but just citizens. Legally speaking, returnees recover national protection once the circumstances justifying their refugee status cease to exist and they return to their country of origin. Nevertheless a gap between the legal

and the social level seems to exist. The State of origin is responsible for the protection of all their citizens equally, but recovering by returnees is not instant, but gradual and it is reflected in the way they progressively situate themselves within the society upon return.

(García Rodicio 2001: 126)

In order to implement Goal 5 established by the Agenda for Protection, the UNHCR Core Group on Durable Solutions proposed in May 2003 the Framework for Durable Solutions for Refugees and Persons of Concern, which includes the so called '4Rs' framework: repatriation, reintegration, rehabilitation and reconstruction.

While recognizing comparative advantages and mandated responsibilities of the respective agencies, the 4Rs programme concept attempts to bring together humanitarian, transition and development approaches throughout the different stages of a reintegration process in a structured manner.

(UNHCR 2003: 3)

It is stated that

the needs of returnees have not systematically been incorporated in transition and recovery plans by governments concerned, the donor community and even the UN system. ... For return and reintegration to be sustainable and the displaced population sufficiently protected, their medium and longer-term needs must be addressed through system-wide consideration and systematic inclusion of this group into the planning and programming of rehabilitation and reconstruction processes.

(ibid.: 9, 11)

In May 2004, UNHCR launched the *Handbook for Repatriation and Reintegration Activities*, which develops the 4Rs framework and is meant to be used as an operational tool for the field. Another instrument that has been developed in recent years is the 'Convention Plus' process that intends 'to improve refugee protection worldwide and to facilitate the resolution of refugee problems through multilateral special agreements' (UNHCR 2004: 1). Although it is an initiative in the first stages of development, it could mean an important step in adapting the refugee regime to the new challenges in refugee protection and, specifically, in voluntary repatriation because

despite their continued relevance, the Convention and the Protocol cannot address all the pressing issues pertaining to refugee protection in today's changing world. These include how durable solutions for refugees can be pursued more effectively and how the responsibility for admitting and protecting refugees can best be shared. For this reason, the United

Nations High Commissioner for Refugees launched the 'Convention Plus' process.

(ibid.)

Despite these current evolving trends, norms and policies regarding the voluntary repatriation framework, efforts are still needed in order to include return within the broader reconciliation process in the country of origin of the refugees. This question is specifically relevant to the Palestinian case because it is the oldest and largest refugee population in the world and the search for a solution to their situation has been protracted for decades. The evolution of the Palestinian refugee case started with the first exodus in 1948. The group of 1948 Palestinian refugees has grown in these last five decades to number, with their descendants, about 5 million persons and they have been displaced in host countries and in the occupied Palestinian territories. Complex legal and political issues have arisen in relation to Palestinian refugees and it is not the aim of this chapter to analyse in depth these issues but to give some clues to situate the given general overview on voluntary repatriation in relation to the Palestinian case.

At legal level, there are important gaps regarding the international protection of Palestinian refugees because

for historical reasons, the Palestinian refugees, alone among refugee communities in the world, fall outside the protective regime of the office of the United Nations High Commissioner for Refugees (UNHCR). UNRWA provides relief and humanitarian aid, but is not constitutionally or politically empowered to provide needed protection.

(United Nations Commission on Human Rights 2001: 30)

This situation has led to the fact that

the protection gap is significant, both with regard to the protection of Palestinian refugee rights in the context of a future durable solution to the Israeli–Palestinian conflict, and with regard to the protection of immediate economic, social, cultural, civil and political rights, as well as physical protection, in the context of exile.

(BADIL 2004)

In terms of repatriation and the effective implementation of the Palestinian refugees' right to return, paragraph 11 of the United Nations General Assembly Resolution 194[4] establishes the framework for a durable solution to the refugee issue:

the refugees wishing to return to their homes and live at peace with their neighbours should be permitted to do so at the earliest practicable date, and ... compensation should be paid for the property of those choosing not to return and for loss of or damage to property which, under principles of international law or in equity, should be made good by the Governments or authorities responsible.

The right to return enshrined in UNGA Resolution 194, as well as in other instruments of international law, has been constantly denied by Israel, including obstruction to the right of return, denationalization and illegal confiscation of private property and land. Therefore, at political level, there is a confrontation regarding this issue:

> The Israel consensus regards the assertion of any serious demand to implement a Palestinian right of return ... as a decisive complication in the search for 'peace'. The Palestinian approach is more varied and tentative. Some Palestinians do insist that the right to return be fully implemented in accordance with international law . . . . More frequently, Palestinians seem more flexible on this matter, seeking mainly a symbolic acknowledgement by Israel of the hardships associated with the expulsions, some provision for compensation and some possibilities for Palestinian family unification.
>
> (United Nations Commission on Human Rights 2001: 31)

Given the general framework on voluntary repatriation and the specificities of the Palestinian refugee issue, a proposal for a comprehensive understanding of repatriation with a reconciliation approach is very relevant. It is an important step further for current debates on the issue of refugee return, and, specifically, on the Palestinian refugees' return debate.

Why is the reconciliation framework relevant in voluntary repatriation approaches?

Contemporary forced migration movements and refugee crises have mainly been taking place in war contexts or conflict related contexts. These situations are characterized, among other circumstances, by generalized violence affecting the society as a whole, social turmoil, disruption of social and political relationships and socio-economic livelihoods, fragility and breakdown of state institutions and physical destruction and insecurity. The trend in the last decades is that internal conflicts constitute the roots of the majority of the refugee flows. This has meant, from a voluntary repatriation point of view, that return processes of refugees to their countries of origin are more than crossing borders. For the refugee populations they mean a re-encounter with the people and with the country as a whole, which is in a post-conflict situation at the political, legal, social and economic levels. And it is in this post-conflict situation, often characterized by the divisions that the conflict caused, that the notion of reconciliation acquires a special relevance.

Reconciliation has been overused as a 'politically correct' word in humanitarian affairs and post-conflict activities during the last decade, especially after the conflicts that took place in the former Yugoslavia and Rwanda in the 1990s. Nevertheless, there is a lack of conceptual frameworks addressing reconciliation and they are still in evolution. It is stated and generally agreed by experts that

> reconciliation is a burdened and difficult word. For many, it conjures up deeply personal religious overtones. For others, it connotes romantic notions of to 'forgive and forget'. Some question whether it has positive meaning in the political terrain. Others ask whether it is appropriate to speak of reconciliation or restoration in the absence of previous situations, relationships or social realities to which one can realistically return. For some there is no tangible memory of peace. . . . Reconciliation is not a mere romantic or utopian ideal. It is a mode of realism – a serious option for living together in the midst of unresolved conflict. . . . In societies emerging from violent conflict, this kind of political reconciliation is often the only realistic alternative to enduring escalating violence – and of achieving economic, social and related forms of justice. . . . Reconciliation is process, as well as goal.
>
> (Villa-Vicencio 2003)

Conscious of the difficulties in defining reconciliation, and taking into account that different cultures and peoples may understand reconciliation processes in a different way and with different elements, it is important to explain the way the concept is understood in this chapter. It is neither the aim nor the purpose of this chapter to analyse reconciliation. Rather the concept will be pragmatically used in the chapter in terms of trying to operationalize it in the framework of voluntary repatriation. In this way, the concept used is defined as follows:

> The long term social and political process, possibly transgenerational, that opens the path to the establishment of peaceful cohabitation and which lay the ground for conditions to deal with the destructive consequences of conflict and allows for more constructive ways of dealing with existing differences. . . . The wider concept of reconciliation is rights-based and ought to be supported from the State by institutions legitimized by society (top-down processes). It also involves the active recognition of the initiatives of grass-roots actors (bottom-up processes) and their interaction with the above mentioned institutions. This implies providing social and political spaces for such an interaction to take place in a framework of public security.
>
> (UNHCR Spanish Committee/Globalitaria 2004)

Although reconciliation has been mentioned in connection with voluntary repatriation by UNHCR and the international community, practices show that the existing approach is clearly insufficient. Usually the debate, at policy and implementation level, refers to different realities and both phenomena are considered interrelated but independent processes. Taking the Cambodian return process as the reference, I will argue that voluntary repatriation is an integral part of the post-conflict reconciliation process and should be understood as such in order to be a durable solution for refugees when they go back to their country of origin. I also argue that existing voluntary repatriation perspectives focus on top-down processes (juridical–political) while usually ignoring the bottom-up processes (grass-roots and psychosocial) and these perspectives limit the legitimacy of those operations. Including voluntary repatriation as an integral part of the reconciliation process in a post-conflict society is essential in terms of legitimacy and rights implementation from a medium- and long-term perspective. In order to include voluntary repatriation and reconciliation in the connected way understood in this chapter, I will use the term 'return process' more broadly than 'voluntary repatriation operations'. On the one hand, these operations are just one part of the process and, on the other hand, the broader term includes both top-down and bottom-up processes as integral to 'return' and places the emphasis on reconciliation.

A proposal drawn from the Cambodian return process[5]

Theoretical framework from a reconciliation perspective: restorative justice and voluntary repatriation[6]

Based on the 1992–3 Cambodian experience of return as expressed by 286 returnee families interviewed in 1999–2000, and given the limitations that existing analysis and approaches offered in addressing refugee return processes, a new theoretical approach to voluntary repatriation was drawn. This approach used the restorative justice paradigm as the main theoretical source, which is focused on restoring human relationships that have been broken due to a wrong and therefore focused on reconciliation. The conceptual elements

> that apply this paradigm in this analysis are the existence of a wrong, the relational dimension, and the principle of equality in social justice. The root causes forcing people to flee their original country imply a wrong (conflict). Humanity is damaged at a personal level and relationships are broken at a social level, as well as the sense of trust necessary to build them. This wrong needs to be corrected once the circumstances that provoked the situation cease and repatriation is possible.
>
> (García Rodicio 2001: 134)

By applying the restorative justice paradigm to refugee return processes a definition of what is called 'restoration of life'[7] is reached:

> Restoration of life in the country of origin for returnees is the process of re-empowerment for returnees, both individually and communally, under the principles of equality and non-discrimination, in order to rebuild social and economic relationships disrupted by the refugee experience and war. This process is not value neutral but has to be connected to reconciliation.
>
> *Restoration of life in the country of origin for returnees refers to restoration in two dimensions:*
>
> Personal restoration. Re-empowerment of returnees in the country of origin to take decisions affecting their lives in order to live and relate in dignity and equality. It includes two levels of restoration: material and emotional (which includes spiritual). Material restoration takes place through the reasonable realization of the four rights inherent to the basic human right of life: right to food, housing, health and education. Emotional restoration takes place through reconciliation of returnees with their own suffering at a personal level.
>
> Communal restoration. Re-establishment of relationships in the country of origin, taking place in a gradual process of interrelations in the heart of a community marked by the two values of respect and equality (at the different levels of community: family, local and national). It takes place through reconciliation at the community level.
>
> (ibid.: 134–5)

These parameters and conceptualization are used to analyse the return process of Cambodian returnees from 1992 to 1993. They are illustrated in Figure 10.1.

The Cambodian transitional process: the contextualization of the Cambodian refugee return process

Brief historical overview

A brief overview of the Cambodian history shows that the history of Cambodian returnees is a history of 'survivors': survivors of a genocide in which approximately 1.7 million people died, survivors of the US bombings in Cambodia in the context of the Vietnam War, survivors of flight through the Thai–Cambodian border, survivors of refugee camps where refugees were pawns in the hands of different actors in the conflict, and survivors of repatriation. Taking this into consideration, return to Cambodia in 1992–3 was a complex process.

In 1989, UNHCR and the Phnom Penh government signed a document called 'Aide Memoir on Voluntary Repatriation' in which principles and

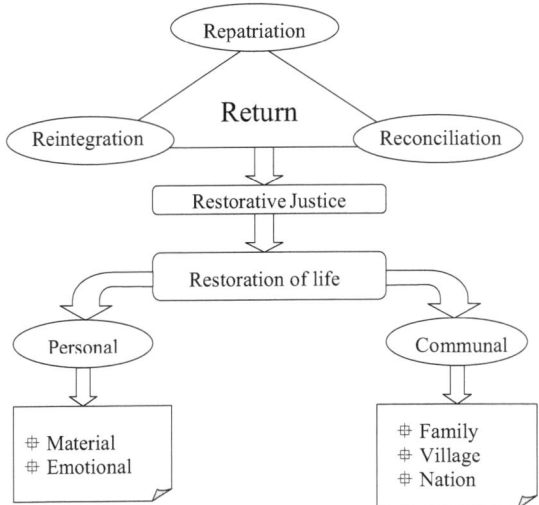

Figure 10.1 Parameters and conceptualization of the return process of Cambodian returnees, 1992–3.

procedures for repatriation were agreed. Therefore in July 1989 the UN Secretary General designated UNHCR as the lead agency to coordinate the repatriation operation. After negotiations, a peace agreement was reached in October 1991, the Agreement on a Comprehensive Political Settlement of the Cambodian Conflict. Repatriation of returnees was an integral part of this Agreement, which stated in its Annex 4, art. 4:

> There must be full respect for the human rights and fundamental freedoms of all Cambodians, including those of repatriated refugees and displaced persons, in recognition of their entitlement to live in peace and security, free from intimidation and coercion of any kind. These rights would include, inter alia, freedom of movement within Cambodia, the choice of domicile and employment, and the right to property.

Upon the signing of the Peace Agreement the United Nations Transitional Authority for Cambodia (UNTAC) was established and the administration of the country relied on their authority until free elections led to the formation of a democratically elected government.

Nevertheless, this was only the first step towards bringing peace to Cambodia as fighting continued in the northwestern part of the country when the Khmer Rouge forces withdrew from the peace process. Returnees were in a country between war and peace. The repatriation operation organized by UNHCR brought back to Cambodia more than 360,000 refugees from the refugee camps in Thailand. The timeframe of this operation was from March 1992 until May 1993, as one of the main objectives of the repatriation operation was that returnees should participate in the first democratic elections in the country, which were set to take place in May 1993. In terms of destination, the majority of returnees opted to return to the northwest provinces, which were areas greatly affected by war and landmines and were politically tense until December 1998.

Although elections took place in 1993 and a coalition government was formed, the turmoil and instability continued in Cambodia. Struggling for power both in political and military terms by the different actors who were fighting during the war was the hallmark of the 1990s. In 1997 a coup took place and a new political and refugee crisis started. Thanks mainly to the international community pressure, democratic elections were held in July 1998 and a new coalition government was formed. In December 1998 the last factions of the Khmer Rouge defected to the Royal Government of Cambodia and the agreement meant that this was the first time for 30 years that Cambodia knew peace. At present, although still in transition and in a post-conflict situation, Cambodia is slowly consolidating the reconciliation process, both at the juridical–political level and at the psychosocial level.

Voluntary repatriation operation: between relief and development

Together with the logistics arrangements for the first phase of the voluntary repatriation operation, UNHCR established under its mandate reintegration programmes for returnees and monitoring activities.

In terms of reintegration, the distribution of responsibilities in the three different phases (relief, reconstruction and development) was reflected in the Memorandum of Understanding between UNHCR and UNDP. While UNHCR would focus on the immediate needs of returnees, UNDP would concentrate on longer-term reintegration. UNHCR designed reintegration programmes for returnees with two components: food for 400 days, which would be provided by the WFP, and a reintegration package. This package included initially two hectares of land per family but the planning was incorrect and these provisions were later changed. Identification of available land was made through satellite images, and important factors, such as landmines or negotiations with the local authorities, were not taken into account: *'However, most of the land identified in this way proved to be not available to returnees because it was not on offer by the authorities, heavily mined, insecure, or in the meantime occupied by others'* (quoted in Robinson 1994: 22). By that time many returnees had chosen their destinations in Cambodia believing that they would receive land and some of them had already returned. In October 1992 new options were designed and adjusted to real possibilities. The distribution of packages was as follows:[8]

- Option A. Agricultural land – 3.0 per cent of the families. This included up to 2 hectares of agricultural land per family, a housing plot, wood for construction of a house frame, US$25 for construction materials and a household/agricultural kit.

- Option B. House – 11.1 per cent of the families. This included a plot of land for a house, wood for construction of a house frame, US$25 to buy thatch and bamboo and a household/agricultural kit.
- Option C. Cash – 83.9 per cent of the families. This included reintegration money, US$50 per adult and US$25 per child under 12, and a household/agricultural kit.
- Option D. Income-generating tools. Removed.
- Option E. Employment – 1.1 per cent of the families. Returnees with UN jobs or other organizations in Cambodia would receive reintegration money to the amount of US$50 per adult and US$25 dollars per child under 12.
- Option F. Family reunion – 0.1 per cent of the families. This option was intended for families of soldiers or Option E returnees who had preceded them into Cambodia. It included money to the amount of US$50 per adult and US$25 per child under 12.

Monitoring also fell within UNHCR's mandate. Nevertheless,

> protection, social service and field officers all spent considerable time in the districts, following up reported problems and assessing needs. But staff limitations and logistical priorities during the movement phase kept UNHCR monitoring activities sporadic and ad hoc.
>
> (Robinson 1994: 58)

These comments were made in May 1994 but similar comments could be cited from the conclusions reached in 2000. The situation of the Cambodian returnees and their process of return, as analysed later in the paper, put into question how this function was addressed by UNHCR in Cambodia and what activities were included in 'monitoring'. At the time of the research in the year 1999–2000, seven to eight years after repatriation, all the UNHCR documents related to the 1992–3 operation were either destroyed or in Geneva and inaccessible so the possibility of analysing these questions through UNHCR documentation was limited. Important questions related to returnee monitoring are still pending in legal and practical frameworks in voluntary repatriation operations. Given the concerns that have come about with the Cambodian case, these questions remain very relevant and should be addressed.

Conclusions of the 1999–2000 study on the Cambodian return process[9]

Personal restoration: material restoration (right to food, housing, health and education)

1   The majority of Cambodian returnees from 1992–3 are a homogeneous vulnerable social group in the Cambodian society in the way their

material restoration has taken place. Integration in Cambodia has not been equal to that of the general population; rather it has only been equal to the most vulnerable groups in society. The evolution of many returnee families in the Banteay Meanchey and Siem Reap provinces shows a progressive disempowerment process since 1992–3 and alerts the entrance of an increasing number of returnees to irreversible cycles of poverty.

2 The way that three of the four rights inherent to the 'right to life' have been realized for returnees since 1992–3 is precarious:

a *Right to food*. Fifty-two per cent of Cambodian returnees from 1992–3 do not have enough food to eat and many others are near the limit established in this study to assess the protection of this right. Consequently, returnees as a group have not realized their basic right to food. Access to food security has not been equal to that of the general population but only similar to that of the most vulnerable groups in society. Statistics are stark: 52 per cent of returnees lack food security whereas in Cambodia as a whole, the incidence of food insecurity applies to only 17 per cent of people unable to meet their basic food needs. The evolution of returnees in terms of food security since return not only has not improved but has become progressively worse, with 30 per cent of returnees not getting by in 1994 and 40 per cent not getting by in 1995. This has been the trend up until now and signals the ongoing increase in the number of families crossing the food poverty line. This situation has led many returnees to take risky coping strategies thus putting them in irreversible circles of chronic poverty.

b *Right to housing*. Seventy-seven per cent of Cambodian returnees from 1992–3 live in inadequate housing within the Cambodian context. As a consequence, the majority have not realized their basic right to housing. Their reintegration in Cambodia in terms of housing is not equal to the situation of the general population, but only to the most vulnerable groups in society. The increasing number of very vulnerable returnee families signals the increasing loss of housing land. Returnees are selling or mortgaging their land for housing in order to cover their basic needs.

c *Right to education*. Seventy-five per cent of the Cambodian returnees from 1992–3 have realized their basic right to education. Their reintegration in Cambodia in terms of education is almost equal to that of the general population, although 10 per cent under the national average. Returnees are very concerned about the education of their children and they make notable efforts to send them to school even if they are facing major economic difficulties in fulfilling their basic needs.

d *Right to health*. The realization of the basic right to health for Cambodian returnees from 1992–3 is relative. Access to health services is the same for returnees as for the general population, but this access is directly related to economic possibilities because of the large private financing of health expenses in Cambodia. The poorest groups are proportionally disadvantaged in their access to health and returnees are among the poorest groups in the society. Their reintegration in Cambodia in terms of health care has not been equal to the general population, but similar only to the most vulnerable groups. The use of risky strategies to cover health expenses is the primary factor leading returnees into a cycle of chronic poverty, which signals an increase in the number of vulnerable returnee families.

3 Returnees are recognized as citizens at the formal level but in reality they are vulnerable citizens considered as a group. Formally their right to food, housing and health is recognized as equal to other citizens. However, the realization of those rights has taken place in a way unequal to that of the general population and only equal to that of the poorest people in Cambodian society.

4 The effective realization of the right to education for the returnees' children is a positive indicator of reintegration of those children in Cambodia. Socialization takes place in schools and parameters of relations and interpretation of reality are learned in connection with other children, which is very important for reconciliation in a post-conflict situation.

Schools built specifically in areas where there are a large number of returnees, and consequently attended chiefly by returnees' children, could have a negative impact on the returnees' children's reintegration into society. A firm conclusion is not possible due to the constraints of this study, but observations suggest that relations with local children do not take place at school and differences are maintained to a greater extent than in places where both returnees' children and local children share the same school.

5 Lack of access to economic resources is the principal factor affecting the returnees' lack of material restoration. Returnees are a social group lacking access to economic resources and their position in society is similar only to the poorest sectors. Economic resources include income generating possibilities and access to land.

In terms of income, 85 per cent of returnees are not earning enough money to cover their basic needs. This vulnerability has an added character because the majority of the returnees live on a hand-to-mouth basis without permanent sources of income.

At the national level 47 per cent of returnee families are within the poorest decile of the society and 82 per cent of returnee families are within the three poorest deciles of the society.

In terms of access to land, 73 per cent of returnees lack access to arable land. The returnees' landlessness is caused by the difficulties in accessing social networks to obtain land and the specific problems returnees experience in obtaining protection for their property rights.

The incidence of landlessness among returnees is much greater than in the general population in Cambodia, which is 13 per cent.

6 In the returnee group there are two social sub-groups, widows and former soldiers' families, who are facing specific reintegration difficulties. They experience a lack of socio-economic opportunities and severe stress with coping mechanisms in relation to their current life conditions in Cambodia.

7 This precarious situation of the 1992–3 returnees has a serious negative impact not only in terms of physical well-being but also psychosocially. Feelings of hopelessness, day-to-day stress and worries about satisfying basic needs are common feelings that returnees experience. These feelings negatively affect their welfare and consequently the way they develop social and economic relationships in the family, in the villages and in society as a whole.

Nurturing and emotional capabilities have been seriously affected by the continuous experiences of war. Facing return to Cambodia under the harsh conditions they are living is a new heavy burden for returnees, which is negatively influencing the way they live and relate.

8 The dignity of 1992–3 Cambodian returnees as a social group is seriously affected by the lack of material restoration in Cambodia after their repatriation. For a large number of returnee families, living in dignity and equality has not been possible in Cambodia up until now.

Personal restoration: emotional restoration

1 The majority of Cambodian returnees from 1992–3 are a homogeneous vulnerable social group in the Cambodian society in terms of emotional restoration. The process of reintegration was constrained by the war conditions until the last Peace Agreement was signed in December 1998. As a result of this and the continuous struggle for survival that many returnees have faced after repatriation, it has been difficult to implement healing mechanisms.

2 A large number of returnee families (60 per cent), feel that they were happier in the refugee camps than they are now in Cambodia. Economic vulnerability and lack of community rebuilding where returnees feel accepted in equal terms are the two main factors affecting these perceptions. Community reintegration has a great impact on the way returnees see their situation in Cambodia. Personal reconciliation is directly related to community reconciliation.

3 History telling is a way of healing at the personal level and a way towards reconciliation at the communal level in Cambodia. Cambodian people were forced to keep silent during the many years of war and therefore suffering in silence has been the way of coping with and surviving the

conflict. The present post-conflict situation is the perfect soil in which to plant the seeds for healing the suffering and the differences of the past.

4 The findings in this study are consistent enough to state that the majority of Cambodian returnees from 1992–3 in the Banteay Meanchey and Siem Reap provinces are and feel themselves to be a vulnerable social group in Cambodian society.

5 The returnee identity is characterized by homogeneity in internal characteristics and external perceptions. Internal characteristics include the shared experience of exile, shared perceptions upon return to Cambodia, their lack of emotional restoration and the socio-economic situations of poverty and the shared sense of identity. External perceptions include the lack of material restoration and the weakness of their communal restoration at different levels of community.

6 This identity has been built and reinforced during the seven to eight years after repatriation. The sense of inclusion that the majority of returnees have is generally limited to the inclusion in the returnee group. Fighting for survival and feelings of exclusion have determined this tendency.

Communal restoration: family, local community and national community.

1 The majority of Cambodian returnees from 1992–3 are a homogeneous vulnerable social group in Cambodian society in terms of communal restoration. The evolution of many returnee families in the Banteay Meanchey and Siem Reap provinces since 1992–3 shows difficulties in the reconstruction of relationships in communities where returnees are located and do not feel included amongst the locals. This situation has evolved towards the reinforcement of the sense of identity of returnees as a group and the establishment of strong links among themselves. It highlights the lack of adequate mechanisms with regard to the inclusion of returnees in the different levels of Cambodian society.

2 *Family community restoration.* Re-establishment of relationships at the family level has been problematic for returnees. Fifty-two per cent of returnees do not have relatives in the same village, 28 per cent do not have relatives either in the village or in the province and 10 per cent do not have any relatives in Cambodia.

   The existence of family relationships, in those cases in which they exist, is an indicator of economic and psychosocial well-being:

   a *Economic.* The presence of relatives in the same village is important in terms of covering emergency situations of food security, housing and health, but not in terms of covering the permanent needs that returnees face due to their serious situation of vulnerability.

   b *Psychosocial.* The percentage of returnees happy in Cambodia is now larger among those returnees that have relatives in the same village than among those that do not have family ties in the village. The recovery of the sense of trust necessary to rebuild relationships in a post-conflict situation is facilitated by the re-establishment of the 'family belonging' links in Cambodia after repatriation.

3   *Local community restoration.* Re-establishment of relationships at the village level has taken different forms and every village could be analysed separately. Nevertheless, there are some commonalties in the way returnees have faced return to village life in Cambodia. It is enough to say that restoration at the village level, in the cases of returnees settled together with locals,[10] has been weak and determined by discriminatory attitudes towards returnees rooted in the conflict. The returnee identity, in some cases inaccurately, refers to a political background, branded on people coming from refugee camps administrated by political factions. This fact accounts for the suspicious way in which local people and local authorities in the villages have looked upon returnees up until now.

4   The meaning of 'community' given by returnees themselves differs according to the different processes of reintegration in the villages. In places where relationships with locals are slowly taking place or in places where all the villagers are returnees, they refer to the village as the community. In places where returnees do not relate with local people they refer to the 'returnee community'.

5   Case studies suggest the existence of three factors influencing local community restoration that have been present in all the villages visited:

   a   Effective involvement of local leaders in the repatriation process. There is a serious concern about the lack of effective involvement of local leaders in the reintegration process of returnees. The effective involvement of an authority with legitimate power has been essential in the way returnees have re-established relationships and in the way the intra-community conflicts between returnees and locals that are somehow inherent to the conflict in Cambodia are properly channelled. Unfortunately, this has not been the case in the majority of the villages visited. In some areas, the lack of effective involvement of local and community leaders has meant the lack of input in the re-establishment of relationships at local level and the consequent evolution towards returnee isolation within the villages in those places.

   b   The existence of shared social spaces in the village. Physical spaces for socializing are essential for the restoration of relationships. In those places where there are pagodas, play yards or any kind of common physical space, contact between people is facilitated. This is an important tool in a post-conflict situation where people feel reticent to meet, even physically, other people and movement has been constrained by war circumstances. In some places where these spaces exist, returnees are slowly re-establishing relationships. A sense of trust slowly grows when people encounter, first physically, then relationally, a way to heal past differences.

c   The active involvement of local populations in the process. In the majority of the villages studied, a large number of returnee families were settled. Taking into account the nature of the Cambodian conflict and the perception by local people about returnees as 'returnees, the enemy', the arrival of a large new group has meant internal conflict between the two groups. Local people have been generally left without a voice in the repatriation process. Reticence in receiving a large group of returnees in the villages is a normal consequence of this fact.

6   Common activities are essential to rebuild relationships. Development activities have been frequently pointed out by returnees as one of the main ways to gather with other people in the village. One of the principal mentions has been 'Food for Work' programmes sponsored by the WFP and ILO. These activities are very positive for the restoration of village level relationships. On the one hand they bring together people that otherwise would not meet and on the other hand they involve both the local and returnee populations equally, in the common development of their village.

Common activities with cultural connotations such as festivals are very important in rebuilding relationships. They constitute a common point of reference for locals and returnees and at the same time they are the cultural elements that bring together populations previously separated by conflict.

7   Socialization of the returnees' children is essential for rebuilding relationships and creating a common history in the villages. Children of returnee families reproduce models of behaviour that they learn from the adults. Many children are living within a returnee identity reinforced by the difficult social and economic circumstances in which their families have to live.

8   Discrimination towards returnees in villages where they settled along with locals took place in the majority of the villages visited. In many places conflicts among returnees and locals arose as an inherent part of the conflict in Cambodia and the different visions, experiences and interests of both groups. Basically they involved the political background of the returnees, who were branded with the politics of the parties administrating the camps, and the lack of access to land by returnees after repatriation.

These conflicts have evolved differently in different places. Conflict resolution strategies developed by returnees include attitudes of keeping silent and patience, attitudes of separation and lack of interrelation with locals and migration to returnee settlements.

9   Solidarity networks indicate commitment to the needs of others and the existence of social bonds. All but one case of this networking were observed among the returnees themselves. Solidarity networks have been built among returnees even if all of them face similar socio-economic

difficulties. They include adoptions of other returnees, food, health care and building of houses for the poorest returnees (chiefly widows).

The fact that networks only exist among returnees and not among locals and returnees (except in one case) indicates weaknesses in rebuilding relationships at the local level with local populations and the strength in building returnee–returnee relationships.

10 *National restoration.* Lack of information by returnees about national issues does not permit firm conclusions. This lack of information is due to the great reluctance shown by returnees in talking about national matters and it is a strong indicator that national restoration has been poor for returnees up until now.

11 There are three indicators that permit the assessment that restoration at the national level has been poor for returnees: personal perception in relation to Cambodia, participation and feelings in relation to national political processes, and secondary migration after repatriation:

a   A majority of Cambodian returnees (64 per cent) do not feel happy in Cambodia now.

b   Participation in political processes at the national level is very high for returnees, with 94 per cent participating in the 1993 elections and 89 per cent participating in the 1998 elections. Nevertheless, there are concerns about their feelings regarding national level decisions. These concerns refer to the general fear that all returnees showed in talking about political matters and to some feelings of exclusion by the national government that some returnees referred to.

c   The incidence of secondary migration after repatriation is very high, with 54 per cent of returnees moving at least once from their original place of settlement. Grounds for this migration include lack of access to economic resources, family reunification and the ongoing conflict in Cambodia until December 1998. Freedom of movement is a basic freedom in a democratic society and includes the right to settle permanently without being compelled to move. The incidence of secondary migration has been very high for returnees and in the majority of the cases has been forced by economic and/or social circumstances.

12 For a large number of returnee families, living and relating in dignity and equality has not been possible in Cambodia up until now.

Conclusion

Existing legal and practical frameworks for voluntary repatriation are not sufficient to address the complex issues related to refugee return processes from a medium- and long-term perspective. Although those frameworks have been evolving during the last decade, as stated by the Agenda for Protection, they are still limited. Development of new approaches and frameworks is needed in order to offer answers to current debates and to explore further voluntary repatriation as an effective durable solution for refugees. All different actors in return processes should participate in the given debates, including those who are generally left outside decision-making processes, such as refugees and returnees themselves.

The return process, as experienced by many Cambodian returnees from 1992–3, indicates that voluntary repatriation should be approached in a holistic way and as an integral part of the reconciliation process inherent to a post-conflict society. Including all the different actors and interests is crucial and finding new ways to make those processes more inclusive is essential. Social dynamics as experienced by the given society as a whole should be carefully taken into account as well as cultural and philosophical understandings.

In general terms, voluntary repatriation operations at present are carried out as a top-down process (juridical–political) and generally ignore social dynamics and civil society initiatives (the bottom-up processes). Including the bottom-up perspective is essential in order to have all actors included in the return process because only then will the given process have sufficient legitimacy from all persons and communities concerned by the complex issues at stake with regard to refugee return. Synchronization of both top-down and bottom-up processes is a challenge that every return process faces and it is something that should be carefully addressed beforehand.

The main conclusion drawn is that the refugee return process is an integral part of the broader reconciliation process in the country of origin of the refugees. This conclusion is especially relevant to Palestinian refugees because the implementation of their right to return is intrinsically part of any possible long-term peace process in the region. The term 'reconciliation' is debated in cases in which there is not previous conciliation, as it could be in the case of Palestine and Israel. In these cases the term 'conciliation' seems more appropriate. Notwithstanding terminological debates, it is important to emphasize that a comprehensive understanding of the right to return of Palestinian refugees with a reconciliation/conciliation approach is very important and it could add new dimensions to actual debates on durable solutions. The comprehensive understanding will include transitional justice issues (such as compensation, restitution, justice questions addressing gross human rights violations and violations of the International Humanitarian Law), the renewal of the social contract and state-building processes, among other issues.

Notes

1 These two norms are generally recognized as part of customary international law so they are applicable and binding in any case of voluntary repatriation, whether a State has signed and ratified those two international instruments or not.
2 At the regional level, the 1969 OAU Refugee Convention is the only binding instrument that explicitly covers voluntary repatriation. It recognizes the vol-

untary character of repatriation and specifies the responsibilities of both the country of asylum and the country of origin.

3 Article 1 of the Statute of the Office of the United Nations High Commissioner for Refugees states: "The United Nations High Commissioner for Refugees, acting under the authority of the General Assembly, shall assume the function of providing international protection, under the auspices of the United Nations, to refugees who fall within the scope of the present Statute and of seeking permanent solutions for the problem of refugees".

4 It is generally agreed by experts that *"the fact that UNGA Res. 194 has been reaffirmed over 100 times is strong evidence of its authority as customary international law on the Palestinian refugee question"* (Akram 2000).

5 Conclusions and analysis presented in this section of the chapter are drawn from the field research the author carried out in Cambodia in the period July 1999–December 2000 (García Rodicio 2000).

6 This theoretical approach is only outlined in this chapter. It has been analysed in greater detail in García Rodicio (2001).

7 The word "restoration" is not used in the strict semantic sense. It does not refer to return to the situation that refugees had before flight, which would be impossible materially, legally and historically. It refers to the process of going back and starting life again in the country of origin while working through the process of exile.

8 Information adapted by Court Robinson based on UNHCR information (Robinson 1994: 23–4).

9 It is fair to emphasize that these conclusions refer to the experiences of return of those returnees who were interviewed by the research team in Cambodia in 1999–2000. They were living in two provinces in the northwest, Banteay Meanchey and Siem Reap. Nevertheless it is considered that the consistency and homogeneity of the results together with observation in other provinces show that these conclusions could be extrapolated to other returnees from 1992–3 in other places in Cambodia.

10 "Locals" and "local people" refer in this chapter to the people who remained in Cambodia during the wars. Differentiation of returnees and people who had not been refugees was not the initial approach of the research but progressively elaborated given the analysis and conclusions reached.

References

Akram, Susan M. (2000) *Reinterpreting Palestinian refugee rights under international law, and a framework for durable solutions*, BADIL – Information and Discussion Brief 1 (Bethlehem: BADIL Resource Center for Palestinian Residency and Refugee Rights).

BADIL (2004) *Closing the gaps: Between protection and durable solutions*. Memorandum presented at the UNHCR Pre-EXCOM NGO in Geneva, Switzerland (Bethlehem: BADIL Resource Center for Palestinian Residency and Refugee Rights).

Boswell, C. (1997) *Voluntary repatriation: A critical analysis (draft)* (Geneva: UNHCR CDR Policy Research Unit).

García Rodicio, Ana (2000) *Restoration of life in Cambodia: 1992–93 returnees in Banteay Meanchey and Siem Reap* (Phnom Penh: Jesuit Refugee Service, Cambodia).

García Rodicio, Ana (2001) "Restoration of life: A new theoretical approach to voluntary repatriation based on a Cambodian experience of return", *International Journal of Refugee Law* 13.

Robinson, Court (1994) *Something like home again. The repatriation of Cambodian refugees* (USA: US Committee for Human Rights).

United Nations Commission on Human Rights (2001) *Question of the violation of human rights on the occupied Arab territories, including Palestine* (New York: United Nations Commission on Human Rights, Report of the Human Rights Inquiry Commission).

United Nations General Assembly (1948) UNGA 194 (New York: United Nations).

UNHCR (2002a), *Global consultation on international protection, 4th meeting. Voluntary repatriation*, EC/GC/02/5 (Geneva: UNHCR).

UNHCR (2002b), *Agenda for protection, A/AC.96/965/Add. 1* (Geneva: UNHCR, General Assembly, Executive Committee of the High Commissioner Programme).

UNHCR (2003) *Framework for durable solutions for refugees and persons of concern* (Geneva: UNHCR, Core Group on Durable Solutions).

UNHCR (2004) *Convention Plus at a glance (as of 14 May 2004)* (Geneva: UNHCR).

UNHCR Spanish Committee/Globalitaria – Peace-building Initiatives (2004) *Summary for the final conference on "Conflicts: Prevention, resolution, reconciliation"*. Analytical document from the 2000–4 International Reflection Process, version presented at the Final Conference in Barcelona, Spain (final version forthcoming) (Madrid: UNHCR Spanish Committee/Globalitaria – Peace-building Initiatives).

Villa-Vicencio, Charles (2003) *The politics of reconciliation* (Cape Town: Institute for Justice and Reconciliation).

11 UNHCR under duress

The reducing power of UNHCR to influence outcomes for Afghan refugees

Peter Marsden

This chapter sets out to demonstrate how UNHCR was compelled to make ever greater compromises on its protection mandate as a consequence of pressures from host governments and also from donors, keen to present the intervention of the international community in Afghanistan as a success story and therefore having a vested interest in refugees from Pakistan and Iran being seen to be voting with their feet.

These pressures led UNHCR to move from a situation in the early 1990s, in which refugees could be said to have freely chosen to re-establish themselves in Afghanistan, to the more recent returns in which there has been a significant degree of coercion from host countries (Turton and Marsden 2002).

A historical outline

Afghanistan is essentially a mountainous desert with isolated river valleys and oases which permit subsistence agriculture based on wheat, barley and pasture. After Sierra Leone, it is the poorest country in the world.

The country sits uneasily between the Middle East, Central Asia and South Asia, with adherence to Islam a dominant characteristic. Ethnically, it is mixed and the borders with its neighbours cut through ethnic boundaries. There are, thus, Pushtuns on both sides of the border with Pakistan, Tajiks looking across to Tajikistan, Uzbeks facing Uzbekistan and Turkmens across from Turkmenistan. Tribal traditions are extremely important within the Pushtun and Turkmen populations. This results in highly conservative attitudes but other sections of the population are not much less conservative.

Tensions arose at the beginning of the twentieth century between those seeking to introduce more liberal attitudes into the country and the more conservative elements. The conservatives prevailed and no further efforts were made to challenge the status quo until the 1950s. By the early 1970s, new intellectual movements had established themselves in Kabul University. One looked to the Soviet model of socialism. The other drew on the radical Islamic thinking of Egypt's Muslim Brotherhood.

The socialist movement staged a successful coup in April 1978 and established the People's Democratic Party of Afghanistan government. This sought to impose reforms but alienated the population through the use of insensitive and, at times, brutal methods. A spontaneous resistance movement aroused concerns in Moscow that the PDPA government might be overthrown and the Soviet Union opted to invade Afghanistan in December 1979. The radical Islamic parties, which had been expelled by the previous Afghan government to Pakistan, took the opportunity to claim leadership of the resistance and took on the collective name of the Mujahidin. Operating both within Afghanistan and through cross-border incursions from Pakistan, the Mujahidin were able to disrupt and undermine the military operations of the Soviet forces. Support was provided, in the form of weaponry and other resources, by the USA, using Pakistan as a conduit but with Pakistan also an active player in supporting particular groups within the resistance.

By 1987, the Soviet government recognised that it was not making any significant progress against the Mujahidin insurgency and was concerned that it could not address major issues within its own borders while it was seriously burdened by its military involvement in Afghanistan. In April 1988, the Soviet Union agreed, through the Geneva Accord, to withdraw its forces from Afghanistan on 15 February 1989.

In spite of the Soviet withdrawal, the Soviet-backed PDPA government was able to remain in power until April 1992. The collapse of the Soviet Union, in 1991, hastened its demise as the resources to keep it afloat were no longer arriving. The UN strove to negotiate a smooth transfer of power to a government of national unity, including elements of both the former Soviet-backed government and the Mujahidin parties. However, certain elements within the Mujahidin resisted any association with the former government and an armed struggle for power broke out immediately between the Mujahidin parties which progressively reduced southern Kabul to rubble over the subsequent three years. The ability of this Mujahidin government to actually govern was therefore extremely constrained.

In response to this failure, Pakistan transferred its support from its protégés within the Mujahidin to a new group, known as the Taliban. The latter drew their support largely from the students of Islamic madrasahs in the refugee camps in Pakistan and sought to create an Islamic state based on Sharia Law. They also drew on the thinking of the Deobandi movement of India which, like the Wahhabis of Saudi Arabia, placed a strong focus on dress and behavioural codes of a particularly puritanical nature.

With support from elements within Pakistan, including radical Islamic parties such as Jamiat-al-Ulema al-Islami, they were able to quickly conquer large areas of southern Afghanistan. Their task was made easier by popular disaffection with the Mujahidin. However, when they took Herat, in western Afghanistan, in September 1995, they were regarded as an occupying force, not helped by their largely Pushtun composition in a Dari speaking city.

The Taliban took Kabul a year later but faced resistance in the Shomali

Valley, to the north of Kabul, which became progressively depopulated as the Taliban and one of the Mujahidin parties, Jamiat-i-Islami, battled for control over the following four years. In the spring of 1997, the Taliban moved on the north of Afghanistan but faced a serious setback, suffering heavy casualties, when they attempted to capture Mazar-i-Sharif in May of that year. They finally took the city in August 1998, followed by the Hazarajat area of central Afghanistan a month later, but had, in the process, incurred considerable enmity from the population. Their subsequent efforts to take the remaining north-eastern corner of the country met with strong resistance but they were able to take the town on Taloqan in September 2000, thus achieving partial success. They made no further progress.

The Taliban became increasingly hard-line and intolerant from 1998 onwards, largely as a consequence of growing international criticism of their regime in the aftermath of the US air strikes on Afghanistan of August 1998. These air strikes, which were a response to terrorist attacks on the US embassies in Nairobi and Dar es Salaam earlier that month, were based on claims that a Saudi militant by the name of Osama bin Laden, who had taken refuge in Afghanistan, had been responsible for these attacks. The US government called on the Taliban to surrender him and their refusal to do so, an inevitable outcome given their power base within a radical Islamic network, led to two sets of UN sanctions against Afghanistan, in October 1999 and December 2000. The US became concerned that military training camps which it had helped set up in Afghanistan during the period of Soviet occupation, to strengthen the Mujahidin resistance, might now be used to train militants to engage in international terrorism.

The terrorist attacks on the World Trade Center on 11 September 2001 resulted in a renewed demand by the US government that the Taliban hand over Osama bin Laden, failing which the US would regard the Taliban as equally responsible for the attacks. The Taliban stood their ground and the US opted to invade Afghanistan in October 2001.

The US was reluctant to use its own forces for ground offensives and so drew on the limited Afghan capacity that existed among the former Mujahidin groups. Foremost among these was Jamiat-i-Islami, which had held out against the Taliban in the north-east. Heavy bombing campaigns by the US enabled Jamiat-i-Islami forces and those of the Uzbek leader, Rashid Dostam (who returned from exile at this point) to oust the Taliban from the north. This was accompanied by reprisals in which thousands of Taliban fighters were killed or imprisoned under particularly harsh conditions. It was also accompanied by punitive action against Pushtun populations resident in the north, who were perceived as having supported the Taliban. Tens of thousands were driven from their homes and many made their way to Pakistan or the Pakistan border area. The US bombing raids also made it possible for Jamiat-i-Islami forces to enter Kabul and to become the de facto power holder in the capital. In Herat, the former ruler of the province, Ismail Khan, was able to re-establish the position he had lost in September 1995, having returned from exile in Iran. The Shi'a Hazara party, Hisb-e-Wahdat, again took control of the Hazarajat and, in the southern provinces, many of the previous power holders from the Mujahidin reasserted themselves. Thus, when the international community helped to form an interim government through the Bonn Agreement of December 2001, its composition largely reflected the power-holding arrangements on the ground. To mitigate these, a number of Afghan professionals were brought in from the diaspora or the aid community to serve as ministers. However, Jamiat-i-Islami ended up with the key ministries of defence, foreign affairs and interior. With strong US backing, a new president was brought in from the diaspora, known as Hamid Karzai.

The new government was quick to establish a blueprint for economic development, through the National Development Framework, but the international community was very cautious in committing resources before the government had built the capacity to manage funds on a large scale. Thus, although it was able, with strong support from the World Bank and others, to build the necessary financial infrastructure, valuable time was lost in demonstrating to the Afghan population that the US-led military intervention would bring quick and tangible results on the reconstruction front.

As a consequence of this, combined with Pushtun resentment over Jamiat-i-Islami dominance, the Taliban were enabled to build a resistance movement in the southern provinces of Afghanistan. The efforts of the US-led forces to confront this insurgency have faced the same difficulties as those encountered by the Soviet Union and little progress has been made. However, the Taliban have been able to engage in an effective campaign of terrorism against those associated with what is seen by them as a US-led government. Those targeted have included members of the new army and police force, government officials, aid workers and construction workers, notably those engaged on US-funded projects. This campaign appears to date from the US intervention in Iraq and demonstrates a similar pattern to that in Iraq. A major consequence has been that the southern provinces have become too dangerous for the aid community to operate in and this has affected the reconstruction process.

The fragmented nature of the power-holding arrangements has undermined the efforts of the government to build a new army and police force and progress on this has been extremely slow. Initiatives to disarm the various power holders have been similarly thwarted. As a result, there is no effective rule of law and a climate of impunity prevails. This means that returning refugees who have legitimate fears that they might be the victims of targeted violence because of previous associations or actions over the period since 1978 are not able to seek effective protection from the state and are therefore highly vulnerable.

The early migrations

The Soviet invasion of Afghanistan of December 1979 created a situation in which an Islamic state had been invaded by a secular one. This placed an obligation on the believer to engage in a religious migration and to take refuge in the neighbouring Islamic states. Pakistan and Iran, which took 6 million refugees between them, accepted responsibility for them as a religious duty.

Those who fled to Pakistan were accommodated in refugee camps the length of the Afghan border. Here they were provided with tents, plastic sheeting, kitchen utensils, wheat and other food commodities. In addition, they had access to health care and education through basic health units and primary schools. Each camp had a supply of piped water which residents drew from taps located in communal areas. Latrines were constructed for individual households, where possible. Some residents were able to benefit from income-generation or vocational training programmes. Over time, refugees built mud or brick houses to replace their tents. Many of the camps were near urban centres where refugees could look for work, mostly in the construction sector.

The camps were used as a base for incursionary movements by the Mujahidin resistance parties into Afghanistan. The parties had recruiting offices in the camps and would also operate their own educational establishments with the aim of producing new generations of adherents to their particular ideologies or creeds. Primary among these were madrasahs or Quranic schools where military training was provided alongside Islamic instruction.

The refugees were not accorded status under the 1951 Geneva Convention, which Pakistan is not a signatory to, nor were they given any documentation, other than ration books, which recognised their position as refugees.

In Iran, the government only permitted the establishment of refugee camps in a few areas at some distance from urban centres and these were used for incursions into Afghanistan. The services provided were similar to those in the camps in Pakistan. However, the vast majority of refugees in Iran were left to fend for themselves in various urban centres or to seek work on the land. They therefore had to find their own housing, normally in particularly poor neighbourhoods. However, they had access to health care and education of a much higher standard than that provided to refugees in Pakistan, through establishments that were part of the mainstream state provision. Refugees were permitted to work, albeit in designated menial occupations and were entitled to state subsidies on basic essentials including food and transport, along with the Iranian population. However, they were not accorded refugee status, even though Iran had signed the 1951 Geneva Convention, but were regarded as Muhajirs or religious migrants.

The early returns

The international community planned for a large-scale repatriation and reconstruction programme in anticipation of the planned withdrawal of Soviet troops in February 1989. It was assumed at the time that the Soviet-backed government would immediately collapse thereafter and that refugees would return en masse. It was reasonable to assume that the refugees would return once the Soviet presence had come to an end but the assumption that the Soviet-backed government would collapse proved to be flawed.

However, the UN set up a new coordination structure, as did NGOs, and drew up plans to accompany refugees to their areas of origin and assist them on arrival. Plans were based on the organisation of huge supply convoys to ensure that returnees had access to food, water and shelter as they travelled. In the event, these plans had to be shelved in favour of an alternative model.

This was based on a new assumption – that refugees would return in relatively small numbers while a Soviet-backed government remained in power and that those who chose to return would benefit from some limited assistance to help with the cost of transport, cover three months' wheat requirements and provide some plastic sheeting and cash.

The view was also taken that it would be beneficial to the long-term return process to undertake some reconstruction work in the areas where the refugees in Pakistan, in particular, originated. It was felt to be important to ensure that those who had remained in Afghanistan were not disadvantaged by not having fled and that reconstruction assistance should benefit entire communities, both those who stayed and those who fled. The international community also took account of the fact that many people had fled within Afghanistan and would need reconstruction assistance when they returned to their villages.

This assistance started in 1990 and was on an extremely small scale. The rural areas became particularly insecure following the withdrawal of the Soviet forces, because of growing divisions within the Mujahidin. They were also extremely fragmented as commanders fought for control at the local level. Aid personnel had to negotiate with one power holder after another as they sought to cover even relatively short distances. These were not conditions which encouraged refugees to return nor were they ones in which the aid community could make significant contributions to the reconstruction of the country. The primary achievement over this period was the success of the FAO in distributing improved wheat seed to farmers in the south-east of the country through a multiplicity of small Afghan NGOs. In addition, some limited work was undertaken by NGOs to clean or improve irrigation systems.

The collapse of the Soviet-backed government in April 1992, following the collapse of the Soviet Union the previous year, removed the obstacle to refugee return. Over the spring and summer of 1992, almost 1 million returned, in spite of the fact that the new Afghan government, made up of different elements of the Mujahidin resistance, resorted to arms almost immediately to settle power struggles.

UNHCR provided assistance to those returning on the basis of the same package of wheat, cash, plastic sheeting, etc. which had been made available to those who had returned prior to April 1992. Refugees surrendered their ration books at designated encashment centres within Pakistan before being given transport to their areas of origin within Afghanistan.

Over the following three years, the rations made available to those still resident in the refugee camps in Pakistan were progressively reduced on the basis of evidence from annual assessment missions undertaken jointly by UNHCR and WFP which indicated that refugees were increasingly able to achieve self-sufficiency through access to the Pakistan labour market. The rations were finally withdrawn in September 1995. Refugees were also required to pay for education, health care and water supply in the camps.

This prompted many refugees living in the camps to present themselves at the encashment centres as potential returnees, receive the assistance package and then seek accommodation in the urban areas of Pakistan.

The returns to Afghanistan also slowed down after 1992 as refugees realised that the new Mujahidin government was not able to provide the necessary security for them to achieve a sustainable return. However, Iran embarked on a three-year repatriation programme in December 1992, similar to that initiated by Pakistan the previous year, and placed particular pressure on those living in the refugee camps along the border to return. The camps were bulldozed to encourage departure.

Over the following years, UNHCR sought to link reconstruction programmes with the repatriation process by recording areas of origin of the refugees living in the camps in Pakistan and encouraging NGOs and other UN agencies to prioritise these areas. One particularly successful initiative involved UNOPS working with a large number of NGOs to ensure a planned process of reconstruction in a town called Khost based on information from UNHCR which indicated that large numbers would be returning there. UNHCR also worked with particular groups of refugees living in the camps in Pakistan to orchestrate reconstruction assistance in their areas of origin as a prelude to their return. UNHCR contracted out projects to NGOs through what were termed Quick Impact Programmes, using funding provided to it by international donors. NGOs also worked in cooperation with UNHCR to target areas of origin, drawing on independent funding from institutional and other donors.

New outflows and internal displacement

The virtual anarchy brought about by the factional conflict in Kabul led to an exodus of people whose homes had been destroyed or who feared the possible consequences of the ongoing violence. Many went to other parts of Afghanistan. Some went to Pakistan or Iran.

There were particular episodes when the violence produced outflows on a very large scale. One of these was in August 1992, which resulted in considerable numbers taking refuge in Mazar-i-Sharif in northern Afghanistan.

Another, more major, was in January 1994 when rockets literally poured onto the capital, leading hundreds of thousands to flee in panic. Pakistan accepted about 40,000 refugees but then closed its borders. The numbers were too great to be easily absorbed by relatives in other parts of the country. However, UNHCR was reluctant to take responsibility for establishing camps in Afghanistan, fearing that this would send a message to Pakistan and Iran that they could expel their Afghan refugee populations and UNHCR would take care of them within Afghanistan. In the event, agreement was reached that the UN coordinating body for Afghanistan, UNOCHA, would set up and manage new camps in the vicinity of Jalalabad in eastern Afghanistan. These remained in being for several years and accommodated around 300,000 people.

The next major outflow was in September 1995, from Herat, in western Afghanistan, to Iran. This was prompted by the capture of Herat by the Taliban, who had emerged as a new power holder in Kandahar the previous November and captured much of southern Afghanistan. Those who fled to Iran were primarily professionals and intellectuals who feared that the puritanical perspective of the Taliban would lead them to target anyone of a liberal persuasion.

When the Taliban captured Kabul a year later, in September 1996, there was a similar exodus of professionals and intellectuals. In addition, large numbers of women left the city in response to the Taliban provision that women could not take employment outside the home. This provision had a particular impact on the capital because the female working population was relatively large there. The failure of the Taliban to pay their civil servants and the harsh penalties imposed by them on people in the street who did not conform to their dress or behavioural codes were added factors in the exodus. Pakistan agreed to receive around 50,000 new refugees from Kabul at this time but then placed new restrictions on Afghans entering the country. The new arrivals were accommodated in Nasirbagh camp, near Peshawar, which had also received the 1994 exodus.

The next wave of refugees from Pakistan was in the autumn of 2000 when the capture, by the Taliban, of the town of Taloqan in the north-east of Afghanistan led 170,000 displaced people to cross the border into Pakistan. As with the previous movements of refugees, Pakistan agreed to provide for the initial group of arrivals but then placed a stop on any new acceptances. Those who came subsequently found their way to a makeshift camp on the edge of Jalozai refugee camp near Peshawar. Here, refugees lived under very basic plastic sheeting and were dependent on charitable donations for food and other requirements. UNHCR was not allowed to register them and was not willing to provide food and other basic essentials without prior registration in case this encouraged refugees living in the urban areas of Pakistan to present themselves as new arrivals from Afghanistan in order to secure food rations. Lengthy negotiations between UNHCR and the Pakistan government finally resulted in agreement that Pakistan would allow new camps to be set up in remote locations in the tribal areas of Pakistan, away from urban centres where refugees might seek work, to discourage people from remaining or seeking to live there. It took many months for UNHCR to establish these camps because they proved to be unsuitable for one reason or another, with security a particular problem.

These camps were not yet operational before another outflow occurred. This time, it was in response to the US military intervention in Afghanistan of October 2001. UNHCR anticipated that, if such an intervention materialised, hundreds of thousands would seek to cross into Pakistan and Iran. Pakistan initially refused to accept entry of those who might flee any US-induced conflict and then, reluctantly, agreed to permit the use of the camps established in the tribal areas. Once these camps were full, refugees were forced to live in temporary camps adjacent to the Afghanistan–Pakistan border on both sides of the border. Conditions in these camps were well below internationally agreed standards and the residents were dependent on charitable handouts for the most part. Finally, UNHCR reached agreement with Pakistan to permit a proportion of those in what was termed the 'waiting area' to be relocated in camps within Pakistan or in a new camp for displaced people at Zhare Dasht, to the west of Kandahar. In April 2004, UNHCR announced that Pakistan had ordered the closure of all the new camps in the tribal areas without provision being made for those evicted to be placed in other camps. UNHCR responded by taking active steps to encourage refugees to return to Afghanistan.

In addition to those who fled to Pakistan and Iran was a relatively small number who opted to take refuge in the USA, Canada, Europe or Australia. The numbers increased markedly following the US air strikes of August 1998, which had the effect of radicalising the Taliban movement. As a consequence, they targeted those they regarded as liberals, whom they perceived as potentially undermining of their objectives. Professionals and intellectuals thus found themselves coming under increasing pressure from the Taliban, with many receiving threats. These threats became increasingly intolerable and prompted growing numbers to leave. The vast majority made their way to north America but many thousands also sought refuge in various European countries.

To these various outflows was added a continuing process of Afghans moving back and forth across the border to look for work in Pakistan or Iran, to look after their land in Afghanistan or to visit or return to their families. It has been a relatively permanent feature of the past 15 years for Afghan families to diversify their earning opportunities by having, for example, some members of the family working on the land, for themselves or others, some members working in one of the urban centres and some working in either Pakistan or Iran (Marsden 1997). Because of the high cost of weddings, a common practice has been for young men to work for up to a year in Pakistan or Iran to earn enough money to marry and establish themselves back in Afghanistan.

The responses of Iran and Pakistan

Iran has always viewed Afghans in a more negative light than has been the case in Pakistan. Afghans have, for decades, been used as a source of cheap labour for the construction industry or to carry out menial occupations such as street cleaning or waste clearance. This has meant that the Iranian population have regarded Afghans with some disdain and Afghans have often been scapegoated for the ills of society and seen as a criminal element. These underlying attitudes have influenced how the population of Iran has responded to the Afghan refugee presence and it has been commonplace for Afghans to be insulted or abused as they sought to survive on a daily basis. Afghans have also been viewed with suspicion by the labour unions because they have undercut the price of Iranian labour. The Iranian government has also exerted much more control over its citizens than that of Pakistan, and Afghan refugees in Iran have found themselves under a significant degree of control and surveillance, with their mobility severely constrained.

As noted above, Iran signed a repatriation agreement with Afghanistan and UNHCR in December 1992 which provided for a return of the 3 million Afghan refugees in Iran over a three-year period. By September 1995, it was clear that the rate of return over the previous two summers had been far below the figures anticipated in the repatriation agreement and the outflow brought about by the Taliban capture of Herat created a situation in which the numbers of people returning could reasonably be expected to show a significant reduction. Iran was also, by this stage, facing a serious downturn in its own economy and viewed the continuing refugee presence as a serious burden.

Iran responded by making daily life for Afghans increasingly difficult. Legal restrictions were placed on the rights of employers to engage Afghans. Afghans were compelled to re-register and were given residence permits of ever shorter duration. Police harassment of Afghans showed a marked increase, with common complaints that the police had picked Afghans up on the street, torn up their permits and transported them by force to the Afghan border or to a detention centre. The conditions in the detention centres were known to be appalling and word quickly spread which discouraged Afghans from being out and about on the streets. This made it more difficult to seek work, as a majority of Afghans were employed in the construction industry and would make for particular parts of town where employers would recruit daily labourers. By this stage, Afghans were also losing access to state subsidies on basic essentials, along with Iranian citizens, with the downturn in the economy. It was also becoming more expensive to access education and health care and the Iranian government would place growing restrictions on access to education, in particular. Afghans would also be subject to daily taunts from their Iranian neighbours. It was also very difficult to secure work, even before the restrictions on employment were tightened. Afghans had to depend on daily labouring and would, typically, only find work for two or three days per week. Those without dependants might be fortunate enough to secure blocks of work on building sites where they would live on site.

This pattern has now existed for almost nine years but with the pressures consistently greater with each year that has passed. In 2002, following the signing of a new repatriation agreement in April 2002, the Iranian government also gave out strong messages on the media advising Afghans that now was the time to return to Afghanistan and that the UN would be there to assist them in their efforts to re-establish themselves in their areas of origin.

UNHCR has found itself almost powerless in relation to the Iranian government. For years it had almost no access to Afghan refugees in the areas where they lived in order to establish their needs or identify any concerns with regard to their treatment by the authorities. When they did become aware of instances of abuse of police power or of forcible detentions or deportations, they were not able to secure any significant change in practice. In part, this was because Iran could point to the fact that the international community had provided very little funding to help provide for the Afghan refugee population. This was a consequence of the difficult relations between Iran and the major Western donors in the years following the overthrow of the Shah and the assumption of power of the Ayatollah Khomeini. It was also because Iran did not want the large visible Western presence that international support for the refugees would entail and wanted international donors to provide it with the necessary funds to enable it to carry the burden on its own. This, the donors were unwilling to do.

UNHCR has therefore had to watch as the Iranian government has placed growing restrictions on the Afghan population without being able to significantly affect the situation for the better.

Pakistan, in contrast, was much more welcoming to Afghans in the early years. A majority of refugees were Pushtuns and found support from fellow Pushtuns on the Pakistan side of the border. In fact, it was not until the outflow of the autumn of 2000 that non-Pushtuns arrived in substantial numbers and this may have been an additional factor in the negative attitude of the Pakistan government at that time.

Pakistan was also disposed to accept the refugees because their presence played into particular agendas that they had, historically, been pursuing. Primary among these was a wish to achieve strategic depth vis-à-vis India by creating an Islamic bloc incorporating Pakistan, Afghanistan and the Central Asian republics. Pakistan had always been preoccupied with India's much greater size since the partition of India when it became independent of Britain in 1947. Pakistan saw an opportunity in the US support for the resistance movement to the Soviet occupation of Afghanistan to seek to establish a compliant government in Kabul. The Pakistan government quite reasonably took the view that the tribal elements in Afghanistan would be extremely unwilling to do Islamabad's bidding and opted to build alliances with the radical Islamic parties which were part of the Afghan resistance movement. The then president of Pakistan, General Zia, was actively engaged, at that time, in building up the power base of the radical Islamic parties in Pakistan, both on the basis of his own sympathies and in order to create a resistance movement which could engage in military incursions into Indian-occupied Kashmir. To this end, he had established a large network of Quranic schools or Islamic madrasahs to bring up a new generation of adherents to radical Islam and potential fighters for the cause. The refugee camps in Pakistan provided a suitable location for such madrasahs to be established. The poverty of the refugees provided a sufficient inducement for them to place their sons in the madrasahs, which provided free food and accommodation and also a small allowance, rather than the other schools set up in the camps. The radical Islamic parties were also allowed to set up offices and educational establishments in the camps and were encouraged to actively recruit resistance fighters to cross the border into Afghanistan and engage in combat against the Soviet forces. Thus, by the time that the Soviet-backed government collapsed in April 1992, the refugee camps had served a very useful purpose. Sympathy for refugees continued during the period of the Mujahidin government, from 1992 to 1996 and during that of the Taliban, from 1996 to 2001. However, the decision of UNHCR and WFP to cease providing rations for Afghan refugees in Pakistan from September 1995 onwards made Pakistan increasingly conscious of the fact that it was shouldering a major burden with little international support. It was also aware of growing protests from its own population over the very visible Afghan presence and over the competitiveness of Afghans in the labour market. Although the ending of rations in 1995 was premised on the assumption that refugees were now self-sufficient, Afghans were finding it extremely difficult to survive in the labour market and were dependent, for the most part, on intermittent daily labouring. A minority had to depend on charitable donations from their fellow refugees. The refugees were thus disposed to accept extremely low wages for the casual work that they did and this inevitably had the effect of undercutting Pakistani labour. The large international presence which accompanied the refugees also had an inflationary effect on housing costs in some areas which made it more difficult for the population of Pakistan to find affordable accommodation. Growing popular resentment was thus making itself felt in the corridors of power and was beginning to manifest itself in the closure of camps towards the end of the 1990s.

The US military intervention in Afghanistan of October 2001 created the fiction that Afghanistan had been 'liberated' and that the international community would create the conditions for political stability and economic recovery. Thus, when Pakistan signed a new tripartite agreement with Afghanistan and UNHCR in March 2002, it set in motion a series of measures which placed increased pressures on Afghans. One of these was the removal of exemption, for Afghans, from the provisions of the Foreigners Act. This meant that Afghans could no longer work without permits (which they could not easily obtain). It also meant that Afghans were subjected to growing police harassment and could find themselves deported. Although this was not happening on the same scale as in Iran, it did make Afghans feel that they were no longer welcome and that they could no longer envisage a long-term future in Pakistan. Afghans were, at the same time, made aware, through the Pakistani media, of pledges by the international community, made at a conference in Tokyo in January 2002, to help in the economic recovery of Afghanistan. Refugees were thus encouraged to think that, if they returned to Afghanistan, there would be plenty of work available. The numbers who returned over the spring and summer of 2002, totalling 1,834,000, reflected this combination of carrot and stick. It should be stressed, however, that there was a serious problem of recycling during the repatriation programme of 2002, with a substantial proportion of returnees being thought to have claimed the assistance package and then returned to Pakistan. Large numbers were also thought to have returned to Pakistan when they had reached their areas of origin or travelled to Kabul and found that the conditions for survival were far worse than they had anticipated.

It should also be noted that the large numbers of Afghans who enter Pakistan and Iran to seek work do so illegally. These illegal migrants are particular targets for the forcible deportations carried out by the police in both countries, deportations which also affect those with documentation.

The responses of donors

Western donors were well disposed to provide for Afghan refugees in Pakistan in the immediate aftermath of the outflows brought about by the Soviet invasion of Afghanistan. There was significant outrage over the invasion and enormous sympathy for the refugees. From 1986 onwards, the US government allocated substantially greater funds to the Afghan resistance and this also meant an increase in funding for refugee programmes. Some funding was also available for cross-border programmes in which cash would be handed over at the border to resistance fighters for charitable handouts to families in particular need. The US was the major provider of wheat for the rations distributed in the camps.

However, in 1993, following the collapse of the Soviet-backed government, the US government ended its funding for Afghanistan and it was left, for the most part, to European governments and the European Commission to maintain funding for the refugees and for reconstruction programmes in Afghanistan The supply of US wheat did, however, continue for the refugee camps, until rations ended in September 1995, and for emergency programmes in Afghanistan. The latter included food for work programmes to facilitate the repair of irrigation and flood protection structures in Afghanistan, in support of refugee return.

Among the European donors, the European Commission played a major role from around 1995 to 2004, in supporting NGOs to undertake long-term integrated rural development programmes. Sweden and Denmark were also large-scale funders of education and water supply programmes undertaken by their national NGOs.

In the aftermath of the US military intervention in Afghanistan, donors were called upon to make pledges for the reconstruction process. $4.3 billion was promised at the Tokyo Conference, a small fraction of the amount allocated more recently for Iraq. However, this was slow to be disbursed and the Afghan Interim Administration set up in Bonn in December 2001 had to survive with very little cash in the early months. This seriously damaged its credibility at a time when early evidence of success in establishing large-scale reconstruction programmes would have gone a long way in building support from the population and facilitating sustainable return for refugees. In the event, progress on the reconstruction front was still slow two and a half years later and the population was becoming disenchanted with the government. This has helped the Taliban rebuild a support base and engage in terrorist activity which has placed the southern half of the country out of bounds for the aid community, thus undermining reconstruction.

New pledges at a more generous level were made at a conference in Berlin in March 2004 but it may now be too late to undo the damage created by the tardy response in Tokyo. The US-led coalition forces appear to be making no headway against the insurgency organised by the Taliban and other radical elements. The Taliban campaign of terrorist activity has also clearly labelled the aid community as associated with what is seen as a US-led state-building process. Even if the US forces were to withdraw after elections provisionally planned for September 2004, as was rumoured at the time of writing, the aid community would have difficulty returning to the southern provinces for some time to come because of this adverse labelling.

Donors have also opted to regard the present Afghan government, for all its serious flaws, as one which they wish to support and strengthen. This is strongly at variance with the position of the international community in relation to the Mujahidin and Taliban governments. In part, this is because European governments have come under increasing pressure to reduce their own refugee populations, of which Afghans have represented an important element. There has therefore been a strong incentive for these governments to present the military intervention in Afghanistan and the Bonn Agreement as having achieved a successful outcome in order to justify a return of Afghan refugees to Afghanistan. This has resulted in extremely optimistic pictures being presented of the situation in Afghanistan over the past two and a half years which have contrasted markedly with the reality in Afghanistan. The prevailing climate of impunity has therefore been disregarded as claims are made that returning refugees can return without fear that they will be victims of violence. In particular, it is claimed that they can return to Kabul where the authorities can accord them protection in spite of the fact that de facto control of Kabul rests with the various militia, whom many of those who fled to the West have good reason to fear.

The then UN High Commissioner for Refugees, Ruud Lubbers, showed himself sympathetic to these concerns of European governments to reduce their Afghan populations and this resulted in highly contradictory statements coming out of different parts of UNHCR. Some statements thus presented a picture of growing insecurity, with serious concerns expressed over the desirability of further returns from Europe, while others suggested that the security situation was improving and that certain areas of the country were safe to return refugees to. Thus, for example, UNHCR issued a statement on 30 November 2003 in which it expressed its concern that, owing to the adverse security situation, it would not be able to adequately monitor the conditions of returnee communities and internally displaced people inside Afghanistan and thus undertake a vital part of its protection work. It added that this included the north and west where, it feared, its reduced presence might 'open up space for increased abuse of the population by local commanders'. The organisation appealed to asylum countries to consider seriously its reduced capacity to monitor situations in many of the provinces and exercise caution when sending Afghans back to locations outside Kabul at this time. However, in April 2004, Lubbers announced that an improvement in stability in parts of the north-east, centre and west of the country meant that UNHCR could start moving towards 'active encouragement of returns' to some selected areas. There had been no significant developments in Afghanistan between these two dates to justify the statement that there had been an improvement in security. In fact, Herat, in the west, has become more unstable.

Western governments have shown themselves to be particularly keen to point to the large-scale return of refugees from Pakistan and Iran in 2002 and, to a lesser extent, in 2003, as indicative of the success of the US intervention (Straw 2004), in spite of documented evidence that the returns were a consequence of significant levels of duress, combined with unrealistic expectations induced by the media.

It is not clear whether the willingness of donors to contribute to UNHCR's repatriation programmes from Pakistan and Iran has been linked to the publication of statements which present the situation in Afghanistan as being conducive to return.

The role of UNHCR in the provision of reconstruction assistance to returnees after 2001

UNHCR found itself in a situation in which it had no choice but to implement what was, in effect, an assisted involuntary return programme. The large scale of the return meant that it was difficult to effect the provision of effective reconstruction assistance except in a few areas of concentrated repatriation. UNHCR could not, therefore, plan to undertake reconstruction programmes in the principal areas of refugee return because there were simply too many. The situation was not helped by the fact that, apart from Kabul and the Shomali Valley to the north of it, refugees were returning in relatively small numbers to each of a multiplicity of areas of origin. UNHCR therefore focused considerable effort on the Shomali Valley, where it was able to support the construction or repair of housing units in an area which had suffered from considerable destruction. In Kabul, the magnitude of the task of rebuilding the southern half of the capital, which had suffered heavy destruction during the factional fighting of 1992–6, was way beyond UNHCR's capacity. The simultaneous existence of a severe drought, which had started in 1999 and was still ongoing at the time of the US military intervention, led NGO programmes to be largely focused on humanitarian relief and there was a shortage of NGO capacity to undertake reconstruction work. The fact that much of southern Afghanistan proved to be increasingly inaccessible to the aid community because of US-led military action in pursuit of the War on Terror further constrained reconstruction assistance.

The orderly process of linking reconstruction assistance to refugee returns, which was an important characteristic of the mid-1990s, has therefore been much less in evidence since 2001. Thus, even though UNHCR has recently embarked upon a new programme aimed at providing reconstruction assistance to specific groups of refugees, this is on a very small scale. UNHCR is faced with a situation in which the vast majority of refugees have disappeared into the void, left to fend for themselves in response to whatever economic opportunities may be available. Where such opportunities have been scarce, families or parts of families have looked elsewhere, either by returning to Pakistan or Iran or by travelling to Kabul in the hope of finding labouring work.

UNHCR is also unable to monitor what happens to returning refugees on more than an extremely limited scale. This is, in part, a consequence of the size of the population which has returned from Pakistan and Iran since the Bonn Agreement, which had increased to 2,296,000 by the end of 2003, and partly because the prevailing level of insecurity makes it difficult for individual members of UNHCR staff to travel around the country or even into the poorer neighbourhoods of Kabul. It is thus not in a position to assess whether individual refugees feel at risk from those who wield power in a situation in which efforts by the government and the international community to build an effective army, police force and judiciary remain at an embryonic stage and there is a prevailing climate of impunity.

The position of the Afghan government

The Afghan government has been extremely unhappy over the large-scale returns from Pakistan and Iran, taking the reasonable view that it should have been given the opportunity to establish itself and build up the infrastructure before being compelled to receive over a million returning refugees. Representations have been made on this issue to both Pakistan and Iran without apparent success.

The government has similarly resisted efforts by Western governments to return Afghans by force. It has therefore been particularly concerned over forcible returns implemented by the British government over the past year. Although these have occurred on the basis of a tripartite agreement drawn up with the UK government and UNHCR, the Afghan government feels that it was under strong political pressure from the UK to sign this agreement and remains unhappy over the returns. It has also received complaints from a number of those who have been forcibly removed.

Efforts are presently being made by the government, with support from UNHCR, to negotiate economic migration arrangements with Pakistan and Iran so that Afghans can freely enter both countries for the purposes of seeking work and be given permits giving them the right to work. Discussions on this are still at an early stage and it is not clear whether the initial resistance to this by both governments can be overcome.

Conclusion

UNHCR has moved from a position in which it was supporting a largely voluntary return over the 1990–5 period to one in which it has come under increasing pressure from Pakistan, Iran and European governments to help reduce their Afghan refugee populations. The dependence of UNHCR on the continued willingness of these governments to allow it to retain a presence has meant that it has been reluctant to take too critical a stance in relation to apparent abuses of refugee protection standards. The relationship between UNHCR and these governments has always been tenuous and has seen difficult periods as UNHCR has sought to challenge particular developments and met with negative responses. It would not appear that UNHCR has ever been able to secure more than marginal policy changes and it has largely found itself compelled to make the best of an ever-worsening situation in relation to refugee protection, to salvage what it can out of the situation. The fact that it has been dependent on funding from Western governments, which have themselves had a vested interest in apparently successful return programmes from Pakistan and Iran to justify an accelerated programme of return of their own Afghan refugees, has placed it under even greater pressure. It would appear that UNHCR has been even less willing to stand up to pressures from donor governments and challenge their asylum policies than has been the case in relation to Pakistan and Iran. It found itself in a particularly weak position when hundreds of thousands of refugees were returning to Afghanistan within three months of the emergence of a new interim government, which had no capacity to govern or provide an adequate infrastructure to support returning refugees. The protection mandate of UNHCR has therefore been very much secondary to its role as an administrator of refugee assistance programmes aimed to effect a smooth transfer of refugees from the host country to Afghanistan.

In seeking to draw comparisons with the Palestinian situation, a number of comments can be made.

Although UNHCR provided an assistance package to returning refugees, in the form of approximately three months' supply of wheat, a minimal quantity of cash (including transportation costs) and a tarpaulin, and also contributed to efforts by the aid community to help returning refugees re-establish their lives (through shelter, water supply, health and education programmes), returning refugees were largely reliant on their own resources in seeking to pursue livelihood and housing options. This pattern can be related to the prevailing consensus amongst those planning for a possible return of Palestinians to the West Bank and Gaza that there should be a minimum level of bureaucratic involvement in such return.

Afghan refugees in Pakistan and Iran made their own decisions as to whether to return based on their expectations of their ability to survive on their return. However, the pressures on them in both countries, manifested in a withdrawal of benefits and entitlements and growing police harassment, was an important contributory factor in their decision-making.

UNHCR's role in moving from a primary responsibility for the care and maintenance of refugees in camps in Pakistan and (to a very limited extent) in Iran to orchestration of a large-scale repatriation programme has not meant that it has become a major player in helping refugees re-establish their lives. UNHCR has sought to orchestrate the combined responses of the Afghan government, UN agencies and NGOs to this need but has had little impact. In part, this has been because the government has also seen itself as increasingly playing this role, but it has also been a consequence of conflicting mandates within the UN system, with responsibility for coordination of development being ill-defined. The net result has been, as noted above, that returnees have benefited from aid programming to varying degrees, with areas of high return being particularly targeted, but they have still been largely dependent on their own resources. It is nonetheless the case that UNHCR has been the most effective of the UN actors in supporting return although NGOs have had the greater impact in the actual delivery of services.

In looking to the potential future role of UNWRA in supporting a return process, it may be that, like UNHCR, it would be in a relatively advantageous position compared with other actors in having an in-depth knowledge of the refugee population but might find itself heavily constrained, in relation to these other actors, in seeking to carve out a role as a development actor. It is likely that one would see the same degree of confusion, in the face of conflicting mandates, roles, responsibilities and policies, in Palestine as has been apparent in Afghanistan.

References

Marsden, P. (1997) *Return and reconstruction: Report on a study of economic coping strategies among farmers in Farah Province, Afghanistan* (London: British Agencies Afghanistan Group).

Straw, J. (2004) *Speech by the Foreign Secretary at the International Institute for Strategic Studies, 28 October 2004* (London: International Institute for Strategic Studies).

Turton, D., and Marsden, P. (2002) *Taking refugees for a ride: The politics of refugee return to Afghanistan* (Kabul: Afghanistan Research and Evaluation Unit).

12 Politically preferred solutions and refugee choices

Applying the lessons of Iraq to Palestine

Michael Kagan

Individual choice is inherent in the right to return, and refugees' capacity to choose for themselves whether to go back to what is now Israel or to accept some other solution will be essential to any rights-based resolution to the Palestinian refugee crisis. Today, for Palestinians the question of choice is only theoretical, since Israel is still denying refugees their right to choose. Yet already the desire by some to predict in advance whether the refugees would in fact choose to return has generated a great deal of debate.[1] For the requirements of international law to be met, refugees must be able to make a free and informed choice between different mixes of return, or settlement elsewhere, plus restitution and compensation.[2] But politically, the abstract right of return is more palatable in Israel if there is some reassurance that most refugees will choose not to repatriate.

Should a rights-based solution to the refugee crisis be achieved, Palestinian refugees will individually bear the weight of these high political stakes. The Palestinian situation is unique in that the political balance of power has thus far been against return, whereas in other refugee situations the trend has been for repatriation. But at a more general level, the Palestinian situation is entirely routine in that the principle of voluntary refugee choice clashes with political pressures from many sides. Although law and UNHCR standards stress that durable solutions should generally be voluntary, the international community typically has a strong preference as to which solution refugees are encouraged to accept.

This chapter looks at the way principles of refugee choice and voluntariness have played out in an ongoing and high stakes case: the repatriation of Iraqi refugees in the first year after the fall of the Ba'ath regime. Shortly after the invasion, UN Security Council resolution 1483 called for the "safe, orderly and voluntary return of refugees and displaced persons" and called on all states to contribute to the implementation of this mandate. Established UNHCR standards similarly call for repatriation to take place only on a voluntary basis. But how well did these standards of voluntariness compare to the actual situation on the ground? UNHCR has officially opposed repatriation to Iraq because of the unstable political and security situation, but at the same time very large numbers of refugees have been returning. In theory, this has been solely the result of refugees' own choices, but often such choices were made in the context of apparent government pressure or without any real alternatives.

In this chapter I first outline and analyze the prevailing UN-established standards of voluntariness in durable solutions. In the next section, I summarize how Iraqi repatriation has taken place in the first year since the war in three countries, Iran, Saudi Arabia, and Lebanon, for which data were available either in the public domain or (in the case of Lebanon) through my personal experience. For each country, I also summarize prevailing refugee protection conditions, in order to establish the context in which refugees chose whether to return to Iraq. I also outline how third country resettlement policy has treated Iraqis over the same period. Following this, I assess the existing UN standards in light of what has happened with Iraqis.

Voluntariness in international durable solutions standards

Of the three standard durable solutions, none can be forced on a refugee, at least not in theory. Most clearly, the principle of *non-refoulement* prohibits forcing a refugee to repatriate. Resettlement to third countries is also not meant to be forced on anyone. Even local integration is in a sense optional, in that most refugees could choose to go home (unless the right of return is denied), or seek a means of traveling elsewhere.

This section will set out the established standards, drawn from international law and UNHCR guidance, of the principle of voluntariness in durable solutions.

Voluntariness in repatriation

International refugee law

The 1951 Convention relating to the Status of Refugees' (hereafter "1951 Convention" or "Refugee Convention") article 33 prohibits states from expelling or returning a refugee "in any manner whatsoever" to territories where his or her life of freedom would be in danger. This principle of *non-refoulement* requires that repatriation be voluntary. The Organization of African Unity's Convention Governing the Specific Aspects of Refugee Problems in Africa (hereafter "African Convention") article 5 makes the point even more explicit: "The essentially voluntary character of repatriation shall be respected in all cases and no refugee shall be repatriated against his will."

Although *non-refoulement* is the foundation of international refugee law, it has its exceptions. Most importantly, although *refugees* cannot be forced to return home, this protection does not apply to former refugees. The Refugee Convention's article 1 (4) provides that refugee status may cease against a person's will if the "circumstances in connection with which he was recognized as a refugee have ceased to exist." This clause is often applied *en masse*, for instance when large number of refugees were recognized *prima facie*, for instance in the recent case of Eritrean refugees in the Sudan. But cessation carries important safeguards for refugees. The change of circumstances test sets a very high standard for cessation. The change must be substantial, truly effective, and durable (Hathaway 1999: 199–205).[3] An asylum state that seeks to invoke cessation bears the burden of proof to demonstrate that sufficient change has actually occurred. In addition to these high legal thresholds, states have demonstrated a great deal of hesitation about invoking cessation, despite its availability in international law. Northern states have only rarely invoked it and have historically linked refugee status with permanent immigration. Even when states have declared protection to be temporary, they have often not actually forced refugees to go home against their will.[4]

The other important exception to *non-refoulement* is security cases. According to the 1951 Convention's article 32, a state may expel a refugee "on grounds of national security or public order," where "there are reasonable grounds for regarding [the refugee] as a danger to the security of the country," or where the refugee is convicted "of a particularly serious crime." However, these exceptions may not be invoked without important due process requirements (Goodwin-Gill 1996: 140). It is also limited by other human rights treaties. The Convention against Torture's article 3, for instance, prohibits forced return "where there are substantial grounds for believing that he would be in danger of being subjected to torture," and does not have the exceptions shown in the Refugee Convention. As with the cessation clauses, the legal limits on the security exception prevent its wide application.

Although forced repatriation is generally prohibited, international refugee law allows voluntary return. The African Convention in article 5, unlike the 1951 Convention, has specific provisions for the rights of returning refugees, such as requiring countries of asylum and origin to collaborate in making return arrangements, and guaranteeing refugees' full and equal reintegration. The 1951 Convention provides under its cessation clauses that refugee status ends when a person "has voluntarily re-established himself in the country which he left," and makes no specific provisions otherwise for repatriation. In the international refugee system, it falls to UNHCR to assist and promote voluntary repatriation.

UNHCR standards

As Fitzgerald notes, refugees often choose to return home when they could legally remain in exile.

> Refugees have a natural inclination to develop ties to the community within which they reside and a human need to build a new life following severe trauma. . . . Conversely, many forced migrants feel such a strong

attachment to their homes that they self-repatriate even before conditions are safe, sparing their state of refuge the delicate task of deciding when to withdraw protection.

(Fitzgerald 1999: 346)

Such voluntary returns are now the international community's preferred durable solution in most refugee crises, and have long been one of UNHCR's core functions. UNHCR has developed a handbook intended to manage them (UNHCR 1996; hereafter "Repatriation Handbook").

By nature, voluntary repatriation involves a balance between two opposing policy mandates. On the one hand, voluntary repatriation should be promoted and facilitated. On the other hand, refugees by definition have good reason to fear for their safety if they return, and have the right to remain abroad. UNHCR's Handbook attempts to maintain this balance through two means. First, repatriation will be promoted only if there is "an overall, general improvement in the situation in the country of origin so that return in safety and with dignity becomes possible for the large majority of refugees." This is a lower standard than the legal test for cessation, but still a bar from promoting return to active war zones or widespread humanitarian disasters. Second, UNHCR has attempted to provide a clear definition of voluntariness.

UNHCR has defined voluntariness as an interplay between two independent factors. First, there must be conditions in the country of origin allowing refugees to make an informed decision to return. Second, the situation in the country of asylum must allow for a free choice by refugees. In general, improved conditions at home should be the "overriding element in the refugees' decision to return rather than possible push-factors in the host country."

Voluntariness in resettlement

Of the three durable solutions, resettlement is the least rooted in firm human rights. Whereas all refugees have the right to return, and refugees generally possess some rights in their host countries, there is no right to be resettled to a third country. UNHCR's Resettlement Handbook (UNHCR 2002a) does not make clear that resettlement is voluntary, although by implication it clearly requires a refugee's consent. Rather than be concerned that refugees will be forced to resettle when they do not want to, the Resettlement Handbook assumes throughout that many refugees who want resettlement will be denied.

By focusing on the prospect of refusing refugees something they want, the Resettlement Handbook is starkly different from the Repatriation Handbook, which focuses on the danger of refugees being forced to accept something they really do not want. The Resettlement Handbook stresses that voluntary repatriation is the preferred solution, and resettlement is the last resort when there are no other options. Substantial sections of the Resettlement

Handbook are devoted to managing refugee expectations in order to reduce disappointment and protest from refugees who are in the end not going to get what they want.

Voluntariness in local integration

In most respects, local integration is not a choice for refugees, unless voluntary repatriation is also available. The emergence of "safe third country" and "irregular mover" rules in international refugee law has meant that refugees are more or less forced to accept the protection offered by the first safe country they reach. If UNHCR determines that local integration is possible there, then it will not promote resettlement.

Still, refugees do have some minimal choices, though they are far from perfect ones.

First, refugees in some circumstances can choose where to flee, hence choosing in which country to integrate locally. But this is hardly a freely chosen choice for most refugees. The exigent need to escape imminent harm, combined with lack of money and inability to obtain travel documents and visas, means that most refugees either have no real choice about where to flee, or can choose only between two or three countries. Whatever "choice" a fleeing refugee can make, it may not be an informed one. If a refugee chooses to go to a particular country because she hears that resettlement is available there, she may end up forced to accept local integration instead.

Second, refugees have the right at any time to choose to return home, and hence abandon local integration. This also is less than a full choice, given that a refugee has a well-founded fear of persecution at home. But it does mean that in theory refugees (with the exception of Palestinians) choose to remain abroad in their host countries.

Voluntariness and politically preferred solutions: a critical analysis

The standards that UNHCR has established for durable solutions are reflections of international refugee politics, or at least attempts by UNHCR to make political realities more humane. This political aspect of UNHR standards can be clearly seen by analyzing UNHCR's durable solutions handbooks through the lens of B. S. Chimni's critical history of durable solutions practices. After surveying the history of durable solutions policy since World War II, Chimni concludes:

> the dominant states in the international system decide from time to time, in the light of their interests, which solution to the global refugee problem should be promoted as the preferred solution.
>
> (Chimni 1999: 17)

Specifically, from the beginning of the Cold War to the mid-1980s, Western states in practice favored resettlement of refugees, motivated by the political fear that refugee returns to the East would be a symbolic victory for Communism. As attention shifted to refugees from the south, government preferences shifted toward repatriation. In this process, Chimni argues, refugees' own free choices have been repressed.

Chimni notes that in the late 1940s Western states were adamant that in theory refugees must have a free choice whether to resettle or repatriate. The Soviet Union had pressured the International Refugee Organization (1947–50) to formally adopt repatriation as the main solution to the postwar refugee problem. Western states insisted that refugees have a free choice, and succeeded in shaping the IRO's practice so that resettlement received more resources. By the 1980s, powerful states dealt with refugee choices in an entirely different way. Instead of insisting on free choice between two options, advocates of repatriation assumed – often without evidence – that refugees in all cases want to return home. Governments and UNHCR looked increasingly for ways in which repatriation could be legally imposed on those who refuse.

Extending Chimni's historical analysis to UNHCR policy, we can see that, as the international community seeks to impose politically preferred solutions on refugees, the principle of choice has been entirely replaced by the more limited concept of voluntariness. If a person has a choice, he can freely decide to take one of at least two options. But voluntariness is more ambiguous. It certainly involves free will, and prohibits overt coercion. But, at least as practiced in durable solutions policy, voluntariness allows for free will to be channeled through lack of alternatives.

Compare the Resettlement Handbook with the Repatriation Handbook. There is nothing at all in UNHCR's Resettlement Handbook suggesting that a refugee will be forced onto an airplane to a third country. As I stated above, UNHCR policy does not conceive of forced resettlement. But what if we apply to resettlement the test of voluntariness suggested by UNHCR in its Repatriation Handbook? UNHCR's understanding of voluntariness in the repatriation context focused on push and pull factors. In repatriation, UNHCR clearly favors pull factors, and emphasizes that refugees should not be pushed out of their host countries. But in resettlement, UNHCR takes the reverse approach. The Resettlement Handbook is emphatic that resettlement is the least preferred option, and can be pursued only when repatriation and local integration fail. The Resettlement Handbook fears that the pull factor of moving to a wealthy third country will make too many refugees want to go. It urges UNHCR staff to advise refugees of their limited resettlement options, so that they will have more realistic expectations.

Unlike in repatriation, in resettlement UNHCR actually prefers push factors. Refugees must have no other options in order to be resettled. Hence, just as Chimni argues that refugee choice is repressed, UNHCR policy tries to prevent refugees from choosing resettlement. Instead, UNHCR policy seeks to prescribe resettlement when nothing else is available, and assumes that refugees will accept it.

Return to Iraq in the first year since regime change

UNHCR policy

Before the US-led invasion of Iraq in April 2003, most attention regarding Iraqi refugees concerned warnings that the impending war would produce hundreds of thousands of new refugees fleeing Iraq. In the event, this did not occur. As the war ended, attention quickly shifted to repatriation of refugees who fled Saddam Hussein's regime before the war.

From the start, and through spring 2004, UNHCR was officially cautious about organizing returns, concerned about the lack of security and continuing instability in Iraq. UNHCR policy has been consistently against any forced returns to Iraq. On 4 July 2003, UNHCR called on governments to extend a moratorium on forcible returns to Iraq, and at the time of writing it has yet to declare the situation stable enough to actually promote repatriation. UNHCR renewed this call on 12 August, this time recommending also that temporary protection be granted to Iraqi refugees and new asylum-seekers. On 14 November, UNHCR extended this policy again, this time "until further notice" (UNHCR Briefing: 14 November 2003). UNHCR repeated this call on 16 March 2004.

The 19 August 2003 bombing at UN headquarters in Iraq obstructed UNHCR's work, forcing all its international staff to leave the country. As of March 2004, UNHCR was relying on 100 national staff in Iraq, guided by international staff working in Jordan and Kuwait (UNHCR, Iraq Operations Update: 9 March 2004). By this time, security concerns had not been resolved, but tens of thousands of refugees had returned anyway. UNHCR reiterated its continued caution, 11 months after the war:

> UNHCR and the Iraqi Ministry for Displacement and Migration (MDM) still consider that conditions in Iraq are not conducive to the promotion of voluntary repatriation to Iraq, but it is clear that many refugees wish to return.
>
> (UNHCR, Iraq Operations Update: 9 March 2004)

Yet, at the same time, UNHCR policy also anticipated large-scale returns. Since most Iraqi refugees had in some manner fled the Ba'ath regime that was now overthrown, there was (and still is) a real possibility that the 1951 Convention's cessation clauses could be invoked once the political situation stabilized. Continued refugee protection for Iraqis has been justified mainly by the generally unstable situation on the ground in Iraq, not on a continued fear of persecution.

UNHCR began putting repatriation programs in place. On 30 April 2003, UNHCR released its Preliminary Repatriation and Reintegration Plan for Iraq (hereafter "Preliminary Plan"). The plan envisioned UNHCR-organized returns both for refugees and people in "refugee-like situations," a category including asylum-seekers, rejected asylum-seekers, and forced migrants who had never applied for refugee status. This was a potentially vast number of people, because in addition to the 400,000 recognized Iraqi refugees world-wide, there were hundreds of thousands of unrecognized Iraqis in Jordan, Syria, and other neighboring countries. In keeping with UNHCR's Voluntary Repatriation Handbook, the Preliminary Plan envisioned a period of assessment and preparation before large scale returns, in which UNHCR would assess security, small number of refugees would visit Iraq to test the waters, and formal repatriation agreements would be negotiated. UNHCR estimated that of the roughly 300,000 recognized refugees and asylum-seekers in neighboring countries (not counting those in Western countries), roughly three-quarters would return "over a relatively short period of time." UNHCR estimated 50 to 60 percent of other Iraqi exiles would return.

At the end of July, UNHCR voiced cautious optimism as it began what was intended to be a slow return program for refugees desperate to go back:

> Many Iraqis are keen to return to their homeland. In response, UNHCR is embarking on a gradual and carefully managed repatriation operation, under which groups of refugees are expected to return from Saudi Arabia and Iran over the next few months. . . . Currently, however, security concerns continue to hinder both refugee return and UNHCR's access to refugee populations living in Iraq.
>
> (UNHCR, Donor Update: Iraq: 30 July 2003)

UNHCR helped 9,000 refugees return over the next seven months, a fraction of the number who actually returned, since many more went back on their own (UNHCR, Iraq Operations Update: 9 March 2004). These organized repatriations may account for fewer than 10 percent of returns to Iraq; the US government estimated in January 2004 that 50,000 to 100,000 had returned since the end of the war.[5]

UNHCR has explained its policy as an attempt to balance concerns about return against refugees' demands to repatriate. In one statement, in January 2004, UNHCR stated:

> UNHCR is not encouraging anyone to go back to Iraq, only facilitating the repatriation of those people who are desperate to go home despite the security problems and precarious humanitarian and economic situation in the country.
>
> (UNHCR Briefing: 6 January 2004)

More recent UNHCR statements have been even more emphatic that any returns are a reaction to the refugees' own demands: "These are people who have been clamouring to repatriate from often desolate refugee camps in order to rejoin their relatives back in Iraq" (UNHCR Briefing: 2 April 2004).

Host countries

Iran

Iran is a party to the 1951 Refugee Convention. Before the war, Iran hosted around half of all Iraqi refugees (200,000), and had the largest refugee population in the world. Around one-third of the Iraqis were Kurds, and the rest mainly Arab (UNHCR, Donor Update: Iraq: 8 July 2003).

Most Iraqis had no special recognition or rights as refugees, and lived with the status of aliens or foreigners. Iraqis received green identity cards, and in isolated cases "refugee booklets." But the identity cards were declared invalid in 2003, and just as the war began Iraqi refugees were supposed to obtain new identity cards. Iraqi Kurds in refugee camps received renewable "white cards." Refugees with identity cards were permitted to work, but only in 16 categories of mainly manual labor. Refugee children were permitted to attend Iranian schools (USCR 2003a).

On 27 May 2003, Iran's official news agency reported the beginning of efforts to repatriate the Iraqi refugees in Iran. Iran's top Aliens' and Foreign Immigrants' Affairs official was quoted saying that repatriation would be voluntary, and that Iraqis could register at offices around the country if they wanted to return. UNHCR officials reacted with caution about organizing any large-scale refugee repatriation because of instability in Iraq, and said, "From our point of view, it is way too early for any large-scale return."[6]

On 15 July, UNHCR reported that 50 to 100 refugees were returning to southern Iraq from Iran every day, a development that UNHCR greeted with concern:

> We are concerned that spontaneous return movements, like the crossings we are seeing at Shalamsha, mean that Iraqis are going back to uncertain situations. Our message to Iraqi refugees is to be patient.
> (UNHCR Briefing: 15 July 2003)

At the end of July 2003, UNHCR continued to be cautious about large-scale returns, but began making arrangements for a pilot convoy of around 100 Iraqis. UNHCR also reported that Iraqis in refugee camps in Iran were eager to return immediately and were resisting infrastructure improvements in the camps.[7]

With Iraq remaining insecure, the pilot convoy still had not left Iran by early September. By this time, UNHCR was in the midst of repatriating refugees from the Rafha camp in Saudi Arabia.[8] Organized returns began slowly by the end of the year, with three convoys of around 500 people between November and December. Yet UNHCR continued to urge Iraqis to wait, given the lack of UN staff in Iraq, the continuing violence there, and the lack of economic infrastructure.[9]

Despite all of this caution, the returns nevertheless became a flood. In early February, UNHCR closed Ashrafi camp, one of Iran's largest, and reported that 50,000 (one-quarter) of the Iraqis in Iran had gone home. UNHCR continued to emphasize that Iraq was not ready for a full repatriation program.[10]

By the end of March 2004, some estimates claimed that around half of the refugees in Iran had returned.[11] UNHCR was organizing three return convoys a week from Iran, carrying 300 to 500 refugees in each. UNHCR's official policy remained unchanged. A spokesperson said, "UNHCR is not promoting repatriation due to the bad security situation inside Iraq, but only facilitating return to those Iraqis that specifically request."[12]

Then, in April 2004, the intensified violence in Iraq forced UNHCR to temporarily delay its return convoys from Iran for around a month (UNHCR Briefing: 6 April 2004). When they resumed on 5 May, UNHCR stressed that it would only repatriate refugees who "insist" on returning, and only to certain relatively secure regions (UNHCR Briefing: 7 May 2004). Finally, in mid-May, UNHCR reported a sudden loss of interest in returning. UNHCR's 18 May briefing stated:

> On Monday, a convoy of returning refugees entered southern Iraq from Iran carrying less than half the number of people who had originally registered to go back. Eighty eight persons opted to stay behind in Iran's Ansar and Matahari camps following news reports of an upsurge in fighting over the weekend in Najaf and Karbala.

At time of writing, in late May 2004, it is too early to say whether this will be a temporary slump in returns or a longer-term chilling of refugee interest in going home to Iraq.

Saudi Arabia

At the end of the 1991 Gulf War, two camps, Artawiyya and Rafha, were set up in Saudi Arabia for around 32,000 Iraqi refugees. In 1992, the residents of Artawiyya were relocated to Rafha, which at the end of 1993 had a population of 28,000. UNHCR operated both voluntary repatriation and resettlement programs from Rafha.

The treatment of these refugees by Saudi authorities was a serious concern. In 1994, Amnesty International reported:

> Over the past three years, the organization has received numerous reports of the arbitrary detention of refugees, their torture and ill-treatment (in some cases resulting in death in custody), possible extra judicial executions and the forcible return of others to Iraq. Various forms of collective punishment have been systematically used against the refugees, particularly in response to protests about living conditions and

treatment by the camp authorities. These have included depriving them of food and water.[13]

Following the US invasion in 2003, UNHCR conducted its first repatriation operation to Iraq from Saudi Arabia. Beginning in late July, UNHCR began repatriating the 5,600 Iraqis who had been at Rafha Camp in Saudi Arabia since the 1991 Gulf War. By December, nearly all of the refugees from Rafha had returned (UNHCR, Iraq Operations Update: 19 December 2003).

Much as in Iran, reports in late spring 2004 indicated a possible change in refugee demands in response to growing instability in Iraq. According to one report, some 480 Iraqis remaining in Rafha want to stay, at least for now (Awaksho 2004).

Lebanon

Of the host countries profiled in this chapter, Lebanon stands out in a number of essentially negative respects. Lebanon is probably the one case in which official authorities encouraged exiles to return, rather than trying to organize the spontaneous returns that were happening anyway. Refugee protection in Lebanon, Syria, and Jordan followed different patterns before the war, and repatriations since have raised different concerns. I am including a summary of the situation in Lebanon because I had personal experience working there in a legal aid program for refugees and asylum-seekers, and I can hence supplement the sparse data that are available in the public domain.

Refugee protection for Iraqis in these three countries was quite different in form than in Iran. Rather than receive a form of group-based identity as refugees as they did in Iran, Iraqis in these states were subject to individualized refugee status determination by UNHCR. UNHCR's application procedures have often been criticized for lack of procedural fairness, and in these countries in particular it was known for noticeably low recognition rates. Many Iraqi exiles never applied at all, and many others were rejected.

As a result, there is relatively little information about the Iraqi forced migrant populations in these countries. Information abut Jordan illustrates the problem. The Jordanian government reported that 305,000 Iraqis were in the country before the war.[14] Only 960 were officially recognized by UNHCR in 2003, though UNHCR also reported 4,243 asylum-seekers, and 1,814 who fled Iraq after the war began.[15] Deportations from Jordan to Iraq had been reported, and in 1997 the UN Committee against Torture ruled that Jordan could not be considered a safe third country for Iraqis reaching Europe.[16]

In Lebanon, refugee protection for non-Palestinians, of whom Iraqis were the most numerous group, had been in crisis for several years when the US and UK invaded Iraq. From August 2000 through February 2001 more than 300 refugees and asylum-seekers were reportedly deported, especially to Iraq.[17] From late 1999 until October 2001, UNHCR was often denied access to detained asylum-seekers and refugees.[18] In May 2002, Amnesty International expressed concern about reports that a new group of 300 Iraqis, including recognized refugees and asylum-seekers, had been deported.[19] The organization concluded: "Amnesty International is concerned that the actions of the Lebanese authorities frequently show a complete disregard for international standards and their own laws in their treatment of asylum-seekers and refugees."

Amnesty International's recent Annual Report for 2003 reported, "There were concerns that convoys organized by the Lebanese authorities to return Iraqis on a voluntary basis to Iraq may have included refugees and asylum-seekers who believed they were at risk of serious human rights violations if returned" (AI 2003).

What lay behind these concerns was a Lebanese government return program in which authorities promoted repatriation even though UNHCR was urging caution. Immediately after the fall of the Iraqi regime the Lebanese government called on Iraqis through broadcast media to register with their embassy in Beirut for repatriation to Iraq. By the end of June, the Lebanese government had twice arranged for convoys of vehicles to carry Iraqis through Syria and into Iraq, carrying in more than 1000 Iraqis. According to press reports, the convoys included Iraqis who were detained by Lebanese authorities, as well as Iraqis who had registered at the embassy (see Frontiers Center 2003).

Although some of the Iraqis had been repatriated directly from detention to Iraq, Lebanese authorities insisted in the press that the repatriations were solely voluntary. UNHCR was publicly silent regarding the government's repatriation program. According to Frontiers Center, a Lebanese human rights center, one detained Iraqi asylum-seeker who had been in the 30 June convoy told researchers that he had been advised by UNHCR to not go home, but "I would have stayed in prison and been tortured if I had not registered my name [for repatriation]" (ibid.). The convoy program paused for several months, resuming again in October.

Third country resettlement policy

Because refugee protection is so fragile in the Middle East, protection for many of the Iraqi refugees in the region had long depended on resettlement. This was especially true in Saudi Arabia, where UNHCR had been gradually resettling refugees from Rafha, and in Lebanon, Jordan, and Syria, where resettlement was the primary (if not the only) durable solution for the relatively small number of Iraqis recognized as refugees by UNHCR.

Yet, resettlement had become problematic even before the Iraq war. After 11 September 2001, the US government temporarily suspended its refugee resettlement program while it devised new security screening measures. The new delays left refugees around the world waiting. By the end of 2002, US resettlement had not resumed in Lebanon, although it had resumed in Egypt and Jordan. Even most of those "tentatively approved" by the Immigration and Naturalization Service in Lebanon before 11 September were still waiting to leave by the end of 2002. A sample of Iraqi refugees stranded in this situation surveyed by Frontiers Center in May 2003 reported that they had been left without access to full information or UNHCR advice during this period (Osmat *et al.* 2003: 42).

In the buildup to the war, it was clear that toppling Saddam Hussein would at least put Iraqi resettlement on hold (see Johnston 2003). According to one report, the US government momentarily suspended its resettlement of Iraqis even before launching the war, in January 2003 (USCR 2003b).

The logic of refugee law more or less ensured that resettlement doors would close once the Iraqi regime changed. Criteria for refugee resettlement to those few states that offer it mirror the international refugee definition. Refugees must have a well-founded fear of persecution in the future. Experiencing persecution in the past is not enough. The problem for many Iraqis who fled the Ba'ath regime is that, to be resettled, one must prove such a risk of persecution on the date of decision by the resettlement country. Hence, an Iraqi who was in danger of political persecution could have been recognized by UNHCR in 2002, but then by the time his file came up for decision by the US, Canadian, or Australian government in mid-2003, the regime he feared was out of power. Even if the situation was not stable enough to apply the cessation clauses, he could not meet the test for resettlement. Hence, the US government reported obliquely in January 2004: "UNHCR is no longer referring Iraqis for resettlement, although it has not issued a Cessation Proclamation, and we expect Iraqi referrals in FY 2004 to be minimal."[20]

Comparing theory with practice in Iraq

Return, with or without security, with or without UNHCR

In other refugee crises, UNHCR has been criticized for promoting repatriation too soon. For instance, the US Committee for Refugees recently raised concerns about preparations for repatriation to Eastern Myanmar.[21] Similar concerns were raised in 2002 about returns to Afghanistan (see Human Rights Watch 2002). UNHCR organized repatriations to Burundi from Tanzania in 2002 despite widespread fighting in the country.[22] But in Iraq, as violence continued long after the fall of Saddam Hussein, UNHCR held the line. Through the end of May 2004, UNHCR continued to say that it was not yet time to actually promote repatriation, and that no refugees or asylum-seekers should be forced home.

The Lebanese government's decision to promote and organize repatriation itself, including of refugees and asylum-seekers in detention, marginalized UNHCR, and probably violated Security Council Resolution 1483 and the principle of *non-refoulement*. UNHCR official silence on this is a significant blemish on its otherwise sound policy of caution about Iraqi returns. Yet Lebanon is a small country in terms of hosting Iraqi refugees.

Paradoxically, given UNHCR's caution, the preliminary estimates of the numbers of people who would return to Iraq appear to have been fairly accurate. UNHCR predicted 75 percent of refugees in neighboring countries would return in a relatively short time. UNHCR did not precisely specify how long a period this meant, but a year after the war around one-half of the refugees may have returned to Iraq, depending on which estimates are to be believed. These returns took place despite UNHCR's position that Iraq was not yet stable enough to promote large-scale repatriation. UNHCR organized some returns, especially as it became clear that people were going back anyway, and many other refugees returned on their own. Rather than promoting return to hesitant refugees, as voluntary repatriation is often conceived, UNHCR was essentially playing catch-up with the refugees.

This situation presented UNHCR with a serious dilemma. Although UNHCR itself did not want to promote return, refugees returning on their own meant return without any organization, without any reintegration assistance, and often return unescorted across minefields and combat zones. In this light, UNHCR's decision to try to organize what was happening anyway seems quite reasonable.

This situation meant that UNHCR could not apply (at least in the first year) the provisions of its voluntary Repatriation Handbook and its Preliminary Plan for Iraq, which were designed to foster informed decision-making by refugees. Since UNHCR was not promoting return, UNHCR was not able to organize information campaigns and short visits by community leaders to test the waters. If any of these measures are eventually put in place, they will only benefit the refugees who remained in exile, not the large number who have already gone back.

Free choice vs. voluntariness vs. desperation

On the face of it, the fact that refugees have appeared to be the main instigators of repatriation to Iraq would seem a reassurance that the returns have been wholly voluntary. I did not conduct any social science research into the perceptions and decision-making of these refugees. Nor do I have any reason to doubt the public account that refugees asked to go home as soon as possible. I would, however, raise doubts as to whether these refugees were making an informed free choice to return. It may be accurate to say that Iraqis refugees were desperate to return home, but questionable whether they freely chose to do so.

There are two main justifications for the Repatriation Handbook's recommendation for a slow buildup to repatriations, during which time refugees are to become more informed about the possibility of returning home. The first is the concern that, unless the cessation clauses of the Refugee Convention apply, there must be safeguards to prevent *refoulement* through coerced returns. The Handbook hence envisions UNHCR closely scrutinizing repatriation preparation to ensure returns are truly voluntary. The second reason is that repatriation programs should promote informed choices by refugees about their futures. The Handbook envisions UNHCR and its partners undertaking an information campaign in refugee communities and interviewing and counseling prospective returnees. Such measures take time.

Even leaving Lebanon aside, the fact that refugees, more than UNHCR, have promoted repatriation does not really resolve the concerns raised in the Repatriation Handbook. First, UNHCR's capacity to fully monitor the returns to Iraq is questionable. Refugees returned on their own in large numbers, at times when insecurity made it difficult for UNHCR to work in Iraq. Since many returned spontaneously, it was difficult for UNHCR to communicate with them before they went back. Second, since UNHCR was not promoting return, there was no organized information campaign and individual counseling in most cases. It is unclear what refugees knew about conditions in Iraq when they chose to go home.

Most critically, it is impossible to know how much Iraqi refugees were "pulled" back by the fall of the Ba'ath regime relative to how much they were "pushed" by poor conditions in their host countries. None of the countries neighboring Iraq had offered Iraqis anything close to the full rights expected for refugees under international law. In some countries, such as Lebanon, refugees had no legal right to residence and lived with constant fear of arrest. In others, such as Saudi Arabia, they were long confined to desert camps. In Iran, the Iraqis had some status recognition, but only partial social and economic integration. Most had no right to work, and many were living in refugee camps. Thus, if we apply the test of voluntariness in the Repatriation Handbook, it would not at all be clear that the pull factors in Iraq were really more influential than push factors in the host countries.

When refugees clamor to repatriate against official advice, it is difficult to argue that the right of *non-refoulement* has been violated, but in the case of Iraq it is also difficult to argue that the criteria for full voluntariness have been met. In light of this doubt, it may be helpful to refine the concept of voluntariness used to define refugee choice in durable solutions. At one extreme, we have involuntary, forced return, which is in most cases illegal *refoulement*. At the other extreme is free, informed choice, as envisioned by the UNHCR Handbook. In the middle ground are cases in which refugees might be said to accept a solution that, for them, is essentially the lesser of two evils.

What was the politically preferred situation?

Earlier in this chapter I introduced the concept of politically preferred durable solutions, in which refugee choice is suppressed by the interests of powerful governments and institutions. As Chimni explains, the politically preferred durable solution in most cases today is repatriation.

Was there a politically preferred solution in the case of Iraq during the first year after the invasion? UNHCR in this case did not actually promote repatriation. On the other hand, it was clear immediately after the invasion that the international community expected Iraqi refugees to be repatriated eventually. Repatriation was the preferred solution, just as Chimni's analysis would predict, but it was officially on hold. Another way to describe this situation is that the refugees were placed in limbo. UNHCR did not actively promote repatriation, but no other solution was made available either. Local integration had never been available. Doors to resettlement closed.

This raises the question: Can a durable solution ever be truly voluntary if there are no available alternatives? UNHCR's Repatriation Handbook does not address the question of providing alternatives. Repatriation should be voluntary, but what if the refugee says no? UNHCR does not in this case hold itself liable to find another solution for a refugee just because he or she has rejected the first option. At best, a refugee can fall back on the protections of international law. In the Refugee Convention, he or she is owed certain civil, social, and economic rights until changes in conditions at home can be shown to be effective, fundamental, and durable. But this is often just theory in the Middle East, where few states have ratified the Refugee Convention and fewer still have implemented all of its provisions.

The soundest analysis is that no choice of a durable solution is free unless the refugee is offered at least one other viable alternative, at least on an interim basis. Otherwise, refugees are simply being asked to accept a *fait accompli*. This does not mean that striving toward voluntariness is pointless in such situations. Being forced suddenly onto a bus in shackles or at gunpoint is extremely disruptive and possibly traumatizing, and doubtless much worse than giving people information and some time to prepare themselves. Even without real alternatives, basic dignity and people's capacity to adjust to a new situation might be preserved. But these important considerations concern *how* a solution is implemented; they should not be confused with the choice over *what* the solution will be.

Conclusion: lessons from Iraq

Assessing UNHCR's standards

In terms of basic concepts, UNHCR's Voluntary Repatriation Handbook does appear useful in the case of Iraq in two key ways, but it also contains an important gap that should be corrected. First, the Handbook stresses that repatriation should not be promoted in situations of violence and instability, and UNHCR deserves credit for generally following this rule in its official policy toward Iraqis during the first post-invasion year. Second, the Handbook's definition of "voluntariness," including attention to conditions both in the country of origin (pull factors) and in the host country (push factors) is a very useful analytical tool for scrutinizing refugee returns. Applying this type of analysis to the case of Iraqis shows how refugees can appear to be making a voluntary choice, when in context they may be acting out of desperation.

On the downside, the Handbook contains a substantial gap in that it does not make the availability of other alternatives a criterion for voluntary repatriation. This is essentially the critique that Chimni makes of durable solutions policy, namely that governments (and UNHCR) insist that they (and not refugees) make the ultimate choice. Without alternatives, refugees are not making a real choice, except to the degree that they can choose to remain in limbo. This bolsters the argument I made above that the concept of voluntariness as used in refugee policy is not really the same as the concept of choice. Voluntariness prohibits overt coercion and requires a measure of free will, but allows governments and/or UNHCR to limit the ways in which refugees can exercise free will. The cautious plan that UNHCR laid out after the invasion does not reflect the way repatriation actually occurred. Rather than refugees choosing their durable solution, it would be more accurate to say that the international community strives to achieve a humane implementation of predetermined solutions. But when free choice is actually required, the information, counseling, and monitoring provided for in UNHCR's existing standards are necessary but not sufficient. Refugees must have real alternatives.

This gap rendered UNHCR's standards largely unworkable in the context of Iraq. Lacking other alternatives, many refugees "chose" the politically preferred solution of return. UNHCR's admirable official hesitation about return was not reflected on the ground, and UNHCR felt pressure to provide some order to returns that were happening anyway. UNHCR's voluntariness standard remained a useful analytical tool, but its practical application was much more limited. The concept of voluntary repatriation to Iraq was at best a means of slowing and managing returns rather than giving refugees a meaningful choice.

Applying the lessons of Iraq to Palestine

To state the obvious, the right to return has not been disputed or denied in Iraq as it has been in Palestine. As with virtually every refugee crisis other than Palestine, the main protection concern with Iraq has been refugees who do *not* want to go home. As Chimni notes at the end of his analysis, the denial of Palestinian return has been against the historical trend. Even though repatriation has increasingly become the preferred solution for refugees (and was preferred at least on paper even in the immediate postwar years), refugees have been denied return in a situation in which they have been pleading for it.

In my analysis, I have sought to focus not on the issue of repatriation specifically, but on the idea that there is usually a politically preferred solution that refugees are pressured to accept "voluntarily." An eventual resolution to the Palestinian refugee crisis might be no different, even if the ranking of politically preferred solutions is not the same.

Individual refugee choice is inherent in UNGA Resolution 194, which refers to "refugees *wishing* to return" and provides for compensation for "those *choosing* not to return." Assuming that international law is finally applied to the Palestinians, it will be essential to guarantee that refugees actually get to exercise this choice. Some concept of voluntary choice will be important for any resolution of the crisis being perceived as just and legitimate.

Israel's resistance to the right to return is the first and primary obstacle to refugee choice for Palestinians. But Israeli policy will not be the only challenge. Neighboring host countries have in many cases been resistant to any local integration for Palestinians, and (especially in Lebanon) have in some cases denied them the most basic human rights. Today's refugees may have limited information about conditions in their homeland 56 years after their (or, in most cases, their parents' or grandparents') expulsion and flight. Just as the denial of the Palestinian right to return has been exceptional, so has the resulting politicization of return. Should return actually become a real choice, this politicization could be an impediment to ensuring free individual choices. Palestinian refugees may feel that their choices about whether to return are reflections of national loyalty. Refugees from other countries form preferences about durable solutions without this added political baggage.

The way Lebanese authorities handled Iraqi repatriation offers another important warning, in no small part because Lebanon has had such a harsh policy toward Palestinian refugees. Lebanon began organizing and promoting ostensibly voluntary return almost immediately after the Iraq war, despite all international official caution. It is not difficult to imagine a situation in which Palestinian refugees are offered a range of choices, return or resettlement, in which some options can be implemented more quickly, while another option might involve a waiting period. If a host government like Lebanon, where refugees already live under a great deal of hardship, were to put heavy pressure on refugees to leave quickly, their ability to make truly free choices would be in doubt.

The question of refugee choice carries even greater importance if an eventual Israeli–Palestinian peace plan is founded on the assumption that many or most refugees will not return. As a political selling point, the right to return would be less threatening to Israel, or at least to some parts of the Israeli political spectrum, if there were reassurance that many refugees would actually not choose to come back. For instance, the left-wing Israeli group *Gush Shalom* (Peace Bloc) has proposed a peace plan in which Israel would acknowledge the right to return "as a basic human right" and would in principle provide "every refugee" a choice between return to Israel and resettlement and compensation elsewhere.[23] Yet, at the same time, the *Gush Shalom* plan envisions a negotiated quota of returnees to Israel. The *Gush Shalom* approach was to some extent reflected in the unofficial Geneva Accords (2003: article 7), although the Geneva Accords lack any explicit endorsement of the right of return. Nevertheless, the Accords include the statement that refugee "choice shall be on the basis of a free and informed decision." Yet this principle of free choice is undermined by a provision that return to Israel would not be an open choice for all. It would be at the "sovereign discretion of Israel," which would set a quota on returnees.

The *Gush Shalom* version offers more hope for refugee rights than the Geneva Accords because of its strong recognition on paper of the right to return. But its reliance on a quota makes this appear to be empty words, and shows the political stakes involved in the way refugees would choose to exercise their rights. The only way such a system could even conceivably be perceived as anything but an infringement on refugee rights is if the agreed quota reflected the real number of refugees who, given a free choice, actually wanted to return. But were this to be the case, the quota itself would be redundant. In practice, a great deal would be at stake in whether the number of refugees choosing repatriation fitted within the agreed quota. Non-return would hence still be the politically preferred solution. If the Iraqi case is any guide, refugees will be under pressure to "voluntarily" accept non-return, even if officially the principle of choice is accepted by all parties.

The case of Iraq indicates that real refugee choice will require more safeguards than those established in international law and UNHCR standards today. Even when official agencies like UNHCR do not officially promote a particular solution, the preferences of powerful governments nevertheless hold a great deal of sway. Hence, any durable solution plan that is contingent on free individual choices must include more safeguards than were in place for Iraqis.

Notes

1 See selection of commentaries in Electronic Intifada, http://electronicIntifada. net/bytopic/195.shtml, under "Refugee polls" (accessed 31 May 2004).

2 See BADIL Resource Centre Commentary (25 July 2003), http://electronicintifada.net/cgi-bin/artman/exec/view.cgi/7/1749 (accessed 31 May 2004).

3 See also UNHCR EXCOM Conclusions No. 69 (1992) para. B, available online at www.UNHCR.ch

4 One of the most famous examples of this phenomenon is the Salvadoreans who were granted Temporary Protected Status in the United States but never actually left the US. See also Bagshaw (1997: 580).

5 Bureau of Population, Refugees, and Migration, Fact Sheet, Refugee Admissions Program for Near East and South Asia (16 January 2004).

6 IRINNews, Iran: Return programme for Iraqi refugees to take time (5 June 2003), available online at www.irinnews.org

7 IRINNews, Iran: Iraqi repatriation awaiting safety guarantees (28 July 2003).

8 IRINNews, Iran: Iraqi refugees waiting for repatriation (4 September 2003).

9 IRINNews, Iran: More Iraqis go home (17 December 2003).

10 IRINNews, Iran: Iraqi refugee camp closed (9 February 2004).

11 IRINNews, Iran: Iraqi refugee repatriation continues (31 March 2004).

12 Ibid.

13 Amnesty International, Saudi Arabia: Unwelcome "guests": The plight of Iraqi refugees, MDE 23/001/1994 (10 May 1994), available online at www.amnesty. org

14 IRINNews, Jordan: Iraqi refugees wait to go home (12 November 2003).

15 Ibid.

16 Avedes Hamayak Korban v. Sweden, Committee against Torture, Communication No. 88/1997.

17 See UNHCR (2002b) at 137 ("Due to the strict application by the Lebanese Government of its immigration legislation, asylum-seekers and persons recognized as refugees by UNHCR risk detention and deportation, often to Syria, on the grounds of illegal entry and residence in the country").

18 Ibid at 134.

19 Amnesty International, "Lebanon: Amnesty International reiterates its concerns on the situation of refugees and asylum-seekers," MDE 18/005/2002 (3 May 2002).

20 Bureau of Population, Refugees, and Migration, Fact Sheet, Refugee Admissions Program for Near East and South Asia (16 January 2004).

21 Joint Letter from the USCR and Refugees International to the Head of UNHCR regarding repatriation of Myanmarese (Burmese) refugees (11 March 2004).

22 "Burundi refugees repatriation on despite heavy fighting: UNHCR," Agence France Presse (22 November 2002).

23 "A draft peace proposal," http://www.gush-shalom.org/archives/peace.html (accessed 26 May 2004).

References

AI (2003) *Annual Report 2003* (London: Amnesty International).

Awkasho, Rashad (2004) "Iraqi refugees want to remain in Saudi Arabia", *Financial Times*, 26 May.

Bagshaw, Simon (1997) "Benchmarks or Deutschmarks? Determining the criteria for the repatriation of refugees to Bosnia and Herzegovina", *International Journal of Refugee Law* 9, p. 566.

Chimni, B.S., "From resettlement to involuntary repatriation: towards a critical history of durable solutions to refugee problems", New Issues in Refugee Research Working Paper No. 2 (Geneva, May 1999), http://www.UNHCR.ch/cgi-bin/texis/vtx/research (follow link to Evaluation and Policy Analysis).

Fitzgerald, Joan (1999) "The end of protection: Legal standards for cessation of refugee status and withdrawal of temporary protection", *Georgetown Immigration Law Journal* 13, p. 343.

Frontier Center (2003) *Refugee protection in Lebanon: Activity report 2003* (Beirut: Frontiers Association).

Geneva Accord Draft Permanent Status Agreement (1 December 2003), available online at www.geneva-accord.org

Goodwin-Gill, Guy S. (1996) *The refugee in international law*, 2nd edn. (Oxford: Clarendon Press).

Hathaway, James C. (1991) *The law of refugee status* (Toronto: Butterworths).

Human Rights Watch (2002) "Closed door policy: Afghan refugees in Pakistan and Iran", Afghanistan, Iran, and Pakistan Series 14, 2 (G) (February), http://www.hrw.org/reports/2002/pakistan/index.htm#TopOfPage

Johnston, Cynthia (2003) "Lebanon's Iraqi refugees in limbo as war looms", Reuters, 10 March.

Osmat, Bashir, Kagan, Michael, and Trad, Samira (2003) "Promises without solutions: Iraqi refugees left in the lurch in Lebanon", *Forced Migration Review* 18, p. 42.

UNHCR, Iraq Briefings and News Stories, http://www.UNHCR.ch/cgi-bin/texis/vtx/iraq

UNHCR, Iraq Operations Updates, http://www.UNHCR.ch/cgi-bin/texis/vtx/iraq?page=planning

UNHCR (1996) *Voluntary repatriation: International protection* (Geneva: UNHCR).

UNHCR (2002a) *Resettlement handbook*, rev. edn. (Geneva: UNHCR).

UNHCR (2002b) *2003 Global Appeal* (Geneva: UNHCR).

UNHCR (2003) Preliminary Repatriation and Reintegration Plan for Iraq (30 April), http://www.UNHCR.ch/cgi-bin/texis/vtx/iraq?page=home

US Committee for Refugees (2003a) *World Refugee Survey 2003* (Washington, DC: USCR).

US Committee for Refugees (2003b) "Iraqi refugee admissions resume, but US refugee resettlement program remains in disarray", press release 24 January, available online at www.refugees.org

Part III

Lessons learnt

13 Palestinian return migration

Lessons from the international refugee regime

Sari Hanafi

Solutions to refugee problems have traditionally been divided into three categories: voluntary repatriation, local integration in the country of asylum, and resettlement from the country of asylum to a third country. The first option might be perceived as the most "natural" option but it is also the most complicated. I prefer to call it "return migration" to emphasize the fact that it is a migration like any other migratory movement. It involves a complex legal framework and institutional arrangements as well as favorable political, economic, and social conditions, and, in addition, the international environment is very important to enable such movement. Since the optimism that surrounded the end of the Cold War, a number of large repatriation operations have taken place and there was hope that lasting solutions might be found for many of the world's refugee problems.

This article has as its objective to look at the lessons for Palestinian return migration that can be drawn from experience elsewhere in the world. It will start by examining the paradigmatic development in the international environment and the historical role of the United Nations High Commissioner for Refugees (UNHCR), what will be called the "international refugee regime." Then I will discuss specific cases of return migration and draw some conclusions regarding eventual Palestinian return.

The international refugee regime

The international refugee regime is a generic regime that was initiated by the 1951 Convention relating to the status of refugees, and amplified by the 1967 protocol, to deal with refugees around the world. Today, 145 states have signed one of these two UN refugee treaties and undertaken to provide protection (in its different forms: permanent, temporary, preventive) and assistance for individuals who have left their home countries and meet the treaty definition of the term "refugee."[1] The implementing institution under the generic regime is UNHCR. When UNHCR began operations in January 1951, it had a staff of 34 people based mainly in Geneva with a budget of about US$300,000. Over the course of the next five decades, the agency grew into a global institution with 268 offices in 114 countries, a staff of more than 5,500 people and a budget of just over US$1 billion. UNHCR currently helps approximately 20 million people around the world (Helton, 2002). This international refugee regime developed and passed through different trends. It should be remembered that the international refugee regime is not only a regime of international law, but one that has also been instrumental in the recent emergence of "refugee studies" as an academic or "applied academic" specialization. Much social scientific research – whether resulting in policy recommendations, development reports, or academic articles – has been conducted in formal connection with (and often funded by) these international organizations (Malkki 1995: 506).

The major historical development of the refugee regime was the emergence of a new paradigm of rights for refugees elaborated against the legacy of World Wars I and II. In the past, Russian, Armenian, and Hungarian refugees were promptly disenfranchised (by having their legal papers revoked) by the new Soviet or Turkish governments, etc. It is important to note that, starting with World War I, many European states began to introduce laws that made it possible for their own citizens to be denaturalized. The first was France, in 1915, with regard to naturalized citizens of "enemy" origins. In 1922, the example was followed by Belgium, which revoked the naturalization of citizens who had committed "anti-national" acts during the war. In 1926, the Fascist regime in Italy passed a similar law concerning citizens who had shown themselves to be "unworthy of Italian citizenship," and in 1933 it was Austria's turn, and so forth, until in 1935 the Nuremberg Laws divided German citizens into full citizens and citizens without political rights.

The second major development is related to globalization as it has affected possibilities for asylum seekers or the choices open to refugees for permanent solutions after the end of conflicts. Refugee movement and mobility should thus be understood in the larger context of globalization and international migration. There are currently some 170 million international migrants who reside outside their countries of birth. This migration trend will continue so long as population growth continues to decline in the more developed regions. As for forced migrants, throughout history most refugee movements have tended to result in permanent exile of a major part of the displaced populations (Rogge 1994: 21).[2] During the Cold War, the international community viewed resettlement as the preferred option; repatriation was incompatible with foreign policy objectives and refugees were often pawns in the superpowers' proxy wars, as in the case of the Afghani refugees used by the United States against the former Soviet Union. Now, however, resettlement is less possible not only because of the rise of anti-immigration sentiments in Europe, Australia, and elsewhere but also as the resettlement procedures have become enmeshed in national security considerations.[3] Apart from special bilateral resettlement initiatives, UNHCR often serves as a gatekeeper in terms of referring individual vulnerable cases to resettling countries (Helton 2002: 185). The 1990s thus became the decade of repatriation. In the few years between the refugee returns to Namibia in 1989 and the returns to Mozambique in 1993–4, UNHCR's role in repatriation operations changed profoundly. In previous decades, UNHCR's involvement in repatriation operations was generally short-term and small-scale and the organization focused primarily on ensuring that refugees returned safely. The repatriation operations in Central America, Cambodia and Mozambique involved a new and broader approach. In each case, UNHCR played a major role in UN peace-building operations, and humanitarian repatriation and peace-building activities became integrated into a wider strategic and political framework aimed at ensuring reconciliation, reintegration, and reconstruction (UNHCR 2000).

Lessons learnt from the refugee return experiences

I will draw some lessons on return migration from the generic regime and the different refugee experiences. The political, sociological, and institutional dimensions of return migration will also be discussed.

Political dimension

What is the relationship between repatriation and conflict? The repatriation process (or at least the possibility of repatriation) is often a central issue in resolving conflicts, including when the conflict is an ethnic one, as in Namibia, Cambodia, Western Sahara, Bosnia, and Rwanda.[4] The non-return of refugees in the Rwanda case has led to a genocide. Barkan (2004) argues that in ethnic conflicts the return of refugees provokes a revival of the conflict and he thus draws the conclusion concerning the Palestinian–Israeli conflict that there should be no return of refugees. He makes extensive use of the Bosnian case. I disagree with his argumentation for two reasons: First, the reason refugees did not return in the Bosnia case was not that it would endanger a resolution of the conflict but because Bosnian refugees did not see a future in their destroyed cities and preferred to stay in other European countries. If Europe decides to implement a Marshall Plan for this post-conflict country, then return will become more significant. Secondly, the nature of the conflict in Palestine/Israel is more colonial than ethnic. By this I mean that one group of people replaced the indigenous population. This remembered legacy is very important and in itself constitutes a cause for the revival of the conflict. Resolving this conflict is to render justice to the indigenous population by allowing them to exercise their right of return and there can be no resolution, even territorially, if Israeli responsibility for the birth of the Palestinian refugee problem is not addressed. The ethnic argumentation could certainly influence Israeli policies in terms of regulating return migration (places where Palestinian returnees can live, land restitution or not, etc.) but it cannot be the *raison d'être* of the return.

The return option cannot be exercised without addressing the question of compensation and land restitution. International experience shows the importance of finding a mechanism that can be quickly launched and which includes provisions for return, integration, land restitution, and compensation. For those desiring to return to long-lost lands and houses, confirmation of title may be crucial, particularly if the property is currently occupied by others. For this purpose, a restitution mechanism could be used to award possession to returning refugees, like the Bosnian Commission for Real Property Claims of Displaced Persons and Refugees (CRPC) established under Annex 7 of the 1995 Dayton Peace Agreement. The Bosnian property commission is a mixed body of international and national commissioners, with three international members appointed by the president of the European Court of Human Rights and six national members, of which four are appointed by the Federation of Bosnia and Herzegovina and two by the Republika Srpska. The commissioners have been supported by some 400 local staff and 12 regional field offices. As of March 2003, CRPC had resolved 81 percent of the 318,780 claims submitted for consideration.[5] This has required a deep investigation into the complicated amalgam of historical legal traditions relating to the registration of property ownership, ranging from methods used under the Austro-Hungarian system to more recent socialist law enactments, in order to confirm title (Helton 2002).

The experience in Bosnia also shows, however, that, while land restitution was partially successful, compensation was very difficult. The Bosnian government did not have the financial resources to contribute to the fund and international donors were not interested in financing individual compensation. Donors were much more interested in rebuilding homes, roads, hospitals, schools, and other public infrastructure (BADIL 2003).[6]

When it comes to the Palestinian case two problems must be acknowledged.

The first is the fact that the large majority of Palestinian property claims seem to concern less than five dunums of land. This means that the cost of a claim could be more expensive than the amount of compensation (Tamari 2005). This could be resolved with lump sum agreements, as some international experience suggests. In fact, there is a long history of using international claims tribunals to settle disputes, many dealing with alien property. From the Jay Treaty of 1794, between the United States and Britain, until World War II, claims tribunals were often used to effect war reparations. Such tribunals, however, came to be considered too slow and expensive, leading increasingly to the use of lump sum agreements. These involved state-to-state payments, with the claimant state expected to distribute funds to individuals and the paying state obtaining a categorical release from its obligations (Helton 2002).

The second problem concerns practical complications regarding the investigation of title relating to Palestinian property, due to the loss of such titles. Oral history may thus play an important evidentiary role in any claims program. Claimants often face great difficulties in proving their claim due to the length of time that has passed, the destruction or loss of documentary evidence during a war or the fact that the claimant was a peasant who worked the land without owning it. The use of oral history would not be unprecedented. All claims programs addressing injustices from the Nazi era and World War II take these difficulties into account and apply relaxed standards of proof in their proceedings. Three programs were established with the help of the International Organization for Migration (IOM) to deal with such claims. The first is the Claims Resolution Tribunal for Dormant Accounts (CRT I) that was established in 1997[7] to resolve claims to dormant accounts (accounts opened in Swiss banks by non-Swiss nationals or residents that have been dormant since 9 May 1945) that were made public by the Swiss Bankers Association in July and October 1997.[8] The second program is the Claims Resolution Tribunal – Deposited Assets Claims (CRT II). After completion of all claims filed to accounts published by the Swiss Bankers Association, the Claims Resolution Tribunal in a different process undertook to process another 32,000 claims from Nazi victims or their heirs to assets deposited in Swiss banks in the period before and during World War II. These claims were filed following the settlement of the Holocaust Victim Assets class action litigation in the US District Court for the Eastern District of New York.[9] The relevant provision in the rules of procedure applies a relaxed standard of proof, as in article 17.[10] The last program is the Property Claims Commission at the German Forced Labor Compensation Program. This commission was established to determine property claims filed as part of the German Forced Labor Compensation Program and applies a similarly relaxed standard of proof.

Whereas all these three programs operate on the basis of written proceedings and there are usually no oral proceedings, written statements by claimants providing information about family history based on oral narratives that claimants heard from family members have been considered sufficient to render a claim plausible. This is so, in particular, if the information provided by the claimant matches other information available, such as archival information or, as in the case of the claims processes before the Claims Resolution Tribunal, undisclosed information contained in bank records.

Furthermore, oral history together with other historic research may also provide important reference material for decision makers as to what happened at certain times and in certain areas. In the above-mentioned claims programs, such reference material has lad to the development of certain assumptions, for example regarding the treatment of particular claimant groups in a certain area at a certain time or regarding the causal connection between the loss suffered by the claimant and the actions by the relevant authorities, thus relieving claimants of the burden of having to show it in each individual case.

These three programs set up a precedent in the history of compensation for victims of conflict and it should provide a very interesting case study to prepare land restitution and compensation for Palestinians. But although the precedent allows the use of oral history, oral history and oral narration should be always linked to some kinds of documentary evidence. The objective of the use of oral history is to fill the gaps and also help decision makers understand the extent of some problems and their psychological dimension.[11]

Sociological dimension

The sociological dimension of return concerns the nature of the modes and forms of the repatriation process, but before I get there I will deal with the question of numbers repatriated in post-conflict areas, as they raise some methodological problems.

Working with UNHCR's data on refugee movements, one quickly sees that the number of refugees returning to their countries of origin (once return is possible) is far less than the number who choose resettlement in the host country or in a third-party state. According to UNHCR statistics for 2002, only 21 percent of refugees exercised their right of return (2,252,804 returnees), and that year was exceptional as Afghanis constituted more than 80 percent of the returnees: of the 3,828,852 Afghan registered refugees, 47 percent returned, mainly from Pakistan, Iran, and Tajikistan. In many places, statistics on return hide a lot of problems. For instance, the statistics are based on border crossings, whereas anthropological verification shows that refugees often become internally displaced, as in the case of PLO returnees to the West Bank and Gaza Strip. In addition, sometimes refugees do not stay long after returning.

There are several reasons behind the rather small percentage of return, chiefly the structure of the global labor market and insecurity in the post-conflict area. The Bosnian case provides some insights: even before the ink was dry on the 1995 Dayton Peace Agreement a vigorous debate was under way about return.[12] Eight-and-a-half years after the signing of the agreement, it is uncontestable that real and tangible progress on the return of Bosnian refugees and internally displaced persons (IDPs) has been made. Close to one million former refugees and IDPs have returned to their prewar homes and municipalities in Bosnia and Herzegovina (B&H), out of an estimated 2.2 million persons forcibly displaced during the war. As of May 2004 (UNHCR 2004), these returns significantly include some 411,970 so-called minority returns (to places where another ethnic group, typically Serb, is dominant) constituting 18.7 percent of the total number of refugees, in addition to the 543,000 so-called majority returns: persons who returned to municipalities where their own ethnic group is in a majority. However, this general progress has made more apparent the plight of those for whom return in safety and dignity remains problematic. A large number of people remain displaced within the region and are in need of a durable solution. These include some 125,000 refugees from B&H who are in neighboring Serbia, Montenegro, and Croatia, and some 45,000 refugees outside the region, as well as some 350,000 IDPs (UNHCR 2003). Thus 18.7 percent of the total number of B&H

refugees and IDPs really constitutes a small number returning to a place with a different majority ethnic group, whereas the return to areas of the same ethnic group is much more significant.

The partial return of refugees can be explained both by the context shaping international relations between states and by the social change refugees underwent in exile. In recent debates inside the UNHCR, the question has been raised whether the return option is indeed the most popular option for refugees.[13] While repatriation was played down during the ideological confrontation of the Cold War, it emerged with renewed vigor in the 1990s. UNHCR even declared the 1990s as the decade of repatriation. However, somehow repatriation was romanticized and the nature of refugees in the world changed. Many refugees (like the Burmese Muslims) showed resistance to returning,[14] while others who were technically not stateless preferred to become so rather than to return to their homeland, as in the case of Polish and Romanian Jews who stayed in France or Germany at the end of World War II, or the case today of victims of political persecution and those for whom returning to their homeland would endanger their survival (Agamben 1997: 2).

In this context, many studies in forced migration have criticized UNHCR's tendency to favor repatriation and force refugees to go home.[15] While UNHCR has always recognized as part of its mandate the need to ensure that refugees are not forced back against their will to their countries of origin, this has not always been evinced in practice; see for example the UNHCR rations denied to Mozambicans in South Africa or Eritreans in Sudan. "Voluntary" repatriation sometimes is a "cover for forced return, or to impede return" (Barkan 2004: 7) and repatriation from Western countries is generally a failure. Even when Iraqi or Afghani refugees were offered financial incentives by governments to return very few were willing to do so. While it is clear that refugees were closely involved in the preparation and planning stages of the repatriation process, some research also shows that the concept of voluntary repatriation has been applied too broadly and loosely. In many cases, the lack of suitable alternatives obliges refugees to cooperate in their repatriation (Dumper, forthcoming). Thus, repatriation is mostly involuntary.

Social change in exile also plays a major role in any decision to return. Protracted refugee statuses create new ties in host countries. Rural people become urban and in many receiving countries women are empowered more than their sisters who stay in Southern countries. The lesson to be learned for the Palestinian case is that one should disconnect partially the question of the right of return from the sociology of return. Rosemary Sayigh noted that the return of Palestinians has been subject not only to push factors from the host country, but also to a collective desire for return on the part of the refugees (Sayigh 1977). Daniel Warner (1994: 160), however, disputes the latter interpretation, challenging the "idealized" and "nostalgic" image of voluntary repatriation. Over time, he argues, dispersal distorts the meaning of community and with it the memory of the homeland (Zureik 1997: 80). The "making strange" of the asylum country often corresponds to the assumption that the homeland or country of origin is not only the normal but the ideal habitat, the place where one fits in, lives in peace, and has an unproblematic culture and identity. But one should be careful not to romanticize and idealize the exile and the diaspora as some authors have done.

Up to now, I have talked about repatriation as if people are permanently on the move from place to place. In fact, repatriation takes different forms including an ephemeral form like that of many African refugees which was labeled "periodic repatriation." There are many parts of Africa where refugees have crossed a border but stay close to it in anticipation of a speedy return. In many cases, they remain in the same ethnic region or in areas into which they may have traditionally migrated on a seasonal basis (Rogge 1994: 31). This form of repatriation could eventually be relevant to Palestinians who prefer to reside in Palestinian territories, or close to Jordan or Egypt, rather than Israel for fear of ethnic friction with the Jewish majority. Any deadline for refugees to choose their place of permanent settlement will fail if the peace process does not create a flexible time–space framework.

Institutional arrangements

The international community has in the past set up both institutional arrangements and legal regulations to deal with refugees and asylum seekers. However, although alleviating the humanitarian aspect of the problem of refugees, these do not sufficiently address refugees' political identity and thus the question of return. Many experiences show that investment by the international community to support return is very limited,[16] and thus the large majority of refugees return without any significant help from international organizations. Significant repatriation efforts over the recent past have included Cambodia, where between March 1992 and April 1993 UNHCR repatriated an estimated 370,000 refugees at the cost of some US$128 million. In Mozambique, some 1.7 million refugees (from six neighboring countries) returned home from 1992 to 1996, an effort upon which around US$150 million was spent. In the case of Namibia, over 40,000 refugees were repatriated by UNHCR at a cost of US$36 million (Helton 2002).

In terms of specific institutional arrangements for return migration, the international community shows an inclination toward regional conferences bringing together the country in conflict, generating the refugees, and its neighbors in order to prepare the region to allow refugees the choice between resettlement and repatriation.

The different experiences of the international regime suggests that Palestinians should avoid depending on one organization alone. I propose here that UNHCR and IOM be responsible for the return of refugees or their resettlement in third countries, as they have the most experience in such work, while the United Nations Relief and Works Agency (UNRWA), UNDP, and the World Bank should be in charge of integration of Palestinian refugees who want to stay in their host countries. UNRWA should also extend its mandate to include temporary protection (Akram and Rempl 2003). The PLO, the PNA, and UNRWA could create an overarching institution with three functions: 1) a support and advice unit for refugees to guide them to the best solution on a case-by-case basis; 2) coordinating the work between these organizations; 3) responsibility for fundraising for the whole process. For the first function especially, this umbrella group should work closely with the popular committees in the camps and the different NGOs dealing with the refugee populations.

For resettlement in third countries, what is needed is legislation rather than institutional arrangements. A more serious impediment to a significant resettlement effort concerns the difference between the Palestinian definition of a refugee and the general definition elaborated by the UNHCR. The immigration and refugee laws of the main resettlement countries generally incorporate the UN refugee standard. If Palestinian refugees are to be re-settled in significant numbers, then adjustments will probably have to be made in numerous national legal systems. Potential resettling governments will thus have to review their laws and make any necessary amendments in order to establish new or expanded humanitarian admissions that would cover Palestinians (Helton, forthcoming).

Economic dimension

If some returnees will consume the resources of the place to which they return, others will bring capital and expertise sufficient to generate improvements to the country's economy. Some studies have demonstrated that the capital influx and investment that accompany the return of professionals generates investment. This type of investment is significantly different from the classical model of remittances studied in the Arab world (Hanafi 2001), which were dominated by limited economic benefits and negative effects of migration, weak investment of remittances in productive activities, and inflation provoked by the transfer of currency (Saad Al Din and Abdel Fadil 1983; Fergany 1988).[17]

Contrary to studies that view returnees as a future burden on Palestinian society[18] and that studied the absorptive capacity of Palestinian refugees from a narrow and short-term economic perspective, other studies have shown great potential benefit from the absorption of returnees, considering the new dynamics and positive externalities that might be established by their return (Van Hear 1997). The Oslo transition period generated a high rate of growth in the Palestinian territories. Gross domestic product and gross national product before the *intifada* were higher than in neighboring countries, with the exception of Israel. If this level is regained, the Palestinian territories will attract refugees at least from Jordan and Egypt, especially if family members contribute at the initial stage. Some Palestinians might also move from the Gaza Strip to the West Bank, where income is higher.

This also applies to Israel, where future government policy will determine whether Palestinian workers, engineers, and IT professionals can take up or resume residence there.

Many studies, like those of Nicholas Van Hear (1997), have provided us with very enlightening conclusions drawn from several case studies about return migration as a generator of employment that also encourages an economy to flourish. Van Heer studied four return experiences. The first was the case of the 50,000 Asians who were expelled from Uganda in 1972 and a subsequent limited return (some 7,000) two decades later, which was an important factor in the recovery of the Ugandan economy. The second case dealt with the forced exodus of 300,000 ethnic Turks from Bulgaria to Turkey in mid-1989. In this case, external assistance aided integration greatly. The third case concerned the exodus of 350,000 of Palestinians from Kuwait and other Gulf States, most of whom went to Jordan. The mass migration from Kuwait and the Gulf represented a 10 percent growth in Jordan's population, increasing it to approximately 3.8 million. While the immediate consequences of the mass arrival were negative and disruptive, some longer-term benefits with great potential for the national economy became apparent within the first two years. Two factors played a major role in the positive economic impact: First, the majority of returnees were well-educated and skilled professionals who immediately entered the labor market; secondly, the migration was accompanied by a large influx of capital (estimated at some US$1.5 billion – Central Bank of Jordan in 1992). The economic behavior of the returnees and the manner of their social integration could tell us much about what to expect in the territories. In all these three cases, external assistance was a positive factor in integration. In comparison, the expulsion of 800,000 Yemenis from the Gulf states in the late 1990s, with no external assistance, showed a negative impact on the society of origin.

We can also draw lessons from the Israeli experience. Israel had a high rate of investment during the peak period of migration. Between 1950 and 1955, the investment rate was 13 percent, and during the waves of Soviet Jewish migration between 1988 and 1992 the rate reached 13.6 percent (Naqib 2003: 45).

Conclusion

Finally, I would conclude that the lessons from the international refugee regime and from different return migration experiences indicate not only the likely volume of repatriated refugees but also the pattern of this return migration.

The political, social, economic, and institutional dimensions of return migration vary from case to case, according to the timespan of exile and the nature of the political conflict. In spite of this diversity, there are always themes repeating: the return of refugees does not mean the return of the whole refugee community; in almost all cases the conflict cannot be settled without resolving the refugee component; the return of refugees is not necessarily an economic burden for the place of origin; return is not necessarily a permanent movement but it is part of a transnational movement in which returnees maintain social, economic, and political ties to their previous host country; the "homeland" is no longer a concept which refers exclusively to the place of origin. This last issue especially needs more attention.

The return of refugees, as many experiences have demonstrated, is a new migration. Thus it is by definition a complex process of economic, social, and cultural adaptation and integration with the new conditions of the place of origin while keeping some ties with the previous place. This is especially so when refugee status has been protracted. Rural people have become urban, and women are empowered in many receiving countries, much more than their sisters who stay in some Southern countries. The lesson to be learned for the Palestinian case is that one should partially disconnect the question of the right of return from the sociology of return.

Notes

1 A refugee was defined as a person who, "owing to a well-founded fear of being persecuted for reasons of race, religion, nationality, membership of a particular social group or political opinion, is outside the country of his nationality and is unable or, owing to such fear, is unwilling to avail himself of the protection of that country."

2 Rogge refers to Norwood (1969), who demonstrated this argument with his exhaustive treatise on religious refugees in history. He refers also to Simpson (1939) with his review of Europe's refugees during the inter-war years, and Proudfoot (1956) and Vernant (1953) with their examinations of the population displacements brought about by World War II (Rogge 1994: 21).

3 The contemporary discourse on immigration, which makes of the asylum seeker an "outsider inside," is based on the sovereign myth and its body politic that conceives of the state as a container, as a "body endangered by migrants" who "penetrate" its borders (Bigo 2002: 68–9).

4 In other cases repatriation did not become central, e.g. Nicaragua, Mozambique, Lebanon, and Guatemala.

5 The CRPC completed its work in 2004.

6 In fact, land restitution is important even if the refugees and displaced persons did not wish to return to their homes of origin. In this case they "were able to repossess their property and then place the property on the open market for sale or exchange. In the end this procedure provided refugees and displaced persons with more money than they might have received from a state or international compensation process and it proved to be a less complicated and more efficient process. With dividends from the sale of their properties, refugees and displaced were able to build or purchase a new home and start a business elsewhere" (BADIL 2003).

7 In September 2001, the Tribunal completed the resolution of all 9918 claims it had received. Information about the Tribunal, including some sample decisions, can be found at www.crt-ii.org/_crt-i/

8 Regarding the relaxed standard of proof, Article 22 of the Tribunal's Rules of Procedure:

"The claimant must show that it is plausible in light of all the circumstances that he or she is entitled, in whole or in part, to the dormant account. The Sole Arbitrators or the Claims Panels shall assess all information submitted by the parties or otherwise available to them. They shall at all times bear in mind the difficulties of proving a claim after the destruction of the Second World War and the Holocaust and the long time that has lapsed since the opening of these dormant accounts.

"A finding of plausibility requires, inter alia, that all documents and other information have been submitted by the claimant regarding the relationship between the claimant and the published account holder that can reasonably be expected to be produced in view of the particular circumstances, including, without limitation, the history of the claimant's family and whether or not the published account holder was a victim of Nazi persecution; and that no reasonable basis exists to conclude that fraud or forgery affect the claim or evidence submitted; or that other persons may have an identical or better claim to the dormant account."

9 The claims resolution process is still ongoing and further information can be found at www.crt-ii.org. Source: interview with IOM officers.

10 Article 17 elaborates on the standard of plausibility and the source of information:

"1. Standard of Plausibility

"Each Claimant shall demonstrate that it is plausible in light of all the circumstances that he or she is entitled, in whole or in part, to the claimed Account.

"2. Sources of Information for Determinations

"In making determinations on Admissibility and Awards, the CRT shall use, to the maximum extent possible, the records and files available under Articles 3–6, the information submitted by the Claimant, and, to the extent that the CRT deems relevant, other sources of information. Other sources of information may include, but are not limited to, records of the Austrian State Archives and archives of other government records of the New York State Holocaust Claims Processing Office, reports of the Independent Commission of Experts Switzerland – Second World War (the 'Bergier Commission'), and any other historical and factual material available to the CRT. The CRT shall at all times bear in mind the difficulties of proving a claim after the destruction of the Second World War and the Holocaust and the long period of time that has elapsed since the opening of the Accounts." Source: IOM.

11 For example, the fund for compensation of Jewish property in Eastern Europe has a list of account holders from Jewish organizations. In the case of one doctor, residing in Vienna, someone claimed that the doctor was his uncle; he attempted to prove the relationship by some information about him but he did not have any written evidence. IOM accepted this narration as it was linked to documentary evidence (the list of account holders). In the same vein, if someone tells IOM that his uncle was not able to practice his profession as a doctor in the Nazi era, IOM can crosscheck this claim with the law in the area where he used to live.

12 Bosnia-Herzegovina, with a population of 4.3 million, was one of six republics of the former Federal State of Yugoslavia. Following the collapse of the communist system in Eastern Europe, Yugoslavia disintegrated and war broke out between the ethnically mixed populations of Bosnia-Herzegovina. Serbian support for minority Serbs in Bosnia-Herzegovina led to the expulsion of Muslim and Croat Bosnians from those areas. There was also conflict between Muslim and Croat forces. By 1992, 95 per cent of Muslim and Croats in eastern Bosnia and Herzegovina had fled their homes and over 2.2 million people became displaced or refugees.

13 UNHCR was criticized for acquiescing in the coerced return of refugees to

Rwanda in 1996, a violation of the duty under international law not to return a refugee to a place where s/he might experience persecution (Helton 2002: 22).

14 In late 1978, some 200,000 Burmese Muslims, who had earlier fled to Bangladesh averring persecution by Burmese authorities, began to return to Burma. This repatriation took place a little over a year following the refugees' arrival. Only after protracted negotiations between the two governments (Bangladesh and Burma) did Burma finally concede to a repatriation plan. However, when the plan was implemented there was near total resistance among the refugees against returning (Rogge 1994: 23).

15 Barbara Harrell-Bond (1989) and Fabienne De Le Houérou (forthcoming).

16 In 2001, Afghani refugees were given around US$50 per family for repatriation (Helton 2002: 182).

17 In 1978, a sample survey conducted by Khader and Badran in Jordan found that about half of the remittances from Jordanian workers in Kuwait were channeled towards investment purposes, including 20.5 percent to education alone (Khader and Badran 1987: 41; cited by Husseini 2000).

18 See for example the European Union report, commissioned in 1999, Prospects for Absorption of Returning Refugees in the West Bank and the Gaza Strip, the Institute of International Economic Relations (Tsardanis and Huliaras 1999).

References

Agamben, Giorgio (1997) "We refugees", available online at http://www.egs.edu/faculty/agamben/agamben-we-refugees.html

BADIL Resource Center (2003) "Refugee return and real property restitution in Bosnia-Herzegovina – Lessons learned for the Palestinian case", Press release, 28 January, available online at www.badil.org

Barkan, Elazar (2004) "Repatriating refugees and crossing the ethnic divide: A comparative perspective. Refugee repatriation". Presented to the International Conference on Process, Patterns and Mode of Transnationality. A Comparative Perspective, Palestinian Diaspora and Refugee Center, Shaml (Ramallah, Palestine) and International Migration, Spaces and Societies, Migrinter (Poitiers, France), 6–7 March.

Bigo, D. (2002) "Security and immigration: Toward a critique of the governmentality of unease", *Alternatives: Global, Local, Political* 27 (1), pp. 63–92.

Dumper, Michael (forthcoming) "Comparative perspectives on the repatriation and resettlement of Palestinian refugees: The cases of Guatemala, Bosnia and Afghanistan", in E. Benvenisti, Ch. Gans and S. Hanafi (eds.), *Israel and the Palestinian refugees* (Heidelberg: Max Planck Institute for Comparative Public and International Law), pp. 1–22.

Fergany, Nader (1988) *Sa'yan wara' al rizq. Dirasa maydaniyya 'an hijret al masriyyin ll'amal fi al aqtar al arabiyya (Striving for subsistence)* (Beirut: Centre d'études de l'unité arabe).

Hanafi, Sari (2001) *Hona wa honaq: nahwa tahlil lil 'alaqa bin al-shatat al-falastini wa al markaz (Here and there: Towards an analysis of the relationship between the Palestinian diaspora and the center)* (Ramallah: Muwatin, Jerusalem: Institute of Jerusalem Studies) (in Arabic).

Harrell-Bond, Barbara (1989) "Repatriation: Under what conditions is it the most desirable solution for refugees? An agenda for research", *African Studies Review* 32 (1), pp. 23–44.

Helton, Arthur (2002) *The price of indifference. Refugees and humanitarian action in the new century* (Oxford: Oxford University Press).

Helton, Arthur (forthcoming) "End of Exile: Practical Solutions to the Palestinian

Refugee Question", in E. Benvenisti, Ch. Gans and S. Hanafi (eds.), *Israel and the Palestinian refugees* (Heidelberg: Max Planck Institute for Comparative Public and International Law).

Husseini, J. (2000) "Current socioeconomic status of the West Bank camp refugees". Paper presented to Shaml Workshop "Palestinian Return Migration: Socio-economic and Cultural Approaches", Ramallah, 2–4 March.

Khader, B., and Badran, A. (1987) *The economic development of Jordan* (London: Croom Helm).

Le Houerou, Fabienne (2006) *Living with your neighbour: Otherness and proximity between outsiders and the possessed. Forced migrants in Egypt and the Sudan* (Cairo: AUC).

Malkki, L. (1995) *Purity and exile: Violence, memory and national cosmology among Hutu refugees in Tanzania* (Chicago: University of Chicago Press).

Naqib, Fadl (2003) "Absorption of the Palestinian refugees: Economic aspect". Unpublished paper (Ramallah: PRC).

Rogge J. R. (1994) "Repatriation of refugees", in T. Allen and H. Morsink (eds.), *When refugees go home: African experiences* (London: UNRISD James Currey), pp. 2–34.

Saad al Din, Ibrahim, and Fadil, Mahmud Abdel (1983) *Intiqal al 'amalah al 'arabiyya (The movement of Arab labor)* (Beirut: Center of Arab Unity Studies).

Sayigh, Rosemary (1977) "Sources of Palestinian nationalism: A study of a Palestinian camp in Lebanon", *Journal of Palestinian Studies* 6 (4), pp. 29–43.

Tamari, Salim (2005) "Palestinian refugee property claims: Compensation and restitution", in Ann Lesch and Ian Lustick (eds.), *Exile & return. Predicaments of Palestinians and Jews* (Philadelphia: University of Pennsylvania Press), pp. 246–60.

Tsardanidis, Charalambos, and Huliaras, Asteris (1999) "Prospects for absorption of returning refugees in the West Bank and the Gaza Strip". Institute of International Economic Relations, unpublished report. December.

UNHCR (2000) *The state of the world's refugees: Fifty years of humanitarian action* (Oxford: Oxford University Press).

UNCHR (2004) *UNHCR Global Report 2004* (Geneva: UNCHR).

UNCHR (2003) *UNHCR Global Report 2003* (Geneva: UNCHR).

Van Hear, Nicholas (1997) *New diasporas: The mass exodus, dispersal and regrouping of migrant communities* (London: University College London Press).

Warner, Daniel (1994) "Voluntary repatriation and the meaning of returning home: A critique of liberal mathematics", *Journal of Refugee Studies* 7 (2/3), pp. 160–74.

Zureik, Elia (1997) "The trek back home: Palestinians returning home and their problem of adaptation", in Are Hovdenak et al. *Constructing order: Palestinian adaptation to refugee life* (Jerusalem: FAFO, Institute for Applied Social Science), pp. 189–221.

14 Global perspectives on Palestinian refugee repatriation

Michael Dumper

Having examined some of the broader themes in Part I and delved into a range of case studies in Part II, where does this leave our discussion on the relevance of international practice to the Palestinian context? This final chapter will draw together both the insights derived from the bird's-eye view and the more microscopic perspective. There will be four parts. The first part summarises Part I and attempts to place the study of Palestinian refugee repatriation programme in its context. The second will examine some of the challenges posed by comparative study and policy transfer. The third will focus on the main issues that can be derived from the case studies. The final section will attempt to apply them to the Palestinian case and draw up a 'toolbox' for the design of a repatriation programme.

Contextualising the study of Palestinian refugee repatriation

The study of repatriation programmes has been until recently a neglected element in refugee studies, largely because of a focus on other stages in the refugee 'cycle' of expulsion/exile/return. In this volume, Black has identified the existing studies as having two main characteristics: first, being dominated by policy-orientated studies; and second, a tendency towards exceptionalism in that there has been less interest in comparative or interdisciplinary studies and more of a focus on the refugee experience in isolation from its broader context.

In addition, another important context was identified by Fagen, who high-lighted the fact that the current debate on repatriation comes at the end of an evolutionary cycle in UNHCR thinking which posited repatriation as a good in itself. As a result of the experience of repatriation programmes in the early 1990s, by the end of the decade and in the early 2000s the discussion considered whether there should be less of an emphasis on a return to the place of origin and more on a homeland. This was not just a result of political difficulties involved in the eviction of secondary occupants or in the re-creation of demographic mixes of the *status quo ante*. It was also a realisation that in many cases exiles brought with them new skills and had acquired social and economic networks and aspirations which made a return to the place of origin both unfeasible and unwelcome to them. The longer the exile, the more this might be the case. As Hammond has written elsewhere, the refugee is not simply 'matter out of place' and thus being put 'back into place' by repatriation. Indeed, given the often changed environment and political and social conditions in the country of origin, repatriation is 'more of a new beginning than a return to the past' (Hammond 1999: 229).

Nevertheless, both Fagen and Black contend that, despite the refinement in how repatriation may be defined in the international community, the post September 11 period has brought renewed emphasis on security. In this context repatriation will remain the preferred option for the international community. Fagen has also highlighted that research into the long-term impact of repatriation on the host community, on the country of origin and on the refugees themselves is still in its early stages and academics and policy researchers have yet to come to a firm conclusion as to its relative costs and benefits. One factor which is clear, however, is that the whole process from planning to execution to consolidation takes a great deal of time, possibly up to a decade.

Brynen and Klein have supplied the regional and political contours in which the debate over repatriation has occurred in the Arab–Israeli conflict. Brynen draws attention to the fact that it was not until the late 1990s that significant resources were devoted by the Palestinian Administration and NGOs to the details of repatriation and the economic, social and political challenges of absorbing returning refugees. Hitherto, the focus had been on political rights, principles and institutional mechanisms that would be acceptable to both Israel and the host countries. Largely as a result of external prompting, from the World Bank, the EU and the Canadian government, the PA Ministry of Planning began to draw up possible scenarios for camp rehabilitation, new housing and economic measures to ease the absorption of large numbers of returned refugees. Much of this work has been shelved in the early 2000s because of more pressing demands on its time as a result of the second *intifada* and the Israeli re-occupation of the West Bank. Klein outlined the shifting terms of the debate in the negotiations between Israel and the Palestinians. Through his analysis of the informal negotiations, or track two diplomacy, one can see that, while extremely limited, the room for manoeuvre is broader than one might expect if one merely accepted the formal positions of each party.

A final context was not part of any of the chapters, but came up frequently in the workshop discussion and in the dissemination tour. This was the changing nature of popular responses to the idea of repatriation and return. On the Palestinian side, the prospect of the PLO offering compromises to the Israelis which undercut the right of return and refugee choice precipitated the formation of popular committees for 'the Defence of the Right of Return' and a global coalition of such groups encompassing the Middle East, Europe and North America. To some extent one can draw some parallels here with the Guatemala case where Guatemalan refugees, dismayed at the content of the agreements being drawn up between the Mexico, Guatemala and UNHCR in 1987, formed the 'Permanent Commissions' to articulate their interests in any repatriation programme and rejected the existing agreement. It is premature to make any conclusions about the lasting impact of the Palestinian Right of Return groups but there is no doubt that since the Camp David summit in 2000, they have galvanised resistance to the growing orthodoxy that Palestinian repatriation would be solely to the OPTs and acted as a brake on Palestinian concessions in this regard.

For Israelis, the second *intifada* in the OPTs, and the support it received from Palestinians with Israeli nationality and the pattern of suicide missions carried out by Palestinian resistance groups, has meant that the absorption of Palestinian refugees inside Israel, even if dressed up as family re-unification, has completely dropped off the agenda. Instead, apart from a small minority (such as Zochrot and Bat Shalom), the majority of the Israeli 'peace camp' has joined with the mainstream in its support for further separation between Israelis and Palestinians through the unilateral Israeli withdrawal from the Gaza Strip and the construction of the wall down the West Bank.

Before we turn to the main themes and principles that can be drawn from the case studies, at this point it is important for the reader to be made aware of some of the methodological problems in making comparisons and embarking upon policy transfer. The process is more complex than it might first appear and scholars have had to tread carefully to avoid erroneous assumptions and faulty lesson drawing exercises. We therefore need to clarify what is meant by making comparisons, drawing lessons and policy transfer.

Is it possible to make effective comparisons and policy transfers?

There are four main benefits to be derived from undertaking a comparative study. First, it contextualises the description of political phenomena in a given country or case study. By studying a number of similar cases scholars can both avoid an ethnocentric bias and place events and patterns within a broader perspective. The study of democracy, for example, is enriched when one examines its variety across time and place and one is therefore able to distinguish what are the essential elements of democracy from cultural accretions. Second, comparison allows a degree of classification in which separate cases can be grouped together and characterised. For example, by studying revolutionary activity across the world one learns that to some extent it is associated with a specific social and economic base. The main actors can be tenant farmers or sharecroppers, urban or rural etc., and this allows some classification of types of revolutionary activity. This process both simplifies discussion and encourages a focus on distinctive features that can be held in common.

Third, once cases have been contextualised and classified, comparative scholars are able to look for explanatory factors by a process of hypothesis-testing. Why has such an activity or pattern existed and what are the main reasons? By this process, relationships between variables (key actors, environmental conditions, socio-economic groupings etc.) can be suggested and demonstrated. For example, the hypothesis that voter participation in a democratic political system increases in countries of high per capita GNP can be tested in groups of culturally mixed countries with different levels of per capita GNP. Finally, an important objective in comparative studies is the ability to make predictions based upon the generalisations constructed and observed. Correlations can be extrapolated from certain proven patterns and sequences. If, for example, one has demonstrated the hypothesis that peace is only possible between democracies, the longevity of certain peace agreements can be predicted according to the extent to which two countries can be classed as democratic. In this way, conducting a comparative study of refugee repatriation programmes along the above lines, it should be possible to predict the extent to which a particular programme is likely to achieve certain objectives. Some repatriation programmes will have the same key actors or socio-economic groupings. It may be possible to extrapolate from this to predict the success or durability of others.

Nevertheless, problems with the comparative method still remain. How does one compare situations so diverse as forced migrations and repatriations, which have such disparate features or are so stretched out over time or involve a very large number of variables? Post-conflict repatriation programmes come in many different forms and have such different rates of completion, target groups, economic and environmental conditions and political and legal frameworks that comparisons can be contrived and artificial. Comparisons seem initially terribly unlikely and fruitless. Scholars who have used the comparative method have identified a number of such shortcomings that need to be taken into account.

One major shortcoming is the danger of extrapolating from a restricted number of cases. This is known as the inferential problem. Most scholars do not have the time and resources to study more than a handful of cases. This severely hampers their ability to identify general trends and makes inference from a small number of cases possibly misleading. Another problem is the extent to which it is possible to use the same term in different political, religious and cultural contexts. For example, the description 'class' may not mean the same in a society where family or religious bonds form the basis of an economic unit. A further problem is known as intentionality. In essence this means that many scholars succumb to bias in the choice of case studies in order to strengthen their argument. There is a danger that one selects those cases that bear out one's hypothesis. A final acknowledged shortcoming of the comparative method is the possibility of drift in the levels of analysis, whereby a study based on one level is used to draw comparisons with a study based upon another level. For example, comparing the range of assistance packages in one group of repatriation programmes does not indicate the nature of a compensation agreement. They are different levels of analysis.

It is also important in our discussion to examine terms such as 'lessons drawn' and 'policy transfer'. The notion of lessons drawn and policy transfer has received increasing attention over the past decade, particularly in the sub-field of public administration. This is largely due to technological change that has allowed greater interactions between the policy-making community. However, just as the comparative approach can be problematic, the very notion of lessons drawn and policy transfer is not free of some debate.[1] This becomes apparent once one starts to define the basic terms: what exactly is lesson drawing and policy transfer? Indeed, how does it differ from other forms of policy-making? Surely all policy-making incorporates some element of lesson drawing through evaluations and *post facto* assessments.

Lesson drawing can be neatly summarised as a cause and effect description of a set of actions that an agency, government or supranational body can evaluate to see if they are applicable to another situation. However to draw out its full meaning five different types of lesson drawing have been identified:

- Copying – which is implementing a programme more or less intact.
- Adjusting – where a programme is adopted but adapted for contextual differences.
- Hybridization – in which elements from two different programmes are combined to create a new one.
- Synthesis – where elements from several different programmes are combined to create a new one.
- Inspiration – where a programme provides the intellectual stimulus to develop a new one (Rose 1993: 27).

For the purposes of this discussion and in the light of the points about the uniqueness of the Palestinian case made in the first section of this book, it would seem that it is the last four types of lesson drawing we should largely concern ourselves with.

In turning to a definition of policy transfer, a leading social scientist in public administration has defined it as 'the process by which knowledge of policies, administrative arrangements, institutions and ideas in one political system (past or present) is used in the development of policies, administrative arrangements, institutions and ideas in another political system' (Dolowitz 2000: 3). Dolowitz proceeds to identify two kinds of policy transfer. The first is voluntary adoption, under which he subsumes the process of lesson drawing. Examples of this kind of policy transfer would be the adoption by the UK government of some elements of the welfare-to-work programme in the US, and the adoption by the Spanish government of elements of the German constitution relating to the role of the President. The second kind of policy transfer is coercive transfer, where a government or a supranational body encourages or forces the adoption of a set of policies, such as the structural adjustment programmes imposed on less developed countries by the International Monetary Fund.

Lesson drawing and policy transfer are not always the same process. Lesson drawing is generally a voluntary process and to a large extent is an integral part of policy-making. Indeed some scholars have criticised its isolation from the general field as a separate process in policy-making as misleading and inflating its importance above other elements of the policy-making process (James and Lodge 2003: 184-7). Nevertheless, scholars have tried to identify occasions when the processes are most likely to occur. For example, Rose has suggested seven possible situations where the likelihood of a lessons drawn process is effective (Rose 1993: 118–42):

- the less unique or specific a programme;
- the closer in function and structure of the relevant institutions;
- the greater the equivalence in the availability in resources;
- the simpler the cause and effect structure of the programme;
- the smaller the scale of change attempted;
- the greater the links in jurisdiction between programmes;
- the greater the congruity between programme values and policy-makers.

What is more difficult to measure is the degree of success there is in the transfer of policy. As a result it has been much easier to identify failures. Dolowitz and Marsh have suggested there are three types of failure in policy transfer. The first is 'uninformed transfer'. Here the borrowing country has insufficient information about the policy that is being transferred, with the result that the policy is imperfectly implemented. The second type is known as 'incomplete transfer', where crucial elements of a policy or programme that made the policy or programme a success are not transferred. The final type is 'inappropriate transfer', where insufficient consideration has been given to the social, economic, political and ideological differences between the borrowings and the transferring country, leading to programme failure (Dolowitz and Marsh 2000: 17).

From this brief discussion of the methodological issues one can see that the comparative study of refugee repatriation programmes is not a straightforward exercise. There are methodological problems that can lead to inaccurate hypotheses and conclusions. In addition there are different elements to the lesson drawing process and different types of policy transfer. The diversity and complexity of the case studies to be considered make lesson drawing and policy transfer for the Palestinian case a hazardous undertaking and should be handled with care. Nevertheless, despite the evolution of the Palestinian refugee situation outside the framework of UNHCR, there are many essential elements which can be instructive. In the Palestinian case, lesson drawing and policy transfer is certainly not a question of 'copying' but much more a question of 'inspiration' and 'synthesis'.

Themes drawn from the case studies

We now turn to the main themes that can be drawn from the case studies and from the discussion that occurred in the workshop. These are grouped under five main headings: international involvement, refugee participation, local and regional structures, justice and reconciliation, and alternatives to repatriation.

International involvement

Most refugee returns, certainly since the 1990s, are preceded by a bilateral agreement which is supported by supplementary trilateral agreements, either with UNHCR or a regional body, backed up by guarantees from key international players. Such agreements comprise specific provisions for a repatriation programme. The international community has a role in ensuring that the degree of protection and security in the country of origin is as good as or greater than that in the host country. International safeguards, therefore, need to be translated into the rule of law. An important element in these agreements has been the establishment of a funding mechanism to finance the repatriation programme. Good examples of this pattern are the Cambodian, East Timorese, Guatemalan and Bosnian cases.

The extent to which this is recognised can be seen in the UNHCR Handbook *Voluntary Repatriation: International Protection*, where detailed sections suggest the contents of clauses to be included in any peace agreement including the repatriation of refugees (UNHCR 1996). A brief reading of the handbook illustrates the extent to which the collective expertise of this agency has been pooled and systematised. Chapter 3, for example, entitled 'UNHCR's Role in Voluntary Repatriation Operations', has sections on the importance of compiling a profile of the refugee community and of the country of origin, of being prepared for organised and spontaneous repatriations, of cross-border and cross agency communication and of the elements that need to be incorporated in repatriation agreements (ibid.: 15–40). In other chapters, there are also detailed guidelines on interviewing, registration, computerisation, monitoring, dealing with landmines and dealing with unaccompanied children. The annexes include sample documents on tripartite agreements, travel documents, amnesty declarations and a reproduction of the People-Orientated Planning framework for refugee repatriation. Finally, Annex 1 is a checklist for voluntary repatriation operations divided into three sections: Preparatory and Promotional Activity, Activities in Pre-Departure Phase and Activities in the Movement and Post-Arrival Phase; which are in turn divided into sub-sections of Country of Asylum and Country of Origin (ibid.: A1–A10).

In sum, despite the fact that this document will have been superseded by a number of subsequent evaluations, despite the fact that the regional bureaux of UNHCR will have developed working practices which do not fit into the global schematic presentation offered by the Handbook, and despite the fact that many UNHCR employees and practitioners probably have not read it, the Handbook nevertheless provides a comprehensive survey of the main issues and a useful reference point of the 'lessons drawn' by UNHCR.

In terms of peace agreements the Handbook strongly recommends the formation of a 'tripartite commission' composed of the country of origin, country of asylum and UNHCR (or another lead agency), and the participation of refugees in the formulation of a repatriation programme. The experience of UNHCR is that Tripartite Commissions are

> a good way to build confidence, resolve differences, and secure a level of agreement and commitment to the basic principles of voluntary repatriation. Such commissions and their technical ad hoc or sub-committees also have a role to play concerning the practical aspects of planning, implementing and monitoring voluntary repatriation operations.
>
> (ibid.: 33)

The essential point to recognise in this discussion, then, is that repatriation is not an 'add-on' which is subsidiary to a political agreement between the two protagonists, but an integral part of the agreement which brings with it close international involvement.

Nevertheless, despite the role played by the international community in bringing about an agreement which also addresses the issue of refugee repatriation, what the analysis of the contributors to this book has been able to draw out is that such international involvement is often inadequate and temporary. This has resulted in the poor implementation of the programme causing distress to the returnees and host population alike. It has also resulted in the lack of durability and sustainability of the programme and led to tensions which contain the seeds of further conflict. In order to be effective, the analysis has concluded that international involvement needs to extend beyond both the agreement phase and the programme planning and implementation phase. It needs to extend to broader development assistance that encompasses the transition from repatriation to integration. This has been recognised by UNHCR with its development of the concept of the 4Rs – repatriation, reintegration, rehabilitation, reconstruction.

Yet, as Fagen, and McDowell and Van Hear pointed out in their chapters, implementing such an awareness is often constrained by budgetary issues and the propensity for devising neo-liberal assistance programmes. Donors, UN agencies and other international NGOs (INGOs) have funding and accountability processes which do not allow for flexible and organic development of programmes. For example, a programme is designated by the donor community as either emergency assistance or development assistance and it is funded and subjected to different evaluation and accountability processes. Cross subsidisation is controversial and rare and often stymied by bureaucratic rivalries. In the same way, programmes are devised to accommodate ideological preferences of the funders and not always the needs and cultural norms of the recipients. For example, the broad consensus in the donor community and INGOs is to emphasise and encourage the creation of a civil society. This necessarily undermines the traditional patriarchal/clan structures prevalent in many refugee communities, but it also has the unintended consequence of further deracination. In a refugee context this may exacerbate many of the social and political tensions arising from exile and causes new problems unrelated to the exile or displacement.

At this point it is important to identify the role of regional neighbours in a repatriation programme. Neighbouring countries may have played many roles during the conflict and period of exile both as being on the receiving end of violence and bloodshed but also as host to a large number of refugees leading them to be dragged into a conflict they may not have had much interest in. The roles of Pakistan, Thailand, Mexico, Kenya etc. in the neighbouring conflicts are all examples of this. In addition, neighbouring countries have an interest in the final settlement and its implications for them in terms of the stability of the regime, the future of the refugees they are hosting and their role as transit country. A regional framework which allows for consultation and input in the planned repatriation therefore is a crucial element in the viability of a repatriation programme. Their support is crucial and their lack of cooperation could sabotage an agreed programme.

A further aspect of international involvement that the contributors of this book have highlighted is the role of a lead agency. UNHCR experience and practice, and the analysis of this book, is that the allocation of the role of lead agency to a single institution is essential in a repatriation programme. The alternative is much duplication, a diffusion of objectives, competition over funds, inter-agency rivalries and turf wars leading to a confused response to refugee and development needs. In addition, as Marsden's work on Afghanistan has illustrated, there is some evidence to suggest that the use of historical actors in a given context avoids much time-wastage as new agencies devote effort and resources to establishing themselves.

A multi-agency approach has its defenders who argue that the involvement of many actors is useful in mobilising international opinion and solidarities. It also avoids the dangers of a narrow range of ideological approaches being applied to the repatriation. However, to a large extent these advantages can be incorporated into the lead agency approach. The nomination of a lead agency has not in general led to a monolithic single-agency operation. Rather the lead agency involves a range of actors with different expertise and its role is that of overall direction, relations with state actors and coordination. Furthermore, an important element in a repatriation programme is to ensure that the refugee protection responsibilities of the international community are implemented. This can be more closely monitored and implemented if a single agency has a clear mandate and can be held accountable in what is usually a very confused transition period in terms of state-building and re-integration. Thus international involvement may be an essential component in a repatriation scheme. It offers political guarantees and a measure of enforcement, financial support and funding mechanisms and possibilities for enhanced cooperation and coordination. However, it has to be acknowledged that it comes with structural limitations and ideological conditions.

Refugee participation and capacity generation

There appear to be three main aspects to this theme. The first concerns the nature of the choices available to refugees: to what extent are they real choices and to what extent are they merely choices within a pre-agreed set of parameters, parameters often set by international and regional actors? Clearly, as Kagan has explored, there is a debate within the UN and other refugee agencies as to the content of its concept of *non-refoulement* and the voluntariness of repatriation. As we will see in the next sub-section, the entry of refugees into the regional labour market also produces cases where refugees are reluctant to return even if it is politically possible, due to the paucity of economic opportunities in their country of origin. The underlying issue here is the transparency in which support for refugee return is geared towards certain political outcomes and choices.

The second aspect concerns the mechanisms for refugee involvement in constructing a repatriation programme. As Rodicio and Stepputat have shown, although most large-scale returns are centrally organised by UNHCR and IOM, a sense of ownership in the process or a 'bottom-up' approach is an important element in ensuring a repatriation programme is acceptable and willingly participated in by refugees. Similarly, both Black and Stepputat argued that accurate and up-to-date information is also essential in providing refugees with informed choices about conditions and option in the country of origin and countering the pattern of 'imagined return communities' based on folklore and oral tradition. The case studies in this book and UNHCR experience point to the role that informed choices have in creating opportunities for refugees to be actors rather than recipients in a planned return process.

For example, the UNHCR Handbook clearly stresses the importance of including refugee voices in the formulation of a repatriation programme.

> The refugee community should be kept informed of the progress of repatriation negotiations. Formal representation of the refugee community can be considered. Whenever the refugee community is not directly involved in repatriation negotiations, UNHCR must develop and maintain regular communications with the refugees throughout the process.
>
> (UNHCR 1996: 34)

Thus, the formal and active participation of refugees in planning the logistics of return and integration is regarded as a prerequisite of a durable repatriation programme.

In this connection, the role of the leadership of refugee communities is crucial and can have both a positive and a negative impact. While refugee participation is contingent upon an articulate and organised refugee leadership, which indeed is crucial in mobilising refugee participation, there can also be a tendency for that leadership to be cautious over any changes, such as a repatriation programme, which might lead to a loss of authority and influence. Thus it is important to construct channels of communication which do not result in a repatriation programme that is dominated by political actors but which at the same time elicit the endorsement and support of the leadership.

A third aspect which makes refugee participation an essential part of a repatriation programme is the development of human resources and capacity generation. This is important to provide refugees with the necessary employment and organisational skills for a return. Their repatriation to the place or country of origin can be designed to fit the requirements and possibilities of those places, which themselves may have undergone transformation since the moment of exile, and lead to a more durable programme. UNHCR experience also indicates that it is essential to introduce gender and age perspectives into repatriation programme at an early stage of planning. The involvement of women and other categories of the population in formulating the options and the logistics of return is critical in ensuring that programmes are durable. For example, the provision of assistance packages for the head of household and the delivery of skills training may be constructed in a way that the main recipients are mostly males of certain age. A gender and age awareness at an early stage ensures that unequal and differential access to protection, assistance and services can be addressed.

International experience suggests, therefore, that this issue of refugee participation is not just a fanciful liberal wish-list but an integral part of the effectiveness of a programme in terms of durability and the use of scarce funds. Repatriation programmes require the cooperation of their intended beneficiaries, the refugees. There is little point and a waste of resources if programmes are constructed but cannot be implemented because of their non-cooperation.

Regional and local structures

Many of the case studies in the book highlighted the fact that, dispossession and political disenfranchisement aside, the condition of exile meant that refugees become part of a transnational community establishing new political and social networks and economic exchanges (Hammond, McDowell and Van Hear, Stepputat). In many cases, refugees have entered a regional labour market with camp dwellers providing a pool of labour for the local economy and new investment in micro-finance initiatives. The loss of their land and employment as a result of displacement are exacerbated by the globalisation trends of the past decade, with the result that refugees are often part of the international labour market with its in-built migratory patterns. In these new circumstances, whatever the agreements reached by the political echelon, and however much there is an aspiration to obtain political rights in their country of origin, refugees are less likely to return unless there is a possibility of employment or some form of productive activity in the country of origin. In many cases, refugees have achieved a higher standard of living in exile and have adopted a range of identities as they dip in and out of the economies of the region, the host countries and the country of origin, looking for the most advantageous positions for themselves and their families. In essence, post agreement repatriation programmes need to reflect that refugees wish to regularise their status in the country of origin but not at the expense of sacrificing their freedom of movement in the region. Thus a degree of flexibility is essential for the package to be acceptable.

A second structural issue concerns the phenomenon of what is known in the literature as 'exilic bias'. Clearly the goal of a repatriation programme is the successful reintegration of the returned refugees in their country of origin. Repatriation packages, therefore, normally comprise a mixture of finance, tools, building materials, land grants and support services to assist the returned refugees in establishing new homes and livelihoods. However, repatriation packages, developmental assistance and compensation which are targeted exclusively to returned refugees have been shown to cause both resentment by the host communities and to some extent dependency by returned refugees. The case studies in this book and UN experience show that a 'holistic' development approach which benefits the broader community in which the refugees are being settled, is known to assist integration and to be a more effective and durable approach. Thus a repatriation programme needs to be incorporated into a national programme of development and community assistance.

In this connection, the case studies also indicate that the largest burden of a return process falls on the local and municipal administrative structures in the country of origin. Many local governments and municipal authorities are not equipped to deal with either the numbers of returned refugees or the articulation of their demands by representatives who are often politically sophisticated in relation to their host compatriots. In addition, a large repatriation programme supported by the international community brings with it the demands of the donor community for transparency and accountability and the introduction of new administrative procedures. As Stepputat argues, a return process, therefore, needs to include the upgrade of personnel skills, administrative capacity and infrastructure particularly of the local and municipal authorities.

Justice and reconciliation

The return process is in most cases also a political process of integration by the returned refugees into the political system of the country of origin. A balance has to be achieved between the imperatives of accountability and those of coexistence and reconciliation. The conflict that caused the displacement initially is often deeply rooted in ethnicity, regionalism, religion or class and the displacement itself will have caused deeper suffering and pain. Refugees are unlikely to return if those who caused their displacement are still in power or continue to be able to act in ways unconstrained by the rule of law. A significant 'pull' factor for refugees is evidence of protection for their civil and political rights and of a legitimate political process for resolving differences.

There is a growing body of experience that indicates that, unless the causes and the trauma of both the conflict and the displacement are addressed through a conscious programme of achieving justice and reconciliation, the conflict is likely to arise once again. For this reason, repatriation programmes also require an element of political and social reconciliation (Bell 2000; Welchman 2003). The process of reconciliation often comprises two main elements: retributive justice and restorative justice. Retributive justice focuses on punishment and the bringing to justice of the perpetrators of war crimes and of crimes against humanity through the establishment of War Crimes Tribunals etc. Restorative justice focuses more on the cathartic and healing process involved in encouraging co-existence and social harmony. It can take the form of Truth Commissions, symbolic acts of apology or regret, national museums to recognise traumatic events and experiences, the erection of monuments to victims, key groups or individuals, national remembrance days and so forth.

Alternatives to repatriation

As was discussed in the first chapter and elaborated in many of the other chapters, not all refugees have elected to return to their country of origin. For some integration into the host country has been the preferred option while for others resettlement in a third country has proved to be more attractive. These are choices which should be made in an informed way and are part of the issue of refugee participation discussed above. A third alternative to repatriation has been the option of compensation. Although this book has not included any chapters on compensation, two of the papers at the workshop dealt with the compensation issue and it was a topic raised in many of the other papers and discussed in the plenary sessions.

The compensation issue is a significant sub-field which would require greater analysis and depth than this volume can offer to do it justice. However, for our purpose we should note that compensation as an option for refugees can take two forms: compensation as part of a repatriation programme, and compensation instead of a return. Compensation as part of a repatriation programme can be designed to compensate the returnees either for the loss of their homes through destruction or through its occupation and sequestration. It can be used to direct returnees to especially designated areas in their homeland but not in their place of origin, and it can be used to compensate them for other material losses and for emotional and psychological trauma.

From international practice it is clear that a number of elements are essential. Documentation of registration, of losses, land ownership and so forth has to be kept from the very early stages of the refugee cycle. This requires the involvement of international agencies such as UNHCR and the IOM. International involvement is often required in both the designation of sources of funds and the establishment of bodies to process and allocate funds. A further element in a compensation package is a mix between funds allocated to individuals and funds allocated for collective assistance. Finally, international practice has also identified the need to ensure that gender issues are factored into any compensation packages. For example, if compensation funds are allocated to heads of families, in many cases this may disadvantage women who may not benefit from such a package.

Towards a toolbox for a Palestinian repatriation programme

In the autumn of 2004, as part of my dissemination and feedback tour, I gave a presentation on the main findings of the Exeter workshop in Ramallah, at the Shaml Palestinian Refugee and Diaspora Center. That week the heavens had opened for the first time since the spring and Ramallah was engulfed by rain and mist. I was pessimistic as to the numbers who would turn up to my talk but despite the dark night and the still heavily falling rain the reception room was full. Even though Yasser Arafat had died only the week before and the fragile transition to a new era had only just begun, the audience was focused and the questions were sharp and to the point. The first was possibly the most difficult. It was posed by Khalil Nakhleh, an astute observer of the donor community and senior administrator in a number of Palestinian NGOs (Nakhleh 2003). In response to my characterisation of the objective of the workshop as the assembly of a toolbox for a Palestinian repatriation programme, he asked what was the task envisaged for the toolbox. It was all very well having the tools to put up, say, a set of curtains, but you also needed to know in which house and which room they were to be hung. Were my tools for Palestinian refugee repatriation for repatriation to Israel and their homes or 'repatriation' to a new Palestinian state in the West Bank and Gaza Strip? This quest for greater specificity pointed at a possible flaw at the heart of the project. How useful would my toolbox be if it had either the wrong tools for a task yet to be specified or everything in it bar the kitchen sink?

The answer to Nakhleh's question is that we simply do not know the outcomes of the Arab–Israeli conflict and therefore what options will be available to tackle the refugee issue. There are a range of possible scenarios and a toolbox could be suggested for each. However, the details that differentiate one scenario from another would be critical and yet at the same time pure speculation. The variables are too many, incorporating the regional balance of power, developments in the internal politics of Israel, the generosity of the donor community, the GDP of the new Palestinian state, the policies of the host countries and so on. Detailed scenario-building of this sort was beyond the scope of this project and anything less than this kind of detail would make scenario-building for purposes of assembling a toolbox profitless. *Faute de mieux*, all that is possible here is the general approach adopted by this project.

It is clear that, in the current political conditions, it is unlikely that there will be any significant repatriation in the next five years. Nevertheless, the decline of the option of resettlement in a third country, as discussed above, leaves the other two options that are open to Palestinian refugees – repatriation to an area within historic Palestine and integration into host countries – as the only two viable short- to medium-term options. In this sense repatriation is still a strategy for debate and planning. In sum, a toolbox by definition will contain both some specialist tools and some more general ones to be useful for a range of tasks. The challenge is to assemble the best mix. This sub-section will attempt to do just this by following the same themes identified above and directly relate them to the Palestinian case.

International involvement

It is clear that the involvement of the international community in a peace agreement incorporating the repatriation of Palestinian refugees is a sine qua non of any resolution to the Arab–Israeli conflict. The protagonists have too deep a history of mistrust to believe in an agreement that does not have international guarantors. The good news is that the structures for such an involvement are already largely in place. There is the group known as the Quartet, comprising the UN, US, Russia and the EU, which is attempting to follow on from the failed Oslo process with a three-stage 'road map'. There is the Refugee Working Group set up by the Madrid Peace Conference in 1991 and convened by Canada. And, more distantly, there is the Euro-Mediterranean Partnership set up by the EU in 1995. International involvement can also be seen in the support role played by the EU's Special Envoy to the Middle East Peace Process, Ambassador Miguel Moratinos, in the Taba peace talks in 2001, and the role played by the Swiss government in drawing up the unofficial Geneva Accords in 2003.

However, international involvement is no guarantee that the rights of refugees are protected or that international norms are adhered to. Indeed as Fagen, Marsden and Kagan in this volume all point out, their very involvement can lead to a dilution of refugee rights. It is significant that in both the record of the Taba talks and the Geneva Accords, there was no reference to international practice and the experience of UNHCR. Another significant omission in the Taba talks and the Geneva Accords, and only partially addressed by the Quartet-sponsored 'road map', is the lack of reference for a regional framework that includes the neighbouring and host countries. This is partly a result of Israel's refusal to negotiate on a comprehensive peace agreement, preferring to have a series of bilateral treaties. But it is also partly a result of an inability of the host countries to allow open debate on the future of Palestinian refugees and to agree amongst themselves. The Chatham House initiative, funded by the European Commission, the Canadian International Development Agency and the International Development Research Centre (Canada), in which representatives in refugee host country have met on an irregular basis on matters of mutual concern, has been one attempt to bring such issues into the public domain. However, it is likely that the involvement of more senior echelons will not take place unless powerful members of the Arab League put their weight behind it. This is unlikely in conditions of ongoing Israeli colonisation, political assassination and the construction of the separation barrier.

What international involvement has obtained is a degree of consensus for the need of another tool from the toolbox – international funding for both compensation and repatriation. Both the Taba talks and the Geneva Accords refer to an international fund to cover compensation, although only the Taba talks refer to assistance for repatriation whereas Geneva focuses on funds for development in the new Palestinian state. It is clear that the new Palestinian state will not be able to generate sufficient internal revenues to construct a new state, provide services for the current population rate of growth and simultaneously fund a large-scale repatriation programme (Exeter Refugee Study Team 2001). Even if the physical return is largely spontaneous and self-financed – the distances between camps and their former homes or new homes in the new state are not large – the provision of housing, employment, health and education services would be far beyond the capacity of the new state to provide or to wish to provide. Thus international funding, whether in the form of individual compensation payments, collective payments to be designated for Palestinian institutions responsible for the repatriation and integration of refugees, or as part of an overall development package, will be essential. Brynen in another chapter and the World Bank office in the West Bank have both outlined possible infrastructural requirements and institutional and regulatory mechanisms for the repatriation of some refugees (Brynen 2003: 15–16; World Bank 2003). These include a relocation package, grants to municipalities, housing support for low-income returning refugees, transitional budget support for health and education costs, and modest improvements in the infrastructure of the camps. They estimate that addressing the needs in this way of 500,000 returned Palestinian refugees and of the 650,000 camp residents in the OPTs would cost around US$613 million per annum or US$6.1 billion over a ten-year period. This is an amount that is likely to exceed the capacity or willingness of international donors.

It is at this point that another tool should be brought into use – a caution with respect to the reliance on external donors. As we have seen this can lead to the introduction of a neo-liberal economic agenda when this may not be appropriate. Budgetary support for repatriation and reintegration activities can be a great benefit but it may also bring costs in terms of market-driven priorities being imposed upon state activities, such as we witnessed in Iraq after the US occupation in 2003. In the Palestinian case, the prospect of alternative sources of funding may be marginally greater in that the Arab and Islamic world are likely to be important contributors. Nevertheless, a repatriation programme of any size will require huge inputs from the usual G8 countries and the EU. The task will be to ensure that any conditionality in grant and loan agreements can be challenged through diversifying both sources of support and encouraging existing networks and institutions.

The final aspect of international involvement that can be applied to the Palestinian case is the issue of a lead agency. As explained in the Introduction, a dedicated UN agency, UNRWA, has been responsible for the provision of services to Palestinian refugees. Its future is one of great debate. In terms of its mandate, UNRWA should remain responsible for refugees until they return to their 'homes', which for most refugees will be in Israel. However, following the creation of a Palestinian state, there is an assumption that its services would be gradually transferred to the respective Palestinian ministries and UNRWA would be gradually wound down. Repatriation will be undertaken by a new Palestinian ministry concerned with refugee absorption and immigration with some operational and logistical tasks being contracted out to international agencies (Exeter Refugee Studies Team 2001: 85). This is the thrust of the tentative agreements reached in the Taba talks and in the Geneva Accords. Clearly there is an issue here as to the extent that refugees will accept that they cannot return to their homes and therefore will have their needs met by the new state. It is certainly an opportunity for leverage by the international community, described in Kagan's chapter, in supporting a peace agreement which envisages repatriation to the homeland rather than the home or place of origin. Nevertheless, whatever the scenario that takes place, the experience of the international community suggests that a single agency should be responsible for the logistics, coordination and planning of a repatriation programme and to some extent the reintegration of returned refugees. Indeed, international experience points to the advantages of making use of historical actors with a track record in the area and institutional memory which can be utilised. All these factors point to a reconsidering of the assumption that UNRWA be phased out soon after an agreement. This is the 'UNRWA-plus' option referred to in the Exeter report above and in Brynen's chapter. It is clear that it is a repository of expertise, credibility and legitimacy in the refugee communities and these are valuable assets in a volatile and risky transition period.

Refugee participation and capacity generation

The three tools that can be inferred from international experience are those of transparency, refugee participation in planning repatriation activities and human resource development. In turning to transparency, international experience has shown that, although legal rights to return and restitution may be upheld in the abstract, it has not always been possible to implement them and refugees have often been obliged to settle for less. A return to the *status quo ante* is rarely possible. In this sense Palestinian refugees are fully aware that they cannot expect to be a special case, that is, to be exceptional. This awareness and the creativity in responding to such an impossibility was made very clear to me during my discussions with refugee representatives in the region following the workshop. However, what is important is that the options are transparent and made clear and that they are part of an overall package which is just and therefore acceptable. This may involve actual but limited return, symbolic acts of return and restitution, a mix of return compensation and resettlement to the new Palestinian state. What is unlikely to be acceptable is the absence of any formal recognition of the right of return.

The second aspect is that of refugee participation and creating a sense of ownership.

The fragmented nature of Palestinian refugee communities, the internal divisions along ideological grounds and the restrictions placed upon the opportunities to develop representative channels due to the Israeli occupation and security concerns, has made the articulation and inclusion of refugee voices in the planning of repatriation extremely problematic. As a result of the reaction to both the Geneva Accords and the lesser-known Ayalon–Nuseibeh initiative, where repatriation was discussed largely, although not wholly, in terms of a return to the new state of Palestine in the West Bank and Gaza Strip, there have been greater attempts at inclusion.

Provided that the overall package is seen to be relatively fair and just, channels for refugee participation need to be created. Currently representation of Palestinian refugee concerns are problematic. Existing PLO structures are weak, lack universal legitimacy and are challenged by other groups (International Crisis Group 2004: 14). Conversely, Islamic groups and the Right of Return committees are not integrated into the broader decision-making processes. While new forms of representation are being experimented with, such as by the EU-funded Civitas organisation, these are viewed with suspicion by political elites as an attempt to replace them. If one turns to international experience, one can see in the UNHCR Handbook some useful material on the role it has played in surveying and coordinating refugee concerns. In the Palestinian context and in the light of the UNRWA-plus discussion in the previous sub-section, UNRWA should be considered as a possible vehicle for such activities. A dedicated unit in UNRWA could be set up to fulfil the functions normally taken up by UNHCR in this regard. UNRWA should also, but not exclusively, be considered in the third aspect – that of providing an institutional base for training and the upgrading of skills. To some extent this is already being carried out in its Vocational Training Centres, and programmes could be reconfigured to complement employment opportunities in the places of destination. In both these cases one would need to bear in mind that not all refugees are either camp-dwellers or registered with UNRWA.

Regional and local structures

International practice has highlighted three tools or aspects that concern regional and local issues. The first is the importance of a refugee repatriation programme allowing refugees to retain a considerable degree of flexibility in mobility. As demonstrated by Stepputat and Hammond, in this volume, and Van Hear (2004), during their period of exile refugees have become economic actors in a broader regional market. This is particularly the situation in the Palestinian case with its transnational networks and their embeddedness in the local economies of the OPTs, Jordan and Syria (Hanafi 1996). The very close proximity of all the major Palestinian refugee camps to their likely destinations and the family and political networks that have developed in exile will encourage Palestinian returnees to remain part of the regional labour market. A Palestinian repatriation programme needs to be flexible enough to facilitate this status spectrum. In essence, this points to a period of transition where a refugee is permitted to retain residency status in the host country for a specified number of years while he or she is examining the employment, accommodation and other services prospects in the place of destination. Clearly such a dual status would require regional recognition and might involve the Arab League temporarily suspending clauses in its charter prohibiting dual citizenship.

Although the flexibility element is an important component of a repatriation programme based on economic 'pull' factors, it also has to be recognised that in some situations there are also 'push' factors such as those affecting the Palestinian refugees in Lebanon and possibly Egypt. Here the state has blocked formal access to the local economy and is likely to seek the earliest opportunity to assist in a repatriation programme. It is generally accepted that in a repatriation programme, because of their economic and political conditions, Palestinians from Lebanon would be accorded priority. (One also needs to recognise Jordanian fear of being regarded as a soft option for depositing Palestinian refugees (Masalha 2003: 233).) To some extent this factor gives added weight to the flexibility formula being suggested above as the flexibility implies a degree of graduation and phasing which in turn will allow attention and resources to be devoted to priority cases.

The second tool is the caution against exilic bias. This is where assistance packages and developmental assistance to the returned refugees create resentment on the part of the receiving community. In many respects, the OPTs and Israel are too small for huge regional disparities to develop (Brynen 2003). In addition family networks remain strong and cut across the refugee/non-refugee divide and will allow considerable ripple effects from targeted aid. The wider community will receive benefits from a repatriation programme Nevertheless, as Rodicio described, strong bonds develop between refugee camp-dwellers and these are exaggerated when they repatriate into a new environment. Friction between the returned Palestinian refugees and their neighbours is a very likely outcome. Despite its advantages, a holistic approach to refugee absorption is still relevant in the Palestinian case. This suggests that ideas such as re-using Israeli colonies in the OPTs with their isolation and enclave characteristics for refugee absorption should be discarded, as these will only heighten the sense of otherness that refugees may feel. Similarly, plans for new cities specifically designed for refugees need to be treated with some caution in favour of a more incremental approach through the expansion of existing cities and the infilling of suburbs (Brynen 2003: 8, 10). One should note that, if there is a possibility of refugee repatriation to homes in Israel, there will be little need for this cautionary tool. The assistance packages and developmental assistance available are unlikely to match the per capita income of an employed or welfare assisted Israeli.

The third tool identified is the importance of increasing the capacity of local and municipal structures to deal with large numbers of returned refugees. Some areas will have a greater capacity to physically absorb large numbers of refugees or to offer better services and employment opportunities than others, but they may not have the personnel to deal with refugee requirements such as information and issues over entitlements (World Bank 2003). In addition, a Palestinian repatriation programme will be heavily dependent upon external donor support. This in turn will require greater transparency in procedures and accountability. Most municipal authorities and local governments are not equipped to deal with servicing the requirements of the donor community and their skills will need upgrading. Thus, as well as basic infrastructural provision, human resource development at the lower levels of government will need resources and effort.

Justice and reconciliation

One of the striking responses I received during my discussions with refugee groups in Syria and Lebanon was the degree of emphasis placed on the issue of reconciliation. At two different meetings where I presented a summary of the main findings of the Exeter workshop with a broad section of refugee representatives ranging from Islamic to Marxist groups, this issue came up time and again. It has to be conceded that the approach was not one of mutuality. Israel was unequivocally viewed as the transgressor and an apology and reparation were regarded as due solely from the Israeli side. Indeed, reconciliation was interpreted quite broadly to encompass the entitlement to restitution as well as compensation. To some extent, therefore, the concept of reconciliation in the discourse to which I was exposed was stretched to affirm the sense of grievance of the Palestinian refugee. Nevertheless, what was completely absent in the discourse, which led me to believe that the term was not being used in an entirely self-serving manner, was any notion of revenge or retribution. An apology was due and reparations needed to be agreed before there could be a closure but the desire for punishment was not a current or a demand that ran through any of my discussions.

In this context, then, the last set of tools to do with justice and reconciliation are less far-fetched than it might first appear. International experience has recognised that reconciliation is an integral part of a repatriation programme. For reconciliation to occur, justice also needs to be seen to be done. Without knowing the exact nature of peace agreement which leads to repatriation, it is difficult to delineate possible ways in which justice is seen to be done. Clearly if Palestinian are to return to their homes in Israel, this will be a much larger undertaking in that, not only will there be a need for a series of people-to-people meetings up and down Israel to encourage dialogue and communication and to provide an opportunity for catharsis and healing, there will also need to be an ongoing mechanism to examine the extent to which a Zionist and Jewish state discriminates against the Palestinian citizens by virtue of their being non-Jews. I personally cannot see this taking place in any peace agreement agreed in the next 10–15 years. If repatriation takes place mainly into the OPTs, the reconciliation is less on a people-to-people basis but more on a state-to-state basis.

One can only work from the assumption that the overall package is regarded as just and fair and that certain measures such as continued Israeli colonisation and incursions involving the demolitions of homes will cease. But the basic outlines of a reconciliation pattern can be discerned as comprising elements of restorative justice. This would include a mutual apology for the sufferings caused to each community as a result of the conflict. In addition there would be an Israeli recognition of the injustice committed in 1948. A programme would also be established to explore possible joint narrative of the conflict but also to reduce inaccuracies and material likely to incite hatred in educational literature. A Truth and Justice Commission would be created to hear testimony in public of crimes against humanity and an amnesty would be offered based on confessions. A number of joint activities could be initiated ranging from joint memorial days for the victims of the conflict to cultural exchanges. Indeed, incentives towards joint economic partnerships could be used as the first steps towards greater economic and monetary cooperation. In essence justice and reconciliation are tools to be used both to provide psycho-social healing and to establish a platform for action designed to prevent such conflicts breaking out in violent ways.

Alternatives to repatriation

As already noted, this project and the Exeter workshop were focused on the issue of repatriation and other alternatives were not considered in any depth. The exception to this was the issue of compensation insofar as it touches on the issue of repatriation. It does this in two ways: compensation as part of a collective grant to assist in infrastructure improvements to absorb returning refugees, and compensation to individuals as incentives for certain kinds of relocation behaviour, e.g. to direct refugees to certain geographical areas or employable skills. In both these cases, it is only possible to calculate and distribute the funds due if there has been an agreed system of documentation.

In the Palestinian case, various estimates have been made to the extent of Palestinian material and moral losses (Hadawi and Kubursi 1988). However, there has been insufficient research on the subject for a clear picture to be obtained. In essence, there are three main sources of information on the status of refugees, their property losses and their historical trajectory as individuals. The first is the UN Conciliation Commission for Palestine (UNCCP) archives. These are detailed records compiled in the 1950s and 1960s of almost every Arab-owned parcel of land in Israel (Fischbach 2003). Unfortunately, access to these files, held in the UN offices in New York, is extremely restricted. The second source is the UNRWA archives, which record the geographical, social, educational and health histories of all UNRWA-registered refugees. At present these archives are mostly handwritten and in manually stored files and thus their use for UNRWA staff and researchers is limited (Tamari and Zureik 2001; Nasser 2003). However, considerable work has begun to digitalize and systematise the work to make them useful for policy analysis and compensation research. The third source is the archives of the Israeli Custodian of Absentee Property, whose office was set up in 1950 to manage Arab and Palestinian refugee property (Peretz 1958). This material has had restricted access but recent studies show that it will be useful in determining the exact amounts of real estate transferred to Israeli or Jewish institutions (Nathanson 2003). What is lacking is a comprehensive analysis of these sources for the purposes of establishing compensation claims.

International practice and the experience of agencies such as the International Organization for Migration (IOM) have found that documentation of land ownership and other losses must be carried out almost immediately a displacement occurs to have any certainty of being considered valid. In the Palestinian case, this activity was partially carried out but not in any systematic way, because of the different mandates of the UN agencies concerned and the ad hoc nature of some of the relief work undertaken in 1948. Therefore the challenge for those involved in Palestinian refugee research is to provide the resources to piece together the parts of the jigsaw involving UN, Israeli, Mandate and other NGO sources in order to build as complete a picture as possible (Irving-Jones 2004).

Conclusion

This project has brought to the fore both the challenges and the opportunities in 'transferring best practice' on the issue of the repatriation of refugees. The specificity of each refugee case creates many difficulties in policy transfer. The political agreement arrived at between the protagonists and the regional powers, the nature of the period of exile and the attitude of the host country are all important variables which make policy transfer complex and bounded by caveats. As we have seen, in the Palestinian case there are additional difficulties in the form of a separate UN operation and the character of the Israeli state. Nevertheless, the issue of repatriation, despite all the flaws in implementation that have been discussed, is firmly on the political agenda and will continue to be of relevance to the Palestinian case.

The contributions have therefore achieved two main tasks. At the same time as drawing attention to the complexity and the enormity of the challenges facing the peaceful resolution of the Palestinian refugee issue, by drawing upon international experience they have extended the range of policy options available. While there cannot be any single formula, any 'off-the-peg' repatriation programme, there are common elements running through many of the cases discussed. These encompass preparation, training, capacity-building, flexibility and mobility issues, reconciliation issues and regional and international support, which will form the basis of a programme.

In addition, by disaggregating the whole return process into its component parts, the project also offers two further opportunities. First, it is possible from this work to identify specific elements which can be embarked upon prior to an agreement. These include greater and prior INGO coordination, prototype tripartite agreements on refugee repatriation, improved documentation and databases, human resource development and institutional capacity generation, regional cooperation over migration and resource management, and the development of materials and structures to aid future reconciliation work. Second, such disaggregation engenders a task-orientated approach to the issue. Although certainly not aimed at bypassing the political and legal issues involved, the process of disaggregation does have the effect of both softening the demonisation of the refugee and allowing more creative thinking on how a repatriation programme could be implemented. In this sense, this volume has attempted to act as a channel simultaneously for introducing 'best practice' into the policy discussions and for laying down a future research agenda for academics and policy researchers.

Note

1 I acknowledge the guidance I received from my colleague Oliver James for this section. See also James and Lodge (2003).

References

Bell, C. (2000) *Peace agreements and human rights* (Oxford: Oxford University Press).

Brynen, Rex (2003) "Refugees, repatriation, and development: Some lessons from recent work", IDRC Stocktaking II Conference on Palestinian Refugee Research, Ottawa, 17–20 June.

Dolowitz, D. (2000) "Introduction", *Governance* 13 (1), pp. 1–4.

Dolowitz, D., and Marsh, D. (2000) "Learning from abroad: The role of policy transfer in contemporary policy-making", *Governance* 13 (1), pp. 5–24.

Exeter Refugee Study Team (2001) "Study of policy and financial instruments for the return and integration of Palestinian displaced persons in the West Bank and Gaza Strip". Unpublished study prepared for the EU Refugee Task Force.

Fischbach, M. (2003) *Records of dispossession: Palestinian refugee property and the Arab–Israeli conflict* (New York: Columbia University Press).

Hadawi, S., and Kubursi, A. (1988) *Palestinian rights and losses in 1948: A comprehensive study* (London: Saqi Books).

Hammond, L. (1999) "Examining the discourse of repatriation", in R. Black and, K.

Koser (eds.), *The end of the refugee cycle? Refugee repatriation and reconstruction* (Oxford: Berghahn Books).

Hanafi, S. (1996) *Between two worlds: Palestinian businessmen in the diaspora and the construction of a Palestinian entity* (Arabic) (Cairo: Dar al-Mostaqbal al-Arabi).

International Crisis Group (2004) *Palestinian refugees and the politics of peacemaking*. ICG Middle East Report 22 (5 February 2004).

Irving-Jones, N. (2004) "Refugee property restitution and compensation: The analysis of UN records and their relevance to a negotiated solution to the Palestinian refugee issue". Unpublished PhD proposal submitted to Exeter University.

James, O., and Lodge, M. (2003) "The limitations of 'policy transfer' and 'lesson drawing' for public policy", *Political Studies Review* 1, pp. 179–93.

Masalha, N. (2003) *The politics of denial: Israel and the Palestinian refugee problem* (London: Pluto Press).

Nakhleh, K. (2003) *The myth of Palestinian development: Poliical aid and sustainable deceit* (Jerusalem: Palestinian Academic Society for the Study of International Affairs (PASSIA)).

Nasser, M. (2003) "The Palestine refugee records project", Stocktaking II Conference on Palestinian Refugee Research, Ottawa, 17–20 June.

Nathanson, R. (2003) "Survey of Palestinian refugee real estate holdings in Israel", Stocktaking II Conference on Palestinian Refugee Research, Ottawa, 17–20 June.

Peretz, D. (1958) *Israel and the Palestinian Arabs* (Washington, DC: Middle East Institute).

Rose, R. (1993) *Lesson drawing in public policy* (Chatham, NJ: Chatham House).

Tamari, S., and Zureik, E. (eds.) (2001) *Reinterpreting the historical record: The uses of Palestinian refugee archives for social science research and policy analysis* (Jerusalem: Institute of Jerusalem Studies).

UNHCR (1996) *Voluntary repatriation: International protection* (Geneva: UNHCR).

Van Hear, N. (2004) "Refugee return and reconstruction after war: Class, conflict and forced migration in Sri Lanka and Somaliland". Paper submitted at international workshop on Transferring Best Practice: The Comparative study of refugee repatriation programmes with reference to the Palestinian context, Exeter, May 2004.

Welchman, L. (2003) "The role of international law and human rights in peacemaking and crafting durable solutions for refugees: Comparative comment". Paper submitted to BADIL Seminar in Ghent, May 2003.

World Bank (2003) "Housing and infrastructure: Scenarios for refugees and displaced persons" (Washington, DC: World Bank).

Appendix 1

Transferring best practice: an
international workshop on the
comparative study of refugee
return programmes with
reference to the Palestinian
context, 9–12 June 2004,
University of Exeter, UK

Presenters

Ms Katia Amore
Centre for Research in Ethnic Relations, University of Warwick

Professor Richard Black
Co-Director, Sussex Centre for Migration Research

Gail J Boling, JD
Attorney & independent researcher, Jerusalem University

Professor Rex Brynen
Chair, Middle East Studies Programme, McGill

Dr Mick Dumper
Reader in Middle East Politics, University of Exeter

Dr Patricia Weiss Fagen
*Senior Associate, Institute for the Study of International Migration, Georgetown
University*

Dr Laura Hammond
*Assistant Professor, Department of International Development, Community &
Environment, Clark University*

Dr Sari Hanafi
Sociologist

Dr Nicholas Van Hear
Centre on Migration, Policy and Society, University of Oxford

Dr Mahmoud Issa
Senior Researcher, Danish Refugee Council

Mr Michael Kagan
Lawyer; Instructor, Refugee & Asylum-Seeker Rights Clinic, Tel Aviv University Law School

Dr Menachem Klein
Senior Lecturer, Political Science Department, Bar Ilan University

Mr Peter Marsden
Coordinator, British Agencies Afghanistan Group Project, Refugee Council

Dr Christopher McDowell
Senior Lecturer, Director, Master of Applied Anthropology Programme, Macquarie University

Paul Prettitore
Legal Advisor, The World Bank, West Bank, Jerusalem

Ana Garcia Rodicio
Researcher, Globalitaria Peace-Building

Shahira Samy
PhD candidate, School of Historical, Political & Sociological Studies, University of Exeter

Dr Finn Stepputat
Senior Researcher, Danish Institute for International Studies

Discussants

Karen Koning Abu Zayd
Deputy Commissioner General, UNRWA, Gaza

Ghada Ageel
PhD candidate, School of Historical, Political & Sociological Studies, University of Exeter

Dr Nadje Al-Ali,
Institute of Arab & Islamic Studies, University of Exeter

Ms Eileen Alma
Research Officer, IDRC, Ottawa

Fateh Azzam
Director, Forced Migration & Refugee Studies, The American University in Cairo

Raja Deeb
Coordinator, A'aidoun Group, Damascus

Leila Hilal
Legal Advisor, PLO Negotiations Support Unit

David Jones
Middle East & North Africa Department, DFID, London

Ms Helen Rask,
Community Services Officer, Section on Refugee Women, Children and Community Development, UNHCR

Mr Terry M Rempel
Coordinator, Research & Information, BADIL Resource Centre for Palestinian Residency & Refugee Rights

Roula El-Rifai
Senior Programme Officer, International Development Research Centre, Ottawa

Saji Salameh
Director-General of Department of Refugee Affairs, PLO

Anke Strauss
International Migration Organization

Jaber Suleiman
Aidun Coalition, Lebanon

Dr Lex Takkenberg
Deputy Director, UNRWA, Syria

Munif Traish
City Engineer, Al-Bireh City

Mays Warrad
Secretariat Coordinator, Refugee Coordination Group, Ramallah

Appendix 2

Palestinian refugees, internally
displaced Palestinians and
convention refugees

Figures and notes reproduced with permission from the BADIL Resource
Centre for Residency Rights and Refugee Research.

Table A1 Palestinian refugees, internally displaced Palestinians and convention refugees

Year	Registered 1948 refugees[1]	Estimated non-registered 1948 refugees[2]	Estimated 1967 refugees[3]	Estimated 'other' refugees[4]	Estimated 1948 internally displaced persons[5]	Estimated 1967 internally displaced persons[6]	Convention refugees[7a]
1950	914,000	257,021	–	–	23,380	–	–
1955	905,986	305,260	–	–	40,254	–	1,643,600
1960	1,120,889	362,553	–	–	50,044	–	1,516,000
1965	1,280,823	430,599	–	–	62,215	–	4,368,900
1970	1,425,219	511,417	250,402	37,182	77,346	12,124	2,480,200
1975	1,632,707	607,403	297,400	108,349	96,157	14,205	2,991,200
1980	1,844,318	721,404	352,218	192,875	119,543	16,677	8,894,000
1985	2,093,545	856,802	419,512	293,261	148,616	19,612	11,817,200
1990	2,668,595	1,017,611	498,249	412,491	184,760	23,098	17,228,500
1995	3,172,641	1,208,603	591,763	554,099	229,694	27,239	14,573,600
2000	3,737,494	1,435,441	702,829	722,284	285,557	34,373	12,062,000
2003	4,082,300	1,591,500	779,237	837,991	325,400	38,266	9,671,800

Notes

There is no single authoritative source for the global Palestinian refugee and IDP population. The figures above reflect estimates according to the best available sources. Figures are therefore indicative rather than conclusive. Estimates for 1967 'other' refugees and IDPs are revised from 2002. For more details about the estimates see 'Notes to Table A1' at the end of this chapter.

a   Convention Refugees include all persons considered as refugees under the 1951 Convention relating to the Status of Refugees and of concern to the UN High Commissioner for Refugees (UNHCR). This figure only includes 428,000 Palestinian refugees for 2003.

Notes to Table A1

1. 1948 registered refugees – UN Relief and Works Agency for Palestine Refugees (UNRWA). UNRWA figures are based on data voluntarily supplied by registered refugees. Figures as of 30 June each year. UNRWA registration statistics do not claim to be and should not be taken as statistically valid demographic data. They are collected by UNRWA for its own internal management purposes, and to facilitate certification of refugees' eligibility to receive education, health and relief and social services. New information on births, marriages, deaths and change in place of residence is recorded only when a refugee requests the updating of the family registration card issued by the Agency. UNRWA does not carry out a census, house-to-house survey or any other means to ascertain whether the place of residence is the actual place of residence; refugees will normally report births, deaths and marriages when they seek a service from the Agency. New births, for instance, are reported early if the family avails itself of the UNRWA maternal and child health services or when the child reaches school age if admission is sought to an UNRWA school, or even later if neither of these services is needed. While families are encouraged to have a separate registration card for each nuclear family (parents and children), this is not obligatory. Family size information may therefore include a mix of nuclear and extended families, in some instances including as many as four generations.

2. 1948 non-registered refugees – Derived from *The Palestinian Nakba 1948, the register of depopulated localities in Palestine* (London: The Palestinian Return Centre, 1998), and the average annual growth rate of the Palestinian refugee population (3.5 per cent). The figures do not account for the small number of refugees reunited with family inside Israel.

3. 1967 first-time displaced refugees – Derived from *Report of the Secretary General under General Assembly Resolution 2252 (EX-V) and Security Council Resolution 237 (1967)*, UN Doc. A/6797, 15 September 1967, and the average annual growth rate of the Palestinian population (3.5 per cent). The figures do not include 1948 refugees displaced for a second time in 1967. The figures for 1967 exclude those refugees who returned under a limited repatriation programme in August–September 1967. The figures do not account for Palestinians who were abroad at the time of the 1967 war and unable to return, refugees reunited with family inside the occupied Palestinian territories, or those refugees who returned since 1994 under the Oslo political process.

4. 'Other' refugees – Derived from George F. Kossaifi, *The Palestinian refugees and the right of return* (Washington, DC: The Center for Policy Analysis on Palestine, 1996), based on an average forced migration rate of 21,000 persons per year. Includes those Palestinian refugees who are neither 1948 or 1967 refugees and are outside the Palestinian territories occupied by Israel since 1967 and unable due to revocation of residency, denial of family reunification, deportation etc., or unwilling to return there owing to a well-founded fear of persecution. The figures are based on the percentage of non-refugee Palestinians in the OPTs (57 per cent) and the average annual growth rate of the refugee population (3.5 per cent). The figures do not account for family reunification, those refugees who returned to the occupied Palestinian territories since 1994 under the Oslo political process or a small number of Palestinians from inside Israel who have sought refugee asylum.

5. 1948 internally displaced persons – Derived from initial registration figures from UNRWA in *Report of the Director of the United Nations Relief and Works Agency for Palestine Refugees in the Near East*, UN Doc. A/1905, 30 June 1951, and an estimated average annual growth rate of the Palestinian population inside Israel between 1950 and 2001 (4.2 per cent). According to the Israeli Central Bureau of Statis-

tics, the Palestinian Muslim population inside Israel (which comprises 82 per cent of the total Palestinian population inside Israel) increased annually by 4.4 per cent between 1948 and 2001. Israel Central Bureau of Statistics, 2002. *Statistical Abstract of Israel,* No. 53. A significant number of internally displaced Palestinians received assistance from UNRWA until the Agency turned over responsibilities for the internally displaced to Israel in 1952. The population estimate for 1950 was probably included as UNRWA registered refugees. The figure does not include those Palestinians internally displaced after 1948, conservatively estimated at 75,000 persons. *Internally displaced Palestinians, international protection, and durable solutions.* BADIL Information & Discussion Brief No. 9 (November 2002). The annual average growth rate of the IDP population is upgraded by a quarter of a percentage point to allow for further internal displaced after 1948 due to internal transfer, land confiscation and house demolition.

6 1967 internally displaced persons – The estimate includes persons internally displaced during the 1967 war from destroyed Palestinian villages in the OPTs. This figure is upgraded by the average annual growth rate of the refugee population (3.5 per cent). *Internally displaced Palestinians, international protection, and durable solutions.* BADIL Information & Discussion Brief No. 9 (November 2002). The figure is upgraded to include the average number of Palestinians displaced by house demolition (1,037) each year between 1967 and 2000. The number of Palestinians affected by house demolition is not upgraded according to the average annual population growth because that it is unknown how many IDPs return to their home of origin. The number of IDPs in the occupied Palestinian territories for 2003 is based on the estimated number of IDPs displaced during the 1967 war and the estimated number of Palestinian homes demolished in 2003 as punishment. Table, Demolition of Houses by Years in the al-Aqsa Intifada, B'tselem – The Israeli Information Center for Human Rights in the Occupied Territories (www.btselem.org). The number of Palestinians displaced is based on an average household size of 6.4 persons. Table 3.2.14, Percentage Distribution of Households by Household Size, Average Household Size and Region, 2002. Palestinian Central Bureau of Statistics, 2003. *Statistical Abstract of Palestine No. 4.* The figure does not include the number of Palestinians displaced because of the proximity of their homes to Israeli military checkpoints and colonies (i.e. settlements). The figure also includes the number of persons displaced in 2003 by Israel's separation wall. Palestinian Central Bureau of Statistics, 2003. *Survey on the impact of separation wall on the localities where it passed through.*

7 Convention Refugees – UNHCR, *2003 Global refugee trends, overview of refugee populations, New arrivals, durable solutions, asylum-seekers and other persons of concern to UNHCR.* Geneva: Population Data Unit/PGDS, Division of Operational Support, UNHCR, 15 June 2004. Data reported by UNHCR country offices generally reflect the view of the host country. The statistics are provisional and subject to change. This figure includes approximately 428,000 Palestinian refugees of concern to UNHCR.

Bibliography

Books

Abu Sitta, S. (1999) *Palestinian right to return: Sacred, legal, possible* (London: Palestinian Return Centre).

Agha, H., Feldman, S., Khalidi, A., and Schiff, Z. (2003) *Track II diplomacy: Lessons from the Middle East* (Cambridge, MA: MIT).

Allen, T., and Morsink, H. (eds.) (1994) *When refugees go home: African experiences* (Oxford: James Currey).

Aruri, N. (ed.) (2001) *Palestinian refugees: The right of return* (London: Pluto Press).

Arzt, D. (1997) *Refugees into citizens: Palestinians and the end of the Arab–Israeli conflict* (New York: Council on Foreign Relations Press).

Avineri, S. (1981) *The making of modern Zionism: The intellectual origins of the Jewish state* (London: Weidenfeld and Nicolson).

Basch, L., and Schiller, N. (1994) *Nations unbound: Transnational projects, postcolonial predicaments, and deterritorialized nation-states* (New York: Gordon and Breach).

Beilin, Y. (2001) *Guide for a wounded dove* (Hebrew) (Tel Aviv: Yedioth Aharonoth).

Ben Ami, S. (2004) *A front without a rearguard: A voyage to the boundaries of the peace process* (Hebrew) (Tel Aviv: Yedioth Aharonoth).

Bisharat, G. (1997) "Exile to compatriot: Transformations in the social identity of Palestinian refugees in the West Bank", in A. Gupta and J. Ferguson (eds.) *Culture, power, place: Explorations in critical anthropology* (Durham, NC: Duke University Press).

Black, R., and Koser, K. (eds.) (1999) *The end of the refugee cycle? Refugee repatriation and reconstruction* (Oxford: Berghahn).

Bloch, A., and Atfield, G. (2002) *The professional capacity of national from the Somali regions in Britain* (London: Refugee Action and IOM).

Bowker, R. (2003) *Palestinian refugee: Mythology, identity, and the search for peace* (Boulder, CO: Lynne Rienner Publishers).

Cahana, S. (1996) *Differing and converging views on solving the Palestinian refugees' problem* (Jerusalem: The Hebrew University, The Leonard Davis Institute for International Relations).

Cernea, M., and McDowell, C. (2000) *Risks and reconstruction* (Washington, DC: World Bank Publications).

Chimni, B. (2003) "Post conflict peace building and the return of refugees: Concepts, practices and institutions", in E. Newman and J. Van Selm (eds.), *Refugees and forced displacement: International security, human vulnerability and the state* (New York: UN University Press).

Coles, G. (1989) "Approaching the refugee problem today", in G. Loescher and L. Monahan (eds.), *Refugees and international relations* (Oxford: Oxford University Press).

Collier, D. (1991) "New perspectives on the comparative method", in D. Rustow and K. Erikson (eds.) *Comparative political dynamics: Global research perspectives* (New York: HarperCollins).

Davis, J., and Kaufman, E. (eds.) (2002) *Second track/citizens' diplomacy: Concepts and techniques for conflict transformation* (London: Rowman and Littlefield).

Dumper, M. (2005) "Comparative perspectives on the repatriation and resettlement of Palestinian refugees: The case of Guatemala, Bosnia and Afghanistan", in E. Benvenisti and S. Hanafi (eds.), *Israel and the Palestinian refugees problem* (Heidelberg: Max Planck Institute for Comparative Public and International Law).

Dunkerley, J. (1998) *Power in the Isthmus: A political history of modern Central America* (London: Verso).

Fagen, P. (1993) "Peace in Central America: Transition for the uprooted", in US Committee for Refugees, *World Refugee Survey 1993*.

Fagen, P. (2003) "Post-conflict reintegration and reconstruction: Doing it right takes a while", in N. Steiner and M. Gibney (eds.) *Problems of protection: The UNHCR, refugees and human rights* (New York: Routledge).

Fagen, P. (2003) "The long term challenges of reconstruction and reintegration: Case studies of Haiti and Bosnia Herzegovina", in E. Newman and J. Van Selm (eds.), *Refugees and forced displacement: International security, human vulnerability, and the state* (UN University Press).

Farah, R. (2003) "The marginalization of Palestinian refugees", in N. Steiner and M. Gibney (eds.), *Problems of protection: The UNHCR, refugees and human rights* (New York: Routledge).

Flapan, S. (1987) *The birth of Israel: Myths and realities* (London: Croom Helm).

Foddy, W. (1993) *Constructing questions for interviews and questionnaires : Theory and practice in social science* (Cambridge: Cambridge University Press).

Frederick, C., and Stein, B. (eds.) (1992) *Repatriation during conflict in Africa and Asia* (Dallas, TX: Center for the Study of Societies in Crisis).

Frelick, B. (1997) "Assistance without protection: Feed the hungry, clothe the naked and watch them die", in US Committee for Refugees, *World Refugee Survey 1997*.

Frelick, B. (2000) *Serbia: Reversal of fortune: Yugoslavia's refugee crisis since the ethnic Albanian return to Kosovo* (Washington, DC: United States Committee for Refugees).

Fuglerud, O. (1999) *Life on the outside: The Tamil diaspora and long distance nationalism* (London: Pluto Press).

Gazit, S. (1995) *The Palestinian refugee problem* (Tel Aviv: Jaffee Center for Strategic Studies, Tel Aviv University).

Ginat, J., and Perkins, E. (eds.) (2001) *The Palestinian refugees: Old problems – new solutions* (Brighton: Sussex Academic Press).

Goodwin-Gill, G. (1999) "Refugee identity and protection's fading prospect", in F. Nicholson and P. Twomey (eds.) *Refugee rights and realities: Evolving international concepts and regimes* (Cambridge: Cambridge University Press).

Goodwin-Gill, G. (1996) *The refugee in international law*, 2nd edn (Oxford: Oxford University Press).

Gordenker, L. (1987) *Refugees in international politics* (New York: Columbia University Press).

Hammond, L. (1999) "Examining the discourse of repatriation: Towards a more proactive theory of return migration", in R. Black and K. Koser (eds.) *The end of the refugee cycle: Refugee repatriation and reconstruction* (Oxford: Berghahn Books).

Hammond, L. (2004) *This place will become home: Refugee repatriation to Ethiopia* (Ithaca, NY: Cornell University Press).

Hanlon, C. (1999) "Guatemalan refugees and returnees: Place and Maya identity", in L. North and A. Simmons (eds.) *Journeys of fear: Refugee return and national transformation in Guatemala* (Montreal: McGill-Queen's University).

Hathaway, J. (1991) *The law of refugee status* (Toronto: Butterworths).

Helton, A. (2002) *The price of indifference: Refugees and humanitarian action in the new century* (Oxford: Oxford University Press).

Home Office (2001) *Secure borders, safe havens: Integration with diversity in modern Britain* (London: HMSO).

IOM (2000) *Evaluation of Phase III of the Programme for the Return of Qualified African Nationals* (Geneva: Office of Programme Evaluation, International Organization for Migration).

Israel/Palestine Center for Research and Information (2002) *Yes PM, years of experience in strategies for peace making: Looking at Israeli–Palestinian people to people activities 1993–2002* (Jerusalem: Israel/Palestine Center for Research and Information).

Kelman, H. (2001) "The role of national identity in conflict resolution: Experience from Israeli–Palestinian problem-solving workshops", in R. Ashmore and L. Jussin (eds.), *Social identity, intergroup conflict and conflict reduction* (Oxford: Oxford University Press).

Kimmerling, B., and Migdal, J. (2003) *The Palestinian people: A history* (Cambridge: Harvard University Press).

King, R. (1984) *Return migration and regional economic problems* (London: Croom Helm).

King, R. (2000) "Generalizations from the history of return migration", in B. Ghosh (ed.), *Return migration: Journey of hope or despair?* (Geneva: IOM/UNHCR).

Klein, M. (2003) *The Jerusalem problem: The struggle for permanent status* (Gainesville, FL: University Press of Florida).

Klein, M. (forthcoming) "The negotiations for settlement of the 1948 refugees", in E. Benvenisti and S. Hanafi (eds.), *Israel and the Palestinian refugees problem* (Heidelberg: Max Planck Institute for Comparative Public and International Law).

Koser, K., and Black, R. (1999) "The end of the refugee cycle?", in R. Black and K. Koser (eds.), *The end of the refugee cycle: Refugee repatriation and reconstruction* (Oxford: Berghahn Books).

Landman, T. (2003) *Issues and methods in comparative politics: An introduction*, 2nd edition (London: Routledge).

Larkin, M., and Cuny, F. (eds.) (1991) *Repatriation under conflict in Central America* (Washington, DC: Hemispheric Migration Project of Georgetown University and the Intertect Institute).

Loescher, G. (2003) *Beyond charity: International cooperation and the global refugee crisis* (Oxford: Oxford University Press).

Loescher, G. (2003) "UNHCR at 50", in G. Steiner and G. Loescher (eds.), *Problems of protection: The UNHCR, refugees and human rights* (New York: Routledge).

McCarthy, K. (1996) *The Palestinian refugee issue: One perspective* (Santa Monica, CA: RAND).

McCreery, D. (1994) *Rural Guatemala: 1760–1940* (Stanford: Stanford University Press).

MacDonald, M., and Gatehouse, M. (1993) *In the mountains of Morazan* (London: Latin American Bureau).

McDowell, C. (1996) *A Tamil asylum diaspora: Sri Lanka migration, politics and settlement in Switzerland* (Oxford: Berghahn Books).

McDowall, D. (1994) *The Palestinians: The road to nationhood* (London: Minority Rights Publications).

Malkki, L. (1995) *Purity and exile: Violence, memory and national cosmology among Hutu refugees in Tanzania* (Chicago: University of Chicago Press).

Manuh, T. (2003) "'Efie' or the meanings of 'home' among female and male 'Ghanaian' migrants in Toronto, Canada and returned migrants to Ghana", in K. Koser (ed.), *New African diasporas* (London: Routledge).

Marsden, P. (1999) "Repatriation and reconstruction: The case of Afghanistan", in K. Koser and R. Black (eds.), *The end of the refugee cycle? Refugee repatriation and reconstruction* (Oxford: Berghahn).

Massalha, N. (2003) *The politics of denial: Israel and the Palestinian refugee problem* (London: Pluto Press).

Morris, B. (2004) *The birth of the Palestinian refugee problem revisited*, 2nd edition (Cambridge: Cambridge University Press).

Morrison, J. (2000) *External evaluation of the voluntary return project for refugees in the United Kingdom: 1998–99* (London: Refugee Action).

Nakhleh, K. (2003) *The myth of Palestinian development: Political aid and sustainable deceit* (Jerusalem: Passia).

North, L., and Simmons, A. (eds.) (2000) *Journeys of fear: Refugee return and national transformation in Guatemala* (Kingston, ON: McGill-Queen's University Press).

Palestinian Authority (1999) *Palestinian development plan 1999–2003* (Ramallah: PA).

Peters, J. (1996) *Pathways to peace: The multilateral Arab–Israeli peace talks* (London: Pinter).

Peters, J. (2000) "Europe and the Arab–Israeli peace process: The declaration of the European Council and beyond", in S. Behrendt and C.-P. Hanelt (eds.), *Bound to cooperate – Europe and the Middle East* (Gutersloh: Bertelsmann Foundation Publishers).

Rudge, P., and Kapferer, S. (1999) *Kosovo: Protection and peace building: Protection of refugees, returnees, internally-displaced persons and minorities* (New York: Lawyers' Committee for Human Rights).

Ruiz, H. (1993) "Repatriation: Tackling protection and assistance concerns", in US Committee on Refugees, *World Refugee Survey*.

Salvadó, L. (1988) *The other refugees: A study of non-recognized Guatemalan refugees in Chiapas, Mexico* (Washington, DC: CIPRA, Georgetown University).

Sayigh, Y. (1997) *Armed struggle and the search for state: The Palestinian national movement: 1949–1993* (Oxford: Oxford University Press).

Schirmer, J. (1996) "The looting of democratic discourse by the Guatemalan Military: Implications for human rights", in E. Jelin and E. Hershberg (eds.), *Constructing democracy: Human rights, citizenship, and society in Latin America* (Boulder, CO: Westview Press).

Sher, G. (2001) *Just beyond reach: The Israeli–Palestinian peace negotiations 1999–2001* (Hebrew) (Tel Aviv: Yedioth Aharonoth).

Smith, C. (ed.) (1990) *Guatemalan Indians and the state: 1540–1988* (Austin: University of Texas Press).

Stepputat, F. (2002) "The final move? Displaced livelihoods and collective returns in Peru and Guatemala", in K. Olwig and N. Sørensen (eds.), *Mobile livelihoods: Life and work in a globalizing world* (London: Routledge).

Takkenberg, L. (1998) *The status of Palestinian refugees in international law* (Oxford: Clarendon Press).

Tamari, S. (1996) *Return, resettlement, repatriation: The future of Palestinian refugees in the peace negotiations* (Beirut: Institute for Palestine Studies).

UNHCR (1993) *The state of the world's refugees: The challenge of protection* (Harmondsworth: Penguin).

UNHCR (1995) *The state of the world's refugees: In search of solutions* (Oxford: Oxford University Press).

UNHCR (1996) *Voluntary repatriation: International protection* (Geneva: UNHCR).

UNHCR (1997) *The state of the world's refugees: A humanitarian agenda* (Oxford: Oxford University Press).

UNHCR (2000) *The state of the world's refugees: Fifty years of humanitarian action* (Oxford: Oxford University Press).

UNHCR (2002) *Resettlement handbook* (Geneva: UNHCR).

UNMIK and UNHCR (2003) *Manual for sustainable return* (Pristina: United Nations Mission in Kosovo/United Nations High Commissioner for Refugees).

Van Hear, N. (1997) *New diasporas: The mass exodus, dispersal and regrouping of migrant communities* (London: University College London Press).

Villa-Vicencio, C. (2003) *The politics of reconciliation* (Cape Town: Institute for Justice and Reconciliation).

Webb, P., and Von Braun, J. (1994) *Famine and food security in Ethiopia: Lessons for Africa* (London: John Wiley and Sons).

Wilson, K., and Nunes, J. (1994) "Repatriation to Mozambique", in T. Allen and H. Morsink (eds.), *When refugees go home* (Geneva: UNRISD).

Winter, R. (1994) "Ending exile: Promoting successful reintegration of African refugees and displaced people", in H. Adelman and J. Sorensen (eds.), *African refugees: Development aid and repatriation* (Boulder, CO: Westview).

Worby, P. (1999) *Lessons learned from UNHCR's involvement in the Guatemala refugee repatriation and reintegration programme 1987–1999* (Geneva: UNHCR).

Zinser, A. (1992) *The International Conference on Central American Refugees: Promises, realities and perspectives* (Washington, DC: Hemispheric Migration Project, Georgetown University).

Zureik, E. (1996) *Palestinian refugees and the peace process* (Washington, DC: Institute for Palestine Studies).

Published articles

Al-Ali, N., and Black, R. (2001) "Refugees and transnationalism: The experience of Bosnians and Eritreans in Europe," *Journal of Ethnic and Migration Studies* 27 (4), pp. 615–34.

Alpher, J., and Shikaki, K. (1999) "Concept paper: The Palestinian refugee problem and the right of return", *Middle East Policy* 6 (3): 167–89.

Ammassari, S., and Black, R. (2001) "Harnessing the potential of migration and return to promote development", *Migration Research Series* (Geneva: IOM).

Benvenisti, E., and Zamir, E. (1995) "Private claims to property rights in the future Israeli–Palestinian settlement", *The American Journal of International Law* 89 (2), pp. 295–340.

Black, R. (2001) "Fifty years of refugee studies: From theory to policy", *International Migration Review* 35 (1), pp. 55–76.

Black, R. (2001) "Return and reconstruction: Missing link or mistaken priority in post-Dayton Bosnia and Herzegovina?", *SAIS Review* 21 (2), pp. 177–99.

Black, R. (2002) "Conceptions of 'home' and the political geography of refugee repatriation: Between assumption and contested reality in Bosnia-Herzegovina", *Applied Geography* 22, pp. 123–38.

Chimni, B. (1991) "Perspectives on voluntary repatriation: A critical note", *International Journal of Refugee Law* 3 (3), pp. 541–7.

Constant, A., and Massey, D. S. (2002) "Return migration by German guestworkers: Neoclassical versus new economic theories", *International Migration* 40 (4), pp. 5–38.

Dolowitz, D. (2000) "Introduction", *Governance* 13 (1), pp. 1–4.

Dolowitz, D., and Marsh, D. (2000) "Learning from abroad: The role of policy transfer in contemporary policy-making", *Governance* 13 (1), pp. 5–24.

D'Onofrio, L. (2004) "Welcome home? Minority return in south-eastern Republika Srpska". *Sussex Migration Working Papers* 19.

Emmott, F. (1996) "'Dislocation', shelter and crisis: Afghanistan's refugees and notions of home", *Gender and Development* 4 (1).

Fitzgerald, J. (1999) "The end of protection: Legal standards for cessation of refugee status and withdrawal of temporary protection", *Georgetown Immigration Law Journal*.

García Rodicio, A. (2001) "Restoration of life: A new theoretical approach to voluntary repatriation based on a Cambodian experience of return", *International Journal of Refugee Law* 13.

Garlick, M. (2000) "Protection for property rights: A partial solution? The Commission for Real Property Claims of displaced persons and refugees (CRPC) in Bosnia and Herzegovina", *Refugee Survey Quarterly* 19 (3).

Gmelch, G. (1980) "Return Migration", *Annual Review of Anthropology* 9, pp. 135–59.

Hanafi, S. (2002) "Opening the debate on the Right of Return". *Middle East Report* 222.

Harrell-Bond, B. E. (1989) "Repatriation: Under what conditions is it the most desirable solution for refugees? An agenda for research", *African Studies Review* 32 (1), pp. 41–69.

Harris, S. (2000) "Listening to the displaced: Analysis, accountability and advocacy in action", *Forced Migration Review* 8.

Hastings, L. (2002) "Implementation of the property legislation in Bosnia Herzegovina", *Stanford Journal of International Law* 37.

Hovdenak, A. (2003) "Palestinian refugees: The right to return", *Journal of Peace Research*, 40 (6), pp. 748–49.

James, O., and Lodge, M. (2003) "The limitations of policy transfer and lesson drawing for public policy", *Political Studies Review* 1, pp. 179–93.

Khalidi, R. (1992) "Observations on the right of return", *Journal of Palestine Studies* 21, pp. 29–40.

Khalidi, R. (1995) "The Palestinian refugee problem: A possible solution", *Palestine–Israel Journal* 2, pp. 72–8.

Kibreab, G. (2003) "Citizenship rights and repatriation of refugees", *International Migration Review* 37 (1), pp. 24–73.

Klein, M. (1998) "Between right and realization: The PLO dialectics of 'The Right of Return'", *Journal of Refugee Studies* 11 (1), pp. 1–19.

Lepore, S. (1986) "Problems confronting migrants and members of their families when they return to their countries of origin", *International Migration* 23 (1).

McDowell, C., and Eastmond, M. (2002) "Transitions, state-building and the 'residual' refugee problem: The East Timor and Cambodian repatriation experience", *Australian Journal of Human Rights*, 8 (1), pp. 7–27.

Malkki, L. (1995) "Refugees and exile: from 'refugee studies' to the national order of things", *Annual Review of Anthropology* 24, pp. 495–523.

Matz, D. (2003) "Trying to understand the Taba talks", *Palestine–Israel Journal* 10 (3), pp. 96–105; (4), pp. 92–8.

Moore, D. (2000) "Levelling the playing fields and embedding illusions: 'Post-conflict' discourse and neo-liberal 'development' in war-torn Africa", *Review of African Political Economy* 83.

Petrin, S. (2002) "Refugee return and state reconstruction: A comparative analysis", *New Issues in Refugee Research Working Paper* 66 (Geneva: UNHCR).

Pressman, J. (2003) "Visions in collision: What happened in Camp David and Taba", *International Security* 28 (2), pp. 5–43.

Stein, B., and Tomasi, L. (1981) "Foreword", *International Migration Review* 15 (1–2), pp. 5–7.

Stepputat, F. (1994) "Repatriation and the politics of space: The case of the Mayan diaspora and return movement", *Journal of Refugee Studies* 7 (2–3), pp. 175–85.

Warner, D. (1994) "Voluntary repatriation and the meaning of returning home: A critique of liberal mathematics", *Journal of Refugee Studies* 7 (2–3), pp. 160–74.

Zetter, R. (1988) "Refugees and refugee studies: A label and an agenda", *Journal of Refugee Studies* 1 (1), pp. 1–6.

Zureik, E. (1994) "The Palestinian refugees problem", *Journal of Palestine Studies* 24 (1), pp. 5–17.

Reports, research papers and unpublished studies

Abunimah, A., and Ibish, H. (2001) "The Palestinian right of return", *ADC Issue Paper* (Washington, DC: Arab-American Anti-Discrimination Committee).

Ackerman, L. (2002) *Violence, exile and recovery. Reintegration of Guatemalan refugees in the 1990s – a biographical approach*. PhD dissertation, School of Geography and the Environment, University of Oxford.

Akram, S. (2000) "Reinterpreting Palestinian refugee rights under international law, and a framework for durable solutions". Information and Discussion Brief 1 (Bethlehem: BADIL Resource Center for Palestinian Residency and Refugee Rights).

Akram, S., and Rempl, T. (2003) "Temporary protection for Palestinian refugees: A proposal", paper presented in Stocktaking II Conference on Palestinian Refugee Research, International Development Research Center, Ottawa, June.

AVANCSO (1990) "Assistance and control. Policies towards internally displaced populations in Guatemala" (Washington, DC: Hemispheric Migration Project, Georgetown University).

Babille, M., Barney, I., Brynen, R., Jacobsen, B., Endresen, L., and Hasselknippe, G. (2003) "Finding means: UNRWA's financial situation and the living conditions of Palestinian refugees". FAFO Report 415 (Oslo: FAFO).

BADIL (2004) "Closing the gaps: Between protection and durable solutions". Memorandum presented at the UNHCR Pre-EXCOM NGO in Geneva, Switzerland, September

Ballard, B. (2002) "Reintegration programmes for refugees in South-East Asia: Lessons learnt from UNHCR's experience" (Geneva: UNHCR: Evaluation and Policy Analysis Unit and Regional Bureau for Asia and the Pacific).

Boswell, C. (1997) "Voluntary repatriation: A critical analysis" (draft) (Geneva: UNHCR CDR Policy Research Unit).

Bovenkerk, F. (1974) "The sociology of return migration: A bibliographic essay", The Hague: Nijhoff: Publications of the Research Group on European Migration Problems, 20.

Brynen, R. (2001a) "Planning for demographic change: A discussion paper", draft prepared for the Ministry of Planning and International Cooperation, Palestinian Authority.

Brynen, R. (2001b) "General donor perspectives on the developmental aspects of the refugee issue", draft prepared for the Ministry of Planning and International Cooperation, Palestinian Authority.

Brynen, R. (2002) "The Palestinian–Israeli conflict: A non-paper on political scenarios and refugee implications", non-paper prepared for the refugee donor "No-Name Group".

Brynen, R. (2003) "Refugees, repatriation, and development: Some lessons from recent work", paper presented in Stocktaking II Conference on Palestinian Refugee Research, International Development Research Center, Ottawa, June.

Brynen, R., Alma, E., Peters, J., and Tansley, J. (2003) "The Ottawa process: An examination of Canada's track two involvement in the Palestinian refugee issue", paper presented in Stocktaking II Conference on Palestinian Refugee Research, International Development Research Center, Ottawa, June.

Dumper, M. (2003) "The return of Palestinian refugees and displaced persons: The evolution of an EU policy on the Middle East peace process", paper presented in Stocktaking II Conference on Palestinian Refugee Research, International Development Research Center, Ottawa, June.

Exeter Refugee Study Group (2001) "Study of policy and financial instruments for the return and integration of Palestinian displaced persons in the West Bank and Gaza Strip", unpublished study prepared for the EU Refugee Task Force.

García Rodicio, A. (2000) "Restoration of life in Cambodia, 1992–93: Returnees in

Banteay Meanchey and Siem Reap" (Phnom Penh: Jesuit Refugee Service Cambodia).

Hammond, L., and Bezaiet, D. (2003) "Safara: An assessment of current and future resettlement in Ethiopia". Report for USAID/Ethiopia, Addis Ababa.

Hammond, L. (2003) "Obstacles to regional trade in the Horn of Africa: Borders, markets and production". Report for USAID/OFDA (Washington, DC: USAID/OFDA).

Hammond, L., and Alula, P. (2004) "Framework for monitoring and evaluation of the government of the Federal Republic of Ethiopia's voluntary resettlement programme". Report commissioned by USAID/OFDA Washington for the Multi-Agency Task Force on Resettlement, Addis Ababa.

Hanssen-Bauer, J., and Jacobsen, L. B. (2004) "Living in provisional normality: The living conditions of Palestinian refugees in the host countries of the Middle East" (Oslo: Norwegian Refugee Council, FAFO).

Holt, J., and Mark, L. (1993) "Making ends meet: A survey of the food economy of the Ethiopian north-east highlands". Report published by Save the Children UK (London: Save the Children).

International Crisis Group (1997) "House burnings: Obstruction of the right to return to Drvar", *ICG Bosnia Report* 24.

International Crisis Group (1998) "The Konjic conundrum: Why minorities have failed to return to a model Open City", *ICG Bosnia Report* 35.

Jamal, A. (2000) "Refugee repatriation and reintegration in Guatemala: Lessons learned from UNHCR's experience" (Geneva: UNHCR: Evaluation and Policy Analysis Unit and Regional Bureau for the Americas and the Caribbean).

Kamara, V. (2003) "Accelerated dynamics of resettlement in emerging from conflict Sierra Leone", Field Report, Conflict Stability in West Africa Series, Community Action for Refugees.

Klinov, R. (1995) "Reparations and rehabilitation of refugees". Unpublished draft paper prepared for the refugee project of the Institute for Social and Economic Policy in the Middle East, Harvard University.

Krafft, N., and Elwan, A. (2003) "Housing and infrastructure scenarios for refugees and displaced persons", paper presented in Stocktaking II Conference on Palestinian Refugee Research, International Development Research Center, Ottawa, June.

McDowell, C., and Ariyaratne, R. (2001) "Complex forced migration emergencies: East Timor case study". Report: Option for the Reform of the International Humanitarian Regime Project, University of Oxford, Refugee Studies Centre.

Marsden, P. (1997) "Return and reconstruction: Report on a study of economic coping strategies among farmers in Farah Province, Afghanistan", *British Agencies Afghanistan Group*.

Nijem, K. (2003) "Planning in support of negotiations: The refugee issue", paper presented in Stocktaking II Conference on Palestinian Refugee Research, International Development Research Center, Ottawa, June.

Oxfam/Save the Children (1998) "Listening to the displaced and listening to the returned: A community study". Summary Report (Colombo: Oxfam GB, Save the Children UK).

Razzazz, O. (1997) "From refugees to citizens: Upgrading Palestinian refugee camps". Unpublished paper prepared for the refugee project of the Institute for Social and Economic Policy in the Middle East, Harvard University.

Refugee Consortium of Kenya (RCK) (2003) "UNHCR budget cuts, dealing a death sentence to refugees in Africa", Nairobi.

Robinson, C. (1994) "Something like home again: The repatriation of Cambodian refugees", Bloomington, IN: US Committee for Human Rights.

Save the Children UK (2002) "The household economy approach: A resource manual for practitioners" (London: Save the Children).

Smillie, I. (1998) "Relief and development: The struggle for synergy", Occasional Paper 33, Thomas J. Watson Jr. Institute for International Studies, Brown University.

Stepputat, F. (1989) "Self-sufficiency and exile in Mexico", Geneva: UNRISD Discussion Paper 9.

Stepputat, F. (1992) "Beyond relief? Life in a Guatemalan refugee settlement in Mexico". PhD dissertation, University of Copenhagen.

Tsardanis, C., and Huliaras, A. (1999) "The economic and social absorptive capacity of the West Bank and Gaza Strip". Unpublished study prepared for the EU Refugee Task Force (Athens: Institute of International Economic Relations).

Turton, D., and Marsden, P. (2002) "Taking refugees for a ride: The politics of refugee return to Afghanistan", UNHCR: Kabul, Afghanistan Research and Evaluation Unit.

United Nations Commission on Human Rights (2001) "Question of the violation of Human Rights on the Occupied Arab Territories, including Palestine". Report of the Human Rights Inquiry Commission (New York: United Nations Commission on Human Rights).

UNHCR (1996) "Mozambique: An account from a lessons learned seminar on reintegration" (Geneva: UNHCR).

UNHCR (1997) "Review of UNHCR's phase out strategies: Case studies in selected countries of origin", EVAL 03/1997 (Geneva: UNHCR, Inspection and Evaluation Service).

UNHCR (2003) "Framework for durable solutions for refugees and persons of concern" (Geneva: UNHCR, Core Group on Durable Solutions).

UNHCR (2004) "Convention Plus at a glance" (Geneva: UNHCR).

UNHCR Spanish Committee/Globalitaria – Peace-building Initiatives (2004) "Summary for the Final Conference on 'Conflicts: Prevention, Resolution, Reconciliation'". Analytical document from the 2000–2004 International Reflection Process, version presented at the Final Conference in Barcelona, Spain (June) (final version forthcoming) (Madrid: UNHCR Spanish Committee/Globalitaria – Peace-building Initiatives).

United Nations Relief and Works Agency (2003) "Report of the Commissioner-General of the United Nations Relief and Works Agency for Palestine Refugees in the Near East, 1 July 2002–30 June 2003", United Nations General Assembly, 58th Session, Supplement No. 13, 10 October (A/58/13).

US Committee for Refugees (2001) "World Refugee Survey 2001" (Washington, DC: USCR).

United States, Department of State (2000) "Proposed initiative on Palestinian displaced persons and refugees", unpublished draft.

Whitaker, B. (2002) "Changing priorities in refugee protection: the Rwandan repatriation from Tanzania", New Issues in Refugee Research (Geneva: UNHCR).

Worby, P. (1999) "Lessons learned from UNHCR's involvement in the Guatemala repatriation and reintegration programmes, 1987–1999". Report supported by the UNHCR Regional Bureau for the Americas and the Evaluation and Policy Analysis Unit.

World Bank (2000a) "Palestinian refugees: An overview", unpublished draft.

World Bank (2000b) "Assessment of the absorptive capacity of the West Bank and Gaza in integrating returnees and associated costs: A concept note", unpublished draft.

World Bank (2000c) "Income and employment generation", unpublished draft.

World Bank (2000d) "Social infrastructure: Education, health, social welfare", unpublished draft.

World Bank (2000e) "Donor coordination and implementation", unpublished draft.

World Bank (with Japan) (2000) "Aid effectiveness in the West Bank and Gaza". Report prepared at the request of the Ad Hoc Liaison Committee.

Web articles, reports and research papers

Agamben, G. (1997) *"We refugees"*, http://www.egs.edu/faculty/agamben/agamben-we-refugees.html

Arnon, A., and Kanafani, N. (2004) *"Absorbing returnees in a viable Palestinian state: A forward-looking macroeconomic perspective"*, Discussion Paper 04–01, Monaster Center for Economic Research, Ben-Gurion University of the Negev, http://www.jcpa.org/jl/vp491.htm

BAAG Monthly Review, British Agencies Afghanistan Group, www.baag.org.uk

BADIL Resource Center (2003) *"Refugee return and real property restitution in Bosnia-Herzegovina – Lessons learned for the Palestinian case"*, press release of 28 January, www.badil.org

Black, R., and Koser, K. (2004) *"Understanding voluntary return"* (London: Home Office), Home Office Online Reports, http://www.homeoffice.gov.uk

Brynen, R. (1998) *"Palestinian refugees and the Middle East peace process"*, www.arts.mcgill.ca/mepp/mepp.html or www.prrn.org

Brynen, R. (2000) *"The future of UNRWA: An agenda for policy research"*, Workshop on the Future of UNRWA, Minster Lovell (UK), 19–20 February, http://www.arts.mcgill.ca/MEPP/PRRN/papers/future.html

Brynen, R. (2004) *"The Geneva Accord and the Palestinian refugee issue"*, http://upload.mcgill.ca/icames/genevarefugees.pdf

Chimni, B.S. (1999) *"From resettlement to involuntary repatriation: Towards a critical history of durable solutions to refugee problems"* (Geneva: New Issues in Refugee Research), Working Paper 2, http://www.UNHCR.ch/cgi-bin/texis/vtx/research

Crisp, J. (2001) *"Mind the gap: UNHCR humanitarian assistance and the development process"*, www.UNHCR.ch

Jesuit Refugee Service, *"Dispatches"*, http://www.jrs.net/dispatches/disp.php?lang=en

Klein, M. (2004) *"The logic of Geneva agreement"*, *Logos* 3 (1), http://www.logosjournal.com/klein.htm

Palestinian Authority (2001) *"Pathway toward a Palestinian vision for 2005 and beyond"*, http://www.pna.org

Palestinian Center for Policy and Survey Research (PSR) (2003) *"Results of PSR refugees' polls in the West Bank/Gaza Strip, Jordan and Lebanon on refugees' preferences and behavior in a Palestinian–Israeli permanent refugee agreement"*, http://www.pcpsr.org/survey/polls/2003/refugeesjune03.html

Palestinian Refugee ResearchNet (PRRN) (2000) *"Workshop Report"*, Workshop on the Future of UNRWA, Minster Lovell (UK), 19–20 February, http://www.arts.mcgill.ca/MEPP/PRRN/prunrwa3.html

Tamari, S. (1996) *"Return, resettlement, repatriation: The future of Palestinian refugees in the peace negotiations"* (Washington, DC: Institute for Palestine Studies), Final Status Strategic Studies, http://www.arts.mcgill.ca/PRRN/papers/tamari2.html

UNHCR, Iraq Briefings and News Stories, http://www.UNHCR.ch/cgi-bin/texis/vtx/iraq

UNHCR, Iraq Operations Updates, http://www.UNHCR.ch/cgi-bin/texis/vtx/iraq?page=planning

Foreign language sources

AVANCSO (1989) "Política exterior y estabilidad estatal", *Cuadernos de Investigación* 5, Guatemala.

AVANCSO (1992) "¿Dónde está el futuro? Procesos de reintegración en comunidades de retornados", *Cuadernos de Investigación* 8, Guatemala.

Consejo de Instituciones de Desarollo (COINDE) (1991) *Diagnóstico sobre refugiados, retornados y desplazados de Guatemala* (Cd. de Guatemala: Mimeo).

Fergany, N. (1988) *sa'yan wara' al rizq. dirasa maydaniyya 'an hijret al masriyyin ll'amal fi al aqtar al arabiyya (Striving for Subsistence)* (Beirut: Centre d'Etudes de l'Unité Arabe).

Hanafi, S. (1996) *Between two worlds: Palestinian businessmen in the diaspora and the construction of a Palestinian entity* (French; Arabic; Arabic and French) (Cairo: CEDEJ; Cairo: Dar al-Mostaqbal al-Arabi; Ramallah: Muwatin).

Hanafi, S. (2001) *hona wa honaq: nahwa tahlil lil 'alaqa bin al-shatat al-falastini wa al markaz (Here and there: Towards an analysis of the relationship between the Palestinian diaspora and the center)* (Arabic) (Ramallah: Muwatin; Jerusalem: Institute of Jerusalem Studies).

Ibrahim, S., and Abdel Fadil, M. (1983) *Intiqal al 'amalah al 'arabiyya (The movement of Arab labor)* (Beirut: Centre d'Etudes de l'Unité Arabe).

Le Bot, Y. (1995) *La guerra en tierras Mayas: Comunidad, violencia y modernidad en Guatemala (1970–1992)* (Mexico D.F.: Fondo de Cultura Económica).

Websites

Amnesty International: http://www.amnesty.org/

Human Rights Watch: http://www.hrw.org/

Norwegian Refugee Council: http://www.nrc.no/

Refugees International: http://www.refintl.org/

United Nations High Commissioner for Refugees (UNHCR): http://www.UNHCR.ch

United Nations Relief and Works Agency for Palestine Refugees in the Near East (UNRWA): http://www.un.org/unrwa/

Index